# White Reign

# White Reign

*Deploying Whiteness in America*

**Edited by Joe L. Kincheloe,
Shirley R. Steinberg, Nelson M. Rodriguez,
and Ronald E. Chennault**

St. Martin's Griffin
New York

WHITE REIGN: DEPLOYING WHITENESS IN AMERICA
Copyright © Joe L. Kincheloe, Shirley R. Steinberg, Nelson M. Rodriguez, and Ronald E. Chennault, 1998. All rights reserved. Printed in the United States of America. No part of this book may be used or reproduced in any manner whatsoever without written permission except in the case of brief quotations embodied in critical articles or reviews. For information, address St. Martin's Press, 175 Fifth Avenue, New York, N.Y. 10010.

ISBN 0-312-22475-3

Excerpts from bell hooks, "Representing Whiteness in the Black Imagination," copyright © 1991. From *Cultural Studies,* edited by Lawrence Grossberg, Cary Nelson, Paula Treichler. Reproduced by permission of Routledge, Inc.

**Library of Congress Cataloging-in-Publication Data**
White reign : deploying whiteness in America / edited by
 Joe L. Kincheloe ... [et al.] ; foreword by Michael W. Apple.
  p.  cm.
 Includes bibliographical references and index.
 ISBN 0-312-17716-X (cloth)  ISBN 0-312-22475-3 (pbk)
Whites—United States—Race identity. 2. Whites—United
States—Attitudes. 3. Race discrimination—United States-
-History—20th century. 4. United States—Race relations.
5. Discrimination in education—United States—History—20th
century. I. Kincheloe, Joe L.
E184.A1W395 1998
305.8'00973—dc21                                              98-9625
                                                              CIP

Book design by Acme Art, Inc.
First published in hardcover in the United States of America in 1998
First St. Martin's Griffin edition: February 2000
10 9 8 7 6 5 4 3 2 1

# CONTENTS

## II. Culture and Pedagogy

*To Strom Thurmond, William Bennett, Newt Gingrich,
Trent Lott, Orrin Hatch, and Jesse Helms*

# FOREWORD

## Michael W. Apple

It may be unfortunate, but it is true that many Whites still believe that there is a social cost attached to being white rather than being a person of color. Whites are the "new losers" in a playing field that they believe has been leveled now that the United States is a supposedly basically egalitarian, color-blind society. Since "times are tough for everybody," policies to assist "underrepresented groups"—such as affirmative action—are unfairly supporting "non-Whites." Thus Whites can now claim the status of victims (Gallagher 1995, 194). These feelings are of considerable importance in the politics of education in the United States as well as in many other nations. As it is being shaped by the conservative restoration, whiteness as an explicit cultural product is taking on a life of its own. In the arguments of the conservative discourses that are now circulating, the barriers to social equality and equal opportunity have been removed. Whites, hence, have no privilege. Much of this is untrue, of course. Although undercut by other dynamics of power, there is still considerable advantage to "being White" in this society. However, it is not the truth or falsity of these claims that are at issue here. Rather it is the production of retrogressive white identities.

The implications of all this are politically and culturally profound. For, given the Right's rather cynical use of racial anxieties, given the economic fears and realities many citizens experience, and given the historic power of race on the U.S. psyche, many members of this society may develop forms of solidarity based on their "whiteness." To say the least, this is not inconsequential in terms of struggles over meaning, identity, and the characteristics and control of our major institutions.

How do we interrupt these ideological formations? How do we develop antiracist educational practices that recognize white identities and yet do not lead to retrogressive formations? This is where *White Reign* enters.

If we were to be true to the historical record, whiteness is certainly not something we have just discovered. The politics of whiteness has been enormously, and often terrifyingly, effective in the formation of coalitions that unite people across cultural differences, across class and gender relations, and against their best interests (Dyer 1997, 19). It would not be possible to write the history of "our" economic, political, legal, health, educational—indeed all of our—institutions without centering the politics of whiteness either consciously or unconsciously as a core dynamic. Of course, I am saying little that is new here. As critical race theorists and postcolonial writers have documented, racial forms and identities have been and are constitutive building blocks of the structures of our daily lives, imagined and real communities, and cultural processes and products.[1] What sets *White Reign* apart, however, is that while it is grounded in a clear recognition of these facts, it does not focus on the "racial Other," as most other books do. It places the spotlight of critical scrutiny on the power of whiteness and how it can be understood, interrupted, and transformed.

Let us look at this situation a bit more closely. Race as a category is usually applied to "nonwhite" peoples. White people usually are not seen and named. They are centered as the human norm. "Others" are raced; "we" are just people. Film critic and cultural theorist Richard Dyer speaks to this in his telling book, *White:*

> There is no more powerful position than that of being "just" human. The claim to power is the claim to speak for the commonality of humanity. Raced people can't do that—they can only speak for their race. But, non-raced people can, for they do not represent the interests of a race. The point of seeing the racing of whites is to dislodge them/us from the position of power, with all of the inequities, oppression, privileges, and sufferings in its train, dislodging them/us by undercutting the authority with which they/we speak and act in and on the world (Dyer 1997, 2).

"Our" very language speaks to the invisibility of power relations in our ordinary talk about whiteness. "We" speak of a sheet of white paper as "blank." A room painted all white is seen as perhaps "needing a bit of color." Other examples could be multiplied. But the idea of whiteness as neutrality, as that which is not there, is ideally suited for designating that social group that is to be taken as the "human ordinary" (47).

In the face of this, in the face of something that might best be called an absent presence, a crucial political, cultural, and ultimately educational project is to *make whiteness strange* (Dyer 1997, 4). Thus part of our task in terms of pedagogy, political awareness, and mobilization is to tell ourselves and teach our students that identities are historically conferred. We need to recognize that "subjects are produced through multiple identifications." We should see our project as not reifying identity but understanding its production both as an ongoing process of differentiation *and most important* as subject to redefinition, resistance, and change (Scott 1995, 11).

There are dangers in doing this, of course. As I argue in *Cultural Politics and Education* (1996), having Whites focus on whiteness can have contradictory effects, ones of which we need to be well aware. It can enable people to acknowledge differential power and the raced nature of everyone—and this is all to the good. Yet it also can serve purposes other than challenging the authority of, say, the white West. It can just as easily run the risk of lapsing into the possessive individualism that is so powerful in this society. That is, such a process can serve the chilling function of simply saying "but enough about you, let me tell you about me." Unless we are very careful and reflexive, it can still wind up privileging the white, middle-class woman's or man's need for self-display. Many of these people have such a seemingly endless need. Scholars within the critical educational community will not always be immune to these tensions. Thus, we must be on our guard to ensure that a focus on whiteness doesn't become one more excuse to recenter dominant voices and to ignore the voices and testimony of those groups of people whose dreams, hopes, lives, and very bodies are shattered by current relations of exploitation and domination.

Further, focusing on whiteness can simply generate white guilt, hostility, or feelings of powerlessness. It can actually prevent the creation of those "decentered unities" that speak across differences and that can lead to broad coalitions that challenge dominant cultural, political, and economic relations. Thus, such a focus requires an immense sensitivity, a clear sense of multiple power dynamics in any situation, and a nuanced and (at times risky) pedagogy. One of the things that makes this volume such an interesting contribution is that it is very clear on the importance of articulating a politics and a pedagogy that both avoid these kinds of dangers and act in ways that go beyond them.

To some readers, the issue of whiteness may seem overly theoretical or one more "trendy" topic that has found its way to the surface of the critical educational agenda. Viewing it in this manner would be a grave mistake. What counts as "official knowledge" consistently bears the imprint of tensions, struggles, and compromises in which race plays a substantial role (Apple 1993). Further, as educational theorist Steven Selden (1998) has so clearly shown in his history of the close connections between eugenics and educational policy and practice, almost every current dominant practice in education—standards, testing, systematized models of curriculum planning, gifted education, and so much more—has its roots in such concerns as "race betterment," fear of the Other, and so on. And these concerns were themselves grounded in the gaze of whiteness as the unacknowledged norm. Thus issues of whiteness lie at the very core of educational policy practice. We ignore them at our risk.

As Joe L. Kincheloe and Shirley R. Steinberg put it in their articulate introduction to this book, "the study of whiteness becomes a central feature of any critical pedagogy or multicultural education for the twenty-first century." To counter the retrogressive white identities with which I began this foreword, they call for the reinvention of whiteness and the construction of transformed white identities through a "power literacy" that can contribute to the cause of racial justice and egalitarian democracy. In *White Reign*, the editors have brought together a provocative set of chapters that can assist educators in moving toward these goals.

## NOTES

1. There is a vast literature here. See, for example, Omi and Winant (1994); McCarthy and Crichlow (1993).

## BIBLIOGRAPHY

Apple, Michael W. (1996). *Cultural Politics and Education*. New York: Teachers College Press.

———. (1993). *Official Knowledge*. New York: Routledge.

Dyer, Richard. (1997). *White*. New York: Routledge.

Fine, Michelle, Weis, Lois, Powell, Linda, and Wong, L. Mun (eds.). (1997). *Off White: Readings on Race, Power, and Society.* New York: Routledge.

Gallagher, Charles. (1995). "White Reconstruction in the University." *Socialist Review* 94, nos. 1 and 27, 194.

McCarthy, Cameron, and Crichlow, Warren (eds.). (1993). *Race, Identity, and Representation in Education.* New York: Routledge.

Omi, Michael, and Winant, Howard. (1994). *Racial Formation in the United States.* New York: Routledge.

Scott, Joan. (1995). "Multiculturalism and the Politics of Identity." In John Rajchman (ed.), *The Identity in Question,* 11. New York: Routledge.

Selden, Steven. (1998). *The Capturing of Science.* New York: Teachers College Press.

# Theory and Pedagogy

# Addressing the Crisis
# of Whiteness

*Reconfiguring White Identity in a*
*Pedagogy of Whiteness*

**Joe L. Kincheloe and Shirley R. Steinberg**

Individuals cannot separate where they stand in the web of reality from what they perceive. In contemporary critical social and educational theory, this statement lays the foundation for the concept of "positionality." Positionality involves the notion that since our understanding of the world and ourselves is socially constructed, we must devote special attention to the differing ways individuals from diverse social backgrounds construct knowledge and make meaning. Critical multiculturalists, thus, are fervently concerned with white positionality in their attempt to understand the power relations that give rise to race, class, and gender inequality. Those of us who claim the mantle of critical multiculturalism are concerned with the ways power has operated historically and contemporaneously to legitimate social/educational categories and hierarchical divisions. We also are interested in the ways individuals interact with representations of race, class, and gender dynamics in a variety of pedagogical spheres. Not content with simply cataloging such portrayals, critical multiculturalists take the next step of connecting representations to their material effects. Awareness of such effects is central in the effort to understand the power-saturated, hegemonic process of resource claims legitimation. At this point critical multiculturalists are equipped to describe the contemporary disparity in the distribution of symbolic/economic/educational capital and the reasons it continues to escalate.

With these dynamics in mind, critical advocates of a pedagogy of whiteness examine the various ways that social forces, including language, knowledge, and ideology, shape white identity and positionality in contemporary American life. Drawing on a critical educational tradition that is dedicated to an analysis of the construction of "self," scholars hope to help readers rethink the construction of the white self and the social, moral, and political implications at the end of the twentieth century (Carby 1992; Frankenberg 1993; McMillen 1995). Even though no one at this point really knows exactly what whiteness is, most observers agree that it is intimately involved with issues of power and power differences between white and nonwhite people. Whiteness cannot be separated from hegemony and is profoundly influenced by demographic changes, political realignments, and economic cycles. Situationally specific, whiteness is always shifting, always reinscribing itself around changing meanings of race in the larger society. As with race in general, whiteness holds material/economic implications—indeed, white reign has its financial rewards. The Federal Housing Administration, for example, traditionally has favored housing loans for white suburbs instead of "ethnic" inner cities. Banks have ensured that access to property ownership and capital acquisition for Blacks is severely limited compared to Whites. Over the decades following World War II, unions ignored the struggle for full employment and universal medical care, opting for contracts that provided private medical coverage, pensions, and job security to predominantly white organized workers in mass-production industries. Undoubtedly, unearned wages of whiteness continue. Indeed, critical multiculturalists understand that questions of whiteness permeate almost every major issue facing Westerners at the end of the twentieth century, from affirmative action and intelligence testing to the deterioration of public space. In this context the study of whiteness becomes a central feature of any critical or multicultural education for the twenty-first century (Fiske 1994; Gallagher 1994; Keating 1995; Nakayama and Krizek 1995; Yudice 1995).

## WHITE REASON:
## THE COLONIAL POWER OF WHITENESS

While no one knows exactly what constitutes whiteness, we can historicize the concept and offer some general statements about the dynamics it signifies. Even this process is difficult, as whiteness as a sociohistorical construct is constantly shifting in light of new circumstances and changing interactions with various manifestations of power. With these qualifications in mind, we believe that a dominant impulse of whiteness took shape around the notion of rationality of the European Enlightenment, with its privileged construction of a transcendental white, male, rational subject who operated at the recesses of power while at the same time giving every indication that he escaped the confines of time and space. In this context whiteness was naturalized as a universal entity that operated as more than a mere ethnic positionality emerging from a particular time, the late seventeenth and eighteenth centuries, and a particular space, Western Europe. Reason in this historical configuration is whitened and human nature itself is grounded upon this reasoning capacity. Lost in the defining process is the socially constructed nature of reason itself, not to mention its emergence as a signifier of whiteness. Thus, in its rationalistic womb, whiteness begins to establish itself as a norm that represents an authoritative, delimited, and hierarchical mode of thought. In the emerging colonial contexts in which Whites increasingly would find themselves in the decades and centuries following the Enlightenment, the encounter with nonwhiteness would be framed in rationalistic terms—whiteness representing orderliness, rationality, and self-control and nonwhiteness indicating chaos, irrationality, violence, and the breakdown of self-regulation. Rationality emerged as the conceptual base around which civilization and savagery could be delineated (Alcoff 1995; Giroux 1992; Keating 1995).

This rationalistic modernist whiteness is shaped and confirmed by its close association with science. As a scientific construct, whiteness privileges mind over body; intellectual over experiential ways of knowing; and mental abstractions over passion, bodily sensations, and tactile understanding. In the study of multicultural education, such epistemological tendencies take on dramatic importance. In educators' efforts to understand the forces that drive the curriculum and the purposes of Western education, modernist whiteness is a central player. The insight it provides into the social construction of schooling, intelligence, and the disciplines of psychology and educational psychology in particular opens a gateway into white consciousness and its reactions to the world around it. At the end of the twentieth century, objectivity and masculinity as signs of stability and the highest expression of white achievement still work to construct everyday life and social relations. Because such dynamics have been naturalized and universalized, whiteness assumes an invisible power unlike previous forms of domination in human history. Such power can be deployed by those individuals and groups that can place themselves within the boundaries of reason and project irrationality, sensuality, and spontaneity on to the Other.

Thus, European ethnic groups, such as the Irish in nineteenth-century industrializing America, were able to differentiate themselves from passionate ethnic groups that supposedly were unable to regulate their own emotional predispositions and gain a rational and objective view of the world. Such peoples—who were being colonized, exploited, enslaved, and eliminated by Europeans during that continent's Enlightenment and post-Enlightenment eras—were viewed as irrational and, thus, inferior in their status as human beings. As inferior beings, they had no claim to the same rights as Europeans—hence, white racism and colonialism were morally justified around the conflation of whiteness and reason. In order for whiteness to maintain itself in the privileged seat of rationality and superiority, it would have to construct pervasive portraits of non-Whites (Africans in particular) as irrational, disorderly, and prone to uncivilized behavior (Alcoff 1995; Haymes 1996; Nakayama and Krizek 1995; Stowe 1996). As rock of rationality in a sea of chaos and disorder, whiteness presented itself as a noncolored, nonblemished, pure category. Historically, even a mere drop of nonwhite blood was enough to relegate a person to the category of "colored." Thus, being White meant possessing the privilege of being uncontaminated by any other bloodline. In this context, a mixed-race child often is rejected by the white side of his or her heritage—the rhetorical construct of racial purity demands that the mixed-race individual be identified by allusion to the nonwhite group, as in "she's half Latina" or "she's half Chinese." Individuals are rarely half White.

As French philosopher Michel Foucault often argued, reason is a form of disciplinary power. Around Foucault's axiom, critical multiculturalists contend that reason can never be separated from power. Those without reason defined in the Western scientific way were excluded from power and were relegated to the position of unreasonable Other. Whites, in their racial purity, understood the dictates of the "White Man's Burden" and became the beneficent teachers of the barbarians. To Western eyes the contrast between white and nonwhite culture was stark: reason as opposed to ignorance; scientific knowledge instead of indigenous knowledge; philosophies of mind versus folk psychologies; religious truth in lieu of primitive superstition; and professional history as opposed to oral mythologies. Thus rationality was inscribed in a variety of hierarchical relations between European colonizers and their colonies early on and between Western multinationals and their "underdeveloped" markets in later days. The white claim of cultural neutrality based on the transhistorical norm of reason erased such power relations—in this construction rationality was not assumed to be the intellectual commodity of any specific culture. Indeed, colonial hierarchies immersed in exploitation were justified on the basis of the interplay of pure whiteness, impure nonwhiteness, and neutral reason.

Traditional colonialism was grounded on the deviation of those colonialized from the norm of rationality; thus colonization became a rational response to inequality. In the twentieth century this white norm of rationality was extended to the economic sphere, with the philosophy of the free market and exchange values being considered signifiers of civilization. Once all the nations on earth are drawn into the market economy, then all land can be subdivided into real estate, all human beings' worth can be calculated monetarily, values of abstract individualism and financial success can be embraced by every community in every country, and education can be reformulated around the cultivation of human capital. When these dynamics come to pass, the white millennium will have commenced—white power (white reign) will have been consolidated around land and money. The Western ability to regulate diverse peoples through their inclusion in data banks filled with information about their credit histories, institutional affiliations, psychological "health," academic credentials, work experiences, and family backgrounds will reach unprecedented levels. The accomplishment of this ultimate global colonial task will mark the end of white history. White supremacy will not end, but it will have produced a hegemony so seamless that the need for further structural or ideological change becomes unnecessary. The science, reason, and technology of white culture will have achieved their inevitable triumph (Alcoff 1995; Giroux 1992; MacCannell 1992; Nakayama and Krizek 1995).

Whatever the complexity of the concept of whiteness, at least one feature is discernible—it cannot escape the materiality of its history, its effects on the everyday lives of those who fall outside its conceptual net as well as on white people themselves. This book—indeed, scholarship on whiteness in general—should focus attention on the documentation of such effects. In a critical multicultural educational context, the study of whiteness should delineate the various ways such material effects shape cultural and institutional pedagogies and position individuals in relation to the power of white reason. Understanding these dynamics is central to the curricula of black studies, Chicano studies, postcolonialism, indigenous studies, not to mention educational reform movements in elementary, secondary, and higher education. The history of the world's diverse peoples in general as well as minority groups in Western societies in particular often has been told from a white historiographical perspective. Such accounts erase the values, epistemologies, and belief systems that grounded the cultural practices of diverse peoples. Without such cultural grounding students often are unable to appreciate the manifestations of brilliance displayed by nonwhite cultural groups. Caught in the white interpretive filter, they cannot make sense of diverse historical and contemporary cultural productions as anything other than proof of white historical success. The fact that one of the most important themes of the last half of the twentieth century—the revolt of the "irrationals" against white historical domination—has not been presented as a salient part of the white (or nonwhite) story is revealing testimony to the continuing power of whiteness and its concurrent fragility (Banfield 1991; Frankenberg 1993; Stowe 1996; Vattimo 1991).

As with any racial category, whiteness is a social construction in that it can be invented, lived, analyzed, modified, and discarded. While Western reason is a crucial dynamic associated with whiteness over the last three centuries, many other social forces sometimes work to construct its meaning. Whiteness, thus, is not an unchanging, fixed, biological category impervious to its cultural, economic, political, and psychological context. There are many ways to be White, as whiteness interacts with class, gender, and a range of other race-related and cultural dynamics. The ephemeral nature of whiteness as a social construction begins to reveal itself when we understand that the Irish,

Italians, and Jews all have been viewed as nonwhite in particular places at specific moments in history. Indeed, prior to the late 1600s, Europeans did not use the label Black to refer to any race of people, Africans included. Only after the racialization of slavery by around 1680 did whiteness and blackness come to represent racial categories. At this historical juncture, the concept of a discrete white race began to take shape. Slowly in the eighteenth and nineteenth centuries the association of whiteness with rationality and orderliness developed, and in this context it came to signify an elite racial group. Viewed as a position of power, those who did not possess white identity often sought it. Immigrant workers from southern and eastern Europe in the new American industrial workplaces of the mid-nineteenth century aspired to and eventually procured whiteness; they viewed it as payment for the exploitation of their labor. Such shifts in the nature and boundaries of whiteness continued into the twentieth century. One reason that whiteness has become an object of analysis in the 1990s revolves around the profound shifts in the construction of it, blackness, and other racial identities that have taken place recently.

How are students and other individuals to make sense of the assertion that whiteness is a social construction? How does such a concept inform the democratic goals of a critical multiculturalism? Such questions form the conceptual basis of our discussion of whiteness, our attempt to construct a pedagogy of whiteness. In order to answer them in a manner that is helpful for Whites and other racial groups, it is important to focus on the nature of the social construction process. In this context, media analyst John Fiske's (1993) notion of a power bloc is helpful. The discourses that shape whiteness are not unified and singular but diverse and contradictory. Logical consistency is not found in the social construction of whiteness. Like the work of any power bloc, the discursive construction of whiteness aligns and dealigns itself around particular issues of race. For example, the discourse of white victimization that has emerged over the last two decades appears in response to particular historical moments, such as the attempt to compensate for the oppression of non-Whites through preferential hiring and admissions policies. The future of such policies will help shape the discourses that will realign to structure whiteness in the twenty-first century. These discourses, of course, hold profound material consequences for Western cultures, as they fashion and refashion power relations between differing social groups. Any study of whiteness involves engaging students in a rigorous tracking of this construction process. When informed by critical notions of social justice, community, and democracy, such an operation allows individuals insights into the inner workings of racialization, identity formation, and the etymology of racism. Armed with such understandings, they gain the ability to challenge and rethink whiteness around issues of racism and privilege. White students then begin to develop questions regarding their own identity (Gallagher 1994; Keating 1995; McMillen 1995; Nakayama and Krizek 1995).

## BALL OF CONFUSION: THE WHITE IDENTITY CRISIS

As Whites gain consciousness of the racialization of their identity, some feel guilty about their association with a group that has perpetrated racial oppression. Such shame can be immobilizing to the extent that it interferes with the construction of a progressive white identity that is psychologically centered and capable of acting in opposition to racist activity. Often guilt-ridden Whites in the midst of the identity struggle engage in a form of self-denigration that expresses itself in a conceptualization of nonwhite cultures as superior to white culture—more authentic, natural, sacred. When confronted with the racialization of whiteness, other white individuals react in a very different manner. Given the way conservatism has shaped various cultural expressions in recent years, Whites in crisis often find greater cultural correspondence with right-wing racial codes and articulations of racial anxieties. When conservatives maintain that white people aren't allowed to be White anymore, many young Whites believe that a conspiracy of antiwhite minorities and multiculturalists is repressing their free expression of a white identity. This conviction fans the flames of white anger against non-Whites and ups the ante of racial hostility (Gallagher 1994; Tatum 1994; Winant 1994).

This reactionary form of the new white identity appropriates whiteness as the defiant signifier—the new self. After all the talk, argument, and litigation about race, starting with the civil rights movement in the 1950s and 1960s, right-wing analysts discovered that they could engage in identity politics as well. As it latched on to the whiteness signifier, right-wing identity politics promoted values such as the Eurocentric cultural canon, English-language-only legislation, the symbol of family values, and the work ethic. Melding such virtues with whiteness, right-wing leaders deployed their brand of ethnopolitics in a larger effort to recover white supremacy, as Aaron Gresson labels it. Such an ideological construction expresses itself in increasingly bizarre and paranoid ways, as neo–white supremacists begin to formulate racially deterministic single-bullet theories that blame non-Whites for all social ills and rally white patriots around opposition to practices such as interracial marriage. Since the white gene is recessive, the patriots fear white identity (purity) will be lost in "miscegenation."

The recovery construction comes from all quarters, education included. After *The Chronicle of Higher Education* ran an article describing the proliferation of whiteness studies, Russell Eisenman wrote a letter to the editor that touched on many themes of the recovery rhetoric. Arguing that "whites are victims of a quota system called affirmative action which causes them (especially white males) to be discriminated against, to work (as I have in the past) for an incompetent supervisor . . . " Eisenman felt the need to justify white virtue and competence. Pointing out white people's intellectual contributions, low crime rate, and declining AIDS infection rate, he warned that because of immigration laws, Whites will become a minority in the United States early in the next century. In the spirit of the recovery rhetoric, he concluded that someone must defend white people because in the 1990s they are attacked from everywhere—whiteness studies scholarship and college courses in particular (Eisenman 1995; Gresson 1995; Stowe 1996; Tanaka 1996; Yudice 1995).

How do we deal with the anger of Eisenman and the millions of white males he represents? Indeed, we understand the simple-minded irony of his argument that someone needs to defend white males—the most powerful group by far in contemporary society. But the importance of Eisenman's argument does not rest on its rational basis; its social importance revolves around its emotionality, its perception of Whites under siege, and its white anger. Eisenman is in crisis about his whiteness in a world, a hyperreality, where meaning is lost and depersonalization is the order of the day. Obviously, his whiteness is important to him as an identity, and he is upset by its instability, its vilification by "Others" who have uncovered the complicity of whiteness in their own oppression.

Identity politics take on new importance in a world as fragmented as ours, often emerging as a remedy for alienation and anonymity. Caught in the crisis of whiteness, Eisenman and countless white young people in various Western societies attempt to deal with the perception that they don't have an ethnicity or at least don't have one they feel is validated. Whiteness is in an identity vacuum; critical multiculturalists must help construct a progressive, antiracist white identity as an alternative to the white ethnic pride shaped by the right wing and embraced by Whites such as Eisenman.

A cardinal aspect of the entire conversation about whiteness is the fact that liberal and pluralist forms of multiculturalism and identity politics have not produced a compelling vision of a reconstructed white identity. A critical white identity that renounces its whiteness, feels guilty about it, or seeks merely to court favor among non-Whites is ineffective in the struggle for justice, democracy, and self-efficacy. Here a key goal of a critical pedagogy of whiteness emerges: the necessity of creating a positive, proud, attractive, antiracist white identity that is empowered to travel in and out of various racial/ethnic circles with confidence and empathy. Operating from such a position, Whites would not resent those Latino/a, Asian, and African immigrants who enter their new countries with a clear sense of their ethnic identities. Progressive Whites would value and learn from such immigrants, using such knowledge in a continuous effort to understand the social and cultural forces that shape the way they see themselves and the world. They would understand the social role of marginality in these contexts of racial difference—the localizing power marginality has been able to muster since the late 1960s to help oppressed peoples gain moral and political currency as compensation for their lowly position. This currency is exactly what Whites haven't possessed over the last couple of decades, and it has made them quite uncomfortable. Whites such as Pat Buchanan, William Bennett, Dan Quayle, and letter-writer Eisenman have felt that something was missing in their struggle with the white identity crisis, but they couldn't name it. The moral and political currency provided by marginality provides insight into their struggle.

The white identity crisis is real and cannot be dismissed simply as the angst of the privileged. While it is in part such an angst, it is also a manifestation of the complexity of identity as class and gender intersect with race/ethnicity, an expression of the emptiness of the postmodern condition, and an exhibition of the failure of modernist humanism to respond to the globalism engulfing it. In their attempt to claim the currency of marginality, Whites have referenced their immigrant grand-parents' stories of struggle, assumed the status of European ethnic minorities, and revived ethnic practices long abandoned by second-generation descendants of immigrants. Such efforts cannot solve the identity crisis, for the immigrant experience of marginalization with its linguistic and custom-related alienation is too far removed from the lived world of most contemporary Whites. Indeed, eating moussaka on holidays does not a marginalized Greek immigrant make. Students emerging from such identity struggles or families caught in them often find it easier to discern manifestations of African, indigenous, or Latino racialized meanings in literature, popular culture, and everyday life than white racialized meanings. How could they know what a white racialized meaning (an implicit or explicit reference to how being White affects one's or a group's life) entails when they are unaware of what it means to be White or even Polish, Italian, or Greek? Even when whiteness and white ethnicity are racialized, their specific meaning is still occluded.

Now there are few options for progressive, antiracist young Whites who don't position themselves as "wannabe Blacks" or "wiggers" (a designation for White niggers). Too often they sense that there exists no good reason to be White (Gallagher 1994; Keating 1995; Tanaka 1996; Winant 1994; Yudice 1995). Educator Henry Giroux (1995) points out that popular culture often provides little hope for a critical whiteness, as evidenced in the violence of white youth films such as *Laws of Gravity* (1992), *Kalifornia* (1993), and *Natural Born Killers* (1994). And it doesn't take much racial insight to identify the white nihilism within a movie such as *Falling Down* (1993). In this film Michael Douglas is an average white guy victimized by women and minorities, who blame him for all that is wrong and want compensation from him. He is tortured by Chicano gang members who want a toll for passing through their turf, by lying and scheming homeless people, by Blacks ready to cry "racism" at every juncture, and by bosses who don't care about competence and qualifications (Clover 1993). When white audiences applaud and cheer Douglas's character, D-FENS, as he "opens fire" and leaves a trail of corpses behind him, they are embracing an aesthetic of white nihilism. Such hopelessness assumes there is no alternative for postmodern white people save taking others with them when they inevitably go down (fall down). A critical pedagogy of whiteness rejects such an alternative as it conceives new ways of being White.

## REACTING TO THE IDENTITY CRISIS: WHITES POSITIONING THEMSELVES AS VICTIMS

A critical foundation of this pedagogy of whiteness involves monitoring the white reaction to the identity crisis, and a central feature of that reaction involves the attempts of Whites over the last couple of decades to position themselves as victims. Aaron Gresson (1995) is unambiguous about the white self-portrayal as victim, when he writes about the recovery of white domination by the portrayal of Blacks and other non-Whites as the new oppressors. In this context whiteness is constructed as a signifier of material deprivation and a litany of present-day griev-ances. Everyone but white males get advantages, the argument goes, as non-Whites undermine white progress by exploiting white guilt about a long-dead white racism. Such a rhetorical construction, Gresson con-tends, is a form of vampirism, as Whites positioning themselves as victims suck the blood of moral indignation from Blacks, Latinos, and Native Americans and use it to reposition themselves in the new racial order. "They" won't even let us have our own clubs and white organizations, white students protest, with that blood of moral indignation dripping from their mouths. A pedagogy of whiteness asks why many white students have such difficulty recognizing the long-term white domina-tion of most existing school organizations. Why do they consistently miss this power dynamic?

The same power illiteracy shapes white students' frequent concern with black history or black studies classes. Why can "they" have such classes, while we can't have white history or white studies classes? Such questions emanate from a belief in a color-blind society in which everyone is equal. In this construct, racially motivated organizations are racist because they are exclusive. Often formed as support organizations for nonwhite students that promote the development of social and professional networks, such black, Latino, Native American, and Asian groups help such students negotiate the often-unfamiliar terrain of academia and the professional world. The need for such negotiation is often lost on Whites who do not perceive race neutrality as a way of maintaining an unjust status quo. Formal education rarely addresses the power illiteracy that plagues many white students. Often in our classes we are confronted with white students who equate all forms of prejudice—for example, black racism toward Whites is equal to white racism toward Blacks. White students are shocked to hear us make the argument that white racism holds more serious ramifications for Blacks than does black racism toward Whites because of the power inequities between Blacks and Whites. For example, we tell them, because Whites commonly control access to job hiring and job promotion—not to mention issues such as cultural capital—white racism has a much greater chance of affecting the quality of life of black people.

The color-blind construct—the new discourse of white victimization and its rhetorical reversal—works only if we assume that being White is no different from being any other race or ethnicity. White privilege must be denied even when it is obvious in its reality and its effects. Dangerous historical memories must be erased in a way that severs the connection between white people's contemporary privileged social location with historical patterns of injustice. When such a connection is destroyed, no one can interpret the relationship between white wealth and racial exploitation—the ethical, moral, and political dynamics of such a relationship never enter white consciousness. With such concepts "whited out," Whites can be represented as the victims of racism just as easily as *The National Enquirer* can claim that Bill Clinton made love to an alien. Such a sociohistorical amnesia allows the Supreme Court to assume that racism at the end of the twentieth century is rare, found among a few white supremacist organizations and a number of racist black militants. This collective white denial of privilege inhibits questions and public reflection on how being White may provide benefits. In this era of white recovery, rarely do public figures ask: Do people ever get jobs and promotions because they're white? (Gallagher 1994; Giroux 1992; Gresson 1995; Hacker 1992; McIntosh 1995; Rubin 1994; Winant 1994).

Indeed, one of the great paradoxes of the end-of-the-century Western societies is their ability to deny what is most obvious: the privileged position of whiteness. Using their belief in a just world with equal opportunity, white students maintain the charade of white victimization. Critical multiculturalists intent on implementing a pedagogy of whiteness must understand the social context that constructs the denial while at the same time appreciating the ways of seeing of white students who genuinely feel victimized. Critical teachers, thus, will not be surprised when they encounter white students who vehemently resent multicultural requirements as antiwhite restrictions that subject them to charges of racism merely because they are White. Some white students see such curriculums as burdens and enter the classes with attitudes shaped accordingly. Multiculturalists teaching about whiteness and white privilege will not succeed if they are not ready to encounter such hostility.

## MOMENTS IN THE PEDAGOGY OF WHITENESS

A critical pedagogy of whiteness assumes that over the last two decades, many Whites have experienced a crisis of identity that must be viewed in the larger context of a growing interracial distrust and an expanding disparity of wealth between White and non-White, rich and poor (Sleeter 1995). Such a pedagogy is grounded in the belief that it is in the best interests of white people as a group to study this situation in a manner that helps them appreciate its moral, ethical, and civic dynamics so they can better formulate progressive ways of responding. As white people, working-class Whites in particular, explore their socioeconomic frustrations and anger in this context, a critical pedagogy of whiteness helps them understand the hollowness of the right-wing argument that preferential policies for Blacks and Latinos have undermined their chances for mobility. White people must understand that the right-wing version of global free-market capitalism that has gained ascendancy in the last two decades has undermined both their own and nonwhite opportunities for good work. Indeed, a key dimension of the pedagogy involves refusing to allow right-wing politicians and social leaders to play Whites against non-Whites, rich versus poor, to protect their positions of power.

The pedagogy of whiteness that we propose attempts to connect an understanding of the construction of whiteness to the political and socioeconomic issues raised earlier. In order to accomplish this difficult task, teachers and cultural workers must examine concepts and processes traditionally ignored in academic settings, including invisible power relations and the ways such social forces shape human consciousness. They must develop creative and compelling ways of talking about racial identity, racial privilege, and racial discomfort that allow students and other individuals to name their previously unspeakable feelings and intuitions. This reference to "feelings and intuitions" does not imply that our pedagogy is a "feel-good" one unconcerned with academic rigor. The curriculum envisioned here is very demanding, embracing concepts and analytical methods from history, philosophy, sociology, anthropology, literary criticism, psychology, film studies, political science, economics, education, and cultural studies in its efforts to engage students in self- and sociopolitical examination. For example, students would engage in a variety of case studies in how color lines are drawn, analyzing historical instances such as California's struggle since the mid-nineteenth century to classify its racial groups and the late-nineteenth-century Irish struggle for admission to the fraternity of whiteness. Interestingly, in the Irish case white status was conferred only when they adopted the old residents' antipathy toward African Americans.

As it contextualizes whiteness, this critical study is characterized by particular moments, including the exposé of the invisibility of its social power and privilege, awareness of the way whiteness as an ideological construction cannot be simply conflated with white people, recognition of the power of whiteness to help produce both white and nonwhite subjectivity/consciousness, cognizance of the power of whiteness to dominate through its ability to normalize itself, knowledge of tacit forms of white supremacy and their complicity with mutating, end-of-century crypto-racism, and the appreciation of the necessity of the reconstruction of whiteness and white identity around a stance of progressive antiracism. The moments do not present themselves in some convenient linear unfolding but are *enfolded* into the opaqueness of whiteness itself, expressing themselves here and there like photons in a linear accelerator. Extending the quantum metaphor, the moments are observable only if we ask the "appropriate" questions. Such questions might involve: inquiries into how whiteness functions in the lives of white people—a prerequisite to any attempt to rearticulate white identity; investigations of how whiteness as a signifier will be received very differently by individuals standing at different intersections of various race, class, gender, religious, and geographical axes of identity; or inquests into the ways whiteness as a norm shapes the lives of those who are both included and excluded by the categorization (Nakayama and Krizek 1995; Stowe 1996; Yudice 1995).

One of the most dramatic moments in teaching whiteness involves the effort to identify and make sense of white power. Such an identification process involves encouraging students to understand the white power bloc—the loose alignment of various social, political, educational, and economic agents as well as agencies that work in concert around particular issues to maintain white power. Without trying to elicit guilt and place blame, teaching students about white power involves the difficult task of tracing oppressive historical frameworks that continue in an ever-evolving form to structure the everyday life of all peoples at the end of the twentieth century. Such a process always will be difficult simply because stifling information by which everyday people gain insight into the workings of power is central to the maintenance of power. Those who are privileged struggle to control representations of themselves; the white power bloc, thus, is not comfortable with the study of whiteness. In this context white students from middle/upper-middle-class backgrounds frequently resist a pedagogy of whiteness as a threat to their privilege. When such a pedagogy views the white power bloc from the perspective of the marginalized, palms sweat and blood pressures rise as connections and continuities are highlighted between agents such as the governing board of Texaco, the publishers of many high school history textbooks, agribusiness leaders in southern California, the administrators of the Virginia Military Institute, and Richard Herrnstein and Charles Murray, the authors of *The Bell Curve: Intelligence and Class Structure in American Life.* No secret Oliver Stone–like conspiracy exists between these agents, but they do work in concert at some tacit level for the protection of white and often male privilege.

The highlighting of the white power bloc enables individuals to see the previously invisible role of whiteness as the norm, the standard by which everyone is measured. Thus, another important moment in this education involves denormalizing whiteness. White ways of being can no longer be universalized, white communication practices can no longer be viewed unproblematically as the standard, and issues of race can no longer be relegated to the domain of those who are not White. The analysis of whiteness that we call for involves a cultural reassessment, a cultural commitment to rethinking the basis of multicultural society. In this context, Whites rethink racial imprints that traditionally have been tacitly relegated to a transcultural domain. Operating on the foundation of such a commitment, white people get over their discomfort discussing how they appear to non-Whites, they learn to listen to the perceptions of African

Americans, Latino/as, and indigenous people, who see them as people not to be trusted, and they begin to rethink their lives and worldviews accordingly. Thus, Whites begin to take seriously the poststructuralist imperative to analyze their social and political positions vis-à-vis their whiteness. In this process, white people start to understand that what they "objectively" see may not be as neutral as they originally thought. Their assumptions have shaped their interpretations of perceptions that differ significantly from those of non-Whites (Fiske 1993; Haymes 1996; Keating 1995; Nakayama and Krizek 1995; Tatum 1994).

A central feature of any pedagogy of whiteness, of course, involves the unlearning of racism. Many analysts have found that many white people have grown up with no one to challenge their assumption of white supremacy. Even after they have been exposed to multicultural antiprejudice programs, many Whites report that they have never been asked to reconsider the assumption that being White is better than being non-White. This education induces Whites to ask such a question and to rethink the very notion of race in their lives. In this context it implores all white people, working class and poor Whites in particular, to examine the interests they share with non-Whites. The forces of the global corporate power bloc do not work in the interests of most white and nonwhite people, and the sooner they all understand this political dynamic, the quicker they can begin to put together alliances based on their mutual interests in particular and social justice in general. Teachers and cultural workers who work in this critical educational setting must carefully monitor the effects of such pedagogical interventions. The goal here is not to elicit white feelings of guilt for white racism but to encourage insight into the nature of historical oppression and its contemporary manifestations (Gallagher 1994; Keating 1995; Nakayama and Krizek 1995; Stowe 1996; Thompson 1996; Yudice 1995). Now we are taking our first baby steps in the study and teaching of whiteness; accordingly, we are not sure either of which path to take or of what the effects of our efforts will be. In this situation, we must pay close attention to the themes we engage and the outcomes we help generate.

## REINVENTING WHITENESS

As white students gain an understanding of the power of whiteness, white supremacy, and the mutating nature of contemporary racism, they begin to perceive problems with their traditional civics lessons. The asymmetries of racial power do not fit with the American faith in meritocracy and the rewards of hard work. Individuals react differently to such a contradiction: despair, anger at the situation, anger at the messenger, a sense of mission, the development of a moral compass, the list goes on. . . . Central to a critical pedagogy of whiteness is the development of a healthy, hopeful, justice-oriented response to this paradox coupled with a rethinking of both white identity and the very nature of whiteness itself. Traditional forms of multiculturalism have not offered a space for Whites to rethink their identity around a new, progressive, assertive, counter-hegemonic, antiracist notion of whiteness. Various multicultural social theorists have addressed the issue of the new white identity with little agreement emerging in the process. Although difficult, it is possible to rethink white identity and reinvent whiteness in light of progressive democratic social goals and a critical understanding of social justice.

In this context, teachers of whiteness refuse to allow individuals to assume new identities without extensive analysis. Whites traditionally have devoted little attention to their racial identity, attending to it only after decades of heightened racial and ethnic awareness. A pedagogy of whiteness must understand these historical dynamics and appreciate the ways the white identity crisis has been colonized by conservative Eurocentric monoculturalists. When white students find themselves outside of any ethnic community and opt to build a new one around a mythologized white supremacist tradition, critical educators must be ready to show them they understand the context in which such students are operating and to offer them a progressive alternative. Here a pedagogy of whiteness becomes a contemporary adaptation of educator John Dewey's notion of the goal of a progressive education: to gain command of oneself so as to make positive social use of one's powers and abilities. Thus, the pedagogy promoted here is simply a subtheme of a philosophy of education that concerns itself with cultural identity and the social production of self. In its analysis of white identity, a critical pedagogy of whiteness seeks a new sociopsychological imaginary that offers a new vision for a twenty-first-century whiteness (Dewey 1994; di Leonardo, 1994; Gresson 1995; Grossberg 1995; Tatum 1994; Yudice 1995).

The redefinition of whiteness begins with the simple question: What does it mean to be White? How can we answer this question in a way that allows for a critique and a rejection of the oppression inflicted in the name of whiteness but concurrently creates a space for a progressive white identity that transcends some narrow notion of a politically correct orthodoxy? We are not comfortable with the concept of a new oppositional white identity as a "race traitor" who renounces whiteness. It is unlikely that a mass movement will grow around that concept, as oppositional Whites still would have little to rally around or to affirm. Antiracist Whites in search of a new identity in the late 1990s are still walking into a racial netherworld with few guides or guiding principles. The netherworld can be exciting and affirmational, but it also can be ambiguous and lonesome. Time there can nurture creativity while at the same time undermining traditional support systems and emotional stability. A key feature of a whiteness pedagogy, therefore, involves developing both theoretical and emotional support systems to help courageous white people through this complex transition. Such theoretical and emotional support systems must not be ascetic and punitive, but appealing, affirmative, humorous, sensitive, and aesthetically dynamic. They must draw on the emancipatory productions of many cultures while making use of the most progressive aspects of white culture itself.

The reinvention of whiteness operates outside any notion of racial superiority or inferiority, as it seeks to transverse the terrain of transitional identity. While it confronts white tyranny directly, it avoids projecting guilt onto white students. In the process, it generates a sense of pride in the possibility that white people can help transform the reality of social inequality and reinvent themselves around notions of justice, community, social creativity, and economic/political democracy. These concerns become extremely important in light of the reactions of white students to recent efforts to teach a critical multiculturalism. Many have great difficulty dealing with the despotism of the white norm and the brutality of white racism. Also, many have reacted negatively to such teaching, not as much out of disbelief or rejection but out of frustration as to what to do with their new knowledge. Without a vision of racial reinvention and support for the difficulties it entails, such students have nowhere to go. Their frustration in this context often has turned to cynicism and a descent into nihilism. The importance of an antiracist, positive, creative, and affirmational white identity in this teaching context cannot be overstated.

One white response to white tyranny has involved the attempt to opt out of whiteness, to escape the responsibility that comes with being White. Educational theorist Becky Thompson (1996) describes her personal effort to opt out as an "I don't want to be white stage"—a period where she did not want to associate with white people. In this mind-set white liberal guilt often leads to an essentialist romanticization of non-Whites that grants them a morally superior status. At the same time Whites may be essentialized as racist, bland, and undeserving of respect—given such characterizations, who would want to call themselves White? In this context white people may attempt to appropriate the "oppression status" of nonwhiteness, misreading the oppression of others for their own. This is where, of course, race traitors enter the whiteness studies cosmos—some describe the race traitor impulse as the political wing of the academic analysis of whiteness. We reject such a label and argue that while this is one activist response to white tyranny and the crisis of white identity, it is merely one of many—indeed, one that may be of little value in the larger effort to solve the material and spiritual consequences of racism and the inequality it generates (Jordan 1995; Tatum 1994; Yudice 1995).

Theorist George Yudice (1995) feels uncomfortable with what he considers the easy renunciation of whiteness and the privilege that accompanies it. Whites alone can opt out of their racial identity, can proclaim themselves nonraced. Yet no matter how vociferously they may renounce their whiteness, white people do not lose the power associated with being White. Such a reality renders many white renunciations disingenuous. It is as if some race traitors want to disconnect with all liabilities of whiteness (its association with racism and blandness) while maintaining all its assets (the privilege of not being Black, Latino, or Native American). Such cold, self-interested realities will always be an impediment to wide-scale efforts to forge new white identities. And this is not the only obstacle, as teachers and cultural workers must deal with a variety of social forces that undermine the effort to reinvent whiteness. As teachers teach a pedagogy of whiteness, they are reminded of how new and unusual such a concept must seem to students and how few models exist for transcending mainstream embodiments of whiteness.

## FASHIONING PROGRESSIVE WHITE IDENTITY: IMPROVISATIONS WITHIN A LITERACY OF POWER

As progressive antiracist Whites learn to listen and empathize with non-Whites, they work to overcome the obstacles to reshaping their identity and developing collective solidarity with other nonracist white people. Such a step is central to the struggle for successful multicultural living and the political movement that must accompany it. None of this focus on whiteness and white identity should be taken to suggest that efforts to empower oppressed groups should be de-emphasized. Instead, the goal of a critical pedagogy of whiteness involves the construction of a white identity that is emancipated from the cultural baggage that often has accompanied whiteness and the norm it insidiously establishes. This norm traditionally has involved a rejection of those who did not meet the notion of reason that emerged from the European Enlightenment. Whiteness deployed reason—narrowly defined *Eurocentric* reason—as a form of disciplinary power that excludes those who do not meet its criteria for inclusion into the community of the sociopolitically enfranchised. Understanding such dynamics, those interested in the reconstruction of white identity can engage in the postformal search for diverse expressions of reason.[1] Such a project empowers white students seeking progressive identities to learn about the process of White identity reconstruction, the redefinition of reason, the expansion of what is counted as a manifestation of intelligence, and the phenomenological experience of challenging the boundaries of whiteness.

Such pedagogical work is anything but easy; progressive Whites will require sophisticated help and support to pull them through the social, political, and psychological dilemmas they all will face. In such a context, those attempting to rethink their identity and to address the cultural and institutional racism they encounter always need strong support groups. Progressive Whites, unfortunately, often will find themselves at odds with white colleagues over racial issues that those colleagues deem to have nothing to do with race. In these situations, progressives will face accusations of being unreasonable and not being team players; they will be seen as truculent subversives who don't understand the hallowed traditions of the schools and institutions in which they operate. Individuals in these situations need support groups if for nothing else to help them survive emotionally. They need historical and contemporaneous examples of white antiracists who have engaged in these struggles and who have faced these personal attacks. They need black, Latino, Asian, and Native American supporters as well, who can provide them with other types of insight and support. In this context alliances can be formed between non-Whites and the white support groups that can address a range of problems in unique and creative ways (Alcoff 1995; Brosio 1994; Fiske 1994; Macedo 1994; Shor and Freire 1987; Sleeter 1995; Steinberg and Kincheloe 1997; Swartz 1993; Tatum 1994; Thompson 1996).

In this new pedagogy, the notion of identity itself is reconceptualized, as teachers refuse to view identity as an absolute, fixed essence. Since in a critical constructivist conceptual frame identities are ever changing in relation to power-driven ideologies and discourses, references to "true identities" are deemed oxymoronic. Understanding that identities are always in the process of negotiation, a critical pedagogy of whiteness does not seek to produce closure on the new white identities it engages. While critical teachers listen with interest to cultural theorists Gilles Deleuze's and Felix Guattari's (1986) notion of a postmodern nomadic identity that breaks up racial and cultural hierarchies, they are uncomfortable with its emphasis on the negation of categories of identity. Whiteness education is more interested in identity structures that are informed by a variety of engaged identities, focus on community building, and find grounding in critical notions of justice and democracy. While certain aspects of a nomadic identity can inform the reconceptualization of white identity, its lack of an ethical and a political referent is troubling.

From a critical pedagogical perspective, the refashioning of white identity involves not simply acquiring a new theoretical appreciation or new way of seeing the world. Such an effort involves new modes of living one's life, new methods of relating to the various individuals with whom one comes in contact. This reconceptualization of identity is focused first and foremost on the critical theoretical notion of emancipatory transformation—not in a modernist sense, where the new identity becomes final and authentic, but more in a poststructuralist articulation that understands the new identity as a transitional phase of an ever-evolving notion of self. A pedagogy of whiteness, therefore, seeks to engage students, teachers, and other individuals in an ever-unfolding emancipatory identity that pushes the boundaries of whiteness but always understands its inescapable connection to the white locale in the web of reality. Such a social location demands forms of political analysis and introspection that move Whites to examine, for instance, the privilege of white identity even after they abandon unexamined whiteness.

An emancipatory white identity seen as a process of becoming is catalyzed by explorations of new cognitive possibilities and forms of consciousness that are historically shaped but knowingly adopted. In this context transformation is fueled by familiarity with nonwhite aesthetics, culturally diverse manifestations of intelligence, and subjugated and indigenous knowledge. Many who have written about identity and its transformation have used the metaphor of border crossing to characterize this multicultural dynamic. While there is much to recommend the use of such a term, care must be taken to connect the act of border crossing with a fidelity to critical notions of social justice, democracy, and egalitarian community building. Without such moral and political grounding, the border crosser, like the nomad, can become an agent of the dominant culture who uses his or her knowledge of non-Whites to facilitate their regulation. A pedagogy of whiteness encourages white students to explore and cross the borders, to take advantage of the benefits to cultural bricolage, to interrogate the new perspectives emerging from the ways traditions are reworked on the cultural borders, to study the manner in which common ground is negotiated in a context where differences are accepted and affirmed, and to analyze the effects of all these border dynamics on identity formation.

It is high time that progressives respond to the white identity crisis—the reinvention of whiteness and the construction of transformational white identities are, it is hoped, steps in the right direction. The reconstruction of white identity is important because it affects everyone; dominant white culture imposes cultural meanings on Blacks, Latino/as, Asians, and Native Americans and, in the process helps to shape self-images and consciousness. As a pedagogy of whiteness moves individuals past a quixotic quest for racial authenticity and purity, the analysis of the meaning and pitfalls of hybridity ensues. The term, "cultural *mestizaje*," often used as a concept challenging existing racial categories and representations, can be employed as a heuristic device that induces teachers, students, and cultural workers to study the ways cultural interaction and exchange take place. In a critical context, *mestizaje* becomes not an educational goal as much as a category for careful scrutiny into the forces that reshape culture and influence identity (Alcoff 1995; Haymes 1996; Keating 1995; McLaren 1993; Wellman 1996).

The treatment of *mestizaje* speaks to a central feature of the educational system described here: No fixed educational outcome, specific definition of whiteness, or particular formation of white identity is sought. While all pedagogical activity is carefully framed by a commitment to antiracism, social justice, political and economic democracy, and heterogeneous and egalitarian community building, there is great room for divergence within these categories. The idea of a pedagogy of whiteness is one of the most compelling notions to emerge in decades in the struggle for racial justice. In order to take advantage of the possibilities it offers, we must be vigilant in our efforts to discern potential problems within it. When multicultural education addresses only the Other and the Other's cultural difference, Whites do not have to examine their own ethnicity and the ways it shapes their social outlook and identity. Once this fundamental concept is appreciated, the most difficult pedagogical work begins with the examination of white privilege, the complex nature of whiteness, the dynamics surrounding the white identity crisis, the redefinition of whiteness, and the formulation of an emancipatory white identity.

In this context, people will confront the social forces that have rocked race relations during the last couple of decades. Understanding the history and nature of racism in relation to the sociopsychological impact of the last thirty years on the white psyche, teachers of a critical pedagogy of whiteness develop a "power literacy" that helps them simultaneously negotiate and explain the quagmire of racial interaction in the late twentieth century. Such a power literacy helps white people in the process of reconceptualizing their identity appreciate the fact that a new white identity does not erase the power differences between White and non-White. No matter how loudly Whites proclaim their border identities, their racial hybridity, their commitment to a common humanity, or their fidelity to *mestizaje,* they can still "pass" as white people when they seek employment, job promotions, or even stroll through all-white neighborhoods. The conversation about whiteness and a pedagogy of whiteness is just beginning; judging from the intense interest that it generates, it will not quickly fade away. A study of whiteness that refuses to forget its antiracist and democratic roots lapses into bourgeois self-indulgence, becomes a psychologized attempt to "feel good" about the angst of privilege, loses sight of the power dynamics that shape racial relations, and cannot make a valuable contribution to the cause of racial justice and egalitarian democracy.

# NOTES

1. Postformalism is a theoretical effort to redefine the Eurocentric notions of intelligence and reason by examining such concepts in light of sociopsychological insights from a variety of non-Western cultures; see Kincheloe 1995; Kincheloe and Steinberg 1993.

# BIBLIOGRAPHY

Alcoff, L. (1995). "Mestizo Identity." In N. Zack (ed.), *American Mixed Race: The Culture of Microdiversity.* Washington DC: Rowman and Littlefield.

Banfield, B. (1991). "Honoring Cultural Diversity and Building on Its Strengths: A Case for National Action." In L. Wolfe (ed.), *Women, Work, and School: Occupational Segregation and the Role of Education.* Boulder, CO: Westview.

Brosio, R. (1994). *The Radical Democratic Critique of Capitalist Education.* New York: Peter Lang.

Carby, H. (1992). "The Multicultural Wars." In G. Dent (ed.), *Black Popular Culture.* Seattle: Bay Press.

Clover, C. (1993). "Falling Down and the Rise of the Average White Male." In P. Cook and P. Dodd (eds.), *Women and Film: A Sight and Sound Reader.* Philadelphia: Temple University Press.

Deleuze, G., and Guattari, F. (1986). *Kafka: Toward a Minor Literature.* Trans. D. Polan. Minneapolis: University of Minnesota Press.

Dewey, J. (1994). "My Pedagogic Creed." In A. Sadovnik, P. Cookson, and S. Semel (eds.), *Exploring Education: An Introduction to the Foundations of Education.* Boston: Allyn and Bacon.

di Leonardo, M. (1994). "White Ethnicities, Identity Politics, and Baby Bear's Chair." *Social Text* 41, 5-33.

Eisenman, R. (1995, October). "Take Pride in Being White". [Letter to editor.] *Chronicle of Higher Education* 134.

Fiske, J. (1994). *Media Matters: Everyday Culture and Political Change.* Minneapolis: University of Minnesota Press.

———. (1993). *Power Plays, Power Works.* New York: Verso.

Frankenberg, R. (1993). *The Social Construction of Whiteness: White Women, Race Matters.* Minneapolis: University of Minnesota Press.

Gallagher, C. (1994). "White Reconstruction in the University." *Socialist Review* 24, no. 1-2, 165-187.

Giroux, H. (1995). "White Panic." In C. Berlet (ed.), *Eyes Right: Challenging the Right-Wing Backlash.* Boston: South End Press.

———. (1992). *Border Crossings: Cultural Workers and the Politics of Education.* New York: Routledge.

Gresson, A. (1995). *The Recovery of Race in America.* Minneapolis: University of Minnesota Press.

Grossberg, L. (1995). "What's in a Name (One More Time)?" *Taboo: The Journal of Culture and Education* 1, 1-37.

Hacker, A. (1992). *Two Nations: Black and White, Separate, Hostile, Unequal.* New York: Ballantine Books.

Haymes, S. (1996). "Race, Repression, and the Politics of Crime and Punishment in *The Bell Curve.*" In J. Kincheloe, S. Steinberg, and A. Gresson (eds.), *Measured Lies: The Bell Curve Examined.* New York: St. Martin's Press.

Herrnstein, R., and Murray, C. (1994). *The Bell Curve: Intelligence and Class Structure in American Life.* New York: Free Press.

Jordan, J. (1995). "In the Land of White Supremacy." In C. Berlet (ed.), *Eyes Right: Challenging the Right-Wing Backlash.* Boston: South End Press.

Keating, A. (1995). "Interrogating 'Whiteness,' (De)Constructing Race." *College English* 57, no. 8, 901-18.

Kincheloe, J. (1995). *Toil and Trouble: Good Work, Smart Workers, and the Integration of Academic and Vocational Education.* New York: Peter Lang.

Kincheloe, J., and Steinberg, S. (1997). *Changing Multiculturalism.* London: Open University Press.

———. (1993). "A Tentative Description of Post-Formal Thinking: The Critical Confrontation with Cognitive Theory." *Harvard Educational Review* 63, no. 3, 296-320.

MacCannell, D. (1992). *Empty Meeting Grounds.* New York: Routledge.

Macedo, D. (1994). *Literacies of Power: What Americans Are Not Allowed to Know.* Boulder, CO: Westview Press.

McIntosh, P. (1995). "White Privilege and Male Privilege: A Personal Account of Coming to See Correspondences Through Work in Women's Studies." In M. Anderson and P. Collins (eds.), *Race, Class, and Gender: An Anthology.* Belmont, CA: Wadsworth.

McLaren, P. (1993). "Border Disputes: Multicultural Narrative, Identity Formation, and Critical Pedagogy in Postmodern America." In D. McLaughlin and W. Tierney (eds.), *Naming Silenced Lives: Personal Narratives and the Process of Educational Change.* New York: Routledge.

McMillen, L. (1995, September). "Lifting the Veil from Whiteness: Growing Body of Scholarship Challenges a Racial Norm." *Chronicle of Higher Education,* A23.

Nakayama, T., and Krizek, R. (1995). "Whiteness: A Strategic Rhetoric." *Quarterly Journal of Speech* 81, 291-309.

Rubin, L. (1994). *Families on the Faultline: America's Working Class Speaks about the Family, the Economy, Race, and Ethnicity.* New York: HarperCollins.

Shor, I., and Freire, P. (1987). *A Pedagogy for Liberation: Dialogues on Transforming Education.* South Hadley, MA: Bergin and Garvey.

Sleeter, C. (1995). "Reflections on My Use of Multicultural and Critical Pedagogy When Students Are White." In C. Sleeter and P. McLaren (eds.),

*Multicultural Education, Critical Pedagogy, and the Politics of Difference.* Albany: State University of New York Press.

Steinberg, S., and Kincheloe, J. ( 1997). *Kinderculture: The Corporate Construction of Childhood.* Boulder, CO: Westview.

Stowe, D. (1996). "Uncolored People: The Rise of Whiteness Studies." *Lingua Franca* 6, no. 6 , 68-77.

Swartz, E. (1993). "Multicultural Education: Disrupting Patterns of Supremacy in School Curricula, Practices, and Pedagogy." *Journal of Negro Education* 62, no. 4, 493-506.

Tanaka, G. (1996). "Dysgenesis and White Culture." In J. Kincheloe, S. Steinberg, and A. Gresson (eds.), *Measured Lies: The Bell Curve Examined.* New York: St. Martin's Press.

Tatum, B. (1994). "Teaching White Students About Racism: The Search for White Allies and the Restoration of Hope." *Teachers College Record* 95 , no. 4, 462-475.

Thompson, B. (1996). "Time Traveling and Border Crossing: Reflections on White Identity." In B. Thompson and S. Tyagi (eds.), *Names We Call Home: Autobiography on Racial Identity.* New York: Routledge.

Vattimo, G. (1991). *The End of Modernity.* Baltimore: Johns Hopkins University Press.

Wellman, D. (1996). "Red and Black in White America: Discovering Cross-Border Identities and Other Subversive Activities." In B. Thompson and S. Tyagi (eds.), *Names We Call Home: Autobiography on Racial Identity.* New York: Routledge.

Winant, H. (1994). "Racial Formation and Hegemony: Global and Local Developments." In A. Rattans and S. Westwood (eds.), *Racism, Modernity, and Identity on the Western Front.* Cambridge, MA: Polity Press.

Yudice, G. (1995). "Neither Impugning nor Disavowing Whiteness Does a Viable Politics Make: The Limits of Identity Politics. In C. Newfield and R. Strickland (eds.), *After Political Correctness.* Boulder, CO: Westview.

# Emptying the Content of Whiteness

## Toward an Understanding of the Relation between Whiteness and Pedagogy

### Nelson M. Rodriguez

I have been performing whiteness, and having whiteness performed on me, since—or actually before—the moment I was born. But the question is, what does that mean?
—Ruth Frankenberg (1996)

## INTRODUCTION

I make a dual argument in this chapter: First, "whiteness" has content. While its content changes with context—that is, changes spatially and temporally—mapping terrains of whiteness and interrogating the spaces and logic of such terrains has become vital. Indeed, "mapping whiteness" has the potential not only to raise consciousness about one's own possible complicity in supporting oppressive regimes (that is, living whiteness oppressively); it also positions one to encounter a multitude of critical languages that can be used to rethink and live whiteness in progressive ways. Of course, in order to recognize that whiteness has content, one must first entertain the possibility that such content even exists. On a theoretical level, how might the content of whiteness be understood and/or articulated? In her text, *White Women, Race Matters: The Social Construction of Whiteness,* Ruth Frankenberg offers a theoretical description and justification for the interrogation of whiteness: "Whiteness *does* have content inasmuch as it generates norms, ways of understanding history, ways of thinking about self and other, and even ways of thinking about the notion of culture itself. Thus whiteness needs to be examined and historicized. We need to look more closely at *the content of the normative* and attempt to analyze both its history and its consequences. Whiteness needs to be delimited and 'localized'" (1993, 231, emphasis added).

As Frankenberg makes clear, part of the "work" of whiteness involves generating norms—that is, making things seem or appear natural and timeless so that people accept situations, as well as particular ideologies, without ever questioning their socially and politically constructed nature. To be sure, whiteness, within this context, dissuades people from interrogating what the literary critic Roland Barthes (1973, 11) calls "the falsely obvious." For example, in terms of curriculum, consider the role of the institution of the school in perpetuating the myth that sexuality is only about heterosexuality. In the cultural works that students are given to read, how is it that these very products fashion a "heteronormativity" and in the process generate a fictitious sense of the superiority of heterosexual desire? In the HBO documentary *The Celluloid Closet,* actor/screenwriter Harvey Fierstein shares his experience of growing up in a school culture where heterosexuality was the unnamed norm that pervaded the curriculum: "All the reading I was given to do in school was heterosexual. Every movie I saw was heterosexual, and I had to do this translation. I had to translate it to my life rather than seeing my life." Naming socially constructed norms, then, is one way of interrogating the logic of whiteness and, thus, of being better equipped to get at its content. If, for example, I name heterosexuality as a normalizing system—a "regulatory ideal," as French philosopher Michel Foucault would say—this in turn gives me reason to examine the logic that undergirds such a system as well as to better understand *where* and *how* it attempts to make its arguments for the placing of heterosexuality at the apex of the pyramid of sexual desire.

In addition to arguing that whiteness has content, I offer this second argument: It is necessary to produce "pedagogies of whiteness" as a counterhegemonic act. This is especially so given the way whiteness as a normative discourse can oppress people, especially groups falling outside of the dominant culture; or the way whiteness might legitimate certain epistemologies and ontologies over others to the point where those with less power are silenced; and still more the way whiteness can initiate and maintain historical amnesia. To talk about what would constitute a pedagogy of whiteness is difficult, however, for the direction such a pedagogy might take can and should be multiple. That is, just as whiteness itself changes over space and time, a pedagogy of whiteness also will change depending on the specific circumstances one finds oneself in and the pedagogical focus one wishes to explore and emphasize. However, in my view, it does seem necessary that certain dimensions be consistently considered in any formation of such a pedagogy. I'd like to describe these as a way of discussing the second argument of this chapter first.

As I have already suggested, one dimension would be to focus on interrogating and naming those aspects of normative discourses that are oppressive—oppressive because they attempt to neutralize and even obliterate difference. Thus, this first dimension would be concerned not only with uncovering the hidden curricula of normalizing systems but also would bring to light and teach subjugated histories, that is, histories and knowledges that have long been silenced in the name of socially constructed sacrosanct norms.

Important also in the formation of a pedagogy of whiteness is the attempt to refigure whiteness in antiracist, antihomophobic, and antisexist ways. What I am getting at here is the idea of radically rethinking the very notion of what it means to be White in the late twentieth century so that being White does not become synonymous with guilt or with the erroneous attempt to "trade in" one's white identity for the identity of the "Other." In "Neither Impugning nor Disavowing Whiteness Does a Viable Politics Make: The Limits of Identity Politics," George Yudice (1995, 264) articulates well the project at hand in refiguring white identity:

> The "easy solution," then, implies a strategy of "becoming minor" or "marginal," a superficial maneuver that suggests that nothing is at stake in one's identity if one can easily disavow it. Declaring oneself marginal without experiencing the hardships is, like ubiquity, a feature of privilege.

Nor is the "difficult solution" (i.e., engaging one's white identity as a function of the "dominant culture," which can result in hostility or guilt) much better, for it leaves no project, no positive imaginary for the self. . . . [I]t is necessary to *reinvent* whiteness as the "possibility of a radical white identity that isn't guilty, doesn't eat roast beef, and isn't trying to be black."

Regarding this chapter, two important points can be made from Yudice's comment. First, in terms of education, Yudice is instructive in helping us recognize that a pedagogy of whiteness driven by guilt and/or the impossible request of asking white students to renounce their whiteness in some total sense is doomed for failure. And second, to make part of a pedagogy of whiteness the notion of reinventing whiteness in radical and progressive ways is to help make the point that identities are not static. Indeed, identity is constantly being *updated* as one encounters other identities, histories, languages, and cultural practices. From this perspective, rethinking the very notion of the meaning of white challenges more broadly the limitations of categorical thinking. But I need to return for a moment and be clearer about the "guilt issue" I have just referenced.

While I am for reinventing whiteness in radically progressive ways, and while I am against guilt-tripping pedagogies, I do think an element of *trauma* or *unsettlement* or *bafflement* must accompany any attempt to rethink whiteness in the classroom along progressive lines. While, on the one hand, guilt-ridden pedagogies are debilitating in the sense that they produce reactions such as guilt, anger, withdrawal, and despair, "trauma within pedagogy," on the other hand, can decenter students' identities and ideologies so as to help them connect past injustices not only with how such injustices continue in the present; also, it can get them to understand that changes in the present can be made based on knowledge of the past. In this sense, students gain a sense of hope that they can contribute to a better world by living their whiteness progressively. Trauma within pedagogy attempts not to alienate students because of their whiteness. Instead, it asks them to rethink and rework their identities based on a radical reformulation of their whiteness; it also pushes them to interrogate whiteness critically as a normative discourse. Both attempts suggest a crisis is at issue to which students must be attentive. In their text, *Testimony: Crises of Witnessing in Literature, Psychoanalysis, and History,* Shoshana Felman and Dori Laub (1992, 53) capture the importance of trauma within pedagogy: "I would venture to propose, today, that teaching in itself . . . takes place precisely only through a crisis: if teaching does not hit upon some sort of crisis, if it does not encounter either the vulnerability or the explosiveness of a (explicit or implicit) critical and unpredictable dimension, it has perhaps not truly taught."

Next, any pedagogy of whiteness must be thought of as a *critical* pedagogy of whiteness in the sense that it must deal, in some way, with the issue of power. An examination, for example, of the nexus between power and knowledge in the curriculum might reveal how normative discourses, as found in mainstream curricula, signal attempts by power blocs to socialize students and teachers to accept and validate particular ways of knowing and being. This critical dimension within a pedagogy of whiteness moves teaching and learning away from understanding knowledge only in instrumental terms, that is, something simply to be mastered, to an understanding of knowledge as *ideological.* Such a critical curriculum would focus on how the production of knowledge takes place within unequal terrains of power struggles to name and represent the world, self, and Other. From this perspective, students begin to recognize that existential reality is not the product of divine intervention (that is, "the way things just are"); instead, social reality is made by men and women. Thus, as world-renowned educator Paulo Freire so eloquently notes in *Pedagogy of the Oppressed* (1995, 33), "Just as objective social reality exists not by chance, but as the product of human action, so it is not transformed by chance. If humankind produce social reality, then transforming that reality is an historical task, a task for humanity." Drawing on Freire, then, a pedagogy of whiteness that attempts to grapple with power relations must be driven by a project of social transformation, a project that works toward the redistribution of power and resources along more equitable lines.

Finally, such a pedagogy must examine culture, especially popular culture, for any "political struggle demands attention to culture—understanding what's out there, resisting cultural messages that disempower us, creating and circulating alternative visions" (Rand 1995, 6). Indeed, examining the various cultural sites, practices, and products where whiteness emerges is to politicize and give contextual specificity to whiteness itself. For example, consider how the politics of whiteness converges on the body of the Barbie doll. How, for instance, does Mattel promote a racist ideology by making white Barbie the standard? While it may be argued that Mattel has a line of "ethnic Barbies," this does not negate the fact that "Barbie Other" is still a version of the white standard Barbie. In addition, Mattel also engages in a superficial and depoliticized multiculturalism precisely because it wants to avoid implicating itself for its role in perpetuating "hegemonic discourses, and thereby the dominance of those served by these discourses; [its real concern stems from its capitalistic desire to create markets] to attract more ethnicity-conscious consumers" (Rand 1995, 9). When investigating the politics of whiteness through the cultural product of the Barbie doll, it can be recognized that whiteness itself is not only about race and racism. That is, whiteness also can be configured more broadly as a "normalizing technology" that aids in the production and maintenance of socially constructed standards and norms. "Dyke activist" and art historian Erica Rand, in *Barbie's Queer Accessories* (1995, 9), offers insight into Mattel's "whitening project" when she notes, "Mattel promotes compulsory heterosexuality by making it look like the most natural and attractive choice; it [also] promotes capitalism and the unequal distribution of resources by glamourizing a character with a huge amount of disposable cash and, to understate grossly, a disproportionate amount of luxury items; [finally], it promotes ageism and sexism by suggesting that a beautiful young body is a woman's most valuable commodity." Again, what begins to emerge here is not only the way whiteness politics manifests itself at a particular cultural site, but also the way that site provides a lens for articulating a more sophisticated and nuanced understanding of how that politics cuts across a variety of social axes, including race, class, gender, sexual orientation, and age.

In terms of my first argument, how do we go about mapping something that seems not to be there at all? Indeed, because whiteness has been unmapped for so long in any formal or theoretical way, the task seems daunting.[1] In much of the literature on whiteness, often a sense of frustration and/or "appreciation" for the complexities involved in naming whiteness can be heard. The film critic Richard Dyer, for example, opens his essay "White" (1988, 44) by noting: "This is an article about a subject that, much of the time as I've been writing it, seems not to be there as a subject at all. Trying to think about the representations of whiteness as an ethnic category in mainstream film is difficult, partly because white power secures its dominance by seeming not to be anything in particular." Examining whiteness at the level of the everyday—that is, examining how our very speech acts either reinforce or rupture the invisibility and supposed naturalness of whiteness—cultural theorists Thomas K. Nakayama and Robert L. Krizek (1995, 293) also struggle to name it: "whiteness has assumed the position of an uninterrogated space. In sum, we do not know what whiteness means. . . . The risk of critical researchers, who choose to interrogate whiteness, including those in ethnography and cultural studies, is the risk of essentialism. Whatever whiteness really means is constituted only through the rhetoric of whiteness. There is no true essence to whiteness; there are only historically contingent constructions of that social location." Finally, this appreciation for and understanding of the difficulty in getting at whiteness is also connected to a recognition of the conflictual and shifting nature of the category white. As American studies scholar Ruth Frankenberg (1993, 11-12) explains: ". . . Jewish Americans, Italian Americans, and Latinos have, at different times and from varying political standpoints, been viewed as both 'white' and 'nonwhite.' And as the history of 'interracial' marriage and sexual relationships also demonstrates, 'white' is as much as anything else an economic and political category maintained over time by a changing set of exclusionary practices, both legislative and customary."

Given that whiteness has an *everything-and-nothing* quality, again, where and how do we intervene in the mapping process? To this end, I have drawn on a body of theoretical works on whiteness that cut across disciplinary boundaries. I have purposely sought out articulations and/ or conceptualizations of whiteness from a variety of academic disciplines. I did this for two reasons: First, I wanted to find out if whiteness was and is a concern of the academy in general. Given that I was able to find interpretations of whiteness in such diverse fields as English, sociology, education, film studies, rhetorical studies, feminist/women's studies, African American studies, and communication/media studies, I think evidence clearly exists regarding the academy's interest in this topic. Second, it was my hope that, by examining whiteness across a variety of disciplines, I would find different conceptualizations of it and, at the same time, some similar underlying themes. Concerning the latter, one similar theme found in most of the essays considered here, albeit in their different ways, is the notion of the invisibility of whiteness, of how it maintains its natural, neutral, and hidden position. As Ann Louise Keating, in her essay, "Interrogating 'Whiteness,' (De)Constructing 'Race'" (1995, 904) notes, "Not surprisingly . . . the most commonly mentioned attribute of whiteness seems to be its pervasive nonpresence, its invisibility." Most of the theorists I have read contend that whiteness maintains its invisibility by not being questioned, mapped, interrogated; they also stress the ramifications of such silence. In their essay "De Margin and De Centre," for example, Isaac Julien and Kobena Mercer (1996, 455) draw on Coco Fusco to emphasize the costs of not interrogating whiteness or the category white, saying: "as Fusco argues, 'to ignore white ethnicity is to redouble its hegemony by naturalizing it.'"

Having considered some of the possible intersections between whiteness and education in the attempt to initiate a discourse on what might constitute a pedagogy of whiteness as well as having begun to consider the meanings of whiteness, I'd like now to focus the remainder of this chapter on a theoretical mapping of whiteness. This theoretical detour will attempt to answer in broad fashion the following question: What shape/form does whiteness take (that is, what is whiteness) and/or what "work" does it do (what are its modes of operation and effects) within particular cultural, linguistic, and historical contexts? The emphasis on context here is meant to show that, far from being an essentialized phenomenon, whiteness is socially situated and changes as it encounters new contexts. It is for this reason that no operational definition of whiteness is possible. This emphasis on context is also meant to provide teachers and other cultural workers with a theoretical space for considering how whiteness *in its multiplicity* might be engaged within specific political and pedagogical projects. Keeping these two emphases in mind, then, in the mapping that follows, I offer four conceptualizations of whiteness: The first examines the relation of whiteness to order, rationality, and rigidity; the second examines the strategic rhetoric of whiteness. Examining whiteness in relation to "terror" provides the third mapping. And finally, an understanding of solidarity as the opposite of whiteness concludes the chapter. Two points are necessary at this stage: First, I frame some of the discussion of whiteness within the political struggles surrounding sexuality. I do this to emphasize that whiteness as a phenomenon cuts across social axes; it does not only impinge on matters of race. And second, "coming to terms" with whiteness is both a personal and, at times, painful experience. However, it seems to me that when examining theories of whiteness, it is impossible not to reflect on one's own encounters with it. In other words, reading about whiteness has helped me to "spot" it in my own everyday experiences. For this reason, throughout this essay, and I hope extending the theories offered, are my personal ways of seeing and encountering whiteness. This chapter, then, is part autobiographical.

## MAPPING A TERRAIN OF WHITENESS

### I.

"The fear of one's own body, of how one controls it and relates to it" and the fear of not being able to control other bodies, those bodies whose exploitation is so fundamental to capitalist economy, are both at the heart of whiteness.

—Richard Dyer (1988)

The essay "White" (1988) by film critic Richard Dyer is a pioneering study on whiteness; therefore, I begin a mapping of the terrain of whiteness with it. First, however, we turn to the cultural theorist Stuart Hall in order to set the context for why Dyer's essay is pioneering. In "New Ethnicities," Hall (1996, 446) problematizes the very concept of ethnicity, noting: "The term ethnicity acknowledges the place of history, language and culture in the construction of subjectivity and identity, as well as the fact that all discourse is placed, positioned, situated, and all knowledge is contextual. Representation is possible only because enunciation is always produced within codes which have a history, a position within the discursive formations of a particular space and time." As I read Hall, "ethnicity" is a product of cultural, social, and political forces, which means "a recognition that we all speak from a particular place, out of a particular history, out of a particular experience, a particular culture (447)." Thus no ethnicity can legitimate itself by claiming transcendentiality or universality. Ethnicity is, in other words, *contextual.* What this means is that " 'we are all ethnically located'" (Julien and Mercer 1996, 456). The new ethnicity for Hall, then, can be understood as a kind of "microethnicity"; the concept of ethnicity itself is *decoupled* from its equivalence with nationalism to, as Hall notes, an "ethnicity of the margins, of the periphery" (Hall 1996, 447). However, the problem is that whiteness and white ethnicity have rendered themselves invisible; they have been able to hide, so to speak, from scrutiny by maintaining an *everywhere-and-nowhere* position. The rearticulation of ethnicity, thus, entails "the displacement of the 'centered' discourses of the West [and further] putting in question its universalist character and its transcendental claims to speak for everyone, while being itself everywhere and nowhere" (446). Returning now to why Dyer's essay is pioneering: Through his analysis of representations of whiteness in mainstream film, he shows how elusive whiteness is, if only because it has been interrogated so rarely. However, by contesting the hegemony of whiteness, thus making it visible within the specific context of film, Dyer's article "inaugurates a paradigmatic shift by precisely registering the reorientation of ethnicity that Hall's argument calls for" (Julien and Mercer 1996, 455). Indeed, Dyer's essay is pioneering not only because it registers ethnicity as a construct, but also because it brings to the fore the very idea of the existence of whiteness as well as what whiteness itself might look like. Dyer argues that whiteness has content and attempts to give this content form/shape.

## WHITENESS AS "BOUNDEDNESS," ORDER, AND RIGIDITY

In "White," Dyer names whiteness, and he uses mainstream film as his vehicle for doing so. He understands, however, the difficulty in getting at the phenomenon of whiteness; thus he attempts to approach it by examining representations of blackness in the Hollywood films *Simba, Jezebel,* and *Night of the Living Dead.* These representations of blackness in turn provide a lens through which *whiteness as whiteness* comes into view. The central argument Dyer proposes is that whiteness is associated in these films with rigidity and "boundedness," and that the films imply this by highlighting the supposed looseness inherent to blackness, implicitly revealing, however, not only the *machinery* of whiteness (what it does, how it works) but also its "properties." As Dyer (1988, 47-48) notes, "all three films share a perspective that associates whiteness with order, rationality, rigidity, qualities brought out by the contrast with black disorder, irrationality, and looseness." The essentialist binarism in these films is fictitious; nevertheless, it does provide an opening for showing the form that whiteness might take, thus focusing on it long enough to identify its shape and, consequently, its logics and modes of operation. I'd like to synthesize and analyze here Dyer's explication of *Jezebel,* for through his subtle analysis he shows how the film illustrates well the passing off of white culture as "low affect" by creating an essentialism about Blacks and black culture that is not only fictitious but racist. The irony, however, about *Jezebel* lies with Julie, played by the white star, Bette Davis. Finding herself repressed by the artificially and socially constructed codes of her white culture—that is, by how the culture disallows the white body to experience publicly its own instabilities, desires, and passions—she attempts to transgress such codes and, in the process, reveals whiteness as "white calm."

Julie occupies a conflictual space in the movie because she desires to move beyond the restrictive codes of her white culture. These codes impose a rigidity not only onto the white body in general but also, more specifically, onto the white, *female* body. As Dyer (1988, 56) notes: "*Jezebel* is generally, and rightly, understood to be about the taming of a woman who refuses to live by the Old South's restrictive codes of femininity. . . . The film [thus suggests that Julie's] trajectory is a specifically white, as well as female, one." The dual challenge that Julie faces, then, is to surmount the repressive codes that pervade her white culture in general as well as the strictures that women faced in the Old South during the 1850s. In attempting to transgress these codes, however, Julie's body is juxtaposed to the black, female body. Not only is the black body positioned pedagogically to make whiteness and white culture appear the better by linking them to order and rationality, but in particular the black, female body is used to portray a spatial, racial, and gender location that should not be desired. However, in so doing, the film deconstructs itself, in my view, by possibly evoking in the viewer a desire not for white culture but for the essentialism it has defined for and about Blacks and black culture. Thus, the movie partly undermines its own pedagogical attempt to "educate" about the supposed superiority of whiteness and white culture.

Even though the film quite possibly deconstructs itself, Julie still is not able to transgress fully her bounded situation. Instead, Julie can display opposition that, while temporarily disrupting the codes of her culture, does not enable her to overcome her social situation. As a consequence, she can only move through the boundedness of her white culture by living vicariously through the black characters in the film. Again, the film deconstructs itself in this way but also attempts to make the argument compositionally that blackness is undesirable precisely because it is loose, irrational, and unbounded. In order to see whiteness better within this racial/gender framework, let's turn to a brief examination of a scene where Dyer reveals blackness as unbounded, and, therefore, whiteness as bounded, precisely at the intersection of race and gender. The famous Olympus Ball scene will initiate the example.

In this scene, Julie shows up for the ball in a red, satin dress. The other women wear white. "The immediate scandal is not just the refusal to conform and uphold the celebration of virginity that the white dress code represents, but the sexual connotations of the dress itself, satin and red" (ibid.). This dress, however, is the same one Julie gives to her black maid, Zette, after the ball. In the film, according to Dyer, Zette is drawn to the dress because of its colorfulness. As Dyer notes: "It is precisely its *colourfulness* that, stereotyping informs us, draws Zette—the dress is marked as coloured, a definite, bold colour heightened by a flashy fabric, just as black representation is." (ibid.). Thus the film suggests that color and colorfulness (that is, looseness) are associated with blackness. Indeed, pedagogically the film operates to give the impression that color is associated with the black Other and that living whiteness is about not living blackness. Instead, living white means not showing one's color. As Dyer (56-57) states:

> Thus what appears to be symbolism (white for virginity, colour for sex) within a universally applicable communication circuit becomes ethnically specific. The primary association of white with chastity is inextricably tied to not being dark and colourful, not being nonwhite, and the defiance and vitality narratively associated with Julie's wearing of the dress is associated with the qualities embodied by black women, qualities that Julie as a white woman must not display, or even have.

As *Jezebel* works to warn against Whites becoming like Blacks, by stereotyping Blacks as loose, unbounded, and out of control, the film endorses a racist binarism that not only pushes for the maintenance of the fixed visibility of the Other; that is, the unbounded black body must be controlled. It also pushes for a kind of living for Whites that is associated, as I have argued, with boundedness, order, and rigidity, a white calm that becomes equated with death itself. Indeed, as Dyer (58) has suggested, in the very process of defining its norm as "white calm," whiteness reveals itself as "an imposition, a form of repression of life."

## II.

We need to expose whiteness as a cultural construction as well as the strategies that embed its centrality. We must deconstruct it as the locus from which Other differences are calculated and organized. The purpose of such an inquiry is certainly not to recenter whiteness, but to expose its rhetoric. It is only upon examining this strategic rhetoric that we can begin to understand the influences it has on our everyday lives.

—Thomas K. Nakayama
and Robert L. Krizek (1996)

When discussing issues of racism, sexism, and heterosexism with my undergraduate preservice student teachers, I often make the argument that we are all to a certain extent racist, sexist, and heterosexist. Such claims usually are unsettling. In my attempt to get more specific, I ask them to consider this: "Do you really think it is possible to step fully outside of the history of racism, to remove ourselves from the way this history has inscribed itself on our bodies and in our very speech acts?" This question alarms some students, angers others, and perhaps even traumatizes. There's a moment of silence, and soon I recognize that behind the wall of silence some students are considering (perhaps for the first time) their own past and present involvements in "racist activity." Indeed, a white, middle-class, young woman speaks out, "Yeah, that could be right." She then shares with the class this brief story: "I remember recently listening to a guest black speaker here at the university. As I sat there, I said to myself, 'He's really a smart black man.'" There's another moment of silence, and I begin to hope there has been a kind of consciousness raising among the students.

## THINKING WHITENESS, SPEAKING WHITENESS

How is it that we think whiteness, speak whiteness, and, in this very process, resecure the hegemonic position of whiteness, that is, constantly recenter it as norm? To mark the "black Other" as "smart," in the way this student did, suggests that the black Other's smartness is measured against something else. "Wow, he's a smart black man." But smart in relation to what or to whom? The "what" and the "whom" constitute zones of whiteness. They are the centered and silent eyes that have the power to represent and name the Other. They comprise the yardstick with which others are compared and with which we compare ourselves. Thus part of the project in identifying and challenging the authority and centeredness of whiteness lies in uncovering the forces that produce the binarism, center/margin. What is it that contributes to our overinvestment in the center, thus producing marginal spaces? From this question, another: What entails our deconstructive project? Cultural critics Isaac Julien and Kobena Mercer (1966, 451) suggest this: "It would be useful to identify the relations of power/ knowledge that determine which cultural issues are intellectually prioritized in the first place. The initial stage in any deconstructive project must be to examine and undermine the force of the binary relation that produces the marginal as a consequence of the authority invested in the centre."

In examining "the force of the binary relation," one might begin with thought processes and speech acts. Indeed, at the level of everyday thinking and speaking—that is, in our encounters with individuals and groups— how do we reflect moments of performing whiteness? And in this process, how do we generate, perpetuate, and maintain a fictitious narrative about the superiority of whiteness? In this section, I want to examine several strategies of the discourse of whiteness by specifically drawing on Thomas K. Nakayama and Robert L. Krizek's essay, "Whiteness: A Strategic Rhetoric" (1995). Here they assemble several discourses that constitute for them the space of whiteness. They note: "In order to map a strategic rhetoric of whiteness, we have assembled a multiplicity of discourses. . . . These strategies mark out and constitute the space of whiteness. By marking this territory, we are making the critical move of not allowing white subjectivity to assume the position of the universal subject with its unmarked territory" (298). Examining the way these discourses on whiteness go unchecked in everyday interaction is part of the process of stopping, seeing, and naming whiteness.

## THE EVERYDAYNESS OF WHITENESS

One strategic rhetoric of whiteness emerging at the level of everyday discourse attempts to rationalize, understand, and/or "sell" the category white as simply nothing more than scientific classification. The appropriation of the latter, however, naturalizes the category itself, which is part of the strategy at work here. For example, drawing on ethnographic interviews and survey data, Nakayama and Krizek (1995, 300) show how respondents, when asked such questions as "What does it mean to be white?" go on to articulate that one's whiteness means nothing more than superficial racial characteristics: "'It just classifies people scientifically and not judgmentally.' Within this discourse, 'white' means 'nothing, except that is what color I am.'" As Nakayama and Krizek go on to assert, however—an assertion I believe is correct—the consequences of performing and/or accepting this strategy are devastating, especially in one regard: *Whiteness is drained.* "We see [within this discourse] that whiteness is drained of its history and its social status; once again it becomes invisible. . . . By referencing whiteness through science, the historical and experiential knowledge of whiteness is hidden beneath a scientific category. . . . By conceptualizing white as natural, rather than cultural, this view of whiteness eludes any recognition of power relations embedded in this category" (ibid.). To be sure, within this strategic rhetorical discourse, the place of whiteness within history and the role of history in the production of whiteness enable the category white to have no history, to mean nothing. The rhetorical strategy "I'm just white, you're just black" works to downplay the necessity of keeping alive a subversive memory of critique and resistance by precisely evading the role of history in the production and meaning of whiteness. Consequently, an understanding of present inequities along lines of the unequal distribution of resources and power is lost to a politics of forgetting.

A second strategy: conflating nationality with race. In this discourse, some of Nakayama and Krizek's respondents make the claim that to be White means one is American, or to be American means one is White. For example, one white respondent noted, " 'A lot of times when people think of American, I bet you they probably think of white. They probably think it's redundant.'" (ibid.). When asked about the meaning of whiteness, another respondent stated that "whiteness means 'that I'm of American descent,' or white means 'white American'" (ibid.). The implications of this strategic rhetoric are at least two: First, by conflating Americanness with whiteness, and vice-versa, there is at work here a policing of identity whereby people who engage in and/or adopt this strategic rhetoric attempt to generate a narrative about race that is essentialist and stagnant—a strategy, in my view, used to avoid the messiness of overlap in any discussions about race (that is, the possibility of a white person having black blood). It is also used to name oppressed groups such as Blacks as the Other, by juxtaposing the latter to a fictitiously generated pure and unified white body. If this strategy works to bifurcate the black and white races along clearly (albeit fictitious) demarcated lines, then the broader implication is the relegation of all individuals and groups in the United States that fall outside of the white equals American paradigm to a marginal role in national life, and it is this that constitutes the second implication of this strategic rhetoric. Perhaps most important to keep in mind here with this second strategy is the attempt at downplaying and even removing from history, and thus from memory, the way contributions by people of various races and ethnicities as well as by women and by people of varying sexual orientations have all contributed to the character of what constitutes Americanness. Any attempt to *singularize* national identity across race, class, gender, and sexual orientation lines is a fabrication that attempts to create a hierarchy precisely along any one of these lines. All these lines *intersecting* contribute to American life, not any one of them in isolation.

As an example, consider the role of the institution of literary theory and criticism (and literary theorists and critics). How has such an institution attempted in the past to *racially singularize* the identity of the canon of American literature, and, in turn, how has that attempt influenced the more broadly mistaken belief that whiteness equals Americanness? In *Playing in the Dark: Whiteness and the Literary Imagination,* novelist and literary critic Toni Morrison (1993) takes issue with literary theorists' attempts at singularizing the American literary canon by engaging in a politics of silence regarding the influence of the black presence in shaping and informing our nation's literature. As she explains:

> For some time now I have been thinking about the validity and vulnera-
> bility of a certain set of assumptions conventionally accepted among
> literary historians and critics and circulated as knowledge. This knowledge
> holds that traditional, canonical American literature is free of, uninformed,
> and unshaped by the four-hundred-year-old presence of, first, Africans and
> then African-Americans in the United States. It assumes that this presence
> which shaped the body politic, the Constitution, and the entire history of

the culture has had no significant place or consequence in the origin and development of that culture's literature. Moreover, such knowledge assumes that the characteristics of our national literature emanate from a particular "Americanness" that is separate from and unaccountable to this presence. There seems to be more or less tacit agreement among literary scholars that, because American literature has been clearly the preserve of white male views, genius, and power, those views, genius, and power are without relationship to and removed from the overwhelming presence of black people in the United States. (5)

As Morrison suggests, an exclusionary practice is involved or embedded in whiteness. This presents us with two similar questions: What is the meaning of whiteness? And what does whiteness do? Within the context of our discussion regarding the conflation of nationality and race, it seems to me that whiteness operates to maintain the power of a specific race, class, gender, and sexual orientation grid. Thus, not only does one have to be White to be considered authentically American, but one also must be male and heterosexual. To conflate whiteness with Americanness, then, is to invoke not only the "race issue" but also the entire aforementioned grid in particular strategic ways that maintain asymmetrical power relations.

A final strategy: whiteness in relation to European ancestry. Here Nakayama and Krizek found that the Whites they interviewed understood their whiteness in relation to European ancestry but that this understanding constituted more a need to belong to a group/community than a desire or interest in understanding the political and economic consequences of belonging to the category white. This understanding does give specificity to whiteness; however, it does not necessarily translate into a critical understanding of the history of whiteness or to an understanding of the power and privileges that Whites have by being part of a socially favored group. Thus, in this strategy, issues of power and privilege as they relate to whiteness go unchecked. As Nakayama and Krizek (1995, 302) explain: "These individuals recognize their European heritage and give a specificity to whiteness: 'It means I am descended from European white people.' While this discourse recognizes a part of its historical constitution, 'White, of European descent,' this reflexivity does not necessarily mean that there has been a recognition of the power relations embedded in that history. . . . [Instead] it meets a need

Americans have for community without individual cost." In my view, this strategy works to give the impression that one is engaged in a critical self-reflexivity about one's own historicity, but in reality the reflexivity involved is devoid of any responsibility to understand one's own subject position in the web of reality in relation to where others stand.

In a similar vein, educational theorist Christine Sleeter (1993), in her discussion of the need for a white discourse on white racism in academe, examines the related strategy of equating ethnicity with race. Such an equation evades racism. For example, according to Sleeter, when Whites conceptualize cultural diversity in the United States, "we [sic] usually subdivide White groups by ethnic origins, placing groups such as Germans, Poles, and Scots within the same conceptual plane as African-Americans and Native-Americans. This conceptual plane high-lights cultural heritage" (14). From this perspective, Sleeter arrives at the important conclusion that this equation/strategy removes whiteness itself from scrutiny, as well as an interrogation of white racism, by highlighting cultural heritage to such an extent that issues of inequity and power relations are completely lost to a depoliticized pluralist multiculturalism.

As all of these rhetorical strategies suggest, at the level of everyday discourse and thought, it is possible to support the notion of whiteness as norm, and it is also possible to (un)wittingly maintain the invisibility and naturalness of whiteness. But it is also possible to challenge the spaces and authority of whiteness. Part of the work involved in doing so, however, requires "active memory work" and the recognition of how discourse and the politics of forgetting are linked. That is, we must connect our present-day thoughts and beliefs with historical discourses that have shaped such beliefs in the first place. In order to concretize what I mean, I offer a brief example regarding the intersecting issues of discourse, public memory, history, and patriarchy.

In the *Newsweek* article "White Male Paranoia," journalist David Gates (1993) discusses the "Rush Room" phenomenon, bars and restau-rants around the country where fans of Rush Limbaugh gather daily to listen and cheer on the right-wing radio host. Upsetting the Rush Roomers, among other things, was Clinton's forthright decision to appoint Janet Reno as attorney general. As Gates explains, "Among the Rush Room set, the insistence on appointing the best female attorney baldly and publicly violated the canons of fair play and equal opportunity" (51). What's missing from the Rush Roomers' argument about fair play and equal opportunity, however, is any historical recognition that prior to Janet Reno, there had never been a female U.S. Attorney General. So in terms of fair play and equal opportunity, the Rush Room set positions their argument only in the present, thus sidestepping issues of patriarchy and gender domination as they have existed in the past. Further, Rush Roomers make no attempt to understand how present structural systems continue to uphold male supremacy. In my view, this type of living and thinking only in the present, in the immediate, helps to support dominant regimes, for without a critical recognition of the ways the present is shaped and informed by past inequities there becomes less opportunity for the encouragement of a critical citizenry and, thus, less opportunity to challenge the status quo. This nonreflexivity also opens space for reactionary decisions and procedures, and more often than not it is those who have less power who pay the highest cost, sometimes with their very lives. Thus, tied up with a nonreflexive, reactionary attempt to regain not only male supremacy, as in the Rush Room example, but also white supremacy and heterosexual supremacy is the possibility that the *terror of whiteness* will strike at any moment. Let us now turn to a more focused examination of this particular face of whiteness.

### III.

All black people in the United States, irrespective of their
class status or politics, live with the possibility that they will
be terrorized by whiteness.

—bell hooks (1992)

Two critical questions: What does it mean to know oneself separate from whiteness? And: How does the critical active move of "looking back" provide a way, an inroad, to know (name) whiteness itself in relation to one's own identity politics, as well as to provide a strategy for fighting assimilation and forgetfulness? These are the questions that bell hooks attempts to grapple with when articulating her understanding of whiteness. Indeed, hooks (1992) begins her essay, "Representing Whiteness in the Black Imagination," by reminding us that Blacks look back; that is, they critically examine Whites and whiteness. She reminds us of this when discussing the surprised and sometimes angry reactions that white students have when they find this out. As she explains:

> In [my] classrooms there have been heated debates among students when
> white students respond with disbelief, shock, and rage as they listen to
> black students talk about whiteness, when they are compelled to hear
> observations, stereotypes, etc., that are offered as "data" gleaned from close
> scrutiny and study. Usually, white students respond with naive amazement
> that black people critically assess white people from a standpoint where
> whiteness is the privileged signifier. (339)

That white students sometimes "respond with naive amazement" upon
being exposed to the centeredness of whiteness by Blacks is, in my view,
a manifestation of the extent to which whiteness in its various forms has
become so in place in a multitude of sites in U.S. society and culture,
from the largest of institutions to the tiniest of spaces and crannies. In
other words, whiteness is "so there everywhere" that we rarely question
its spaces, logics, or assumptions. What we often understand epistemo-
logically, for example, seems "natural" and "correct" to us. This deep
investment in Western ways of knowing seems "understandable" not
because the West is better than the Rest, but because for so long the myth
of the inherent greatness of whiteness *has been with us.* As cultural critics
Robert Stam and Ella Shohat (1994, 296) note in their essay, "Contested
Histories: Eurocentrism, Multiculturalism, and the Media," "The resid-
ual traces of centuries of axiomatic European domination inform the
general culture, the everyday language, and the media, engendering a
fictitious sense of the innate superiority of European-derived cultures
and peoples." By bringing to presence, then, the idea that Blacks examine
the culture of white, white people, and whiteness itself with a critical
ethnographic gaze, hooks disturbs the long-held belief that all people
naturally desire and find relevant and meaningful the supposed unique
knowledge that Western culture has to offer. Hooks implicitly disrupts,
in other words, the embedded belief that Europe and America offer the
world some unique source of meaning. More explicitly, however, by
discussing the "look back," hooks sets up her essay around the understanding of what it is that Blacks have seen and are seeing, have felt and
are feeling, when they look back at whiteness: "Collectively black people
remain rather silent about representations of whiteness in the black
imagination. As in the old days of racial segregation where black folks
learned to wear the mask, many of us pretend to be comfortable in the
face of whiteness only to turn our backs and give expression to intense

levels of discomfort. Especially talked about is the representation of whiteness as terrorizing" (341).

hooks's way of seeing whiteness as terror explodes the egotistical, ludicrous, and unfounded belief that whiteness is equated with goodness and blackness with darkness, evil. Thus, as she rightly points out, there is a fantasy about whiteness, and this fantasy hides or removes from conversational circulation the oppressive components of whiteness as well as how it is understood and experienced by those who, for one reason or another, fall outside of the dominant paradigm: "Socialized to believe the fantasy, that whiteness represents goodness and all that is benign and non-threatening, many white people assume this is the way black people conceptualize whiteness. They do not imagine that the way whiteness makes its presence felt in black life, most often as terrorizing imposition, a power that wounds, hurts, tortures, is a reality that disrupts the fantasy of whiteness as representing goodness" (340-341). By naming whiteness as terror, hooks does not wish to create a simple reversal whereby black becomes equated with goodness and white with evil. That is, she is not interested in examining the stereotypes of Whites that are formed by Blacks as a consequence of Whites' stereotypes of Blacks. Indeed, stereotypes of Whites are only one form of representation in the black imagination. Rather, hooks wants to explore how Blacks form their understanding of whiteness as terror as a response to and/or consequence of a history of white supremacy and racism: "I want to focus on that representation of whiteness that is not formed in reaction to stereotypes but emerges as a response to the traumatic pain and anguish that remains a consequence of white racist domination, a psychic state that informs and shapes the way black folks see whiteness" (341).

To do this, hooks returns to memories; she journeys back to a time when whiteness made its *imprint,* an imprint that would carry over into her adult life, an imprint that would be in constant dialogue with her present circumstances. As an example, she notes:

> As a child, I did not know any white people. They were strangers, rarely seen in our neighborhoods. The "official" white men who did come across the tracks were there to sell products, Bibles, and insurance. They terrorized by economic exploitation. What did I see in the gazes of those white men who crossed our thresholds that made me afraid, that made black children unable to speak? Did they understand how strange their whiteness appeared in our

living rooms, how threatening? Did they journey across the tracks with the same adventurous spirit that other white men carried to Africa, Asia, to those mysterious places they would one day call the "third world"? Did they come to our houses to meet the Other face to face and enact the colonizer role, dominating us on our own turf? Their presence terrified me. Whatever their mission, they looked too much like the unofficial white men who came to enact rituals of terror and torture. As a child, I did not know how to tell them apart, how to ask the "real white people to please stand up." The terror that I felt is one blacks have shared. (341-342)

Moving into the past and examining it in relation to the present, especially examining historical points or moments when whiteness made its presence felt, offers pedagogical possibilities/openings for hooks. In other words, it is precisely by confronting whiteness historically—that is, by remembering when and how in the past it made its imprint felt at the level of the personal—that Blacks (and others), according to hooks, can begin to do at least two things: First, this personal confrontation with whiteness allows one the possibility to loosen the terror of history and the role of the terror of whiteness within that history on one's psyche. This counterstrategic move allows one to face the enemy, as it were, to conquer terror through ritual reenactment, and then begin the self-healing process of moving on, of trying to get beyond the trauma of the imprint of whiteness. Second, traveling into the past to confront the imprint of whiteness is to engage in "critical memory work" that not only serves as a self-healing tool but, perhaps more important, becomes a way for never allowing oneself to become too comfortable with whiteness in the present. Indeed, what does it mean to know oneself separate from whiteness, not separating oneself from whiteness or Whites, but fighting for an identity that isn't encompassed by dominating forms of whiteness? This question reflects the crux of hooks's project of possibility in writing "Representing Whiteness in the Black Imagination." To be sure, hooks is calling for making problematic the present by connecting it to the past. What it means to live blackness critically in the face of whiteness in the late twentieth century is partly predicated on recalling those historical terrorizing impositions of whiteness, remembering, that is, historical moments when the terror of whiteness was much more obvious than it is today. Keeping alive those more obvious terrorizing moments of whiteness, without letting them incapacitate, becomes important to maintaining in the present that necessary tension between one's own identity politics and this phenomenon we call whiteness; doing so is necessary because without that subversive memory, we are less likely to resist having whiteness performed on us as well as performing whiteness on others. This is even truer given that spotting moments of whiteness today is no easy matter.

While I want to be sensitive not to dislodge the specificity of hooks's discussion of whiteness as terror in the black imagination, of what that means specifically for Blacks, I can say that I have felt and at times continue to feel whiteness as terror, given my own identity politics as a gay man. That is, I have a shock of recognition when reading hooks, especially when she talks about the *always-possibility* of being terrorized by whiteness. Indeed, to know I might be struck down when walking the streets holding the hand of the man I love is to know deeply that I live daily with the possibility that whiteness might strike, might strike precisely because of what has been socially constructed and legitimated as sexual norm. I'm telling you this because I want to stress the importance of what mapping whiteness can do: In her specific discussion of whiteness as terror, hooks offers me a language with which to rethink my own personal understanding of and relationship to whiteness. In addition, the terror and terrorizing dimension of her understanding of whiteness makes me want to consider how, in that very different way Blacks and gays experience the terror of whiteness, we at the same time can unite deeply, profoundly, and productively based on this "shared" oppression, can create solidarity around our difference so as to fight larger "hate systems." Of course, solidarity building is not limited to gays and Blacks but is a possibility and hope for all people regardless of race, class, sexual orientation, gender, and other such axes. Indeed, understanding that solidarity is the opposite of dominating and oppressive forms of whiteness, not of white people, becomes crucial not only for so-called minority groups but for Whites as well. It also becomes the subject of the following section.

## IV.

I may be secular, but I know holiness when I see it.
One of its names is solidarity, the opposite of whiteness.
The more you claim it, honor it, and fight for it, the less it
costs.

—Melanie Kaye/Kantrowitz (1996)

What is meant by a "whitening project"? And how does the latter dehumanize by its very insistence on (re)centering whiteness as norm? In the attempt to answer these questions, let us turn for the moment to the issue of sexuality and public education. In public schooling, discussion of the diversity of human sexuality rarely takes place. Instead, the moral Right has defined sexuality in the curriculum as compulsory heterosexuality, and if "gay sex," for example, gets discussed at all, it is usually mentioned within the context of AIDS, deviancy, or abnormality. Thus, gays and lesbians, and gay and lesbian sex, become pathologized and/or medicalized within a curricular representational politics that attempts to privilege a particular version of sexuality by pathologizing sexual practices that fall outside of the politically and socially constructed dominant category—"heterosexuality." In "The Impact of Culture and Ideology on the Construction of Gender and Sexual Identities: Developing a Critically Based Sexuality Curriculum," educational theorist James T. Sears (1992) examines the hidden curriculum around the issue of sexuality, a curriculum that attempts to squash sexual diversity by limiting sexuality to a narrowly defined epistemological understanding backed by a disingenuous moral bent:

> Too many school children remain ignorant of the diversity of human sexuality. . . . This plague, so toxic to compassion and common sense, is spread by purveyors of a supposedly moral agenda. But I find the concern of these religious True Believers hardly moral. They do not want to eradicate ignorance and fear; rather they want schools to propagate their skewed concept of morality and sexual orthodoxy. Because they accept the axiom that sexual knowledge may lead to sexual activity, no Tree of Knowledge is welcomed in the Eden of the True Believer. (147)

I lead into a discussion of solidarity as the opposite of whiteness, by way of discussing the limiting and limited position of sexuality held by the moral Right in public education, in order to raise two related broader problematics: How does one take positions on issues without holding either oneself or others "hostage" to those positions? And at what point do one's personal convictions preclude the possibility for and necessity of solidarity building? Within a discourse on whiteness, the latter two questions might be rephrased as follows: How does any attempt to normalize a position represent an act or moment of performing whiteness (that is, imposing a whitening project)? And by not critically examining one's own ethical referents in relation to positions taken, how, then, does a position become or turn into a terrorizing imposition of whiteness to the point where the view of solidarity can no longer be seen? Indeed, in my view, part of what enables solidarity building is the recognition of the limits, possible violence, and uncertainty of any position. I am not suggesting that we cannot or should not take positions; we must take positions on issues in order to act. There must be, as Stuart Hall (1996, 264) tells us, "arbitrary closure." However, no position is free from interrogation either by the person or group declaring the position or by those whom the position might influence. And more important, no position is so absolute that it is free from the forces of other positions. Positions change; they expand; they take on new meaning and life; and they are reworked. This is the case in part because positions are enunciated within language, and language itself is unstable—unstable because it represents a terrain of struggle over meaning carried out within ongoing asymmetrical relations of power.[2] Indeed, no articulation, no speech act, no position, can claim to speak for everyone, can sell itself in some universal way. Positions, therefore, are not only open to interrogation; they are also, in the very act of being interrogated, subject to change. This does not mean, however, that dominant positions or cultural practices are simply free-floating or easy to subvert; yet at the same time, these positions and practices have no necessary or a priori meaning. In order to make better sense of what I have just said, let me expand some on my earlier discussion regarding the moral Right by focusing that discussion on a personal encounter I had with the topic of Christianity. This brief example also will work us back to the main issue of this section: solidarity as the opposite of whiteness as discussed, understood, and experienced by Melaine Kaye/Kantrowitz (1996) in "Jews in the U.S.: The Rising Costs of Whiteness."

Recently a Christian acquaintance told me that I was going to Hell because I had not taken the time out to get to know Jesus. At first, I did not know how to respond. Indeed, how does one critique such an assertion with a language that does not just say, "You're wrong"? In other words, how does one find and use a language of critique and possibility that not only exposes the oppressive dimensions of such an argument but also has the possibility to move the speaker of such an assertion in a direction where solidarity might be possible? Later, after I had some time to "settle" from the assertion, I began to think about this comment within the context of my ongoing work on whiteness. I realized in some sense the whiteness that lubricated this person's argument. That is, his version of Christianity, and the claim for its centeredness, was a moment of performing whiteness. Further, implied in his argument was the idea that anyone can embrace Christianity regardless of "personal specificity," a strategy no doubt for maintaining the "normative" space of Christianity itself. As Kantrowitz explains: "Christians—religiously observant or not—usually operate from the common self-definition of Christianity, a religion any individual can embrace through belief, detached from race, peoplehood, and culture" (122). Christianity, then, as my acquaintance was so carelessly throwing around the term, became for him, even though he did not think of it in these terms, the religious yardstick with which every other religious belief system was to be compared; it became that "(white) point in space from which we tend to identify difference" (Carby 1992, 193). Indeed, there does seem to be a relation between whiteness and Christianity. That is, in addition to normalizing its position by "containing" difference within it, Christianity also attempts to overlook its own oppressive historical moments, both instances illustrating the lack of humbleness necessary for the building of solidarity. Kantrowitz:

> Do white Christians feel kinship with African-American Christians? White slave owners, for example, with their slaves? White Klansman with their black neighbors? Do white Christians feel akin to Christians converted by colonialists all over the globe? Doesn't Christianity really, for most white Christians, imply *white?* And for those white Christians, does *white* really include *Jewish?* Think of the massive Christian evasion of a simple fact: Jesus Christ was not, was never, a Christian. He was a Jew. What did he look like, Jesus of Nazareth, 2,000 years ago? Blond, blue-eyed? . . . [And of course], crusades, witchburnings, and inquisitions. . . . That wasn't *their* Christianity. Their Christianity was a sweet white church and Grandma Jones's special Christmas cookies. (1996, 122).

As Kantrowitz suggests, challenging the normalizing and dehistoricizing processes of whiteness requires constant work at moving away from a desire to position one's thoughts and understandings of self, world, and Other at the center to, instead, a decentered space where, in the very act of taking a position, one also recognizes that such a position is taken not in isolation but within the context of communities that are ever-changing. Thus, what's entailed is a kind of pull and tug, because, on the one hand, individuals and groups are asked, as responsible and active citizens, to take positions on issues; but, on the other hand, the fact that positions live within sites of permanent political contestation suggests that positions always represent "contingent foundations." As a way of emphasizing the notion that positions must be taken "not standing still" and to continue the discussion about how and why this relates to the building of solidarity as the opposite of whiteness, I would like to end by telling the story that Kantrowitz shares about her struggles to locate, build, and define solidarity within the personal context of her intersecting identities as feminist, Jewish, activist, lesbian.

## CONNECTING THE
## PERSONAL WITH THE POLITICAL

In "Jews in the U.S: The Rising Costs of Whiteness," Kantrowitz (1996) makes the argument that Jews, and more generally speaking, humanity, must come together across race, class, gender, and sexual orientation lines. Doing so might even be necessary for survival. She tells the story, for example, of going to Portland, Oregon, on the evening of Election Day, 1992, to fight against Measure 9: "the most vitriolic of the homophobic hate measures, was on the ballot. Measure 9 would have sanctioned discrimination explicitly and violence implicitly; would have banned from public libraries and schools books that deal positively with gay and lesbian experience; would have blocked funding of any public institutions that aided gays and lesbians—for example, AIDS counseling" (133). Many years before, Kantrowitz lived in Portland, and it was there that she came out as a lesbian. Going to Portland, then, was an important move to unite with and be there for the lesbian and gay community. However, her decision to return was also triggered by a deep sense of Jewish history: "I felt like I was returning to Berlin, to the Weimar Republic in 1933 on the eve of the election; I was coming back to be with my people in their time of trouble" (133).

When Kantrowitz arrived, she went to a friend's house where she would stay. Pulling into the neighborhood, one of mixed races and incomes and not especially gay, Kantrowitz saw signs on every lawn. They read: NO ON 9. Upon witnessing this, Kantrowitz began to cry, for she realized that up to then she had had no concept of allies. As she notes: "Even though the friend I was going to stay with was heterosexual, and I knew she'd been working very hard on this issue, I had still somewhere assumed that no one would stand with us—that we would be fighting alone. And I knew this came from my history as a Jew" (133). Continuing her story, Kantrowitz tells how eventually Oregon's Jews stood unanimously against Measure 9: "every synagogue, every community organization and institution, every rabbi" (134). There was one rabbi, however, who refused at first to take a position. While Kantrowitz does not tell us why, one might speculate that the rabbi had *already* taken a position, more broadly, on the issue of lesbian and gay liberation: He either was against it or felt deeply torn over the issue. It is for this reason that he probably did not want to involve himself in the *particular* fight against Measure 9.

This possible angst felt by the rabbi, however, brings us back to my earlier discussion of the necessity to struggle constantly to rework personal positions taken in light of living in a world that is dynamic—such dynamism requires individuals and groups to be open to redefining themselves and their beliefs based on the exigencies and changing social, political, and cultural conditions of particular times and places. And it is this necessary flexibility that partly enables the construction of a politics that works, as Hall (1996, 444) notes, "with and through difference, which is able to build those forms of solidarity and identification which make common struggle and resistance possible but without suppressing the real heterogeneity of interests and identities, and which can effectively draw the political boundary lines without which political contestation is impossible, without fixing those boundaries for eternity." Indeed, as one might speculate, in eventually taking a position to fight against Measure 9, the rabbi probably had to rework his original position on equal rights for gays and lesbians given the context in which he found himself. In other words, he likely knew that maintaining his original position in the face of the imminent legalization of discrimination against gays and lesbians would not only put their lives, but quite possibly the lives of Jews (and others) in jeopardy as well. To be sure, an excerpt from the Oregon Jews' statement against Measure 9 suggests that, tied up with fighting against the specificity of the measure itself, there also was a deep historical recognition of the high costs of remaining depoliticized on any issue that might very well pave the way for mandated discrimination and hatred: "[The Holocaust] began with laws exactly like Ballot Measure 9. Those laws first declared groups of people to be subhuman, then legalized and finally mandated discrimination against them. Comparisons to the Holocaust must be limited. But clearly, this is the start of hatred and persecution that must stop now" (Kantrowitz 1996, 134).

In the foregoing story, whiteness is the opposite of solidarity. But what exactly does that mean? Within the context of solidarity building, whiteness is a set of political, cultural, and social forces linked to relations of domination that have the *potential* to keep individuals and groups from building necessary coalitions that are linked to broader democratic projects. To put it more bluntly: Whiteness in the negative sense is that which separates; it is that which prevents linking particular interests and struggles to the project of a radical democracy. Indeed, the battle against Measure 9 was not just about combating legalized discrimination against gays and lesbians, as many individuals and groups across a variety of social axes from the State of Oregon recognized. The battle had just as much to do with fighting against those forces of whiteness linked to dominance that separate; it was a battle against how such forces potentially can preclude the coalition building necessary for deepening and extending the project of a substantive democracy.

## BY WAY OF CONCLUSION: A FEW NOTES ON REDEPLOYING WHITENESS OTHERWISE

I would like to close with a few brief remarks about whiteness as domination. There can be no doubt that so much of the scholarship within "whiteness studies" has rightly problematized the historically unmarked material and discursive spaces of whiteness as well as shown their links to forms of domination. Such work needs to continue. At the same time, however, we must hold onto whiteness in the sense of committing ourselves to the project of rearticulating it. I say this in the face of a particular theoretical strand within whiteness studies advanced by the "new abolitionists." Their stance calls for the abolition of whiteness. As their slogan exemplifies, "Treason to whiteness is loyalty to humanity." But is it really possible to disavow or simply reject whiteness, just like that? I would think not. I tend to agree with the insight offered by sociologist Howard Winant (1997) where he critiques the new abolitionist project for not taking as seriously as it should the complexities of a social construction model of race. As he notes: "They [the abolitionists] employ it [social construction] chiefly to argue against biologistic conceptions of race, which is fine; but they fail to consider the complexities and rootedness of social construction, or as I would term it, racial formation. Is the social construction of race so flimsy that it can be repudiated by a mere act of political will?" (48). As Winant suggests, rather than trying to erase whiteness altogether, would not rearticulating (one's) whiteness be the better project? To be sure, the problem with attempting to erase whiteness is that it would have to be erased both within social structures and within culture. This to me seems like an impossible project. Again, I agree with Winant when he tells us that:

> whiteness may not be a legitimate cultural identity in the sense of having a discrete, "positive" content, but it is certainly an overdetermined political and cultural identity nevertheless, having to do with socioeconomic status, religious affiliation, ideologies of individualism, opportunity, and citizenship, nationalism, etc. Like any other complex of beliefs and practices, whiteness is embedded in a highly articulated social structure and system of signification; rather than trying to repudiate it, we shall have to rearticulate it (ibid.).

Transforming whiteness will certainly entail much political labor, and within academe many historically separate discourses will need to intersect fruitfully and creatively. Critical and cultural pedagogical discourses will constitute one important intersection for other theoretical and political discourses concerned with rearticulating whiteness. Indeed, how whiteness gets taken up in the curriculum, as well as how it is produced, circulated, received, and analyzed within a variety of cultural pedagogical sites, will have much to do with asking not how to abolish whiteness but what to *do* with it. To put it another way: Most of the content of this chapter has examined what whiteness does. However important such an investigation might be, we must concern ourselves with an equally important question: What can whiteness do?

# NOTES

1. I want to emphasize that even though whiteness has for so long been unmapped and is only now taken on a theoretical urgency of sorts in academe, Blacks have for some time informally examined whiteness as well as the white Other. For example, hooks (1992, 338) describes this informal mapping process: "Although there has never been any official body of black people in the United States who have gathered as anthropologists and/or ethnographers to study whiteness, black folks have, from slavery on, shared in conversations with one another special knowledge gleaned from close scrutiny of white people. Deemed special because it was not a way of knowing that has been recorded fully in written material, its purpose was to help black folks cope and survive in a white supremacist society. For years, black domestic servants working in white homes, acting as informants, brought knowledge back to segregated communities—details, facts, observations, and psychoanalytic readings of the white Other."

2. The contemporary efforts on the part of gays and lesbians to work on and work over the language of marriage illustrates well the instability of language precisely because of its encounters with the ongoing political struggles of individuals and groups to name and represent themselves in ways other than how dominant language sees and defines them.

# BIBLIOGRAPHY

Barthes, Roland. (1973). *Mythologies.* London: Paladin.

Carby, Hazel V. (1992). "The Multicultural Wars." In Gina Dent (ed.), *Black Popular Culture.* Seattle, WA: Bay Press.

Dyer, Richard. (1988). "White." *Screen 29,* 44.

Felman, Shoshana, and Laub, Dori. (1992). *Testimony: Crises of Witnessing in Literature, Psychoanalysis, and History.* New York: Routledge.

Fierstein, Harvey. (1995). Quoted in *The Celluloid Closet.* Rob Epstein and Jeffrey Friedman, directors. HBO presentation.

Frankenberg, Ruth. (1993). *White Women, Race Matters: The Social Construction of Whiteness.* Minneapolis: University of Minnesota Press.

Frankenberg, Ruth. (1996). "When We Are Capable of Stopping, We Begin to See: Being White, Seeing Whiteness." In Becky Thompson and Sangeeta Tyagi (eds.), *Names We Call Home: Autobiography on Racial Identity.* New York: Routledge.

Friere, Paulo. (1996). *Pedagogy of the Oppressed.* New York: Continuum.

Gates, David. (1993, March 29). "White Male Paranoia." *Newsweek.*

Hall, Stuart (1996). "New Ethnicities." In David Morley and Kuan-Hsing Chen (eds.), *Stuart Hall: Critical Dialogues in Cultural Studies,* 446. New York: Routledge.

hooks, bell. (1992). "Representing Whiteness in the Black Imagination." In Lawrence Grossberg, Cary Nelson, and Paula Treichler (eds.), *Cultural Studies*. New York: Routledge.

Julien, Isaac, and Mercer, Kobena. (1996). "De Margin and De Centre." In David Morley and Kuan-Hsing Chen (eds.), *Stuart Hall: Critical Dialogues in Cultural Studies*, 455. New York: Routledge.

Kaye/Kantrowitz, Melanie. (1996). "Jews in the U.S.: The Rising Costs of Whiteness." In Becky Thompson and Sangeeta Tyagi (eds.), *Names We Call Home: Autobiography on Racial Identity*. New York: Routledge.

Keating, AnnLouise. (1995). "Interrogating 'Whiteness,' (De)Constructing 'Race.'" *College English* 57, 904.

Nakayama, Thomas K., and Krizek, Robert L. (1995). "Whiteness: A Strategic Rhetoric." *Quarterly Journal of Speech* 81, 293.

Rand, Erica. (1995). *Barbie's Queer Accessories*. Durham, NC: Duke University Press.

Sears, James T. (1992). "The Impact of Culture and Ideology on the Construction of Gender and Sexual Identities: Developing a Critically Based Sexuality Curriculum." In James T. Sears (ed.), *Sexuality and the Curriculum: The Politics and Practices of Sexuality Education*. New York: Teachers College Press.

Sleeter, Christine E. (1993). "Advancing a White Discourse: A Response to Scheurich." *Educational Researcher* 22.

Stam, Robert, and Shohat, Ella. (1994). "Contested Histories: Eurocentrism, Multiculturalism, and the Media." In David Theo Goldberg (ed.), *Multiculturalism: A Critical Reader*. Cambridge, MA: Blackwell.

Winant, Howard. (1997). "Behind Blue Eyes: Whiteness and Contemporary U.S. Racial Politics." In Michelle Fine, Lois Weis, Linda C. Powell, and L. Mun Wong (eds.), *Off White: Readings on Race, Power, and Society*. New York: Routledge.

Yudice, George. (1995). "Neither Impugning nor Disavowing Whiteness Does a Viable Politics Make: The Limits of Identity Politics." In Christopher Newfield and Ronald Strickland (eds.), *After Political Correctness*, 264. Boulder, CO: Westview Press.

# THREE

# Whiteness Is . . .

## *The Struggle for Postcolonial Hybridity*

### Peter McLaren

**B**y the early twentieth century, European maritime empires controlled over half of the land (72 million square kilometers) and a third of the world's population (560 million people). Seventy-five million Africans died during the centuries-long transatlantic slave trade (West 1993). The logics of empire are still with us, bound to the fabric of our daily being-in-the-world; woven into our posture toward others; connected to the muscles of our eyes; dipped in the chemical relations that excite and calm us; structured into the language of our perceptions. We cannot will our racist logics away. We need to work hard to eradicate them. We need to struggle with a formidable resolve in order to overcome that which we are afraid to confirm exists let alone confront in the battleground of our souls.

The educational Left has failed to address the issue of whiteness and the insecurities that young Whites harbor regarding their future during times of diminishing economic expectations. With their "racially coded and divisive rhetoric," neoconservatives may be able to enjoy tremendous success in helping insecure young white populations develop white identity along racist lines. Consider the comments by cultural critic David Stowe (1996, 74) who writes:

The only people nowadays who profess any kind of loyalty to whiteness *qua* whiteness (as opposed to whiteness as an incidental feature of some more specific identity) are Christian Identity types and Aryan Nation diehards. Anecdotal surveys reveal that few white Americans mention whiteness as a quality that they think much about or particularly value. In their day-to-day cultural preferences—food, music, clothing, sports, hairstyles—the great majority of American whites display no particular attachment to white things. There does seem to be a kind of emptiness at the core of whiteness.

African-American studies scholar Cornel West has identified three white supremacist logics: the Judeo-Christian racist logic, the scientific racist logic, and the psychosexual racist logic. The Judeo-Christian racist logic is reflected in the biblical story of Ham, son of Noah, who, in failing to cover Noah's nakedness, had his progeny blackened by God. In this logic, unruly behavior and chaotic rebellion are linked to racist practices. The scientific racist logic is identified with the evaluation of physical bodies in light of Greco-Roman standards. Within this logic, racist practices are identified with physical ugliness, cultural deficiency, and intellectual inferiority. The psychosexual racist logic identifies black people with Western sexual discourses associated with sexual prowess, lust, dirt, and subordination. A serious question is raised by West's typology in relation to the construction of whiteness: What are the historically concrete and sociologically specific ways that white supremacist discourses are guided by Western philosophies of identity and universality and capitalist relations of production and consumption? West has located racist practices in the commentaries by the church fathers on the Song of Solomon and the Ywain narratives in medieval Brittany, to name just a few historical sources. He also has observed that human bodies were classified according to skin color as early as 1684 (before the rise of modern capitalism) by the French physician François Bernier. The famous eighteenth-century naturalist Carolus Linnaeus produced the first major written account of racial division in *Natural System* (1735).

People do not discriminate against groups because they are different; rather, the act of discrimination itself constructs categories of difference that hierarchically locate people as "superior" or "inferior" and then universalizes and naturalizes such differences. When I refer to whiteness or to the cultural logics of whiteness, I need to qualify what I mean. Here I adopt American studies scholar Ruth Franken-berg's (1993) injunction that cultural practices considered to be White need to be seen as contingent, historically produced, and transform-able. White culture is not monolithic, and its borders must be understood as malleable and porous. According to cultural theorist Alastair Bonnett (1996), whiteness is neither a discrete entity nor a fixed, asocial category. Rather, it is an "immutable social construction" (98). White identity is an ensemble of discourses, contrapuntal and contradictory. Whiteness—and the meanings attributed to it—is always in a state of flux and fibrillation. Bonnett notes that "even if one ignores the transgressive youth or ethnic borderlands of Western identities, and focuses on the 'center' or 'heartland' of 'whiteness,' one will discover racialized subjectivities, that, far from being settled and confident, exhibit a constantly reformulated panic over the meaning of 'whiteness' and the defining presence of 'non-whiteness' within it" (106). According to Frankenberg, white culture is a material and discursive space that: "is inflected by nationhood, such that whiteness and Americanness, though by no means coterminous, are profoundly shaped by one another. . . . Similarly, whiteness, masculinity, and femininity are coproducers of one another, in ways that are, in their turn, crosscut by class and by the histories of racism and colonialism" (1993, 233).

Whiteness needs to be seen as *cultural*, as *processual*, and not ontologically different from processes that are non-White. It works, as Frankenberg notes, as "an unmarked marker of others" differentness—whiteness not so much void or formlessness as norm" (198). Whiteness functions through social practices of assimilation and cultural homoge-nization; it is linked to the expansion of capitalism in the sense that "whiteness signifies the production and consumption of commodities under capitalism" (203). Yet capitalism in the United States needs to be understood as contingently White, since white people participate in maintaining the hegemony of institutions and practices of racial domi-nance in different ways and to greater or lesser degrees. Frankenberg identifies the key discursive repertoires of whiteness as follows:

> modes of naming culture and difference associated with west European
> colonial expansion; second, elements of "essentialist" racism . . . linked to
> European colonialism . . . and segregationism in what is now the USA;

third, "assimilationist" or later "color- and power-evasive" strategies for
thinking through race first articulated in the early decades of this century;
and, fourth, . . . "race-cognizant" repertoires that emerged in the latter half
of the twentieth century and were linked both to US liberation movements
and to broader global struggles for decolonization. (1993, 239)

Whiteness is a sociohistorical form of consciousness, given birth at the
nexus of capitalism, colonial rule, and the emergent relationships among
dominant and subordinate groups. Whiteness constitutes and demarcates
ideas, feelings, knowledge, social practices, cultural formations, and systems of intelligibility that are identified with or attributed to white people
and that are invested in by white people as "white." Whiteness is also a
refusal to acknowledge how white people are implicated in certain social
relations of privilege and relations of domination and subordination.
Whiteness, then, can be considered as a form of social amnesia associated
with certain modes of subjectivity within particular social sites considered
to be normative. As a lived domain of meaning, whiteness represents
particular social and historical formations that are reproduced through
specific discursive and material processes and circuits of desire and power.
Whiteness can be considered to be a conflictual, sociocultural, sociopolitical, and geopolitical process that animates commonsensical practical
action in relationship to dominant social practices and normative ideological productions. As an ideological formation transformed into a principle
of life, into an ensemble of social relations and practices, whiteness needs
to be understood as conjunctural, as a composite term that shifts in
denotative and connotative emphasis, depending on how its elements are
combined and on the contexts in which it operates.

Whiteness in the United States can be understood largely through the
social consequences it provides for those who are considered to be non-
White. Such consequences can be seen in the criminal justice system, in
prisons, in schools, and in the boardrooms of corporations such as Texaco.
It can be defined in relation to immigration practices and social policies
and practices of sexism, racism, and nationalism. It can be seen historically
in widespread acts of imperialism and genocide and linked to an erotic
economy of "excess." Cultural theorist Eric Lott (1993, 482) writes:

In rationalized Western societies, becoming "white" and male seems to
depend upon the remanding of enjoyment, the body, an aptitude for

pleasure. It is the other who is always "excessive" in this respect, whether through exotic food, strange and noisy music, outlandish bodily exhibitions, or unremitting sexual appetite. Whites in fact organize their own enjoyment through the other, Slavoj Zizek has written, and access pleasure precisely by fantasizing about the other's "special" pleasure. Hatred of the other arises from the necessary hatred of one's own excess; ascribing this excess to the "degraded" other *and indulging* it—by imagining, incorporating, or impersonating the other—one conveniently and surreptitiously takes and disavows pleasure at one and the same time. This is the mixed erotic economy, what Homi Bhabha terms the "ambivalence," of American whiteness.

Whiteness is a type of articulatory practice that can be located in the convergence of colonialism, capitalism, and subject formation. It both fixes and sustains discursive regimes that represent self and "Other"; that is, whiteness represents a regime of differences that produces and racializes an abject Other. In other words, whiteness is a discursive regime that enables real effects to take place. Whiteness displaces blackness and brownness—specific forms of nonwhiteness—into signifiers of deviance and criminality within social, cultural, cognitive, and political contexts. White subjects discursively construct identity through producing, naming, "bounding," and marginalizing a range of others (Frankenberg 1993, 193).

Whiteness constitutes unmarked patriarchal, heterosexist, Euro-American practices that have negative effects on and consequences for those who do not participate in them. Inflected by nationhood, whiteness can be considered an ensemble of discursive practices constantly in the process of being constructed, negotiated, and changed. Yet it functions to instantiate a structured exclusion of certain groups from social arenas of normativity.

Whiteness is not only mythopoetical in the sense that it constructs a totality of illusions formed around the ontological superiority of the Euro-American subject; it is also metastructural in that it connects whiteness across specific differences; it solders fugitive, breakaway discourses and rehegemonizes them. Consumer utopias and global capital flows rearticulate whiteness by means of relational differences.

Whiteness is dialectically reinitiated across epistemological fissures, contradictions, and oppositions through new regimes of desire that connect the consumption of goods to the everyday logic of Western democracy. The cultural encoding of the typography of whiteness is achieved by remapping Western European identity onto economic transactions, by recementing desire to capitalist flows, by concretizing personal history into collective memory linked to place, to a myth of origin. Whiteness offers a safe "home" for those imperiled by the flux of change.

Whiteness can be considered as a conscription of the process of positive self-identification into the service of domination through inscribing identity into an onto-epistemological framework of "us" against "them." For those who are non-White, the seduction of whiteness can produce a self-definition that disconnects the subject from his or her history of oppression and struggle, exiling identity into the unmoored, chaotic realm of abject Otherness (and tacitly accepting the positioned superiority of the Western subject). Whiteness provides the subject with a known boundary that places nothing "off limits" yet that provides a fantasy of belongingness. It's not that whiteness signifies preferentially one pole of the white-nonwhite binarism. Rather, whiteness seduces the subject to accept the idea of polarity as the limit-text of identity, as the constitutive foundation of subjectivity.

Whiteness offers coherency and stability in a world in which capital produces regimes of desire linked to commodity utopias where fantasies of omnipotence must find a stable home. Of course, the "them" is always located within the "us." The marginalized are always foundational to the stability of the central actors. The excluded in this case establish the condition of existence of the included. Thus we find that it is impossible to separate the identities of both oppressor and oppressed. They depend on each other. To resist whiteness means developing a politics of difference. Since we lack the full semantic availability to understand whiteness and to resist it, we need to rethink difference and identity outside of sets of binary oppositions. We need to view them as coalitionist, as collective, as processual, as grounded in the struggle for social justice.

While the entire range of discursive repertoires may come into play, jostling against, superseding, and working in conjunction with each other, white identity is constructed in relation to an individual's personal history, geopolitical situatedness, contextually specific practices, and his or her location in the materiality of the racial order. In other words, many factors determine which discursive configurations are at work and the operational modalities present.

Bonnett (1996, 98) notes that a reified notion of whiteness "enables white people to occupy a privileged location in anti-racist debate; they are allowed the luxury of being passive observers, of being altruistically motivated, of knowing that their 'racial' identity might be reviled and lambasted but never actually made slippery, torn open, or, indeed, abolished." He further notes: "To dismantle 'blackness' but leave the force it was founded to oppose unchallenged is to display both a political and theoretical naiveté. To subvert 'blackness' without subverting 'whiteness' reproduces and reinforces the 'racial' myths, and the 'racial' dominance, associated with the latter" (99).

Ian F. Haney-López's book, *White by Law* (1996), offers a view of white transparency and invisibility that is at odds with sociologist Charles A. Gallagher's thesis that Whites are growing more conscious of their whiteness. López cites an incident at a legal feminist conference in which participants were asked to pick two or three words to describe themselves. All of the women of color selected at least one racial term, but not one white woman selected a term referring to her race. This prompted theorist Angela Harris to remark that only white people in this society have the luxury of having no color. An informal study conducted at Harvard Law School underscores Harris's remark. A student interviewer asked ten African Americans and ten white Americans how they identified themselves. Unlike the African Americans, most of the white Americans did not consciously factor in their "whiteness" as a crucial or even tangential part of their identity.

López argues that one is not born White but becomes White "by virtue of the social context in which one finds oneself, to be sure, but also by virtue of the choices one makes" (1996, 190). But how can one born into the culture of whiteness, one who is defined as White, undo that whiteness? López addresses this question in his formulation of whiteness. He locates whiteness in the overlapping of *chance* (features and ancestry that we have no control over, morphology); *context* (context-specific meanings that are attached to race, the social setting in which races are recognized, constructed, and contested); and *choice* (conscious choices with regard to the morphology and ancestries of social actors in order to "alter the readability of their identity) (191).

In other words, López maintains that chance and context are not racially determinative. He notes that:

> Racial choices must always be made from within specific contexts, where the context materially and ideologically circumscribes the range of available choices and also delimits the significance of the act. Nevertheless, these are racial choices, if sometimes only in their overtone or subtext, because they resonate in the complex of meanings associated with race. Given the thorough suffusion of race throughout society, in the daily dance of life we constantly make racially meaningful decisions. (193)

López's perspective offers potential, it would seem, for abolishing racism since it refuses to locate whiteness only as antiracism's "Other." I agree with Bonnett when he remarks that "to continue to cast 'whites' as anti-racism's 'other,' as the eternally guilty and/or altruistic observers of 'race' equality work, is to maintain 'white' privilege and undermine the movement's intellectual and practical reach and utility" (1996, 107). In other words, Whites need to ask themselves to what extent their identity is a function of their whiteness in the process of their ongoing daily lives and what choices they might make to escape whiteness. López outlines—productively in my view—three steps in dismantling whiteness. They are worth quoting in full:

> First, Whites must overcome the omnipresent effects of transparency and of the naturalization of race in order to recognize the many racial aspects of their identity, paying particular attention to the daily acts that draw upon and in turn confirm their whiteness. Second, they must recognize and accept the personal and social consequences of breaking out of a White identity. Third, they must embark on a daily process of choosing against Whiteness. (1996, 193)

Of course, the difficulty of taking such steps is partly due to the fact that, as López notes, the unconscious acceptance of a racialized identity is predicated upon a circular definition of the self. It's hard to step outside of whiteness if you are White because of all the social, cultural, and economic privileges that accompany whiteness. Yet whiteness must be dismantled if the United States is to overcome racism. Cultural critic George Lipsitz remarks: "Those of us who are 'white' can only become part of the solution if we recognize the degree to which we are already part of the problem—not because of our race, but because of our possessive investment in it." (1995, 384)

The editorial in the book *Race Traitor,* puts it thus: "The key to solving the social problems of our age is to abolish the white race. Until that task is accomplished, even partial reform will prove elusive, because white influence permeates every issue in US society, whether domestic or foreign. . . . Race itself is a product of social discrimination; so long as the white race exists, all movements against racism are doomed to fail" (10).

I am acutely aware that people of color might find troubling the idea that white populations can reinvent themselves by making the simple choice of not being White. Of course, this is not what López and others are saying. The choices one makes and the reinvention one aspires to as a race traitor are not "simple" nor are they easy choices for groups of Whites to make. Yet from the perspective of some people of color, offering white people the choice of opting out of their whiteness could seem to set up an easy path for those who don't want to assume responsibility for their privilege as white people. Indeed, there is certainly cause for concern. Historian David Roediger (1994, 16) captures some of this when he remarks: "whites cannot fully renounce whiteness even if they want to." Whites are, after all, still afforded the privileges of being White even as they ideologically renounce their whiteness, often with the best of intentions. Yet the potential for nonwhiteness and antiwhite struggle is too important to ignore or dismiss as wishful thinking or associate with a fashionable form of code switching. Choosing not to be White is not an easy option for white people; it's not like deciding to make a change in one's wardrobe. To understand the processes involved in the racialization of identity and to consistently choose nonwhiteness is a difficult act of apostasy, for it implies a heightened sense of social criticism and an unwavering commitment to social justice (Roediger 1994). Of course, the question needs to be asked: If we can choose to be non-White, then can we choose to be Black or Brown? Insofar as blackness is a social construction (often "parasitic" on whiteness), then I would answer yes. Theologian James H. Cone, author of *A Black Theology of Liberation* (1986), urges white folks to free themselves from the shackles of their whiteness. He writes: "If whites expect to be able to say anything relevant to the self-determination of the black community, it will be necessary for them to destroy their whiteness by becoming members of an oppressed community. Whites will be free only when they become new persons—when their white being has passed away and they are created anew in black being. When this happens, they are no longer white but free" (97).

But again I would stress that becoming Black is not a "mere" choice but a self-consciously political choice, a spiritual choice, and a critical choice. To choose blackness or brownness merely as a way to escape the stigma of whiteness and to avoid responsibility for owning whiteness is still very much an act of whiteness. To choose blackness or brownness as a way of politically misidentifying with white privilege is, on the other hand, an act of transgression, a traitorous act that reveals a fidelity to the struggle for justice. Lipsitz sums up the problems and the promise of the abolition of whiteness as follows:

> Neither conservative "free market" policies nor liberal social democratic reforms can solve the "white problem" in America because both of them reinforce the possessive investment in whiteness. But an explicitly antiracist pan-ethnic movement that acknowledges the existence and power of whiteness might make some important changes. Pan-ethnic, antiracist coalitions have a long history in the United States—in the political activism of John Brown, Sojourner Truth, and the Magon brothers, among others—but we also have a rich cultural tradition of pan-ethnic antiracism connected to civil rights activism . . . efforts by whites to fight racism, not out of sympathy for someone else but out of a sense of self-respect and simple justice, have never completely disappeared; they remain available as models for the present. (1995, 384)

Cultural critic George Yúdice (1995, 268) gives additional substance to Lipsitz's concerns related to coalition building when he points out some of the limitations of current identity politics: "The very difficulty and imagining a new social order that speaks convincingly to over 70 percent of the population requires critics to go beyond pointing out the injustices and abuses and move on to an agenda that will be more effective in transforming structures. What good is it to fight against white supremacy unless whites themselves join the struggle?"

The key, Yúdice maintains, is to center the struggle for social justice on resource distribution rather than identity. "Shifting the focus of struggle from identity to resource distribution will also make it possible to engage such seemingly nonracial issues as the environment, the military, the military-industrial complex, foreign aid, and free-trade agreements as matters impacting local identities and thus requiring a global politics that works outside of the national frame" (280). The work of critical multiculturalists attempts to unsettle both conservative assaults on multiculturalism and liberal paradigms of multiculturalism, the latter of which, in my view, simply repackage conservative and neoliberal ideologies under a discursive mantle of diversity. In undertaking such a project, I have tried in a modest way to advance a critical pedagogy that will service a form of postcolonial hybridity.

Critical multiculturalism as a point of intersection with critical pedagogy supports the struggle for a postcolonial hybridity. Cultural critic Guillermo Gómez-Peña (1996, 7) captures the concept of postcolonial hybridity when he conceptually maps what he calls the "New World Border": a great trans- and intercontinental border zone, a place in which no centers remain. It's all margins, meaning there are no "Others," or better said, the only true "Others" are those who resist fusion, *mestizaje,* and cross-cultural dialogue. In this utopian cartography, hybridity is the dominant culture: Spanish, Frangle, and Gingonol are linguas francas; and monoculture is a culture of resistance practiced by a stubborn or scared minority. (7)

A revolutionary multiculturalism must engage what scholar Enrique Dussel (1993) calls "the Reason of the Other." The debates over modernity and postmodernity have a different set of valences in Latin America for *los olvidados,* for the peripheralized, for the marginalized, and for the wretched of earth. Dussel writes about this distinction from his own Latin American context:

> Unlike the postmodernists, we do not propose a critique of reason as such but we do accept their critique of a violent, coercive, genocidal reason. We do not deny the rational kernel of the universalist rationalism of the Enlightenment, only its irrational moment as sacrificial myth. We do not negate reason in other words, but the irrationality of the violence generated by the myth of modernity. Against postmodernist irrationalism, we affirm the "reason of the Other."

What I am advocating is a revolutionary multiculturalism that moves beyond the ludic, metrocentric focus on identities as hybrid and hyphenated assemblages that exist alongside or outside of the larger social totality.

Revolutionary multiculturalism, as I am articulating the term, takes as its condition of possibility the capitalist world system; it moves beyond a monoculturalist multiculturalism that fails to address identity formation in a global context and focuses instead on the idea that identities are shifting, changing, overlapping, and historically diverse (Shohat 1995). Revolutionary multiculturalism is a politics of difference that is globally interdependent and raises questions about intercommunal alliances and coalitions. According to cultural theorist Ella Shohat, intercommunal coalitions are based on historically shaped affinities, and the multicultural theory that underwrites such a coalitionist politics needs "to avoid either falling into essentialist traps or being politically paralyzed by deconstructionist formulations" (177). She articulates the challenge as follows:

> Rather than ask who can speak, then, we should ask how we can speak together, and more important, how we can move the dialogue forward. How can diverse communities speak in concert? How might we interweave our voices, whether in chorus, in antiphony, in call and response, or in polyphony? What are the modes of collective speech? In this sense, it might be worthwhile to focus less on identity as something one "has," than on identification as something one "does." (ibid.)

Living in Los Angeles is like being encrusted in a surrealist hallucination. Yet as I look at the city from this café window, things don't seem that bad: Kid Frost pulsates through the airwaves, a 1964 Chevy Impala cruises the street in all its bravado lowrider beauty; the sun is shining bountifully on brown, black, and white skin (albeit prematurely aging the latter); my gas tank is full and the ocean is reachable before the heat gets too heavy and the freeway too packed. I'll take the 405 toward Venice, searching for that glimmer of light in the eyes of strangers, seeking out that fertile space to connect, looking for the vacant lots of their souls where the foundation of a new public sphere can be fashioned out of the rubble of concrete dreams.

## BIBLIOGRAPHY

Bonnett, Alastair. (1996). "Anti-Racism and the Critique of White Identities." *New Community,* 22, no. 1,: 97-110.

Cone, James H. (1986). *A Black Theology of Liberation.* New York: Orbis Books.

Dussel, Enrique. (1993). "Eurocentrism and Modernity." *Boundary* 2, 20, no. 3, 55-77.

Frankenberg, Ruth. (1993). *The Social Construction of Whiteness: White Women, Race Matters.* Minneapolis: University of Minnesota Press.

Gómez-Peña, Guillermo. (1996). *The New World Border.* San Francisco: City Lights Bookstore.

Haney-López, Ian F. (1996). *White by Law: The Legal Construction of Race.* New York: New York University Press.

Hicks, Emily. (1991). *Border Writing.* Minneapolis: University of Minnesota Press.

Ignatiev, Noel and John Garvey (eds.). *Race Traitor* (1996). New York: Routledge.

Lipsitz, George. (1996). "It's All Wrong, but Its All Right: Creative Misunderstandings in Intercultural Communication." In Gordon Avery, Ian F. Haney, and López. *White by Law.* New York: New York University Press.

———. (September, 1995). "The Possessive Investment in Whiteness: Racialized Social Democracy and the 'White' Problem in American Studies." *American Quarterly* vol. 47, no. 3.

Lott, Eric. (1993). "White Like Me: Racial Cross-Dressing and the Construction of American Whiteness." In Amy Kaplan and Donald E. Pease (eds.), *Cultures of United States Imperialism.* Durham, NC: Duke University Press.

McLaren, Peter (1995). *Critical Pedagogy and Predatory Culture.* New York: Routledge.

Novik, Michael. (1995). *White Lies, White Power: The Fight Against White Supremacy and Reactionary Violence.* Monroe, ME: Common Courage Press.

Radhakrishnan, R. (1996). *Diasporic Mediations.* Minneapolis: University of Minnesota Press.

Roediger, David (1994). *Towards the Abolition of Whiteness.* New York: Verso.

Shohat, Ella. (1995). "The Struggle Over Representation: Casting, Coalitions, and the Politics of Indentification." In Román de la Campa, E. Ann Kaplan, and Michael Sprinker (eds.), *Late Imperial Culture.* New York: Verso.

Stowe, David W. (1996). "Uncolored People: The Rise of Whiteness Studies." *Lingua Franca* 6, no. 6, 68-77.

*The Boston Globe,* January 26, 1990.

*Time* (February 20, 1995), "Banker to Mexico: 'Go get 'em.'" p. 9.

West, Cornel. (1993). *Keeping Faith: Philosophy and Race in America.* New York: Routledge.

Yúdice, George. (1995). "Neither Impugning nor Disavowing Whiteness Does a Viable Politics Make: The Limits of Identity Politics." In Christopher Newfield and Ronald Strickland (eds.), *After Political Correctness: The Humanities and Society in the 1990s.* Boulder, CO: Westview.

# FOUR

# Is the Benign Really Harmless?

*Deconstructing Some*
*"Benign" Manifestations of*
*Operationalized White Privilege*

**Frances V. Rains**

Reaching back into the last century, and into the early part of this century, racism was raised as problematic for its victims (Douglass 1855/ 1969; Jackson 1881/1993; Winnemucca Hopkins 1883/1969) and as being institutionally embedded within our society (DuBois 1903/1990; Woodson 1933). As this century draws to a close and we stand on the brink of a new millennium, there is still much discussion of racism (Altbach and Lomotey 1991; Anzaldúa 1990; Davis 1983; Hull, Scott, and Smith 1982; McCarthy and Crichlow 1993; Morrison 1992; Omi and Winant 1986; Trinh 1989; Williams 1991) and how it functions in numerous areas in our society.

Within the last decade there also has been work that breaks ground on issues of whiteness within our society (Feagin and Vera 1995; Frankenberg 1994; McIntosh 1992; Roman 1993; Sleeter 1993). There is a freshness to such endeavors, since they mark the willingness of white scholars to begin to examine the location and power of whiteness in our society. This scholarship has not come easily, as cultural critics Hernán Vera, Joe R. Feagin and Andrew Gordon (1995) note: "One difficulty in studying the white self is that, until recently, it was an invisible and non-researched category, even difficult to name and not perceived as a distinctive racial identity. Even today, most white Americans either do not think about their whiteness at all or else think of it as a positive or neutral category" (296). Naming whiteness has provided an opportunity to examine an aspect of our society that was not seriously considered in the past by most scholars.

Yet for all the generation of theory on racism and on whiteness, there remains a surprising disconnection of these issues to the ways in which we behave and act toward each other. It is what I call the "vaccination effect." That is, there appears to be an inoculation of distancing that enables the readers of the theories to neutralize the impact of such issues on their everyday interactions. It is as if, once racism or whiteness is mentioned, the theoretical vaccinates the individual from the practical. It is similar to what Ana Tiscornía, an artist from Uruguay, proclaims in her artist statement regarding her society's response to sexism. She writes,

> Our society is machista [sexist]; very machista and hypocritical, but very good at putting on a "good front," especially in the artistic, politically progressive and intellectual circles in which I move. With the way the left embraces certain lines of thought, the privileged intellectuals develop abstract concepts . . . one would think that they would reject machista tendencies. Lamentably in this case, theory is not compatible with practice, and more than awareness is needed to transform daily habits.

While Tiscornía is discussing machista, her notion that there is a sense of putting on the "good front" is what often happens with issues of racism. The dialogue on racism becomes the front, symbolizing perceived concern. In the process of developing this perceived concern, however, symbol has too often been confused for substance. Dialogue becomes a means of vaccinating oneself against having to take action based on this concern. Personal responsibility and personal action too easily become anesthetized. In short, the "front" can lead to "dysconsciousness." Educator Joyce E. King (1991) asserts that dysconsciousness "is an uncritical habit of mind (including perceptions, attitudes, assumptions, and beliefs) that justifies inequity and exploitation by accepting the existing order of things as given. . . . It is not the *absence* of consciousness (that is, not unconsciousness) but an *impaired* consciousness or distorted way of thinking about race as compared to, for example, critical consciousness" (emphasis in original, 135). The front for dealing with racism becomes a dysconscious means of ignoring the intricacies embedded in this society's racist history, structures, and behaviors.

Although the civil rights movement and the legislation that followed may have driven many overt acts of racism underground, institutionalized racism and acts of white privilege continue to add subtle complexities to the issues of racism within our society. Much of the scholarship just cited has been an effort, on the part of some academics of color and white academics, not to lose sight of the need to continue to work on the issues. Theory alone, however, as Tiscornía suggests, is not enough. Unless some visible application of theory is evidenced, awareness can too easily become an endpoint rather than a beginning.

My intent is to bring the theoretical into the practical by examining the everyday world of academe. Many of the theories and discussions on racism and white privilege, after all, are generated in the academy. However, as cultural theorist Ruth Farmer (1993) suggests, "[i]n the academic community, much is written about racism, race dynamics, and racial attitudes, yet little is done about these same issues personally, departmentally, or institutionally. Race is viewed abstractly" (210). It is hypocritical to espouse the importance of race theories on the one hand and then turn a blind eye to the daily, personal interactions that center on racial dynamics on the other. The academy, then, presents an interesting location from which to bring the practical and the theoretical together.

The purpose of this chapter is to build on work already in place by drawing a connection between racism and white privilege. Also, several ways that seemingly benign daily habits of white privilege operate in the context of the academy will be deconstructed as a means of making the "practical" real. Is the benign really harmless? I argue that it is not. I maintain that unless we, as an academic community, are willing to examine our own house and proverbially "get it in order," we run the risk of being hypocrites about the very issues we profess to know well enough to write about, simultaneously alienating the audience we most desire to reach with our theories. If our theories are meant for our society, then what responsibility do we have to model what it is that we theoretically envision?

## THE RELATIONSHIP BETWEEN
## RACISM AND WHITE PRIVILEGE

> Snow-blindness. White solipsism: To think, imagine, and
> speak as if whiteness described the world.
>
> —Adrienne Rich (1979)

I posit that white privilege is the invisible corollary to racism—invisible in the sense that there are many who do not "see" how the two are connected. In this way, racism remains a label reserved for a derelict few, the relationship of white privilege and racism remains unexamined, and the status quo remains woefully in tact.

White skin privilege and the advantages that accompany it are not necessarily obvious to those who are white and middle class (McIntosh 1992). The privileges acquired by being a person of light skin color are so institutionalized that they do not appear to be "privileges" at all. As author Katherine Weiler (1988) asserts, "since white privilege is so much a defined part of U.S. society, whites are not even conscious of their relationship of power and privilege. In U.S. society, white is the norm; people of color are defined as deviating from that norm" (76-77). In this sense, many Whites do not conceive of themselves in racialized terms, even though their race matters very much in the "social pecking order" in which "power, prestige, and respect are distributed" (Dalton 1995, 108). This belief of "white is the norm" is so engrained it remains obscured from view, as natural as the air we breathe but do not see. This inability to see something that truly affects *all* of our lives contributes to the invisibility of white privilege as a corollary to racism.

This invisibility is further compounded by what educational theorist James Scheurich (1993) recognizes as a contradiction of perspectives between educated Whites and people of color.[1] By extension I would broaden the notion of white academics to also include white students in the academy. Scheurich (1993) begins:

> Few would disagree that racism continues to be a serious social problem.
> More problematic for many white academics is the judgment that the
> academy itself is racist. . . . I argue that the judgment that the academy is
> racist is frequently misunderstood by us white academicians because our

socially learned investment in individualism eclipses our awareness of our racial positionality.

. . . Highly educated whites usually think of racism in terms of the overt behaviors of individuals that can be readily be identified and labeled. A person who does not behave in these identified ways is not considered to be a racist. Within this perspective, racism is a label for individuals not for social groups. . . . People of color, on the other hand, usually experience racism differently. . . . [t]hey are constantly reminded by words, deeds, and unconscious gestures that they are out-group members because they experience themselves collectively and historically as being treated differently based on their skin color. . . .(5-6)

These contrasting viewpoints, seeing racism as an individualistic or as a subtle yet pervasive experience, lead to a difference in the construction of racism.

When racism is constructed as individualistic, it is much easier to think that it has no relationship to the vast majority of Whites, inside or outside of the academy. Undergirding this construction is a logic that alleges individuals who are not engaged in overtly racist behaviors are not racist. Comments made about racists or racism simply do not pertain to them. Such a construction of racism as overt, individualistic behavior provides a cloak of immunity from scrutiny.

Immunity carries with it a certain power, for being immune means not having to be mindful of that from which one is exempt. The complicity in racism that privilege provides remains nameless and unnoticed. The responsibility that comes with the location and role of white privilege can be denied. However, as educational theorist Laura Pérez (1993, 269) states " . . . power produces not only oppression but its opposition—and opposition, in turn, avails itself of power's blind spots and loopholes." The indelible marks that racism leaves on the lives that it touches provide a different construction of racism that offers to pull back the cloak of immunity to reveal the blind spots in how white privilege connects to racism through the maintenance of the status quo.

Racism often has been taught with an emphasis on the negative outcomes. That is, the focal point often is centered on how racism functions to the disadvantage of people of color. Yet rarely is there acknowledgment of how half of the lesson is missing. Racism is not only about negative outcomes; it is also about the hidden benefits to be gained from maintaining a system of racial inequalities (Feagin and Vera 1995; Frankenberg 1994; McIntosh 1992; Rains, 1995; Roman 1993). Who benefits from racist practices? How does racism serve to unjustly advantage some at the cost of disadvantaging others? In her reflective analysis, cultural theorist Peggy McIntosh (1992) explains:

> I have come to see white privilege as an invisible package of unearned assets that I can count on cashing in each day, but about which I was "meant" to remain oblivious. White privilege is like an invisible weightless knapsack of special provisions, assurances, tools, maps, guides, codebooks, passports, visas, clothes, compass, emergency gear, and blank checks. Since I have trouble facing white privilege, and describing its results in my life, I saw parallels here with men's reluctance to acknowledge male privilege. Only rarely will a man go beyond acknowledging that women are disadvantaged to acknowledging that men have unearned advantage, or that unearned privilege has not been good for men's development as human beings, or for society's development, or that privilege systems might ever be challenged and *changed.* (emphasis in original, 71)

As long as racism is perceived as *only* having negative outcomes, then the inequalities that exist within our society can be dysconsciously recast in such a way that the racial positioning in the social hierarchy and the set of advantages conferred upon those born with white skin privilege can be ignored.

The failure to analyze the invisibility of white privilege as a corollary to racism has prevented us from dealing effectively with racism. While there are overt acts of racism that cry out for attention, racism does not function in isolation. Rather, it is the subtler, "benign" acts of white privilege and the hidden benefits that accrue from unearned racial advantages that sustain the status quo and, in turn, sustain racial inequality. It is this status quo maintenance, in conjunction with white privilege, which makes racism more difficult to eradicate.

The task of deconstructing white privilege is not an easy one. Any analysis of either racism or white privilege is typically fraught with tensions, deeply rooted emotions, and intertwined histories. After all, 500 years of domination as a social group has contributed to the invisibility of white privilege and how it functions to maintain the status quo. Such a length of time in the top position of the racial hierarchy could certainly reinforce dysconsciousness toward one's own membership of race as well as one's own racialized location. Educational theorist Leslie Roman (1993) suggests that the invisibility of white privilege serves to "hide [whites] in the light of reflexive exposure . . . while obscuring their own structural locations, ethical responsibilities and epistemic standpoints" (75). As our nation struggles with affirmative action backlash and a social and political climate that appears to be headed toward retrenchment of racial divisions, it would seem that the ivory tower of the academy cannot remain exempt from such struggles.

The academy is deemed the place within society where the boundaries of knowledge and understanding are expected to be expanded. Where better to begin than in the academy, the place where the theories on race and racism are generated? By deconstructing some of the "benign" acts of white privilege in the status quo maintenance in the academy, it is hoped that the insights will bring us one step closer to dismantling racism.

## DECONSTRUCTING SOME "BENIGN" ACTS OF OPERATIONALIZED WHITE PRIVILEGE

Unequal power relations and racialized locations within the social hierarchy are preserved through the maintenance of the status quo. Often when white privilege is being discussed, the focus is either at the theoretical level or at the broader social level (Dalton 1995; Feagin and Vera 1995; Roman 1993). The personal level may be more difficult and challenging to examine for it threatens to be too direct and to infringe upon that which is held more sacred, confidential, and private. Yet by examining the personal level of how white privilege functions, often a more concrete and practical understanding can be gained (Cruz 1995; McIntosh 1992). By offering to deconstruct how the status quo is maintained through a variety of dysconscious, "benign" manifestations of white privilege in the academy, it is hoped that the collective "we," as academics, can begin to move beyond the dialogue of politically correct rhetoric toward informed actions and behaviors that reflect our ability to practice what we preach, to apply the theoretical to the practical in our everyday lives in the academy.

I draw upon my own experiences as a woman of color in the academy as well as the experiences of other academics of color (Carty 1992; Cruz 1995; Farmer 1993; Mindiola 1995; Ng 1993; Padilla 1995; Pérez 1993; Rains 1995; Reyes 1994a, 1994b, Russell 1992; Slack, Rains, Collay, and Dunlap 1994; Trask 1993; Williams 1991) as a means of identifying five "benign" reactions and responses white academics or students frequently give when issues of race or racism are brought close to home.[2] Often these benign responses and reactions reflect a "shields-up" approach, accompanied by a sense that bringing such issues from the abstract to the concrete is just too close for comfort. By deconstructing these seemingly benign responses and reactions, the cloak of immunity that is possible with white privilege is pulled back, exposing an dysconscious effort to maintain the status quo. The five benign reactions/responses are as follows:

- The sense-of-entitlement reaction
- The citation-of-exceptions response
- The well-I-can't-speak-for-(fill in the blank w/color) response
- The sense-of-guilt reaction
- The color blind and racial neutrality responses

The sense-of-entitlement reaction personifies the myth of meritocracy espoused by some white faculty and white students (Chan and Wang 1991; Cruz 1995; Rains 1995; Reyes and Halcón 1991; Tatum 1992). In a time of tightening budgets and affirmative action backlash, this reaction sometimes is used when race/racism are discussed in the context of jobs, scholarships, or other competitive opportunities. The white people who use this reaction typically say that they have "done all of the right things," so the just rewards should be there for them. They *deserve* the rewards because they have worked hard. Implicit in this type of seemingly benign reaction is the perception that some people of color are "taking away" these "earned" rewards from some entitled Whites. The implication is that some people of color who may have received the rewards somehow *did not earn* them, or are "less deserving" than some Whites. This "benign" reaction, however, assumes that via location, a.k.a. white privilege, the rewards are somehow *white* rewards to begin with. This false sense of entitlement preserves and perpetuates the status quo by ignoring the advantages gained through the system of *dis*advantaging others.

Pérez (1993) explains how this sense-of-entitlement reaction sometimes gets played out in academe. She states:

> . . . there has been a widespread anti-affirmative action backlash, some of whose scenarios are all too common in the day-to-day practices of higher education institutions. In my recent experiences, for example, it has become more common to hear or be told by leftist and liberal students and faculty of their resentment of colleagues supported by affirmative action funding and hiring policies; their doubts concerning their minority peers' academic merit and credentials; or of their suspicion of the importance of their intellectual work, minority focused or otherwise. Within this climate all minority students and professors identified as such are felt to be *and* feel suspect in ways that others are not, and in ways that are disempowering: Do they really deserve to be here, or are they here as mere tokens? Is their work really important? Is it intellectually and/or theoretically sophisticated enough? . . . But further, all minorities are suspected of unfairly benefiting from affirmative action policies, and thus, through the circular logic of racism, we are tainted yet again, precisely because we have been socially constructed as minorities. Academic minority scholarships or fellowships are not taken as serious indicators of intellectual talent but dissolved into an indistinguishable pool of financial aid. In the minority experiences at the university, it becomes a commonplace that one is guilty of some kind of intellectual inadequacy or incompetence until one proves otherwise, or until one successfully deploys a politics or assuagement; that is, until one's politics—conservative or progressive—are approved. (272)

Some academics of color encounter this sense-of-entitlement reaction not only among some of their white colleagues, but also with some of their white students. For example, a woman faculty member of color at a large Midwestern research university illuminated how this sense of entitlement reaction has played out with some of her white graduate students. These students were concerned about internship opportunities in her department. Their complaint to her had been that *all* the internships were going to "minority students." She reported:

My white students believe that they've done all the right things, so there should be a job waiting for them on the other end! And they don't understand that the fact that we're in an economic recession means that they're NOW encountering the same kinds of obstacles that people of color and poor people have ALWAYS encountered! But these kids who believe that "my" job is there and that Black person or that Latino or that Asian is going to "take MY job" because of Affirmative Action, is a complex misunderstanding. It tells us a lot about privilege. You have to be a very privileged person to ASSUME that there's a job there waiting for you, and that all you have to do is "X", "Y", and "Z" and your job will be there. But certainly, when you're white and you're middle class, you have those expectations! (Rains 1992, 45)

This type of reaction, whether from white faculty or students, reflects an assumed set of invisible guarantees. Not only do these guarantees imply an inordinate amount of privilege, but also they simultaneously minimize the connection of white privilege to "the ways in which institutionalized whiteness confers upon whites (both individually and collectively) culturally, political, and economic power" (Roman 1993, 72).

Five hundred years of *white* affirmative action has created a blind spot in the sense-of-entitlement reaction. The white-is-norm perspective that such a legacy fosters enables those who espouse this "benign" reaction to ignore how for 500 years the meritocracy that was available to many Whites was commonly unavailable to large bodies of First Americans,[3] African Americans, Latinos, and Asian Americans. Currently, meritocracy does not hold true for large numbers of people of color who work just as hard and expend inordinate amounts of effort and energy toward earning just rewards. Moreover, the invisible yet often expected set of guarantees that this sense-of-entitlement reaction generates, at the same time, works to reinforce and uphold the status quo.

A second way that white privilege functions to maintain the status quo is through the citation-of-exceptions response. This "benign" response is sometimes used when the social, political, economic, educational, or cultural inequalities within our society are the focus of discussion. With this response, the white academics who utilize it stress that individuals of color exist who have managed to pull themselves up by their proverbial bootstraps. The implication of this hypothetically benign response is that hardships can be overcome with merely enough individual effort. It further implies that since this "exceptional person" made it, then it is "easy" for all people of color to make it—if only they had a strong enough desire to do so (Caplan 1994). This type of response neglects the systemic or collective nature of some of the hardships being discussed.

An example of this response comes from my own experience at the American Educational Research Association Conference held in San Francisco (April 1995), where I attended a "women's" session. Out of 81 women present at this particular session, I counted only 6 women of color. During that session, we broke into smaller groups to share some of our experiences with the given topic. Being the only woman of color in my small group, when it was my turn, I began to discuss how my experiences as a person of color differed fairly dramatically from those being shared by the primarily upper-middle to middle-class white women. My experiences had been less positive and were somewhat painful—they had not led to the cherished memories held by the other women in my group. However, before I could complete more than a few sentences, I was interrupted by a "powerful" white woman. She was well connected at the conference and held a status position within the organization. She cut me off, saying "Yes, but, Frances, You made it," as she patted me on the knee.

In essence, the benign citation-of-exception response (in this case, the exception being myself) acted in the group to do three things. First, the emphasis on my "success" shifted the focus away from the points I was trying to help others in the group understand regarding the difference in how our racial and economic positioning influenced the nature of our experiences. Second, by dysconsciously shifting the focus, any perceived concerns about status quo were potentially blocked. The status quo, therefore, remained viable and intact. Finally, beyond shifting the focus, this "benign" response simultaneously delegitimized the value of my experiences.

The citation-of-exceptions response becomes an effective tool for maintaining the status quo. If one accepts that civil rights, and affirmative action have "worked," then it is easier to accept the problems encountered by people of color to be the responsibility of the individual. From the advantage of a privileged position, it is the individual who simply must exercise due initiative, thereby fitting in neatly with the meritocracy myth. What this perspective succeeds in doing is to remove from view the underlying "flaws of American society—flaws deeply rooted in historic inequalities and long-standing cultural stereotypes. How we set up the terms for discussing racial issues shapes our perception and response to these issues" (West 1993, 3). As long as the struggles and issues that people of color experience are viewed as individual "problems," then the responsibility rests with people of color "to do all of the 'cultural' and 'moral' work necessary for healthy race relations" (ibid.). The blind spot that emerges from this dysconsciously benign response reveals a sense of denial. That is, the status quo is maintained partly through the denial of many Whites to examine how white privilege contributes to the inequalities that exist for many. Not only is there a denial of the enormous effort, personal and cultural sacrifices, and distance the individual of color may have had to traverse in order to "make it," but further, there is a denial that systems of inequality perpetuated by the status quo and the power positioning of many Whites make the pathway for other individuals of color to "make it" on a larger scale next to impossible. With this response, the "victim," once blamed, becomes the scapegoat for finding the solution. Complicity through white privilege remains invisible and deniable, thereby maintaining the status quo.

The status quo is also maintained by white privilege through a third "benign" response. The well-I-can't-speak-for (a color) response has been used by some white academic feminists (Roman 1993) and may occur in women's sessions within large conferences in one's field, or at women's conferences. Initially, this presumably benign response may be interpreted as reflecting a new sensitivity to the differences between white women and women of color. The response also is used in reference to curricular decisions. Cultural critic Audre Lorde (1984) explains how this response emerges in the field of women's literature:

> As white women ignore their built-in privilege of whiteness and define woman in terms of their own experience alone, then women of Color become "other," the outsider whose experience and tradition is too "alien" to comprehend. An example of this is the signal absence of the experience of women of Color as a resource for women's studies courses. The literature of women of Color is seldom included in women's literature courses and almost never in other literature courses, nor in women's study as a whole.

All too often, the excuse given is that the literatures of women of Color can only be taught by Colored women, or that they are too difficult to understand, or that classes cannot "get into" them because they come out of experiences that are "too different." (117)

Embedded within this benign response is an assumption that the nature of the experiences and literatures of women of color is too "strange" (read: "different" from the white majority) to be able to relate to. Since the experiences of women of color are so different, the argument goes, many white women cannot possibly teach about women of color or the theories, scholarship, and literature written by academic women of color. While this argument seems plausible on the surface, many white women teach literature written by men without ever having a sex-change operation. White women scholars do not have to be British or male to teach Shakespeare, for example. To take this example a step further, rarely is the teaching of Shakespeare considered to be advocating or "speaking for" him.

The blind spot of the Well-I can't-speak-for (a color) response comes in the form of a dismissal that absolves the speakers from any responsibility for learning and understanding the work of people of color. As sociologists Himani Bannerji, Kari Dehli, Susan Heald, and Kate McKenna and black feminist Linda Carty (1991) assert, "perceiving the issue as just a matter of who can speak for whom can also offer a way out of dealing with the complexity of women's experience and women's oppression. It permits white women *to forget about non-white women* since, 'we have no right to speak for anyone but ourselves.' This reading of the political and theoretical critiques of white feminism can be used to *justify ignoring the majority of women in the world* together. The very idea that anyone has to speak for someone else is a problem" (9). This type of response can legitimize indifference and ignorance in the name of political correctness.

Even more troubling is the hidden message this sends to students— that the literatures, scholarly work, or issues of people of color are not worth exploring, learning about, or understanding. The well-I-can't-speak-for (a color) response reifies the status quo, dysconsciously vanishing the location of white privilege, as Leslie Roman (1993) suggests, "The question of scholars working within such contexts, who now confront the crisis of representation, is not whether the subaltern can speak.

Instead, it is whether privileged (European and North American) white groups are willing to listen when the subaltern speaks and how whites can know the difference between occasions for responsive listening and listening as an excuse for silent collusion with the status quo of racial and neocolonial inequalities" (79).

The fourth "benign" way that white privilege operates to maintain the status quo materializes in the sense-of-guilt reaction. This reaction often occurs after a person of color has been asked to share her or his perspectives/experiences on issues of race/racism. Implicit within this seemingly benign reaction is the external positioning of the locus of control for guilt feelings. The person of color becomes responsible for the white person's guilty feelings.

An example of this reaction in action occurred at a conference I attended where there had been a keynote panel of color, each member addressing their respective experiences with racism. When the panel had finished, they opened up the session for questions and comments from the floor. Immediately a white woman stood up. She was sobbing. It took her a few minutes to regain her composure. Then she blurted out, "But I feel so guilty when you talk about this!" and she proceeded to sob some more before she sat down.

In the matter of a few minutes, this white woman had managed to shift the entire focus of the session away from the points the panelists of color generated, points that were grounded in very painful, personal accounts of how racism had affected their lives. The attention had been diverted, the audience no longer concerned about the purpose of the panel. Instead, the entire audience was focused upon the crying white woman and her needs.

The status quo was maintained successfully through this seemingly benign reaction. By dysconsciously shifting the focus away from the topic of racism, this type of reaction emphasizes an external locus of control. That is, by viewing the "guilty feelings" as a consequence of hearing the points made by the panelists of color, the panelists become "responsible" for her reaction, a variation on the blame-the-victim scenario. When the locus of control is perceived as external, it removes any responsibility from the person utilizing this reaction for having to respond to the points the panelists were making. It eliminates any internal need to respond to the topic. The "guilty feelings" become an immobilizer to responsibility. Yet as Adrienne Rich (1979, 281) points out, "[t]here is a profound difference between actual guilt—or account-ability—and guilt feelings."

The blind spot here reveals the problematics of how this presumably benign reaction transforms the discussion by the panelists into a concern for how the reactor feels (Williams 1991). In the process, the sobbing and guilt-ridden feelings of the white woman alleviate her from having to actually "do" anything about what she has heard, either in terms of her own behaviors or in terms of original focus of the panel. In the meantime, the panelists have a double burden. Not only must they consider how much risk to take in sharing intimate details of what are often very personal and sensitive issues to an audience that may reflect the privileged and the powerful in our society, but they must further consider diluting racial issues in order to protect the audience from their own feelings. Williams (1991, 64) shares insight into the perspective of those who must choose to speak or keep silent: "Though there is certainly an obligation to be careful in addressing others [the audience], the obligation to protect the feelings of the other gets put above the need to protect one's own; the self [person of color] becomes subservient to the other, with no reciprocity; and the other becomes a whimsical master." Personal feelings and risk of the disempowerment become secondary in deference to the feelings and needs of the already empowered. Guilt feelings, then, become a stabilizer of the status quo and a deterrent to accountability.

Finally, another way that white privilege operates to maintain the status quo is through the "color-blind" and "racial neutrality" responses. These two responses may appear to be the most "benign" of all. After all, what could be the harm in not seeing color or race?

These reactions are most likely to occur when there are discussions of race or racism. The "color-blind" response often is used in a sweeping and generalizable way. It goes something like this: "You know, some of my best friends are (a color/ethnicity), but I don't see their color. . . . I treat all my friends the same." The "racial neutrality" response is often more personally directed and typically goes like this: "Gee, I don't think of you as (a color/ethnicity)." Implicit within the first response is an effort to be "nondiscriminatory" combined with an abiding sense of political correctness. Implicit within the second response is a compliment. An example of the "benign" color-blind response emerged from my qualitative study on the professional lives of women faculty of color at a large research university (Rains 1992), where one of the participants in the study shared her experiences of collegiality. She recalled:

> Well, one time. . . when I first came here, it was after a departmental meeting, and I was getting ready to leave, when a white colleague came up to me and clearly wanted to "chat." What was interesting was this person came up to me, all confidential-like, and began to quietly say that she was so glad that I was here because she couldn't believe that it had taken so long for the department to finally get a Black in the department!! She leaned real close and said, "You know, I don't know what all the fuss has been about you coming here." And I thought to myself, "Oh, so there's been a fuss, now, has there?" But I didn't say that to her. Dr. ——— went on. She said, "I really don't. I mean, I don't see color. I treat everybody the same. So, I just don't know what all this fuss is about!!" Not, mind you, a warm hello, or "how you doing?" but, an "I don't see color" routine. Can you imagine?! She didn't ask how I felt about being in an all-white department, or was I doing okay. She just wanted to get that off her chest and let me know that she was colorblind. Like that is supposed to make me feel better. Especially now that she had let the cat out of the bag that the rest of the department wasn't exactly thrilled to have me here! So, there are things like that that go on all the time.

Grounded in such an outwardly "benign" response by this participant's white colleague is an attempt to "demonstrate" equal treatment as well as remove from the realm of possibility the white reactor's possible connection to (overt) racism. American studies scholar Ruth Franken-berg (1994, 76) points out, however, "This discursive repertoire is organized around evading difference or acknowledging it selectively, rather than literally not 'seeing' differences of race, culture, and color." Embedded in the "benign" response of color-blindness are both uncon-scious defensiveness and denial. The unconscious defensiveness works to safeguard the reactor from harmful definitions or accusations. For example, in this age of political correctness, it is possible that some Whites may fear being labeled as "racist" if they somehow "see" color. These individuals have confused color recognition with quality of treatment. That is, for the Whites who engage in this "benign" response of color-blindness, the misguided assumption is one of "if I don't see the color, race, or ethnicity of the subject, then I am absolved of any responsibility or accusation of unequal treatment."

Moreover, this "benign" response works to deny and, therefore, erase the identity of the subject(s) of the response. It denies persons of color their right to have their own identities as well as the values, histories, contributions, language and richness of such identities. "Color-blind-ness" is a luxury that only those who are very secure in, and dysconscious of, their own racialized position of whiteness and power can have. This privilege of whiteness trivializes the substance and weight of the inter-twined histories of Whites and people of color, ignores the poor quality of treatment that many people of color encounter, and denies many people of color their right to their respective identities, while it safeguards how the individual white person engaged in this response may appear in the name of political correctness. Together, the dysconscious defensive-ness and denial of this "benign" response function to maintain the status quo while absolving the white reactor's responsibility for any relationship to "race" that his or her location carries.

The "racial neutrality" response is similar to the "color-blind" response but with a slight twist. In this response, there is less dysconscious defensiveness, less focus on the needs of the individual white reactor; instead, there is more emphasis on the denial of race and color. For example, Williams (1991) shares how the "benign" response of "racial neutrality" has been used by some of her colleagues in the academy. She relates:

> A man with whom I used to work once told me that I made too much of my race. "After all," he said, "I don't even think of you as black." Yet sometime later, when another black woman became engaged in an ulti-mately unsuccessful tenure battle, he confided to me that he wished the school could find more blacks like me. I felt myself slip in and out of shadow, as I became nonblack for purposes of inclusion and black for purposes of exclusion; I felt the boundaries of my very body manipulated, casually inscribed by definitional demarcations that did not refer to me. (9-10)

This response attempts to neutralize the race of the person being discussed. This happened to me in April of 1996, at the American Educational Research Association conference where, during a frank discussion on race, a white woman sat across the table from me and said,

"But, Frances, I don't think of you as Indian." It was meant to be a compliment.

Embedded in this "benign" response of racial neutrality is the desire to universalize whiteness in an attempt to absolve racial differences. It is benignly assumed that such a comment is a compliment. The implication here is that the person of color is being thought of as "white" and that he or she would be complimented to be considered such.

The blind spot within this presumably benign response obscures from view the issue of who defines whom. The stereotypic definitions that the white reactor may harbor may be used as a standard of measure in determining whether the particular person of color "fits" within the white-prescribed boundaries of those definitions. Applied to the previous example, since I did not "fit" the white woman's narrowly prescribed definition of a First American, then from her standpoint, she thought of me as non-Indian. The comfort, indifference, and power with which she was able to erase my identity exude the dysconsciousness of her privileged location in the social hierarchy. Erasure of a person of color's identity, through poor fit with stereotypic definitions, is a disempowering act. Karen Russell (1992), the daughter of a Boston Celtic basketball star, placed the responsibility back upon the empowered when she remarked, "I would hope that people wouldn't have to negate my race in order to accept me"(83).

## CONCLUSION

If there is no struggle, there is no progress. Those who profess to favor freedom, and yet deprecate agitation, are men *[sic]* who want crops without plowing up the ground. They want rain without thunder and lightening. They want the ocean without the awful roar of its many waters. This struggle may be a moral one, or it may be a physical one, or it may be both moral and physical, but it must be a struggle. Power concedes nothing without a demand. It never did and it never will.
—Frederick Douglass (1855)

In many dialogues on racism and race issues, the perception of being a "nonracist" becomes so overwhelmingly important in an often "politically correct" environment that it has overshadowed the need to examine how privilege and power function to maintain the status quo. Appearance eclipses substance, and the complicity that white privilege generates as a corollary to racism is denied.

Certainly, in such times, it would be easier to assume that the seemingly benign is really harmless. When benign responses and reactions are analyzed, however, they reveal blind spots in how such acts of operationalized white privilege ignore the power, location, and role that white privilege plays in maintaining unequal relations.

Focusing on the advantages of white privilege can be difficult. Discussions can become heated very quickly, tempers can flare easily, and encountered rebuttals can range from fear and guilt, to delegitimizing the work or personhood of the individual who may dare to raise the topic. When that person is of color and the audience is predominantly White, this risk seems even more eminent. Clearly, it would be easier to leave it be, to not raise it as a topic of exploration. Yet to keep silent is to contribute to cultural hegemony, to contribute to certain forms of domination, to leave value systems that sustain certain power structures in place. Racism will not disappear by sweeping it under the rug, nor will ignoring white privilege in any way reduce its tyranny or subordination of others.

How, then, to overcome this stumbling block to progress? While ultimately it would be great to have people move beyond dialogue to incorporate understandings gained from new insights into their daily practices, it would appear that the academy is not ready for that yet. Therefore, in preparation for practice, there first must be listening to each other, learning from each other and from more in-depth exploration of study, and efforts to understand situations and circumstances very different from our own. The academy is a good place to begin. We, as academics, are trained to learn. What we must do is break down the barriers that prevent us from listening to each other, from having compassion for each other, and from being willing to put new knowledge into practice.

There is a need for multiple dialogues. White scholars need to talk with other white scholars to begin to understand the implications of their behaviors. These dialogues need to bring to the forefront the hidden and not-so-hidden costs to others and, most important, the hidden benefits that accrue due to their racialized positioning and privilege in a society that is very color conscious. Further, these dialogues should consider how to move beyond issues of guilt or retribution.

Scholars of color need to talk to other scholars of color to begin to address what can be done to bridge such understandings without malice or ill will. These discussions need to foster ideas of how to prevent a downward slope of blame. Scholars of color are by no means monolithic, and such discussions, while sometimes occurring within a group, need to expand across different ethnic groups.

Furthermore, white scholars and scholars of color need to have dialogues with each other. Defensiveness, denials, accusations, guilt, blame, and dysconsciousness have no room in such dialogues and must be left at the door. These dialogues must occur with a sense of trust, a sense of the risk each side brings, a willingness to explore these risks to begin to open ourselves up to understanding each other. What might such a dialogue look like?

I initiated such a dialogue at the American Educational Research Association conference in April of 1996. It was an attempt to bring some of the most active and brilliant minds in the field of education together. I invited 20 female scholars to participate as cofacilitators. Ten were white women scholars, ten were women scholars of color. The former held various ranks within the academy, representing various parts of the United States and Canada. The latter, also of varying ranks, represented Asian American, Asian Canadian, Latinas, African American, and First American women. These scholars were asked to review, in advance, a series of readings that I sent to each of them.

At the conference, these cofacilitators were paired, one white woman scholar and one woman scholar of color together respectively, in order to divide the audience of 250 people into 10 groups. While the "small groups" were much larger than I had anticipated due to the large attendance, members had the opportunity to literally participate in the dialogue. The dialogue did not get as far as I had hoped due to time constraints, but the feedback indicated that this humble attempt to begin to discuss such issues as racism and privilege was, indeed, valuable. While the proposal to continue the dialogue at the next conference was rejected (because it was not a research-focused presentation), I hold fast to the idea that there is merit in initiating more in-depth dialogues.

Moreover, more learning needs to take place. As scholars we are lifelong learners; our success depends on it. Many white scholars need to learn more about how our histories, that of people of color and white people in this society, are intertwined. Indeed, our democracy has been built on the backs of multitudes of nonwhite peoples and poor white ethnic groups. More learning needs to take place that goes beyond the "celebrations of diversity" that too often emphasize the decorative, the cuisines, or the exotic. Instead, learning must occur that not only builds on the contributions and richness of the various groups that have played a part in the development of this society but that also analyzes the vast systemic inequities that continue to exist for large parts of our society.

It also means that many scholars of color need to learn more about histories other than their own. Many have learned their own histories but know little to nothing about another group of color's history. When there is an understanding that goes beyond the history of a single group, there are new possibilities of discovery. Shared oppressions, similar resistive acts, different ways of approaching problem solving might be discerned. Such learning has the potential to expand understanding of different worldviews, of the conflicts that have divided us, and of how we might begin to bridge understanding.

Finally, it is not enough to be compassionate. Action, practice, the ability to demonstrate understanding—we ask this of our students; dare we ask less of ourselves?

We must begin to move beyond responses and reactions that perpetuate the status quo. Haunani-Kay Trask (1986), a Native Hawaiian political activist, in her analysis of white feminism points out:

> In these times, it is simply inefficient for white feminists to protest that they are not women of color and therefore cannot understand racism. Neither is it sufficient to acknowledge a racist heritage—and then fail to move toward changing a racist society. By analogy, feminists would not allow men simply to agree that they are sexist without insisting on a change of behavior. The same, then, must hold for white feminists. . . .The questions of race and racism cannot be pushed to the back of the theoretical or political bus any longer. (179)

Lip service or superficial attempts to appear "nonracist" are no longer enough. The location of white privilege as an invisible corollary to racism must move beyond acknowledgment. As we approach a new millennium, the time has come to move beyond issues of guilt, defensiveness, and avowed ignorance. "Giving up white privilege begins with a giving up of white inaction" (Trask 1986, 180).

## NOTES

I am indebted to my colleague Dr. Patrick McQuillan for his willingness to read a draft of this chapter and offer his earnest insights regarding the implications of this work.

1. Each of the terms "White" and "people of color," is more diverse than is implied by the use here. It is acknowledged that neither term represents a monolithic or even a cohesive group. It is not the purpose here to debate, nor expound upon the diversity within each group.

2. This is not to be construed as a definitive list of "benign" reactions and responses. Rather, these five identified manifestations of white privilege are being analyzed as a way of beginning to "unpack" the ways that privilege is operationalized in supporting the status quo.

3. Here I purposefully use "First American" in preference to "Native American" or "American Indian." It must be noted that I do *not* speak for all Native peoples; instead, I am engaging in the empowerment of voice to take personal responsibility for naming in a way that, similar to the First Nations of Canada, makes clear the history of location and precedence. The label "Native American" emerged from the ivory tower, and has been perpetuated by scholars and the "politically correct." Meanwhile, many of the Native Nations whom this label is supposed to "honor" continue to use their Native Nation affiliations primarily, and secondarily use either "Indian" or "American Indian." In spite of Columbus' navigational error in judgement, it is time to clarify both location and precedent with regard to these lands.

## BIBLIOGRAPHY

Altbach, P. G., and Lomotey, K. (eds.) (1991). *The Racial Crisis in American Higher Education.* Albany: State University of New York Press.

Anzalda, G. (ed.). (1990). *Making Face, Making Soul, Haciendo Caras: Creative and Critical Perspectives by Women of Color.* San Francisco: An Aunt Lute Foundation Book.

Bannerji, H., Carty, L., Dehli, K., Heald, S. and McKenna, K. (1991). Introduction. In H. Bannerji, L. Carty, K. Dehli, S. Heald, and K. McKenna (eds.), *Unsettling Relations: The University as a Site of Feminist Struggles.* Boston: South End Press.

Caplan, P. J. (1994). *Lifting a Ton of Feathers: A Woman's Guide to Surviving in the Academic World.* Toronto: University of Toronto Press.

Carty, L. (1992). "Black Women in Academia: A Statement from the Periphery". In H. Bannerji, L. Carty, K. Dehli, S. Heald, and K. McKenna (eds.) *Unsettling Relations: The University as a Site of Feminist Struggles.* Boston: South End Press.

Chan, S. and Wang, L. C. (1991). "Racism and the Model Minority: Asian-Americans in Higher eEducation. In P. G. Altbach and K. Lomotey (eds.), *The Racial Crisis in American Higher Education.* Albany: State University of New York Press.

Cruz, D. M. (1995). "Struggling with the Labels that Mark My Ethnic Identity. In R. V. Padilla and R. Chávez Chávez (eds.) *The Leaning Ivory Tower: Latino Professors in American Universities.* Albany: State University of New York Press.

Dalton, H. L. (1995). *Racial Healing: Confronting the Fear Between Blacks and Whites.* New York: Doubleday.

Davis, A. Y. (1983). *Women, Race and Class.* New York: Vintage Books.

Douglass, F. (1855/1969). *My Bondage and My Freedom.* New York: Dover Publications.

DuBois, W. E. B. (1903/1990). *The Souls of Black Folk.* New York: Vintage Books.

Farmer, R. (1993). "Place But Not Importance: The Race for Inclusion in Academe." In J. James and R. Farmer (eds.), *Spirit, Space and Survival: African American Women in (White) Academe.* New York: Routledge.

Feagin, J. R. and Vera, H. (1995). *White Racism: The Basics.* New York: Routledge.

Frankenberg, R. (1994). "Whiteness and Americanness: Examining Constructions of Race, Culture, and Nation in White Women's Life Narratives." In S. Gregory and R. Sanjek (eds.), *Race.* New Brunswick, NJ: Rutgers University Press.

hooks, b. (1989). *Talking Back: Thinking Feminist, Thinking Black.* Boston: South End Press.

Hull, G. T., Scott, P. B., Smith, B. (eds.). (1982). *All the Women Are White, All the Blacks Are Men, But Some of Us Are Brave: Black Women's Studies.* New York: The Feminist Press at the City University of New York.

Jackson, H. H. (1881/1993). *A Century of Dishonor: A Sketch of the United States Government's Dealings with Some of the Indian Tribes.* New York: Indian Head Books.

King, J. E. (1991). "Dysconscious Racism: Ideology, Identity, and the Miseducation of Teachers." *Journal of Negro Education* 60, no. 2, 133-146.

Lorde, A. (1980/1984). "Age, Race, Class, and Sex: Women Redefining Difference." In A. Lorde (ed.), *Sister Outsider.* Freedom, CA: The Crossing Press.

————. (1979/1984). "The Master's Tools Will Never Dismantle the Master's House". In A. Lorde (ed.), *Sister Outsider.* Freedom, CA: The Crossing Press.

McCarthy, C. and Crichlow, W. (eds.). (1993). *Race, Identity, and Representation in Education.* New York: Routledge.

McIntosh, P. (1988/1992). "White Privilege and Male Privilege: A Personal Account of Coming to See Correspondences Through the Work in Women's

Studies." In M. Andersen and P. H. Collins (eds.), *Race, Class, and Gender: An Anthology.* Belmont, CA: Wadsworth Publishing Company.

Mindiola, T., Jr., (1995). "Getting Tenure at the U." In R. V. Padilla and R. Chávez Chávez (eds.), *The Leaning Ivory Tower: Latino Professors in American Universities.* Albany: State University of New York Press.

Morrison, T. (ed.). (1992). *Race-ing Justice, En-Gendering Power: Essays on Anita Hill, Clarence Thomas, and the Construction of Social Reality.* New York: Pantheon Books.

Ng, R. (1993). "'A Woman Out of Control': Deconstructing Sexism and Racism in the University." *Canadian Journal of Education* 18, no. 3, 189-205.

Omi, M., and Winant, H. (1986). *Racial Formation in the United States.* New York: Routledge.

Padilla, R. V. (1995). "MEMOrabilia from an Academic Life." In R. V. Padilla and R. Chávez Chávez (eds.), *The Leaning Ivory Tower: Latino Professors in American Universities.* Albany: State University of New York Press.

Pérez, L. E. (1993). "Opposition and the Education of Chicana/os." In C. McCarthy and W. Crichlow (eds.), *Race, Identity, and Representation in Education.* New York: Routledge.

Rains, F. V. (1995). "Views from Within: Women Faculty of Color in a Research University." Unpublished doctoral dissertation, Indiana University, Bloomington.

———. (1992). *Women Faculty of Color and Their Experiences of Collegiality, Research, and Teaching in a Research University.* Unpublished raw data.

Reyes, M. de la L., (1994, a, April). *Radical Interventions: Difference, Identity, Voice, Agency, Subversion in Educational Praxis.* Paper symposium presented at the annual meeting of the American Educational Research Association, New Orleans, LA.

———, (1994, b, April). *Interruption, Racism, and Sexism: White Women, Women of Color and the Preparation of Teachers.* Paper symposium presented at the annual meeting of the American Educational Research Association, New Orleans, LA.

Reyes, M. de la L., and Halcón, J. J. (1991). "Practices of the Academy: Barriers to Access for Chicano Academics." In P. G. Altbach and K. Lomotey (eds.), *The Racial Crisis in American Higher Education.* Albany: State University of New York Press.

———. (1988). "Racism in Academia: The Old Wolf Revisited." *Harvard Educational Review* 58, no. 3, 299-314.

Rich, A. (1979). "Disloyal to Civilization: Feminism, Racism, Gynephobia (1978)." In A. Rich (ed.), *On Lies, Secrets, and Silence: Selected Prose 1966-1978 .* New York: W. W. Norton.

Roman, L. G. (1993). "White is a Color! White Defensiveness, Postmodernism and Anti-Racist Pedagogy." In C. McCarthy and W. Crichlow (eds.), *Race, Identity, and Representation in Education.* New York: Routledge.

Russell, K. K. (1992). "Growing Up with Privilege and Prejudice." In M. Andersen and P. H. Collins (eds.), *Race, Class, and Gender: An Anthology.* Belmont, CA: Wadsworth Publishing Company.

Scheurich, J. J. (1993). "Toward a White Discourse on White Racism." *Educational Researcher* 22 , no. 8, 5-10.

Slack, P. J., Rains, F., Collay, M., and Dunlap, D. (1994, April). "Can We Rebuild the AERA House Using the Same Old Tools? The Academic Vampire Chronicles—Chronicles III. (A Reader's Theatre on Life in Academia.)." Presented at the meeting of the American Educational Research Association, New Orleans, LA.

Sleeter, C. (1993). "Advancing a White Discourse: A Response to Scheurich." *Educational Researcher* 22, no. 8, 13-15.

Stanfield, J. H. (1985). "The Ethnocentric Basis of Social Science Knowledge Production." *Review of Research in Education* 12, 387-415.

Tatum, B. D. (1992). "Talking About Race, Learning About Racism: The Application of Racial Identity Development Theory in the Classroom." *Harvard Educational Review* 62 no. 1, 1-24.

Trask, H. K. (1993). *From a Native Daughter: Colonialism and Sovereignty in Hawai'i.* Monroe, ME: Common Courage Press.

———. (1986). *Eros and Power: The Promise of Feminist Theory.* Philadelphia: University of Pennsylvania Press.

Trinh, M. H. (1989). *Woman, Native, Other.* Bloomington: Indiana University Press.

Vera, H., Feagin, J. R., and Gordon, A. (1995). "Superior Intellect?: Sincere Fictions of the White Self." *Journal of Negro Education* 64, no. 3, 295-306.

Weiler, K. (1988). *Women Teaching for Change: Gender, Class and Power.* New York: Bergin and Garvey Publishers.

West, C. (1993). *Race Matters.* Boston: Beacon Press.

Williams, P. J. (1991). *The Alchemy of Race and Rights: Diary of a Law Professor.* Cambridge, MA: Harvard University Press.

Winnemucca Hopkins, S. (1883/1969). *Life Among the Piutes: Their Wrongs and Claims.* Bishop, CA: Chalfant Press.

Wolverton, T. (1983). "Unlearning Complicity, Remembering Resistance: White Women's Anti-Racism Education." In C. Bunch and S. Pollack (eds.), *Learning Our Way: Essays in Feminist Education.* Trumansburg, NY: The Crossing Press.

Woodson, C. G. (1933). *The Mis-education of the Negro.* Philadelphia: Hakim's Publications.

# FIVE

# America's Racial Unconscious

## The Invisibility of Whiteness

**Monica Beatriz deMello Patterson**

But what on earth is whiteness that one should so desire it?
Then always, somehow, some way, silently but clearly, I am
given to understand that whiteness is the ownership of the
earth forever and ever, Amen!
—W. E. B. DuBois (1920)

Cultural theorist Edward Said (1989) writes that America's influence
on the rest of the world is heavily dependent on the cultural discourse,
the knowledge industry, the production and dissemination of texts,
textuality, and culture—not culture as a general anthropological realm
but specifically that of a Eurocentric culture of whiteness. It is this culture
that exists invisibly, colorless, undefined by geographical or psychological
descriptions. This culture exists within the boundaries of the United
States and has been socially constructed and is historically specific. We
can theorize about this culture and place it inside of the petri dish of
examination in which the dominant usually place the marginalized. But
this examination rarely calls into question the position of the dominant
cultural group. It merely defines a culture while reducing any historic

incidents to facts. Whiteness, as American studies scholar Ruth Frankenberg (1993, 239) defines it, is the culture that the dominant peoples of the world possess; it was created socially and structurally by a society. Whiteness can be defined by several strong features including capitalistic market society structure; belief in progress and science, possession of modern concepts of family and societal group structures based on individualism, competition, social mobility, and belief in Eurocentric cultural, philosophical, and economic superiority. In a phrase, whiteness refers to ways of living that are discursive practices that were formed out of a culture associated with Western European colonial expansion.

According to Frankenberg (236), "Whiteness signals the production and reproduction of dominance rather than subordination, normativity rather than marginality, and privilege rather than disadvantage." She continues: "We need to displace the colonial construction of whiteness as an 'empty' cultural space, in part by refiguring it as constructed and dominant rather than as norm. Without reconceptualizing culture, we run the risk of reifying and dehistoricizing *all* cultural practices, valorizing or romanticizing some while discounting others as not cultural at all" (243). How can we displace these seemingly permanent placements within the dominant ideology in our teaching philosophies and practices?

The ideology of whiteness becomes actualized and normalized to the point of invisibility by way of language, media culture, and schooling. In spite of its invisibility, whiteness does possess content. Frankenberg (231) explains: "However, whiteness *does* have content in as much as it generates norms, ways of understanding history, ways of thinking about self and other, and even ways of thinking about the notion of culture itself." As whiteness becomes another signifier of Westernization, it becomes a mode of imperial colonialism by attempting to alter those deemed Other who stand in its way. Since we know that cultures of racist discourse exist, we need to create an overarching ideology that states that the Other is being measured against, compared to a normalized, accepted form of goodness, wholeness, to what is normal, familiar, and civilized.

In this chapter, I will attempt to interrogate the social construction of whiteness through a more global perspective. Making a direct connection between the concept of whiteness and Western expansion in the non-Western world, I contend that students of the West can better understand mechanisms of cultural oppression in the Third World by understanding the silence, normativity, and invisibility of the construction of whiteness. There exists a need to bring these two understandings together to realize the complicity that whiteness plays not only in the creation of oppression in the Third World but also in the entire Western world in the name of multi/monoculturalism and education/suppression for all. By tying these two themes together, those engaging within the walls of the education system (academia) will be better able to critically examine their own involvement with imperialism in the Third World as well as their collusion with the same mechanisms of oppression within our own borders.

The following is a comparison: I will describe as revealed in the work of education anthropologist Stephen Harris the worldview of the northern Australian Aborigine people. Contrast will be drawn between that and the Western worldview wherein lies Truth and Reason and Goodness, the undergirding of white ideology. This description does not intend to be all-inclusive or to essentialize the Aboriginal ideology to all non-Western peoples. Research in the area of the cultural hegemony of whiteness can help educators place themselves outside of their belief systems, if only for a moment, to understand the discursive practices and expressions of whiteness, "stripping them to reveal the underlying presuppositions, embodiments of interests, aims and projections of exclusion and subjection (Goldberg 1990, xii). This discussion acts as a step in the never-ending process of interrogation.

In observing relations between Aboriginal peoples of northern Australia and the European Australians, Harris (1990, 52) writes: "The differences between cultures are not merely ones of degree, but are more fundamental." His text, *Two-Way Aboriginal Schooling: Education and Cultural Survival,* reveals distinct ideological differences that help us understand how dominant Western, white worldviews disrupt life-sustaining vernacular communities. Schooling in this context imparts one knowledge or set of values, beliefs, and ways of knowing that are produced from a Eurocentric, white cultural history. It acts to replace the ideology that existed prior to the placement of that transplanted educational system. Now let us turn to the vernacular culture or way of knowing the world belonging to the Other, which is viable, unique, and hopeful, yet incompatible with the dominant ideology of Euro-centric whiteness.

## THE DREAMING

Aborigines regard the European Australians as delinquent Aboriginal people who need to be handled with a lot of patience, while the latter regard the former as delinquent Australians who need to be Westernized (Harris 1990, 18). This example reveals basic differences in how each culture conceptualizes the way people relate to each other, to the Other, and to the universe. The beliefs of both groups do not lie on a hierarchical continuum of views, one placed higher than the other. Instead, the two belief systems lie parallel to each other, possibly intersecting, but definitely existing uniquely in their own evolutionary tract. Harris (21) quotes Muta, a Mutimbata Aborigine: "White man him go different. Him got road belong himself."

The Dreaming is a term Aborigines feel to be the closest English phrase to describe their worldview. It is not a historic or temporal concept; rather it refers to their origins and ways of maintaining human life. Aborigines also use a second English word, law, to define their worldview, but when this term is used in speech it is consciously chosen in response and resistance to the threat they feel from outside forces on their culture— specifically on the threat to The Dreaming. The Law refers to how Aborigines feel about their culture's positioning in relation to the dominant culture today. Both of these expressions describe "differences in perceived causation, and in perceptions of time, how to view space, the nature and origins of human relationships, the nature of belief, and the nature of the earth" (22).

## SPIRITUAL VERSUS POSITIVISTIC THOUGHT

A spiritual rather than a scientific approach to the world is the first characteristic that defines both The Dreaming and The Law. What is believed is given more credibility and priority than what can be proven or understood. The basis for proving or understanding lies in another way of proving not based in fact. Since spiritual belief is completely integrated into human daily activity, the powers that guide and direct the world are believed to exist as a kind of second nature with all human life. The powers are not regarded as an outside, alien force to be reckoned with and controlled.

The powers come from the living earth whose energy contains spiritual origin, causation, and meaning. Harris (1990, 23) writes: "It is easy for a non-Aboriginal to see that a blade of grass, or an earthworm is alive in a different way than a dog or human. . . to an Aboriginal person, the earth is alive to about that same degree of difference. They may not express it this way, but particular parts of the earth come closer to having ears and eyes and feelings which can be offended or supported, and a conscious intelligence, than is the case in non-Aboriginal perceptions." Proof or understanding comes from occurrences produced by these powers; Westerners may regard them with skepticism and conclude that their origins, not based in scientific fact, thus are wrong.

When events occur that cannot be explained by modern science, Aborigines relate to them as natural expectations. Many of these occurrences have been witnessed and documented by Westerners traveling or working in northern Australia (Morgan 1994). Miraculous healing, sightings of spirit beings, messages from animals or birds are all natural and expected occurrences in *The Dreaming*. To people who are comfortable only with empirical, positivistic causation, such occurrences are mysterious, abnormal, and strange. To Eurocentric Westerners, reality is only what is measured, controlled, and repeated. Mysticism, intuition, and spiritual assumptions are cause for suspicion and doubt. With this understanding, we can begin to see that whiteness as a culture can, at best, clash with others in the classroom. The kind of thought that Western schooling attempts to reproduce will not allow Aboriginal children to grow up Aboriginal.

## RELATEDNESS
## VERSUS COMPARTMENTALIZATION

*The Dreaming* contends that the vitality of the earth is consistent with the degree of relatedness between specific places, people, kinship, and spiritual belief and expression. People come to exist in physical form through the union of their eternal spiritual form, a particular locality, and the spiritual form's manifestation within the body of a woman. Aboriginal culture has adopted what we know scientifically about conception into its belief about the nature of physical life. The male role in birth influences the timing of conception. "Conception seen in this light establishes a relationship with the land because the spirit-embryo belongs to particular parts of the land" (Harris 1990, 24). The child's parents are connected to a particular part of the land; thus, the child is related to the parents not only through the human form but also through a connection to the land.

Each person is regarded as having a human parent as well as a parent in the land. Aboriginal peoples view this relation to the earth as Westerners might perceive their relation to a biological mother, father, sister, or grandfather. To Aboriginal people, the land is their mother or father. If forced to leave the land, they feel like orphans—removed from their parents. "In effect, the land owns them as much as or more than they own the land" (24). This attitude is an extremely fundamental belief in *The Dreaming* and one that is not easily internalized or at least comprehended by Eurocentric Westerners.

The Aboriginal peoples enact a celebration on the land as an indication that the land is fertile—capable of sustaining growth and producing birth. It is a sign that the earth is alive and that the creators are doing their work. Ceremonial life is also illustrative of the relatedness of symbolic representation in *The Dreaming*. Symbols take on the actual life of what they signify. For example, a dancer is not merely mimicking a kangaroo but becomes that animal for the duration of the dance. The symbolism also defines an individual's relationship to the land as revealed when Aboriginal men call to another close relative using the word "country." Evidence of this connection is revealed over and over in the symbolic life of the Aborigine.

Harris (25) retells the story of one individual who remarks: "Can't you see? You are killing our minds," when confronted with the ever-present threat of oil drilling and mining occurring on the land. This suggests a physical connection to the land, as well as the aforementioned symbolic one. Aboriginal people consider the land part of their corporeal selves. Symbolic storytelling contains the power to keep the land alive. Aborigines who have left their land keep it alive by telling stories about it, maintaining their kinship systems, and performing ceremonies. "It's alright, our singing looks after the land. We can do it from a long way," says one Pilbara elder (ibid.).

In *The Dreaming*, land, kinship, and spiritual life cannot exist separate from each other. Each aspect is viewed as having connection to the others and cannot exist in isolation. This relatedness exists in direct opposition to how the West chooses to compartmentalize aspects of human life. Areas such as religion, kinship, or land can be discussed easily without making any kind of connection to the others. "It is also impossible to talk about this interrelatedness without seeing that Aboriginal perceptions of time and space are not constrained in the same way as those of non-Aborigines" (27)."

Value is placed on relatedness rather than on quantity in *The Dreaming*. Value also lies in one's position in a group as one's sense of self-worth is inscribed out of his or her connection and relation to the group. This identity attachment to the group infuses a sense of cooperation with other group members. Competition does exist, but plays a role only in mate choice, determination of who has the best voice, who is the best dancer, and who is the more generous provider. Individuality is encouraged, but within established areas so that it poses no threat to the group or extended family loyalties. Notions of individualism—striving for individualistic gain away from the group—are not aspired to by Aborigines in *The Dreaming*. Their ideals of communal responsibility exist in direct opposition to this pervasive component of the culture of whiteness.

Eurocentric Westerners compartmentalize to organize society. We set up dualistic relationships between work/play, spiritual/civil, corporeality/functionality, home/school. These distinctions are presented to Aboriginal children in schools. For example, teachers expect Aboriginal children to relate to them in terms of their role as teacher and transmitter of necessary skills and knowledge. Teachers do not view personal character as important, while to their Aboriginal students it is pivotal: "Information is often valuable in terms of who is giving it" (26). Here we see another example of how the priority of relatedness, as an important manifestation of *The Dreaming*, is out of step with the priorities of Western schooling.

## CYCLIC VERSUS LINEAR TIME PERCEPTIONS

"When the creator beings traveled across Australia making the hills, rivers, springs, people, flora and fauna, [it] occurred in the cyclic time frame of past-continuous. It happened in the distant past, but also is still happening today" (Harris 1990, 29). This passage gives us insight into a view of time that seems almost ambiguous to Eurocentric Westerners. The Aboriginal view of history and present time is so close that there almost appears to be no difference. The Western linear view of the past creates a different sense of time that works counter to *The Dreaming*. Harris describes how, according to Western carbon dating techniques, the Aboriginal presence dates back 20,000 years. Yet according to Aboriginal spoken history, the oldest lineage existed merely 200 years ago. To Westerners, this disparity in actual time is important, but the difference in time does not impress itself on Aboriginal consciousness. "This time orientation is in stark contrast to that of Westerners, particularly the better educated, upper middle class groups, who not only have a linear quantified view of the past, but think and plan a great deal and a great distance into the future (27)." Aboriginal peoples do make future plans, such as for a marriage or ceremony, but not to the extent that Western, Eurocentric peoples do. To Westerners, time, like space, needs to be filled up.

Time in *The Dreaming* exists more in a cyclic pattern rather than a linear one. Aborigines view their histories and generations of family as constantly "coming around" (Stanner 1979; as cited in Harris 1990, 27). This physically manifests itself in the repetitious use of the same names every three generations in the Aboriginal languages of Oenpelli and Milimgimbi. In this same way the kinship categories repeat themselves every seven generations. This cyclical attention to related-ness of time and history gives a more complete view on existence than does the Western view.

## BEING VERSUS
## DOING BEHAVIORAL CONTENT

Bain (1972, 1979; as cited in Harris 1990, 28) describes the differences in the being/doing dichotomy of Aboriginal/Eurocentric cultures as the interactional/transactional dichotomy. Interactional behavior implies an emphasis to be placed on being, on relatedness, on the personal. Transactional behavior implies emphasis placed on the distinction between one's professional or working life and one's personal life. Such behavior is comprised of a series of transactions devoid of any personal responsibilities to the other. In the culture of whiteness, emphasis is placed on personal relationships only when it is a means to an end. To Aborigines, the actual shared experience, the working together, or the interaction itself is what is valued—the goal of the relationship.

This attention to personal interaction has manifested itself in economic relationships between Aborigines and Westerners. Bain (1979; as cited in Harris 1990, 30) describes how Aborigines place more importance on the personal relationship than on the accuracy of quantities when engaging in business transactions (In fact, Harris notes that Aboriginal language has very few concepts or words delineating quantity.) These differences are not merely due to poor communication but to harboring different priorities centering on the interaction/transaction dichotomy. One Aboriginal man told Bain that operating from a transactional framework is like having no relations.

The being/doing and interactional/transactional contrasts explain yet another vital aspect of *The Dreaming*—the relationship of the Aboriginal to the natural environment. People can relate to their surrounding environment in two ways. The first way is to make things happen or to manipulate, and the second way is to fit oneself in with what is there or to respond. Aboriginal communities exist in one of the driest ecosystems on the planet. In response to their surroundings and as a survival technique, Aborigines have come to be hunters and gatherers. Agricultural use of the land would be possible only with high use of technological inputs or high levels of manipulation. Part of the Aboriginal response to nature includes a highly developed system of reliance and reciprocity. *The Dreaming* defines strong connection to community and kin; importance is placed on personal relationships so that people can rely on the extended family and community members in times of need. Aboriginal communities depend on each other for support and aid in times of need and expect to help others when they have surplus to share. This survival-based practice has become an ethic—Aborigines refrain from and are opposed to manipulating nature.

Western schooling teaches transactional behavior and a philosophy of doing, quantifying, and manipulation. These values work in direct opposition to the values taught in the Aboriginal community and home and offer an obvious potential for conflict between school, community, home, and student.

## CLOSED VERSUS OPEN SOCIETY

The way that *The Dreaming* places value on the past and future is related to the Aboriginal belief that the most significant event to have happened in history was the creation of the land, the ceremonies, the people, and the social system. Since this event has already occurred, there is no need to expect a greater event; thus, Aborigines do not think about development and progress or believe in better things coming in the future. The future, according to *The Dreaming*, should contain more of the same.

Conformity, an anthropological term used to describe differences between traditional and Western societies, is useful in our discussion about *The Dreaming*. All societies are regulated by a certain degree of conformity; without this no society could function. Aboriginal culture contains a greater degree of organic conformity than exists in Western societies. According to Harris (1990, 31): "[I]n Aboriginal society, there is a prescribed network of relationships and ways of believing and operating. Although there is deviation from this system, the ideal and the norm are much closer than in [Western] societies in the sense that the ideal and the prescribed system dominates consciousness." Even though there is room for difference, creativity, and individuality in Aboriginal society, the variation occurs without ever rejecting the validity of the ideal. For instance, the way that marriages are arranged within the community is often challenged and rearranged according to the preferences of those involved, yet they are still arranged in a prescribed fashion. Additions to their culture from outside Western influences, such as rock music or dancing, are not viewed as challenges to their way of life. This is because the additions do not challenge the validity of their ideal. Obligation to family and religious beliefs, however, is not optional.

The nonaggressive nature of *The Dreaming* creates the possibility for cultural destruction in defending their position from outside forces. Aboriginal peoples are not overly concerned with explaining their beliefs and practices to those who are not Aboriginal because they assume that Others are as versed in *The Dreaming* as they are. "Aboriginal membership in a closed society is consistent with their philosophy of being rather than doing, their value of live and let live" (32). This leads to an unfair struggle, as they are unable to defend themselves against stronger, more influential cultural workers such as Western-oriented educators and social workers.

In a more closed society, knowledge is connected more closely to context and situations, not to theories or ideas. Spear construction is a case that points out this phenomenon. Spears are chosen depending on acceleration, trajectory, and distance. The use of a device called a *woomera* indicates knowledge of leverage, and choice of specific spears over others indicates knowledge of the relationships among height, length, and force. Even though this example describes knowledge of highly involved physical properties, this knowledge is confined to the context in which it is used. Users do not generalize these facts to any other context.

How the Aborigine relates to life events is another quality indicative of a closed society. In *The Dreaming,* people accept situations as that which life gives them. As Harris quotes Stanner (1979; as cited in Harris 1990, 33): "I do not at all say that pain, sorrow, and sadness have no place in Aboriginal life, for I have seen them all too widely. All I mean is that [the Aborigines] seem to have gone beyond, or not quite attained the human quarrel with such things." They view the source of conflict from outside of their beings, from outside of their control. With this way of relating to their problems, they are unable to infer that problems could come from within or are due to internal, individual causes. The latter is a truly Eurocentric, open society conception of how to view life. "It is only when people feel a degree of internal control over their destiny that they begin to quarrel with it" (33).

The Aboriginal culture has begun to exhibit change arising from outside its closed society. Some groups are beginning to take responsibility for other groups with whom they are not related. Some Aboriginal groups also have begun articulating *The Law,* their values and priorities, to outsiders. Doing so has necessitated theorizing about their present situation, including learning how to express it to outsiders.

The last, most striking example of change concerning Aboriginal closed society involves the interaction of the Christian faith with the faith of the Aborigines. In some parts of the Northern Territory, Christians and Aborigines are engaging in a kind of blending of the two faiths to produce a mutual coexistence. Traveling Christian preachers from Aboriginal communities are able to persuade other Aborigines to learn the Christian beliefs. These individuals are passionately committed to the Aboriginal way yet preach the words of Christian faith. Until recently, *The Dreaming* existed in direct opposition to Christianity.

These three examples describe how the Aboriginal culture has evolved to resist change from the outside through an effort to control it. Evidently, the closed nature of the society has not kept Aborigines from identifying the causes of struggle and oppression from Eurocentric influences and learning what they need to do in order to fight those forces. The responses represent what they regard as valuable about *The Dreaming*.

The relationship of Aboriginal culture—closed society—to Eurocentric culture—open society—helps to illustrate how Western forms of schooling influence the thoughts of the Aborigine, thus, *The Dreaming*. As the examples of internally induced change suggest, Aboriginal groups wish to maintain their ways in spite of how dominating the white, Eurocentric influence may be. What is also suggested is that Aboriginal groups do not wish their society to become the open society that the Western world is. This is evident since they resist the West's total influence by learning how to relate to the West on the West's terms.

## CONTRASTING VIEWS OF WORK AND ECONOMICS

Aboriginal perceptions of work are very different from those of Westerners. In Western society, a close relationship exists between the land, labor, and wealth. Even though ethics that may originate with religious beliefs influence the Western economic system, that system is still viewed as secular, impersonal, and mechanistic. Resources are considered devoid of spiritual content and impersonal, and those belonging to the government are presented as a whole belonging to the people. Work is deemed a moral responsibility of the people in the West. This idea has arisen out of modern conceptions of time, Darwinism, and progress. The work ethic instills in Westerners a sense of future: Hard work will create a better future.

Aborigines, on the other hand, believe that the present social and economic order is fine, since *The Dreaming* revolves around a past-continuous time orientation. According to Harris (1990, 35): "They believe that a perfectly acceptable social order is already present without need of further evolution or progress and that work is only a means to social or religious ends and never in itself a moral matter or matter of personal identity."

Work is one of the major components of the Eurocentric economic system. For Aborigines, there exists no separation between work and living. The word for work, *djaama*, was introduced into the language in the eighteenth century by a visitor; today it is used to refer to the work done for the European Australians. In *The Dreaming*, work is closer in meaning to participation. In the same way that participation is crucial to ritual, it is also a necessity for productivity. Productivity is also tied very closely to ritual. This becomes clear when we see that the Aboriginal word for ceremony is business. The Aboriginal word *wukirri*, meaning "write" is the word used for school. Participation is also highly important in this realm of life as schoolchildren place value in the ritual of "non-cognitively demanding work, such as copying lots of writing from the [chalk] board."

To a Westerner, the institutions of work, economy, and schooling are interrelated and mutually dependent. School is the place where students are prepared to participate in the economy. This understanding arises from a faith and belief in a positivistic relationship to work, resources, the economy, and schooling. The Aborigine views a similar relationship among the three institutions, believing in goals of participation, maintaining meaningful relationships, ritual activity, and cooperation with nature.

## VIEWS OF AUTHORITY

An important distinction between remote Aboriginal society and Eurocentric Western society is the function in the latter of a bureaucracy and a government made up of subagencies. Individuals fill the positions within these constructs in an impersonal and temporary manner. The construct that is permanent is the office itself, as roles are filled regardless of an individual's needs and rights. In a bureaucratic structure, the filling of the position becomes most important.

In the West, the private lives of individuals are shaped by the highly organized, structured, impersonal, and quantified systems of this bureaucratic organization. The basis for authority lies within this construct: Authority has been effectively taken from the people and placed within the government or bureaucracy. Laws are then created describing the relationship of power with the people and their world.

In Aboriginal society, authority generated through societal structure is attained in a different manner altogether. Here society is structured and ordered through egalitarianism and a blending of ritual authority with the obligations and partiality due to ties of kinship. Aboriginal ritual life is organized around relationships with the land from where ownership of ceremonies come. Authority is given to individuals depending on factors such as birth order, intelligence, forcefulness, and beauty of singing voice. Ritual authority is viewed as that chosen by *The Dreaming*, that which is not human-made. Authority obtained through the ritual world is not directly interchangeable or necessarily related to the civil world, yet it is the only form of authority that can override the loyalty to close relatives in the secular world. Seniority in the secular world may increase chances of gaining authority in the ritual world.

One example of the smaller-scale nature of Aboriginal governing concepts occurs today with the presence of land councils. In the Northern Territory, three councils preside over and are responsible for representing the needs and voice of more than fifty communities of Aboriginal peoples. This modern construct of pan-Aboriginal identity and authority exists, yet with frequent rebellions and dissension of individual groups. *The Dreaming* explains to Aborigines that authority is located in a specific localized place and that a large council cannot speak for the needs of local groups.

Aboriginal definition of authority is more closely related to the Eurocentric concept of nurturance. When a man teaches a young boy the role that he will assume once he reaches the appropriate age, he views his relationship to that boy as one of "looking after" or of nurturing. The knowledge passed onto the young man is knowledge he needs to be married and begin the next stage in life. The passage is extremely important to their culture. Authority given in this manner cannot be easily transferred into a Western situation, as has been attempted by area employees, businesses, and land councils. As Harris (1990, 37) describes: "The checks and balances between the forces of individual autonomy, authority, kinship loyalties and the ethics of generosity and cooperation, which counterbalance each other at the family or small group level, are not strong enough to operate effectively on a wider scale."

The Eurocentric school curriculum and system readies its students for integration into a large-scale, bureaucratic society where authority comes from an office and where the individuals filling the positions in those offices have no connecting loyalties to people with whom they have completed transactions.

## THE DREAMING AND SCHOOLING

What's this white man's education all about? Education for what? To destroy my people? To destroy the land? *Our* education, Aboriginal education, was for survival, for getting along with each other and all the creatures. Theirs was to try to make us be like them.

—Art Davidson (1992)

Western schooling imparts one knowledge—one worldview—that denies the knowledge and worldview that was there in the first place. This worldview is distinguished from others by several features including: a scientific, fact-based approach to truth; corporeal and spiritual separation from the land; compartmentalization of areas of life; use of linear time frames and quantifiable concepts; emphasis on function and transactions rather than on being and interactions; manipulation of the environment; open societal structure; secular, mechanistic, and impersonal economic systems; work ethic; authority placed in bureaucratic offices separate from the people; and placement of individuals in positions of authority through a bureaucratic process, not through kinship loyalties, acts of generosity, intelligence, or other personal attributes.

The hidden curriculum, that which teaches students what are the valuable ideological attributes of the dominant society, "rubs off over time even though it may not be deliberately taught" (Harris 1990, 3). It teaches values, attitudes, and what is regarded as normal. Accompanied by English-language instruction, which imparts its own hidden curriculum, values are transmitted through seating arrangements and student grouping. These practices ignore Aboriginal social avoidance rules and preferred gender and age roles. Cooperative behaviors common in Aboriginal communities are discouraged to stimulate individual learning. Use of English names and words carries with it the message that Aboriginal ways are not important enough to follow in school and can be easily broken without any consequences. The messages the schools send to the children is that their parents' culture and ways are backward, nonmodern, and doomed to die.

Even a bilingual education program is loaded with Western lessons. English language usually is placed higher on a learner achievement scale than the Aboriginal language. Often this is reflected in the way students are tested. In another more insidious way, bilingual programs use the Aboriginal language to teach Eurocentric ways of thinking.

Aboriginal ways are very different from Western ways. Harris (9) describes the two as "antithetical—consisting of more opposites than similarities." Even though official Australian government policy toward Aborigines has changed to cease practices that force assimilation, Eurocentric schooling inherently reproduces Western culture. As Harris quotes Stanner (ibid., 11): "This means that the Aborigines must lose their identity, cease to be themselves, become as we are. Let us leave aside the question that they may not want to, and the possibility. . . that very determined forces of oppression will appear. Suppose they do not know how to cease to be themselves? People who brush such a question aside can know little about what it is to be Aboriginal."

Adaptation, change, and regeneration can exist while Aboriginal identity remains intact without denying the reality of cultural change. Researchers have noted forms of resistance as Aborigines have learned to fight and hang onto *The Dreaming*. I believe that this fight also must be a message to the West, to the educational policy makers in the capital, to the individual of goodwill that Eurocentric schooling transplanted from the West into the non-West locations imposes an alien culture on another. The attempt to colonize the minds of indigenous, non-Eurocentric-thinking peoples like the Aborigines of northern Australia will be met with resistance. As yet another indigenous voice stated: "Please, try to fathom our great desire to survive in a way somewhat different than yours" (Yúpik elder; quoted in Davidson 1990, 3).

## TEACHING WHITENESS IN THE WEST

Whiteness as a pseudonym for Westernization and Eurocentrism is a learned ideology. Sociology informs us that education structures exist in order to prepare individuals to become part of the society they live in. When we base our curricular content and design on only a Eurocentric approach toward histories, we avoid a vital component in a multicultural education.

We need to expose whiteness as a cultural construction, as well as the strategies that embed its centrality. We must deconstruct it as the locus from which other differences are calculated and organized. The purpose being here, to expose the rhetoric or logic of whiteness. It is only upon critically examining this strategic rhetoric that we can begin to understand the influences it has on our everyday lives and, by extension, our research and teaching. (Nakayama and Krizek 1995, 297).

I believe that a hole exists in the logic of the multicultural curriculum. For me, the missing piece that is needed in classroom debate and dialogue is space for exploration of positionality. Cultural theorist Gayatri Spivak calls to the "quiet other" that exists within us all. It consists of that which is not constructed from a need to make the Self whole, yet that which "is the voice of the other in us" (Spivak as cited in McGee 1992, 123). This aspect of positionality allows one to view relational constructs from the side of the Other, to see the intersubjective space that binds subject to subject through language. Perhaps Spivak's theoretical stance is what teachers need to help them to fill in the gap. This process produces a blank space to allow for new interpretation, thinking, and theory that students may not have conceived previously. Through a call to the "quiet other," a revelation of socially constructed histories is possible. Yet how do students become aware of their own activeness in that construction? "Rather than evade his or her position within hegemonic culture, the Western individual should display it, expose it, question it, and put it into relation to the 'third world' culture he or she needs to hear. This is the first step toward unlearning the privileges of imperialist culture" (124).

The challenge to multiculturalism is to marry its goals with a politics of location or positionality, to aid students in the personal interrogation of position. This may not be comfortable and may never be neutral. In fact, it will reactivate the curricular project. Interrogating one's positionality should not be fashionable or faddish. It can *not* be easy; if one is not careful, one may lose sleep over it. German-Jewish philosopher and literary critic Walter Benjamin describes a perspective sense of alienation and melancholia acquired by the postcolonial subject once that individual acknowledges the historicity of eternal truths, specifically of the truths and values that masked the domination of Western culture (McGee, 154). Benjamin's condition of melancholia is not reserved for subjects of the Third World or for members of internal colonies located within the borders of the First World. Melancholy is an inevitable stage in self-interrogation that arises when the psychological clash, rehash, reform also occurs in the mind of the privileged subject.

Frankenburg (1993) discusses how Eurocentric people tend not to be aware of their own culture and the implications that this has on their lives as well as the lives of those who are non-white, non-Western, non-Eurocentric. She states: "Whiteness, as a set of normative cultural practices, is visible most clearly to those it definitively excludes and those to whom it does violence. Those who are securely housed within its borders usually do not examine it" (228). Individuals can become self-interrogative by recognizing that a Eurocentric ideology is learned and can be imposed onto another through mechanisms in our society such as schooling, media, language, and policy.

My use of Harris's description of Aboriginal ways of knowing is not merely intended to be a trip into the exotic but a part of this more fully defined multiculturalism. Harris's research effectively decodes the encrypted characteristics of whiteness otherwise deemed nonexistent. If we seek to include study of other ways of knowing in our classrooms and research, we can begin to open up a new space for possibility. For once we have defined the Other, we inadvertently reveal ourselves. Through this practice, we reveal that whiteness can be defined very specifically as an ideology socially and historically situated that is controlled by institutions invested in power and distribution of resources and is personally, locally, and globally located; thus, it is *not* invisible.

## BIBLIOGRAPHY

Davidson, Art. (1993). *Endangered Peoples.* San Francisco: Sierra Club Books.

Frankenberg, Ruth. (1993). *The Social Construction of Whiteness: White Women, Race Matters.* Minneapolis: University of Minnesota Press.

Goldberg, David Theo (ed.). (1990). *Anatomy of Racism.* Minneapolis: University of Minnesota Press.

Harris, Stephen. (1990). *Two-Way Aboriginal Schooling: Education and Cultural Survival.* Canberra, Australia: Aboriginal Studies Press.

McGee, Patrick. (1992). *Telling the Other.* Ithaca, NY: Cornell University Press.

Morgan, Marlo. (1994). *Messenger Down Under.* New York: HarperCollins.

Nakayama, Thomas K. and Krizek, Robert L. (1995). "Whiteness: A Strategic Rhetoric." *Quarterly Journal of Speech* 81, 291-309.

Said, Edward W. (1989, Winter). "Representing the Colonized: Anthropology's Interlocuters." *Critical Inquiry* 15, 205-225.

Stauffer, Robert B. (1979). "Western Values and the Case for the Third World Cultural Disengagement." In Krishna Kumar, (ed.), *Bonds Without Bondage: Explorations in Transcultural Interactions.* Honolulu: University of Hawaii Press.

Verhelst, Thierry. (1987). *No Life Without Roots: Culture and Development.* London: Zed Books.

Yapa, Lakshman. (1991, Summer). "Theories of Development: The Solution as Problem." *Research and Exploration.*

# SIX

# Youth, Memory Work, and the Racial Politics of Whiteness

**Henry A. Giroux**

## RACE, WHITENESS, AND THE CRISIS OF YOUTH

**A**merican society increasingly produces a social frenzy through the highly charged rhetoric of moral panic and political rage about the notions of race and identity and the state of youth culture. Releasing itself from its political and moral obligations to working-class youths and youths of color, the American public continuously enacts punishment-driven policies to regulate and contain such youths within a variety of social spheres. For instance, surveillance has replaced a politics of caring as jobs disappear, public services in the inner cities are abandoned, and the criminal justice system takes the lead in regulating large numbers of youths marked by class and racial subordination.

Racism feeds this attack on kids by targeting black youths as criminals while convincing working-class white youths that Blacks and immigrants are responsible for the poverty, despair, and violence that have become a growing part of everyday life in American society. Racism is once again readily embraced within mainstream society. As the gap between the rich and the poor widens and racism intensifies, neoconservatives and liberals alike enact legislation and embrace policy recommendations that undermine the traditional safety nets provided for the poor, the young, and the aged. As the realities of high unemployment, dire poverty, bad housing, poor-quality education, and dwindling social services are banished from public discourse, working-class youths and youths of color are offered a future in which they will be earning less, working longer, and straining to secure the most rudimentary social services. As American society reneges on its traditional promise of social and economic mobility for the marginalized and disadvantaged, it accelerates its war on the poor, immigrants, and Blacks while simultaneously scapegoating young, especially urban, black youths as a substitute for addressing the economic and political factors that undermine the possibility for a multiracial society and the formation of broad-based political coalitions. Within the current historical conjuncture, talk about youth is inextricably linked to discourses about whiteness and the growing threat the latter faces from people of color. Working-class white youths may appear troubled and troubling in the national media, but the problems they face, according to the dominant media, have less to do with the economy or the dismantling of the welfare state than with the corrupting influence of hip-hop culture, the spread of crime by urban black youths, and the undermining of public schools in the urban center by kids of color. Rarely does one find in the popular media a sustained critique of how racism works to marginalize white working-class youths while demonizing youths of color. White youths who succumb to the "pathologies" of communities of culture are seen as either the product of dysfunctional families, as in Oliver Stone's film *Natural Born Killers,* or as poor and vulnerable to the corrupting influence of black youth culture, as in Larry Clark's film, *Kids.* Outside of Hollywood representations of such racist and demeaning stereotypes, a dominant culture seizes on identity politics in order to claim that white folks are under siege by hordes of urban youths, mostly black, threatening to tear down the moral fabric of society with their renegade music, drug dealing, and welfare cheating. Within this scenario, whiteness becomes both unfrozen and defensive, self-assertive and hostile. Lost from this discourse are the much-needed attempts to hold whiteness up to the same self-scrutiny afforded to alleged communities of color.[1]

While it is imperative to understand the rise of racism and the current attack on youths within the context of past and current historical conditions, it is also crucial to experience one's relationship to the present from the inside, as part of an ongoing dialogue between oneself, the past, and the emergence of a present that dispenses with the obligation to remember. More specifically, it is crucial to remind ourselves that any discourse about youth is simultaneously a narrative about the ideologies and social practices that structure adult society. Such narratives become useful pedagogically and politically when used to provoke and interrogate history—especially the history of the much-maligned 1960s and the emergence of the often-celebrated Reagan-Bush period beginning in the 1980s—in order to enable the past to become part of a broader dialogue in understanding the current circumstances shaping the lives of young people.[2] Of course, kids bear the burden of such a past more directly than adults do since they generally are in a much weaker position to modify or transform the effects it leaves on their bodies and psyches. This is not meant to suggest that kids bear the effects of generational attacks in the same way—effects vary depending on how one is situated in the class/race/gender nexus. But the legacy of the culture of Reaganism does not merely limit the power of agency and sour the willingness of young people to transform the conditions they inherit, it also provides the pedagogical grounds for memory work—that is, individual and collective inquiries into how public memory about the 1960s, narratives of whiteness, and the Reagan-Bush eras are written and used to legitimate the racially coded and oppressive policies that currently frame not only a eugenicist-based politics of whiteness but also a widespread conservative movement aimed at regulating the schools, courts, and families as well as the medical and health professions. (See D'Souza 1995 and Murray and Herrnstein in 1994 for examples of racial politics.)

The starting point for such memory work is twofold. First, it begins with a recognition that the category of youth is constituted across diverse languages, cultural representations as well as racial and class-based experiences. Moreover, the multiplicity and contradictions that work within and across generations are both historically specific and subject to continuous change. Youth is a fluid historical and social construction as well as a space, location, and embodiment in which the personal and social intersect and give meaning to the particularities of individual and social differences. The second feature of memory work is more personal and begins with the recognition that understanding youth and racial identity as lived experience demands, in part, an inquiry into the formative conditions of my own white, working-class youth as it was lived out within the overlapping boundaries of racial and class divisions that fueled my entry into the 1960s and, later, into the long march through the Reagan-Bush eras.

This inquiry is not meant to be confessional. Instead, I want to reconstruct how my own experience of youth differs from that of a generation of contemporary working-class youths whose experiences are constructed within vastly disparate political, cultural, and economic conditions. Most notably, excavating my own experiences of youth prompts me to be attentive to how youth and the interface of race and class are signified and lived out differently across various historical conjunctures. For instance, memories of growing up in the late 1950s and early 1960s recollect for me a period of time that seemed more open, a period when dreams of social and economic mobility did not appear out of reach as they do for so many young people today. On the other hand, race and class divisions in my youth were rigidly defined around most cultural, social, and political fronts. Today's youths confront a different set of circumstances. Both working-class and black kids face the threat of dead-end jobs, unemployment, and diminished hopes for the future. Moreover, they locate themselves within a culture that is more porous, fluid, and transit. Hip-hop culture, for example, provides a style, a language, a set of values, and diverse modes of behavior that cut across racial and class divisions. Young people today live in an electronically mediated culture in which channel surfing—moving quickly from one mode of communication to another—becomes the primary method by which they are educated. Such conditions have not only refigured the class and racial landscapes of today's youths, they have redefined how adult society names and treats young people at the end of the century. For example, the attack on youth and the resurgence of a vitriolic racism in the United States is, in part, fueled by adult anxiety and fear over the emergence of a cultural landscape in which cultural mobility, hybridity, racial mixing, and indeterminacy increasingly characterize a generation of young people who appear to have lost faith in the old modernist narratives of cultural homogeneity, the work ethic, repressive sublimation, and the ethos of rugged individualism. Youth as menace symbolizes both a collective fear and the changing face of America—a change characterized by diverse public cultures, racial spaces, languages, media cultures, and social relations. Youths more than any other group appear to represent the emergence of new forms of community, national identity, and postmodern citizenship. The changing conditions that signify youths, especially working-class and black youths, have not been lost on conservatives such as Allan Bloom, Jesse Helms, William Bennett, and Bob Dole. Youths, in this discourse, have been shaped by what is perceived as a serious moral and intellectual decline as a result of the student movements of the 1960s and the leveling ideology of democratic reform movements that embrace multiculturalism, political correctness, feminism, and other "anti-Western" influences. According to conservatives such as Robert Bork (1996, B7), youths have been corrupted by "tribal loyalties," "voguish nonsense," and "anti-rationalistic enterprises" that threaten to usher in "a barbarous epoch."

## MEMORIES OF WHITENESS

How does a reconnection with a past practice support a disconnection from a present practice and/or a development of a new one?

—Hal Foster, (1996)

As a young kid growing up in Providence, Rhode Island, I was always conscious of what it meant to be a white male. Whiteness was a defining principle shaping both how I named and negotiated the boundaries my friends and I traveled when we went to school, played basketball in gyms throughout the city, and crossed into alien neighborhoods. Being white and male were crucial markers of our individual and collective identities, yet we were also working class, and it was the interface of race and class that largely governed how we experienced and perceived the world around us. Of course, we hadn't thought deeply about race and class in a critical way; we simply bore the burdens, terrors, and advantages such terms provided as they simultaneously named the world and produced it.

In my working-class neighborhood, race and class were performative categories defined in terms of events, actions, and the outcomes of struggles we engaged in as we watched, listened, and fought with kids whose histories, languages, styles, and racial identities appeared foreign and hostile to us. Race and class were not merely nouns we used to narrate ourselves, they were verbs that governed how we interacted and performed in the midst of "Others," whether they were middle-class kids or black youths. Most of the interactions we had with "Others" were violent, fraught with anger and hatred. We viewed kids who were black or privileged from within the spaces and enclaves of a neighborhood ethos that was nourished by a legacy of racism, a dominant culture that condoned class and racial hatred, and a popular culture that rarely allowed Blacks and Whites to view each other as equals. Everywhere we looked, segregation was the order of the day. Community was defined within racial and class differences and functioned largely as spaces of exclusion, spaces that more often than not pitted racial and ethnic groups against one another. Solidarity was based mostly on the principles of exclusion, and race and class identities closed down the promise of difference as central to any notion of democratic community.

When college students walked through my Smith Hill neighborhood from Providence College to reach the downtown section of the city, we taunted them, mugged them on occasion, and made it clear to them that their presence violated our territorial and class boundaries. We viewed these kids as rich, spoiled, and privileged. We hated their arrogance and despised their music. Generally, we had no contact with middle-class and ruling-class kids until we went to high school. In the 1960s, Hope High School (ironically named) was a mix of mostly poor black and white kids, on the one hand, and a small group of white, wealthy kids on the other. The school did everything to make sure that the only space we shared was the cafeteria during lunch hour. Black and working-class white kids were generally warehoused and segregated in that school. Tracked into lifeless courses, school became a form of dead time for most of us—a place in which our bodies, thoughts, and emotions were regulated and subject either to ridicule or swift disciplinary action if we broke any of the rules. We moved within these spaces of hierarchy and segregation deeply resentful of how we were treated, but with little understanding and no vocabulary to connect our rage to viable forms of political resistance. We were trapped in a legacy of commonsensical understandings that made us complicit with our own oppression. In the face of injustice, we learned to be aggressive and destructive, but we learned little about what it might mean to unlearn our prejudices and join in alliances with those diverse Others who were oppressed.

Rather, the everyday practices that shaped our lives often were organized around rituals of regulation and humiliation. For instance, the working-class black and white kids from my section of town entered Hope through the back door of the building, while the rich white kids entered through the main door in the front of the school. We didn't miss the point, and we did everything we could to let the teachers know how we felt about it. We were loud and unruly in classes, we shook the rich kids down and took their money after school, we cheated whenever possible, but more than anything, we stayed away from school until we were threatened with being expelled. While class registered its difference through a range of segregated spaces, race was more problematic as a register of difference. Like the black kids in the school, our bodies rather than our minds were taken up as a privileged form of cultural capital. With few exceptions, the teachers and school administrators let us know that we were not bright enough to be in college credit courses but were talented enough to be star athletes or do well in classes that stressed manual labor. Both working-class Whites and Blacks resented those students who studied, used elaborate, middle-class language, and appeared to live outside of their physicality. We fought, desired, moved, and pushed our bodies to extremes, especially in those public spheres open to us—the football field, the basketball court, and the baseball diamond.

As a working-class white kid, I found myself in classes with black kids, played basketball with them, and loved black music. But we rarely socialized outside of school. Whiteness in my neighborhood was a signifier of pride, a marker of racial identity experienced through a dislike of Blacks. Unlike the current generation of many working-class kids, we defined ourselves in opposition to Blacks, and while listening to their music we did not appropriate their styles. Racism ran deep in that neighborhood, and no one was left untouched by it. But identities are always in transit, mutate, change, and often become more complicated as a result of chance encounters, traumatic events, or unexpected collisions. The foundation of my white racist identity was shaken while I was in the ninth grade, in the last year of junior high school.

I was on the junior high basketball team along with a number of other white and black kids. The coach had received some tickets to a Providence College game. Providence College's basketball team had begun to receive extensive public attention because it had won a National Invitation Basketball tournament; moreover, the team roster included a number of famous players, such as Lenny Wilkens and Johnny Eagen. We loved the way in which these guys played; we tried to emulate their every move into our own playing styles. Getting tickets to see them play was a dream come true for us. Having only two tickets to give away, the coach held a contest after school in the gym to decide who would go to the game. He decided to give the tickets to the two players who could make the most consecutive foul shots. The air was tense as we started to compete for the tickets. I ended up with two other players in a three-way tie, and we had one chance to break it. As I approached the foul line, Brother Hardy, a large black kid, started taunting me as I began to shoot. We exchanged some insults and suddenly we were on each other, fists flying. Then I was on the floor, blood gushing out of my nose; and the fight was over as quickly as it started. The coach made us continue the match, and, ironically, Brother Hardy and I won the tickets, shook hands, and went to the game together. The fight bridged us together in a kind of mutual esteem we didn't quite understand but respected. Soon afterward, we starting hanging out together and became friends. After graduating from junior high school, we parted ways and I didn't see him again until the following September, when I discovered he was also attending Hope High School.

I made the varsity my sophomore year; Brother Hardy never bothered to try out. We talked once in a while in the school halls, but the racial boundaries in the school did not allow us to socialize much with each other. But that soon changed. The second month into the school year I noticed that during lunch hour every day, a number of black kids would cut in front of white kids in the food line, shake them down, and take their lunch money. I was waiting for it to happen to me, but it never did. In fact, the same black kids who did the shaking down often would greet me with a nod or "Hey, man, how you doin'?" as they walked by me in the corridors as well as the cafeteria. I later learned that Brother Hardy was considered the toughest black kid in the school, and he had put out the word to his friends to leave me alone.

During the week I played basketball at night at the Benefit Street Club, situated in the black section of the city. I was one of the few Whites allowed to play in the gym. The games were fast and furious, and you had to be good to continue. I started hanging out with Brother Hardy and on weekends went to the blues clubs with him and his friends. We drank, played basketball, and rarely talked to each other about race. Soon some of my friends and I were crossing a racial boundary by attending parties with some of our black teammates. Few people in our old neighborhood knew that we had broken a racial taboo, and we refrained from telling them.

I couldn't articulate how my crossing the racial divide gradually served to challenge the white racism to which my body had grown accustomed, but it slowly became clear to me in those formative years that I had to redefine the modalities of my whiteness as I moved within and across a number of racially defined spheres. I had no intention of becoming a black wannabe, even if such an option existed in the neighborhood in which I grew up, and, of course, it didn't. But at the same time, I began to hate the racism that shaped the identities of my white friends. My crossing the racial divide was met at best with disdain and at worst, with ridicule. Crossing this border was never an option for Brother Hardy and his friends; if they had crossed the racial border to come into my neighborhood, they would have been met with racial epitaphs and racist violence. Even in the early 1960s, it became clear to me that such border crossings were restricted and took place only with a passport stamped with the legacy of racial privilege. My body was relearning about race and identity because I was unlearning the racist ideologies that I took for granted for so long. But I had no language to express how I felt, nor did I understand how to reject the notion that to be a working-class white kid meant one had to be a racist by default.

The language of racial identity, whiteness, and differences that I inherited as a kid came from my family, friends, school, and the larger popular culture. Rarely did I encounter a vocabulary in any of these spheres that ruptured or challenged the material relations of racism or the stereotypes and prejudices that reinforced race and class divisions. I assumed rather than challenged the commonplace presumption that the dominant public sphere was white. It was only later as I entered the 1960s, that I discovered, in the midst of the civil rights and antiwar movements, languages of dissent and possibility that helped me to rethink my own memories of youth, racism, and class discrimination.

My own sense of what it meant to be a white male emerged pedagogically and performatively through my interactions with peers, the media, and the broader culture. The identifications I developed, the emotional investments I made, and the ideologies I used to negotiate my youth were the outcome of educational practices that appeared either to ignore or to denigrate working-class people, women, and minority groups. Culture, especially popular culture, became the educational medium that supplied the texts to negotiate everyday life, especially as such texts provided the categories of meaning through which our identities, values, and desires were mobilized. The act of listening and watching various media provided a combination of knowledge and drama that legitimated the social roles we occupied as kids as well as the range of possibilities through which we could imagine something beyond the world in which we lived. The trauma I associated with negotiating between the solidarity I felt with Brother Hardy and my class friends suggests that education works best when those experiences that shape and penetrate one's lived reality are jolted, unsettled, and made the object of critical analysis. In looking back on my experience moving through the contested terrains of race, gender, and class, it is clear to me that power is never exerted only through economic control, but also through what might be called a form of cultural pedagogy. Racism and class hatred are learned activities, and as a kid I found myself in a society that was all too ready to teach it.

## PERFORMATIVE INTERPRETATIONS AS PEDAGOGICAL PRACTICE

Looking back at my own journey through a culture steeped in racist and class divisions, I was very fortunate to have had the opportunities to challenge some of the dominant cultural practices shaping my perception of my white racial identity. While the racial boundaries among contemporary youths are more fluid, young people inhabit a society that is indifferent to their needs while it scapegoats them for many of the problems caused by deindustrialization, economic restructuring, and the collapse of the welfare state. Those youths who have come of age during the culture of Reaganism that began in the 1980s are increasingly used as either a bait for conservative politics—blamed for crime, poverty, welfare, and every other conceivable social problem—or "defined in its relation to processes and practices of commodification" (Grossberg 1994, 27). The attack on youth coupled with an insurgent racism in America has transformed the field of representations, discourse, and practices that shape youth into a battleground. Targeted as dangerous and irresponsible, youngsters face a future devoid of adult support, maps of meaning, or the dream of a qualitatively better life for their own families.

At issue is how youth and race are constructed within new realities that offer both a warning and a challenge to all educators concerned both with analyzing whiteness and racial identity and furthering political and economic democracy in the United States. But this is more than a matter of naming or bringing to public attention the scandal that constitutes the conservative attack on youth and the insurgent racism that parades without apology across the American landscape. There is also the matter of what French philosopher Jacques Derrida (1994, 51) calls "performative interpretation." That is, "an interpretation that transforms the very thing it interprets." As a pedagogical practice, "performative interpretation" suggests that how we understand and come to know ourselves and others cannot be separated from how we are represented and imagine ourselves. How youth and race are imagined can best be understood through the ways in which pedagogy weaves its "performative interpretation" of youth within all those myriad educational sites in which electronic technologies are redefining and refiguring the relationship among knowledge, desire, and identity. Youth and racial identity are constituted within and across a plurality of partially disjunctive and overlapping communities—such communities or public spheres offer creative critiques and possibilities even as they work to constrain and oppress youths and others through the logic of commodification, racism, and class discrimination. This suggests that educators must begin to reclaim the political as a performative intervention that links cultural texts to the institutional contexts in which they are used, critical analysis to the material grounding of power, and cultural production to the historical conditions that give meaning to the places we inhabit and the futures we desire.

At a time of insurgent racism and violence against young people, it is necessary for educators to begin to understand the ways in which youth and race function in diverse cultural sites within particular pedagogical and political discourses. At stake here is more than simply providing a critical reading of different cultural texts or the languages that construct them. On the contrary, I am more concerned about how such texts contribute to our understanding of the expanding pedagogical and political role of cultural spheres that often are treated as if their only purpose were to provide entertainment or promote consumerism. Central to such a concern is how such spheres can be rearticulated as crucial pedagogical sites actively shaping how youths are named and produced in this society. In this instance, youth becomes more than a generational marker, it also becomes an ethical referent reminding adults of their political, moral, and social responsibilities as public citizens to address what it means to prepare future generations to confront a world we have created. The growing demonization of youth and the spreading racism in this country indicate how fragile democratic life can become when the most compassionate spheres of public life—public schools, health care, social services—are increasingly attacked and abandoned. Part of the attempt to undermine those public spheres that provide a safety net for the poor, children, and others can be recognized in the ongoing efforts of the right to "reinstall a wholly privatized, intimate notion of citizenship" (Nelson and Gaonkar 1996, 7). In the new world order, citizenship has little to do with social responsibility and everything to do with creating consuming subjects. Such a constrained notion of citizenship finds a home in an equally narrow definition of pedagogy and the racial coding of the public sphere. In the first instance, pedagogy is defined by conservatives so as to abstract equity from excellence in order to substitute and legitimate a hyper-individualism for a concerted respect for the collective good. In the second instance, it is presumed in both the media and in the representations that flood daily life that the public sphere is almost exclusively white. Blacks are rarely represented as a defining element of national identity or as an integral presence in the various public spheres that make up American life. Reduced to the spheres of entertainment and sports world, Blacks occupy a marginal existence in white America's representation of public life, largely excluded from those public spheres in which power and politics are negotiated and implemented. While the immediate effects of this assault on public life bear down on those most powerless to fight back—the poor, children, and the elderly, especially those groups that are urban and Black—in the long run the greatest danger will be to democracy itself—and the consequences will affect everyone. Now is the time for educators to address these critical issues and once again to assert that the vocation of teaching is about the responsibility for witnessing, combining intellectual rigor with social relevance, and sustaining those public spheres where democracy can flourish and sustain itself.

## NOTES

1. Of course, a body of recent work on whiteness does attempt to engage critically what it means to be White in historical, political, and psychological terms. Some representative examples of recent scholarship on whiteness include: Roediger (1991); Saxton (1991); hooks (1992); Ware (1992); Frankenberg (1993, 1997); Morrison (1993); Winant (1994); Allen (1994); Omi and Winant (1994); Roediger (1994); Ignatiev (1995); Pfeil (1995); Ignatiev and Garvey (1996); Dyer (1997); Hill (1997); Fine, Weis, Powell, and Wong (1997); Wray and Newitz (1997).

2. This is not to ignore that some of the most important work on whiteness has been developed in historical studies but to suggest that more work has to be done in which whiteness is addressed as a formative narrative in the work of those white theorists who construct themselves as scholars of "whiteness." An excellent example of such work that does not translate into self-help formulas can be found in Wray and Newitz (1997).

## BIBLIOGRAPHY

Allen, Theodore. (1994). *The Invention of the White Race*. London: Verso.

Bork, Robert. (1996, October 11). "Multiculturalism Is Bringing Us to a Barbarous Epoch." *Chronicle of Higher Education*.

Derrida, Jacques. (1994). *Specters of Marx*. New York: Routledge.

D'Souza, Dinesh. (1995). *The End of Racism*. New York: Free Press.

Dyer, Richard. (1997). *White*. New York: Routledge.

Foster, Hal. (1996). *The Return of the Real*. Cambridge, MA: MIT Press.

Frankenberg, Ruth. (1993). *White Women, Race Matters*. Minneapolis: University of Minnesota Press.

Frankenberg, Ruth (ed.). (1997). *Displacing Whiteness*. Durham, NC: Duke University Press.

Grossberg, Lawrence. (1994). "The Political Status of Youth and Youth Culture." In *Adolescents and Their Music*. Jonathon S. Epstein, ed. New York: Garland. 25-45.

Hill, Mike (ed.). (1997). *Whiteness: A Critical Reader*. New York: New York University Press.

hooks, bell. (1992). *Black Looks: Race and Representation*. Boston: South End Press.

Ignatiev, Michael, and Garvey, John (eds.). (1996). *Race Traitor*. New York: Routledge.

Ignatiev, Noel. (1995). *How the Irish Became White*. New York: Routledge.

Morrison, Toni. (1993). *Playing in the Dark*. New York: Vintage.

Murray, Charles, and Herrnstein, Richard (1994). *The Bell Curve: Intelligence and Class Structure in American Life*. New York: Free Press.

Nelson, Cary, and Gaonkar, Dilip. (1996). "Cultural Studies and the Politics of Disciplinarity: An Introduction." In Cary Nelson and Dilip Parameshwar

Gaonkar, (eds.), *Disciplinarity and Dissent in Cultural Studies*. New York: Routledge.

Omi, Michael, and Winant, Howard. (1994). *Racial Formations in the United States from the 1960s to 1990s*. New York: Routledge.

Pfeil, Noel Fred. (1995). *White Guys*. London: Verso.

Roediger, David. (1994). *Towards the Abolition of Whiteness*. London: Verso.

———. (1991). *The Wages of Whiteness*. London: Verso.

Saxton, Alexander. (1991). *The Rise and Fall of the White Republic*. London: Verso.

Ware, Vron. (1992). *Beyond the Pale: White Women, Racism, and History*. London: Verso.

Winant, Howard. (1994). *Racial Conditions*. Minneapolis: University of Minnesota Press.

Wray, Matt, and Newitz, Annalee (eds.). (1997). *White Trash*. New York: Routledge.

# SEVEN

# "They Got the Paradigm and Painted It White"

*Whiteness and Pedagogies
of Positionality*

## Frances Maher and Mary Kay Thompson Tetreault

### INTRODUCTION

So when they met, first in those chocolate halls [of Garfield
Primary School] and next through the ropes of the swing,
they felt the ease and comfort of old friends. Because each
had discovered years before that they were neither white nor
male, and that all freedom and triumph was forbidden to
them, they had set about creating something else to be.
—Toni Morrison (1974)

This quotation from Toni Morrison's novel *Sula* opened one of the
chapters from our book, *The Feminist Classroom* (1994), a study of 17
classrooms in 6 colleges and universities across the country. We chose it
because it captured one of the central interpretive frames of our research,
which explored how feminist professors and their students "set about
creating something else to be" by taking as their explicit subject matter

the histories, experiences, and aspirations of women, people of color, and other groups previously ignored or trivialized by the academy. Along with our professor and student participants, we engaged in a process of bringing these perspectives to light and explored their implications for the social construction of classroom knowledge.

This quote also invites an examination of what it means to be "White." *Sula* explored some of the complex ways in which students from the dominant white culture began to learn about themselves from these newly emerging voices. One white male student's definition of his identity was bound up with and expressive of a deep-rooted sense of entitlement based on gender and class as well as race. Reflecting on the importance of taking a course that addressed both sexism and racism, he went into great detail about being a minority in a class composed of a majority of African Americans, both female and male, and a small group of white women:

> Never in my life have I ever been ashamed of being an upper-class white male . . . I don't have anything to gain by having Black and white equal. I feel like if it happens, I'll still have a good life, a profitable life. And if women stay home or not, you know like men want them to . . . I can gain, like mankind gains, or womankind, but personally I don't have to deal with that. I'm an upper-class white male; I'm the boss . . . If you're born and you could have your choice of what you wanted to be, white male would probably be the choice, because that's the best thing to be. (Maher and Tetreault 1994, 196)

This student, "Mark Adams,"* was in a class entitled "Women and Literature" taught by an African American woman and emphasizing texts by women of color. Having thought that everything about the context in which this student was learning was therefore "right," we now began to notice that learning about the lives and works of African American women left Mark's own position intact and unexplored. Could a different emphasis in this class have challenged his belief that in this society white and male "is the best thing to be"?

---

* In cases where we used a pseudonym because we were unable to obtain permission or decided to do so for reasons of privacy, we have placed the pseudonym in quotation marks the first time it appears.

We now see both these quotations as revealing the standpoint from which Mark and many other Whites consciously or, more often, unconsciously look at the world. We began to wonder how to address in our work the implications of seemingly ingrained assumptions of white privilege such as Mark's, amid the persistence of racial oppression and the growing racial alienation of our society. Among the most powerful frameworks for maintaining the superiority of dominant voices, in the classroom as elsewhere, is the failure to understand the workings of whiteness: how assumptions of whiteness shape and even dictate the limits of discourse.[1] Because both we and our informants were looking for previously silenced voices, we did not always see the persisting powers of the *dominant* voices to continue to "call the tune" in the classroom— to maintain the conceptual and ideological frameworks through which these new voices were distorted or not fully heard. Much of the ideological power of whiteness stems from its being hidden as "normal," "an invisible package of unearned assets" that Whites "can count on cashing in on each day, but about which they were meant to remain oblivious" (McIntosh 1992).

Moreover, as pointed out by several writers, whiteness operates at different levels simultaneously. In spite of our culture's tendency to construct everyone as an individual, whiteness is not simply an individual identity along the lines Mark suggested. By the institutionalization of physical appearance as social status, all whites gain special advantage over those marked "Black" or "people of color." Thus, whiteness is a marker for a location of social privilege as well. To understand whiteness as a social position is to assign everyone, not only people of color, differentiated places in complex and shifting relations of racialized and gendered hierarchies.

But whiteness is more than identity and position. It is also a pervasive ideology justifying this dominance of one group over others. Whiteness, like maleness, becomes the norm for "human," the basis for universality and detachment; it is the often silent and invisible basis against which other racial and cultural identities are named as "Other," measured and marginalized. In comparable formulations, authors such as Becky Thompson (1997) and white women challenging racism have distinguished among "whiteness as description," referring to the assignment of racial categories to physical features; "whiteness as experience," referring to the daily benefits of being white in our society; and finally "whiteness as ideology," referring to the beliefs, policies, and practices that enable Whites to maintain social power and control. Whiteness may be further defined, in media theorist Elizabeth Ellsworth's (1997) recent work, as "instead of a fixed, locatable identity, or even social positioning, . . . a dynamic of cultural production and interrelation." Because whiteness is *not* an essentialized identity but rather a "product of history and power relations," it is constituted and reconstituted by social activity; both stable and unstable, it is always "more than one thing and never the same thing twice."

In college classrooms, as in other settings, whiteness operates on all these levels. It is both assumed and continually in need of assertion, always being constituted as it is simultaneously being challenged and resisted. Moreover, in terms of the classroom in particular, whiteness is also a central defining feature of the academy's practices of intellectual domination, those ways of constructing the world through the lenses of the traditional disciplines. *The Feminist Classroom* began with the following quote from American poet and feminist critic Adrienne Rich: "When those who have the power to name and to socially construct reality choose not to see you or hear you, whether you are dark-skinned, old, disabled, female, or speak with a different accent or dialect than theirs, when someone with the authority of a teacher, say, describes the world and you are not in it, there is a moment of psychic equilibrium, as if you looked into a mirror and saw nothing."[2] By evoking the academic mirror's assumptions of whiteness and maleness, Rich named two major attributes of the universalized perspective that scholarly pursuits both depart from and aim for. Intellectual domination often is couched in the language of detachment and universality, wherein the class, race, and gender position of the "knower" is hidden or presumed irrelevant. When instructors, as well as those students most likely to dominate class discussions, are White, the common silence about their own social positions exaggerates their power to universalize their own particular perspectives. Moreover, even egalitarian, democratic discussion practices often simply allow the most vocal students to take over; again, in white-dominant settings, these are most likely to be white students.[3]

What new questions, therefore, do we need to ask as teachers and classroom researchers in order to expose Mark's and others' classroom experiences as complex reflections of and reactions to the racialized power relations of our society? How are assumptions of whiteness lodged in the academy's ideological frameworks, in professors' and students' exercise of intellectual domination in the classroom, and how do these assumptions work to shape classroom knowledge? How is whiteness produced and resisted as a function of the ongoing production of classroom meanings, and what role does it play in the students' construction of their own places within racial as well as class and gender hierarchies?

We organized *The Feminist Classroom* around four themes of analysis: mastery, voice, authority, and positionality. Of the four, positionality is the most salient here. Positionality is the concept, advanced by postmodern and other feminist thinkers, that knowledge is valid only when it includes attention to the knower's position in any specific context (Maher and Tetreault 1994, chap. 1). While always defined by gender, race, class, and other significant dimensions of societal domination and oppression, position is also always evolving, context-dependent, and relational, in the sense that constructs of "maleness" create and depend on constructs of "femaleness"; "blackness" and the term "of color" are articulated against ideas of "white." The constructs "teacher" and "student" are positional as well, in that they too represent shifting relationships — of authority, expertise, and empowerment. The classroom is one important arena where these relational networks are susceptible to critique and change, if they are explored rather than ignored, individualized, or universalized.

In the book we called for "pedagogies of positionality," for approaches to teaching in which these complex dynamics of difference and inequality could be named and examined. We looked at the ways our teachers approached class discussions to ensure that the whole range of student voices could be heard. More broadly, we explored the efforts of our professor participants to claim a new kind of professorial authority, one that was neither enacted on the basis of hierarchical notions of scholarly expertise nor relinquished in the name of a common "sisterhood" with their students. Rather, they often saw their authority as positional, based on their own histories and engagements with scholarly work, and they consciously attempted to model themselves as knowers and learners evolving with their students. Encouraged by their teachers, students often became authorities for each other around specific topics or texts (ibid., chap. 5).

What we ignored in our analyses, however, was the role of whiteness in helping to shape all these relations of dominance in the classroom, including the relations of authority. We did not see the ways in which thoroughgoing "pedagogies of positionality" must entail teachers' and students' conscious excavations of whiteness as well as other forms of dominance in their many dimensions and complexities. In a sense, our use throughout *The Feminist Classroom* of a "methodology of positionality," one in which we continually revisited our work and our own position with new perspectives gained from new experiences and insights, allows us now to write a new "last chapter" as both an extension and a reversal of the book. We can now use whiteness as a lens to examine some of our classroom portraits as well as our own positions anew (ibid., chap. 7).

Many of the discussions in *The Feminist Classroom* reflect the assumption, although often challenged by the teacher, that whiteness is a normal condition of life rather than a privileged position within networks of power. It appears a safe, well-marked path, more powerful because it is invisible, that allows even discussions of race to slide effortlessly forward as notations of features of "the Other."

We examine several situations in which whiteness begins to come into focus as a position of privilege. The path of discussion becomes much more bumpy and painful than when whiteness is assumed as the racial norm, but the critique of the relations of oppression necessary to a positional understanding of whiteness becomes more possible. In each of these classes, we look at the ways in which the professors, the white students, and the students of color are challenged to reposition themselves in order to allow whiteness to surface as an issue. Indeed, in the second situation—not by coincidence one in which the teacher and the majority of participants were people of color—whiteness is consciously identified as a means for participants to proceed with the construction of knowledge on their own terms. In both of these situations, we see the participants actively struggling to deploy "pedagogies of positionality," in that they are naming and exploring the societal relations of race, gender, culture, and power that they are reproducing and reframing through the discussion. We also have come to understand that confronting issues of whiteness necessitates conscious interventions on the part of teachers, interventions that might challenge their commitments to an uncomplicated classroom democracy.

## WHITENESS AND THE
## RESISTANCE TO INTELLECTUAL DOMINATION

The professor who helped us to see most clearly how intellectual domination is tied to whiteness as well as to issues of classroom processes and power relations taught history and gender studies at Lewis and Clark

College.[4] Integral to Grey Osterud's idea of feminist processes in the classroom was a sharing of her authority with her students. She saw the sources of her authority as lying in her identity as an explicitly positioned subject, enacting commitments as a feminist and a socialist, rather than in her scholarly expertise. Nevertheless, only a wrenching shift of the power relations in her classroom made it possible for the processes of white intellectual domination to be challenged there.

Worrying about a gender studies class in which about half the students were silent, Osterud assumed at first that the quieter students just needed time to become equal participants, not realizing that they felt unprepared to join a discussion that presumed so much prior knowledge and experience. Thus her use of democratic classroom processes, by which she meant to enable students to become authorities for each other, also meant that a few more verbal students were dominating the others, and these were members of the dominant white culture. In exploring their own experiences, these students often avoided and resisted the experiences of others. Osterud (1987) said about this issue:

> The culture of our gender studies program validates personal experiences and suppresses the expression of differences that challenge other peoples' perspectives. People feel empowered to speak of their own experiences, and construct theory on that basis, and that is good. But they do not feel impelled to include other people's experience in their explanatory frameworks, . . . and when the other people insist that their experiences too must be taken into account, they respond with barely concealed hostility. . . .

To illustrate these problems and their relation to whiteness, we turn to Osterud's class, "Feminism in Historical Perspective/Feminist Theory," which enrolled 30 students (six of whom were men and three of who were students of color) in the spring of 1987. A small number of theoretically minded seniors were taking over class discussions, and their distinctive discourse was incomprehensible to the rest of the students.[5] This pattern was broken by two women of color who complained openly in class; one was Beth Sanchez, a student who described herself as "mixed Latina and Native American." Her frustration with these seniors led her to a critique of the "academic realm" as one of domination and subordination, one in which "you can be in the 'not knowing' position or you can be in the 'knowing.'" Academic discourse constricts "what we really mean and puts a real limitation on how we communicate." She said, "Sometimes I go to class thinking, That was a bunch of theory, and feeling like the more abstract people are looking down on me, which I think is a product of their own insecurity and insensitivity."

Osterud was conscious of the situation, one she described as "in violation of feminist classroom processes and that had to be stopped." But she refused to use her authority as a teacher to solve the problem of students' participation, in either the large or small groups. She waited for more than a week for the students to clarify the problem together so that they could come up with a solution together. She told us: "I could see it, but I could not do anything about it. Maybe some teachers could if they are authoritarian, but I knew that anything I did that was directive would defeat the whole purpose . . . they had to realize there was a problem and . . . break open the process."

Although she responded with a number of alternatives about the structure of the class and the course readings, Osterud insisted that the students needed to take collective responsibility for the large-group discussion. The students agreed that they would plan the reports from the small groups and the subsequent agenda for the large one. They also agreed to choose one of themselves to chair the large-group discussion each day. Osterud convinced them that this was a necessary condition for the whole group to respond to students' needs, so that they could look to one another rather than to her for responses to their comments. This repositioning of Osterud's authority would, as she put it, "free me from the role of orchestral conductor to become an 'expert participant' in the discussion; I could try to clarify matters or pull things together instead of eliciting the expression of opposite points of view or setting up controversies as I had been doing." The next full-group discussion was the one that follows; it was begun and extended by students without much input from her.

Thus, the students themselves came up with a solution regarding their own responsibility for the class. We believe that the earlier revolt against a few seniors created a climate in which some of the formerly quieter students could bring issues of racial and gender oppression and invisibility into the classroom. An active reformulation of the discussion dynamics in the class set the stage for an overt discussion of social positions, or the relations of oppression. The discussion, led by three students of color, concerned the absence of race in feminist theory and their own need to create explicit racial and ethnic identities. While the book contains part of the discussion, we missed the continuing assumptions of whiteness that framed the discourse.

We now want to return to this class to look at how the white students' construction of gender and racial oppression worked to mask the naming of whiteness as a social position and as an oppressive aspect of feminist theory. We also want to illustrate the ways the students of color challenged those students by insisting on exploring the need to name themselves, to give themselves identities, and how the pervasiveness of whiteness as a dominating conceptual apparatus frustrated their efforts. We can see here how whiteness is actively constructed and maintained even as it is resisted; how, in Ellsworth's formulation, it is "always more than one thing, and never the same thing twice."

The discussion began with some observations by Cheryl Ibabeo, a Filipino American, about the absence of women of color in Sheila Rowbotham's book, *Woman's Consciousness, Man's World,* because discussions of the black movement focus on men and discussions of women focus on white women. "Most of the feminist literature that I've come across doesn't say a lot about racism." A white male student, "Ned Sharp," responded by pointing out that the problem lay in the connections between experience and theory; specifically Rowbotham's "extolling of individual experience" and "looking for too-generalized similarities between us . . . which overlooks problems like race." He then added: "If she never had to entertain race and it never crossed her mind once, I would indite her methodology, her starting from personal experience," implying that no one who started from personal experience (that is, no white person, therefore, no one) would have to deal with race. The problem of race for feminism is posed only by black women; when they disappear, there is no "race."

The other white students' reactions to these points were to push for a general theory of gender that would unite all women across their different experiences, without having to pay attention to particular forms of oppression and dominance, namely whiteness and white racism, that would disrupt that unity and cast them into oppressor roles. One white female student, for example, wanted to know "how you can maintain the diversity but still get some kind of unity." Another resisted the loss of women as a "distinct" group, saying: When "women's issues are intermixed with racial issues and oppression . . . women [that is, *white* women] get lost in the shuffle."

But Ned continued to worry about both the necessities and the perils of beginning with individual experiences. To him theory ought to broaden out by connecting "personal experiences" of oppression; giving groups a "common battle to fight," or "linking up with someone who is similarly oppressed and slog through the bog," as he said at other points. He worried that "increasingly narrow experiences" would result, as if combining all the different oppressions cancels out each one: "I think my question about women's consciousness earlier was, is this an attempt to erode class [unity]? I think you can just assume it was answered yes and was also an attempt to erode racial barriers—but what comes out of [talking about gender and race] is an increasingly narrow experience." Ned seemed to understand that individual experiences in and of themselves are at best a starting point of analysis, and he was reaching for a more structural analysis. However, he overlooked the complex relations of oppression and dominance hidden by whiteness and maleness not being marked as social positions—only the "oppressed" position is marked.

Thus, the feminism of all these white students, based on assumptions of whiteness, did not include any consciousness of being white. Race was seen as an exclusive (and obstructive) property of black women only. Indeed, for Ned, gender belonging only to women also obstructs unity. Moreover, while they were able to construct black women as members of a social group, not individuals, the white students could not see that white people, too, were not simply individuals with common personal experiences but differentially placed members of an unequal social order.

But there was another discussion going on, led particularly by Cheryl and "Ron Underwood," an African American male. In it the prevailing assumptions of whiteness operated not only as unacknowledged social location but also as active ideology—where whiteness was a key feature of a normalized and unmarked "center" of intellectual discourse. Both Cheryl and Ron later in interviews acknowledged that they were very aware of working to raise the white students' consciousness around issues of race. In response to comments like those just cited, Cheryl tried to show how looking at people of color exposed the intellectual dominance of the white academy and its distance from the real world.

CHERYL: It makes me wonder if we're not being too theoretical and abstract when we don't consider those things. It makes me wonder if this isn't just a bunch of you know intellectual masturbation and what action is going to come out of it, if we're not going to be diverse about what we're going to be concerned about and be realistic about it.

JANA (white female): Some great chasm between the community and society?

CHERYL: Yeah, but if I weren't here to voice those concerns, and if this weren't Lewis and Clark—we are not black people in this class and I keep thinking to myself 'cause I'm a suburban kid, I'm not an urban kid. And I just think, well, God, this is all great, but how do we apply it.

Cheryl attributed the lack of attention to racism to the culture of Lewis and Clark. She said in an interview: "I've been at this college for a long time and it's predominately all White. People aren't really dealing with the issue of racism." Her comment about "we are not black people in this class," while seeming to ignore Ron's presence, was perhaps also about the impossibility of encountering the many aspects of "blackness" in a context where the complexities and varieties of other cultures are erased by the black/white duality imposed by the dominant discourse. "Black" could be apprehended only as "not white," seen only on white terms. Her notation of "suburbia" could be read as an observation that everyone in the school, being middle class, is "passing" on the terms of white culture, but that "race" is more than physical description. It also must be structural and tied to social class. Finally, she may be reflecting a deeper confusion, tied to the ambiguous racialization of Asian Americans within the dominant discourse: In a black/white universe, where does a Filipina belong?

A few minutes later Ron tried another tack, beginning a discussion of the need to construct identities outside the margin: "In a way to get at the center you have rings of light to bring to light what is marginal and spread [it]. And the only way to do that being a woman or being a black person whose experience is marginalized, you've got to talk about that experience, you have to establish some kind of identity."

He was trying to push gently at the limits of the white students' understandings, to help them look at identities relationally, as situated positions implicating both Whites and people of color. But his quote illustrates the silent workings of whiteness, in that the center is not named. The white students continued to insist on marking race as a concern only for Blacks, so that unity could occur only through transcending race or "doing it for them."

NED: Or we never have a common battle to fight? If we're not all suburbanites together then we can't fight the same battle?

"LAURIE": If a white person defines black struggles that's not an answer, so somehow we have to if we're White or if we're privileged or if we're male or whatever that that kind of people have to somehow empower others to do it instead of doing it for them.[6]

As the discussion proceeded, Cheryl and Ron, joined by Beth, made comments that suggested that they also were continuing to struggle specifically against whiteness as a form of intellectual domination. But because they cannot yet identify the center of knowledge production as white, they cannot fully articulate a language of their own to produce a different knowledge.

CHERYL: But [oppressed groups] all have to form an identity first . . . in a lot of ways it doesn't exist, in that it is so *threatened* given. (Emphasis added)

RON: I think it's *dangerous* to form the question of whether we have the wherewithal to form groups without first knowing who you are.

CHERYL: You know, just part of it is the individual knowing his or her cultural experience, historical experience.

A few comments later:

BETH: I think one thing interesting about learning political language that the mainstream culture understands [is] so that you can as an oppressed group be validized. But once you learn how to communicate, then I think it is necessary to go back to your own language, your own identity, your own culture and I guess they, we, the marginal people, face sort of a problem on the one hand to be autonomous and form an identity and reevaluate it on the other hand, be able to communicate to . . .

RON: So there will always be a double consciousness, sisters under the veil.

To Cheryl's point that most feminist theory is written by white women "with their ideologies and values," Ron replied, "But that's the whole point, that's how language is used to oppress people. People close the doors and talk about all this stuff, and I'm saying that theory provides a key to that door—it also presents a way of changing meaning, changing the way things are."

In the face of unspoken assumptions about whiteness as the norm, the students of color struggled to name it instead as a position and thus "get at the center." Beth pointed out that the "political" "mainstream" language (that is, the dominant language, the language of whiteness) validates other groups' identities, only to simultaneously marginalize them—so "you have to go back to your own language." The idea that they were unable to articulate was that if the center could be named and positioned as white, then the processes of "forming groups," of knowing one's "cultural and historical experience," would be shared by all groups and would not be the task of only the marginalized. A language exposing the positional operations of power relations could be developed, by which all "cultures" could be constructed and deconstructed relationally. The key is undertaking a conscious discourse of whiteness, theorizing whiteness, and thus "changing language" in order to change meaning and "to change the way things are."

It was not that the students of color did not understand what they were up against here. Ron clearly understood that the oppressor has a position. He said in an interview: "The position of the oppressor is the most inflexible. A person who is in an oppressed position will idealize what is above him. [The oppressor] objectifies everything. I just think that oppressed people . . . are better at ripping apart the disguises than creating them. The oppressors are greater at creating them."

Beth and Cheryl also saw the problem as tied to whiteness. The numerical and intellectual dominance of white students on campus contributed to Cheryl's wish that "we would try to imagine ourselves to be something other than white, upper-class people." She and Beth both felt "cultural alienation on campus because the majority of students in the class are White and. . . . overlooking a lot, a lot of things that are conscious but can't be formed into academic lingo and come out in weird ways or don't come out."

In our book we noted that "the white students [avoided] confronting their own position as whites, [as] they repeatedly objectified, generalized about, and posited the unknowability of the 'Other'" (Maher and Tetreault 1994). We pointed out that "white students' resistance to theorizing their 'whiteness'—to being caught in the racial matrix—

hampered the students of color in their aim of articulating their ethnic identities." In our tentative grasp of these issues, however, we underestimated the power of whiteness as ideology, as the assumed basis of a governing intellectual framework, in part precisely because it was not confronted or named directly; we have returned to read between the lines.

The professor herself, Grey Osterud, broke her customary classroom reticence when interviewed. She said later:

> [During the discussion of Rowbotham's book,] when a few minority students were trying to raise the issue of race, I found myself violating the cardinal rules of feminist pedagogy. I got angry and argued with the class; I think I told one student that she was wrong and another that her position was morally indefensible; . . . I behaved in a manner that we might usually term authoritarian, and I was glad that, as a teacher, I had some power to support the minority students' right to be heard. It felt wonderful to get the issue out into the open, with all the conflicting feelings involved. I felt that night that all those things which I stand for and which are validated by the structure of the course were being used to say that the race issue was not crucial or to make excuses for people. I always try to cut the ground out from under that.

In this case, "pedagogies of positionality" involve the teacher taking an active stand in support of the minority of students of color. Indeed, only in situations where people of color were a majority, as in the next class, was the topic of whiteness explicitly taken up in class discussions.

## RESISTING INTELLECTUAL DOMINATION: A WHITE AUTHOR AND A BLACK AUDIENCE

We now turn to a class where the majority of students and the teachers were people of color. What problems are caused for people of color because the "crucial problem" of whiteness is left unnamed and unresolved? In classes like these we can see more fully the effects of unanalyzed whiteness on the ways in which people of color framed their own views of the world, in resistance to and outside those the dominant white culture accorded them. African American students at Spelman College, for example, affirmed the value of constructing knowledge from their own standpoint, against "truths" of white social scientists that claimed they were "deviant" and "pathological." They complained about being prevented by white stereotypes from living the normal, complex lives of "ordinary" middle-class people. One said: "I always hear people talk about NBC as the Negro Broadcasting Company [laughter], because they always tend to try, well, this is a stereotype, they try to cater to black struggles, but it's not necessarily that realistic, because we go from *Good Times* to *Cosby,* and there is no middle."

In our original reading of the class, we emphasized the struggles of the participants to forge their own knowledge. But in emphasizing this new knowledge, we minimized the role of whiteness. This professor and her students had to come to terms with whiteness, almost before they could go about "creating something else to be." The following discussion explored the ways in which a white author used an African American figure for his own critique of white society. This was a class at Emory, a large, elite, and predominantly white southern university, in which Gloria Wade-Gayles, a visiting African American female literature professor, was teaching "Images of Women in Literature" to a group mixed by both race and gender. The 26 students included 13 African American women, 7 African American men, 4 white women, and 2 white men. This professor was more direct than Grey Osterud in constructing a classroom discourse committed to the exploration of societal inequalities. She made a point of consciously exposing the racial and gender stereotypes embedded in the dominant culture's views of black and white women. For example, one day she gave a summary of the learning process she wanted them to go through, stressing the importance of revealing what is on your mind so that stereotypical assumptions can be named and confronted. She said:

> The problem is that the culture tells you these things again and again and you internalize them, and you make an effort to find the cases that support what you've been programmed to believe. Liberation is liberation of the mind. You liberate your mind. Then you change society. But you can't liberate your mind until you examine honestly what has been put in your mind.

In *The Feminist Classroom* (Maher and Tetreault 1994) we noted that this setting, in looking at white privilege, may have simply made the white students in the class appreciate their positions more; the white male student, Mark Adams, quoted earlier, was in this class. However, a few days later, in spite of these difficulties, whiteness was emphatically named as a problem. The following discussion, centering on Dilsey, the mammy figure in William Faulkner's *The Sound and the Fury*, shows the students beginning with an analysis of an African American central character, a victim of racial oppression, and then shifting to a focus on the perpetuators of that oppression, in this case Faulkner himself. In the course of uncovering the meanings in the book, the students discovered that Faulkner, while critiquing white society, was not writing for or to African Americans but for white people. Paradoxically, they found that African American readers are shut out of a literary treatment that explores white racism.

The way into Faulkner's view of Dilsey had been paved by lengthy observations, directed by the professor, into the many ways that the author emphasizes, subverts, and ultimately exposes the toxic effects of racism on a decaying white southern culture. For example, Wade-Gayles had a student read aloud a passage where the family son, Quentin Compson, goes north to Harvard, and reflects on his changed views of African Americans:

> When I first came East I kept thinking, You've got to remember to think of them as coloured people, not niggers. . . . And if it hadn't happened that I wasn't thrown in with many of them, I'd have wasted a lot of time before I learned that the best way to take all people, Black or white, is to take them for what they think they are, then leave them alone. That was when I realized that a nigger is not a person so much as a form of behaviour; a sort of obverse reflection of the white people he lives among. (105)

Wade-Gayles initiated the following discussion by soliciting their reactions to the stereotype of the mammy figure. She asked them, "What do you want to say to Dilsey?" Immediately a black female spoke up, perhaps expressing the view of a black child whose mother must care for Whites: "It doesn't seem she cares about her own children as much as she does about Quentin" (the white family son). The first speakers were African American: Eugene Williams, "Kathy Kennedy," and "Michael Cash," whose "explanations" for Dilsey's failure to nurture her own children ranged from fear that Whites might take them away, to the idea that her job entailed ignoring them in favor of the white children.

KATHY: Maybe she doesn't want to get too attached, maybe they'll get rid of her kids. She still has this mind-set not very different from slavery. . . .

EUGENE: I agree—even though it was the 1920s, she did have that mind-set that . . . goes from generation to generation so the time we are dealing with is something like slavery. Look at what it did to African American lives! You really can't put a time limit on that. But she totally forgot about the nurturing of her children.

MICHAEL: I felt that she didn't love her children, in fact I would go as far as to say that she more or less did not give them a stable beginning whatsoever, she criticized everything they did. . . .

KATHY: It's not her fault that she has to take care of those other children!

EUGENE: Regardless of what the social constraints are or whatever, she's a mom, and she could nurture them in some way. It is obvious that she has the capability to nurture. Why couldn't she do it with her own children!?

MARK (white male): It seems like it's more of a job, though, isn't it? Wouldn't it be her job to do that? It would be like any other job, when the job's over you're not like what you were on the job.

JAMES: But that's the thing—it's not just a job!

More discussion of Dilsey's relationship with the Compson family ensued, during which the professor pointed out that Faulkner made Dilsey "the moral conscience of the novel," and that "she is also a stereotype."

WADE-GAYLES: She's positive—I mean, be honest. The negative images are the images of the white people! I mean, give Faulkner credit. . . . She's the moral conscience of this novel, and we, the readers, are supposed to say this is positive.

In our analysis of this class in the book, we focused on the African American students' identification with Dilsey's children and concluded that the reason Dilsey was so objectionable was: "not so much because her portrayal in the novel seemed to them to contradict stereotypic notions of women as nurturing; rather, it was because of the whole history of the merging of femaleness and racial identification in slavery."

Could the black students' anger also have been focused on the unspoken racialized assumptions of the white students, namely their unproblematic location of Dilsey in the servant role, leaving "normal" mothers as white women taking care of their own children? A few days earlier, the students in this class revealed that their constructions of the "good" mother were racially positioned, as they took up the question of whether Blacks or Whites were better mothers. One black female said, "When I see a [white] child acting up, I think, if I was a black mother, I wouldn't let my child run around like that," to which a white female replied, "I just haven't heard that [said]."

In spite of the attempts by the white students to locate Dilsey unproblematically in her servant role, the students of color were able to uncover "literary whiteness"—to position Faulkner as a writer not for a universal, normative, and unnamed audience but specifically for white readers. We now see also that these students were resisting the connection of a certain kind of motherhood with black racial identity, namely that Blacks "mother" Whites, not their own children. More broadly, they were displaying the resentment they felt once again, both in the way Dilsey acted and in the way Faulkner appropriated the figure of a black woman to be the conscience of a white family, Blacks were being made to live for Whites and not on their own terms. The African American students' discussion of Dilsey reveals their struggle to perceive themselves, just as the Spelman students, as "normal," as children with all the expectations of American children in middle-class nuclear families in the late twentieth century. Confronting Faulkner's "universal appeal" of hiding assumptions of whiteness as the center of his normative universe was important for them in order to reconsider these issues in their own lives. In giving Faulkner a specific social position, they could claim a valid one of their own.

## CONCLUSION

In this new, "last chapter" for our book, we have returned to our themes of "pedagogies" and "methodologies" of positionality, using the construct of "whiteness" to examine positions of dominance rather than, as in our book, marginalities. We have focused here on largely unacknowledged assumptions of whiteness as a key aspect of the dominant culture and how these assumptions interact with constructions of gender, class, ethnicity, and race to shape the construction of classroom knowledge. We have seen whiteness operate both differentially and simultaneously, as "always more than one thing"; it has been physical description, individual identity, social position, ideology, and, throughout, a "dynamic of cultural production and interrelation" operating "within a particular time period and place, and within particular relations of power" (Ellsworth 1998, 31).

In Grey Osterud's classes at Lewis and Clark, the white students initially sought a theoretical unity of all the oppressed. Based on physical description as marker for social location, white students and students of color assigned "race" to minorities, especially to Blacks, while staying oblivious to the Whites' position as Whites. Thinking about whiteness as ideology, we can see how the conceptualization of race as a bipolar construct, with Black and White as the two poles, operated to make all "difference" oppositional in nature, so that black lives could not be normal, but only the obverse or the exception to those of Whites— whether in Faulkner or *The Cosby Show*. Also caught in this dualism, the Asian, Filipina, and Hispanic students in Osterud's class lacked any appropriate "mirror" for their identities. Yet these students probably were enabled to speak up as much as they did by the earlier revolt against a classroom atmosphere that, while ostensibly democratic, actually rewarded the most vocal students and the ones most trained in discourses of the dominant culture. This class shows how "positional pedagogies" may entail necessary reconfigurations of classroom dynamics in order to allow students of color to be heard at all.

Nevertheless, both discussions show the pervasive power of whiteness as a feature of the intellectual dominance of the academy, wherein the universalized knower and known are always assumed to be White. Each discussion represents whiteness at many more levels than we have captured here, through layers of personal, political, and ideological constructions and assumptions, and through discourses of gender and class as well as race.

In employing the shifting lenses occasioned by our methodologies of positionality, we also have to come to terms with the fact that we now "see" dynamics in our data hidden from us before. Yet to "recognize" (or "re-see") those dynamics positions us partly as expert detectives, who want to "get it right" this time around. We see more clearly the importance of continuing to learn about ourselves, to interrogate our own social positions of privilege, and to use that knowledge to inform our research, our teaching, and our professional practice.[7]

Finally, beginning to be able to understand and "track" whiteness in these ways, as constructed socially and historically, allows us to think about the possibilities of revealing its various operations so as to challenge and renegotiate its meanings—in Roy's words, "to change language, change meaning, and change the way things are." While classrooms often not only reflect but also impose the dominant culture's ideological frameworks, they also may function as somewhat sheltered laboratories where those frameworks may be exposed and interrogated. One hope thus lies in students (and professors) becoming genuine authorities for each other as they are explicit about themselves as positioned subjects with respect to an issue or a text. As this chapter has shown, however, many of the steps toward these kinds of awareness are tentative. Often they are undertaken, at some risk, by people occupying subordinate positions. The students of color in Osterud's class speak of danger and threat in looking at their own identities.

In relation to whiteness in particular, increasing numbers of teachers have begun to use the literature on whiteness with students—both Whites and students of color—to help them see themselves and each other differently: not as individuals whose relations to racism must be either "innocent" or "guilty" but as participants in social and ideological networks. While these networks are not of their own making, they nevertheless can come to understand and challenge them. Several of these teachers, such as Elizabeth Ellsworth, Beverly Tatum, and Sandra Lawrence, have written about this work with students, as have several of our teacher participants. As Bev Clark, one of our participants, once told us, "My students don't live their whiteness, I don't live my whiteness. I'm working hard to see how to do that."

A glimmer of hope we would like to pursue may lie in a final comment by Mark Adams, the white male student quoted at the beginning of this chapter. Mentioning that an older African American woman student named Blanche Burch in Wade-Gayles's class had become an authority for him, he told us that the professor:

. . . seems like she's teaching on more than one level. She's teaching me just to open my eyes, but with Blanche it's totally different because she has open eyes. Blanche is ten steps ahead of me in understanding all this. . . .

This class could easily have ended up all black women, but it's important for me to be in there because I have to understand it. I can't understand it when I am in a nice little fraternity house, predominantly white men from North and South. It's good for me and maybe if I take something from this and go home and sit with my roommates and talk about it and open it up there, rather than keep it in the classroom . . . it seems like we need it for us. We need it and [other] white males and females probably need it just as much.

Gloria Wade-Gayles left us with a message, one that we now see exhorts Whites to understand whiteness and to work from that position: "Black women need to understand how special they are. For Whites, you need to understand what you can do working as a white American, one who can make a difference."

## NOTES

Thanks to all our participants, especially those included in this chapter, whose contributions in the form of classroom dialogues in some cases go back ten years. Thanks also to Gloria Wade-Gayles and K. Edgington for commenting on this chapter. A longer version is forthcoming in the *Harvard Educational Review*.

1. Privileges accorded people because they are middle or upper class, male, and heterosexual also are often unacknowledged and operate in similar ways. In this chapter we focus on whiteness, while noting ways that it intersects with other forms of privilege in the different vignettes that we explore.
2. We first saw this quote from Adrienne Rich in a paper by Renato Rosaldo (1988).
3. This phenomenon is widely acknowledged most often with relation to male and female students; however, it operates with students of color as well.
4. Lewis and Clark College is known for its strong gender studies program and an institutional pedagogy focused on student perspectives as learners. A hallmark of their pedagogy was the practice of beginning with the students' questions rather than the common approach of asking the professors' questions.
5. Other issues present beset this and many other feminist classrooms: how to attend to theory by getting students to think theoretically without separating theory from their personal experience and feminist practice; how to enable the students to set their own agenda; and how to deal with the disparate discourses in a class that arise from, in the professor's words, "that real separation, the gap between inside the classroom and the real world of personal experience out there."

6. Laurie Lester's quote had new meaning when we learned that she had unresolved issues with her father, who achieved upward mobility through the military, married a middle-class white woman, and denied ties to his father, who is a Northwest Indian.

7. We also see again the value of the community of feminist scholars our book and other work has created. It was in a final interview with Angela Davis that we first learned about the whole field of scholarship on whiteness, in the form of Ruth Frankenberg's work (1993) examining the constructions in white women's life narratives. Grey Osterud's observations that we had treated positionality only as it arises from marginality, thus concealing the dominant position, became another nagging issue that would not go away. The last-minute perusal of articles by Neil Gutanda, Elizabeth Ellsworth, and Sandra Lawrence gave us new insights into this work.

## BIBLIOGRAPHY

Ellsworth, Elizabeth. (1997). "Double Binds of Whiteness." In Michelle Fine, Lois Weis, Linda Powell, and L. Mun Wong (eds.), *Off White: Readings on Race, Power, and Society.* New York: Routledge.

Ellsworth, Elizabeth. (1996, Fall). "Working Difference in Education." *Curriculum Inquiry.* v. 26 no. 3.

Faulkner, William. (1946). *The Sound and the Fury.* New York: Random House.

Frankenberg, Ruth. (1993). *White Women, Race Matters: The Social Construction of Whiteness.* Minneapolis: University of Minnesota Press.

Lawrence, Sandra. (1994). "Beyond Race Awareness, White Racial Identity and Multicultural Teaching." In Maher, Frances A., and Tetreault, Mary Kay. (1994). *The Feminist Classroom: An Inside Look at How Professors and Students Are Transforming Higher Education for a Diverse Society.* New York: Basic Books.

McIntosh, Peggy. (1992). "White Privilege and Male Privilege: A Personal Account of Coming to See Correspondences Through Work in Women's Studies." In Margaret Anderson and Patricia Hill Collins (eds.), *Race, Class and Gender: An Anthology.* Belmont, CA: Wadsworth Publishing Co.

Morrison, Toni. (1974). *Sula.* New York: Alfred A. Knopf.

Osterud, Nancy Grey. (1987). "Teaching and Learning about Race at Lewis and Clark College." Unpublished.

Rosaldo, Renato. (1988). "Symbolic Violence: A Battle Raging in Academe." Paper presented at the annual meeting of the American Anthropological Association, Phoenix, AZ.

Rowbotham, Sheila. (1973). *Woman's Consciousness, Man's World.* New York: Penguin.

Thompson, Becky, and White Women Challenging Racism. (1997). "Home Work: Anti-Racism Activism and the Meaning of Whiteness." In Michelle Fine, Lois Weis, Linda Powell, and L. Mun Wong (eds.), *Off White: Readings on Race, Power, and Society.* New York: Routledge.

# EIGHT

# Educating the White Teacher as Ally

## Connie Titone

If only we could rise up against the killer of man's dreams. But sometimes, the killer of dreams is in us and we do not know how to rid ourselves of it. It is the apathy of white southerners that disturbs me; and may I add this apathy is north and west of our region too. There are so many people who are determined not to do wrong but equally determined not to do right. Thus they walk straight into Nothingness.

—Lillian Smith, 1897-1966

**A**s a white teacher, I worry that in many high school and college classrooms we are not confronting one very serious difficulty: We are not fighting hard enough to help white students abandon racism and define a positive racial identity. I worry that so many people at schools of education are absolutely determined not to do wrong when it comes to multicultural, anti-racist work but are equally resolute not to do right.[1] We white educators have to educate ourselves, "to combat, actively and directly, the racism in other White people" (Malcolm X 1987, 371), and we cannot do that by keeping our tongues tied when it comes to white racism. We must take on the leadership roles that are required to combat pathological whiteness and eradicate racism accompanied by all of its negative academic effects. When we do not, too many students and faculty walk uninterrupted into Nothingness.

Our personal identities and our professional ones are inextricably connected. To create exemplary professionals, we have to be self-actualized individuals—or at least be working on it. We have to attend systematically to our students' personal development at the same time that we work on their professional development. In a school of education, the determination not to do wrong can create the impression of knowledge, polish, peace, and skill in individuals. However, white educators who have the professional look but not the identity development of antiracist teachers cannot accomplish the difficult adaptive work required to move us ahead into the new century. It is no easy task to help white students unlearn racism, to teach an individual the skills he or she needs to be an ally to oppressed peoples and to other white people.[2] It is a challenge to create ways for our racial identities as allies to inform our professional identities as teachers. This challenge is the focus of this chapter, and I offer some of my own personal and professional insights as cases in point.

## RACIAL SOCIALIZATION
## OF A WHITE SOUTHERNER

I was born and grew up in Louisiana to Italian-speaking, Sicilian parents with little formal education. They taught me that I should assimilate into mainstream U.S. culture (that is, "speak English and become American"), to pursue with all seriousness my education, and to make the system as it existed work for me. Indeed, I have achieved many of the goals they had for me and have gained much in this process, but this has been accomplished at considerable cultural expense to myself (Rodriguez 1982). As one profound example, I could never communicate directly with any of my grandparents and have lost all connection to my family's past.

During my childhood, I reached the point of being inwardly outraged by all racist practices and systems but did not know how to disrupt or destroy them. I was living in an openly segregated and racist environment more than one-third of which was Black. With the arrival of my reading skills, I also began to read my world. The "colored" and "white" drinking fountains at the downtown Sears and Roebuck on

Texas Avenue embodied what I saw as the tangible absurdity of my artificially, yet very completely, divided community. It was not a particularly dramatic event that kept my agitation alive but rather the daily, consistent, silent sickness I perceived in white people. As an adolescent, the gentle back door of cruelties I witnessed from "nice white people" scared me. Their hypocrisy deeply offended my sensibilities and my intelligence. I feared the seeming inevitability that my own attitudes and actions might become similarly shaped. As I reflect on it now, I see that growing up, I resisted the pressing conformity of a racist socialization I was receiving from my community. At the same time, I could not maintain the silence we were keeping on these issues. Soon I summoned the courage to speak out against the inconsistencies. My challenges fractured the accepted paradigm, and I was called dangerous by my father, my friends, and my Sunday school teachers.

I had absolutely no positive, white, antiracist role models to emulate or with whom to discuss these issues. My life provided no public space for thinking critically, and even though I could see through some of the "big lies" (Macedo 1993), I did not escape the more subtle indoctrination that was to come. I came to adulthood never realizing that "White" had been socially constructed just as "Black" had been and that I too had been racialized. All of my experiences and my knowledge—and, equally impor-tant, the experiences and knowledge I did not have—were preparing me for a life's work and a particular type of teacher identity that converged with my personal identity. I have proceeded through at least two models of teacher identity as the changes in my personal racial identity have occurred: the white savior and the multicultural intellectualist. I am now attempting to practice from a third, the white teacher as ally.

## MODELS OF PROFESSIONAL WHITE TEACHERS

### The White Savior

In the early years of my official teaching career, which I began in the mid 1970s, I thought my noblest social contribution should come from merely teaching African American, Cajun, and Vietnamese adolescents to succeed academically. These were "the Others" in our Louisiana schools. Unconsciously I incorporated the lessons of my parents into my teaching agenda: I believed that if I cared enough about my students, I could teach them to assimilate into mainstream ways of speaking and acting, learn the given Eurocentric curriculum, gain access to the social and economic system as it was, and thus be successful. I assumed that students would best accomplish these tasks on *my* culturally familiar terms, not theirs. I defined my professional self as one who could "save" certain children from the prescribed, inferior future that awaited them— from their blackness or "Otherness." Thinking I was doing good work, and believing in the good I was doing, I eagerly persisted in that role for more than a decade.

I shudder now to think of how my own faulty development—one that could not see any difference between rightness and whiteness— stunted the growth of my students of color, how I miseducated them as I had been miseducated. Oddly enough, though I understood my own lack of positive, white role models, I was blind at the time to the possibility of intentionally becoming one myself for my white students and colleagues.

With this feeling of superiority over my students and of blind confidence in my teaching ability, but lacking the varying perspectives and the role models I needed, I left Louisiana in the late 1980s to continue my professional development in the North at a highly esteemed university. Quite an accomplishment—the southern, Italian American woman from a working-class background entering a doctoral program at such a privileged place. I was initially intimidated by my surroundings and expected much. Disappointingly, the formal aspects of my train-ing—even at this highest level of study and in this most respected of institutions explicitly committed to "issues of diversity"—neither actively informed nor passively encouraged my development as a bud-ding white, antiracist teacher. Rather, I learned to understand multicul-tural issues from an intellectual perspective and to leave at the door my outrage and my expectations of finding white, antiracist role models whose pedagogy and practice I might emulate.

## The Multicultural Intellectualist

I was well instructed when it came to studying the educational research related to issues of diversity. I learned to conceptualize "the Other" as a cultured being and to respect and to affirm "them." I learned about internalized oppression and its effects on students' self-esteem. I studied Delpit (1988) and de la luz Reyes (1992); from them I learned the data on learning styles and linguistically different discourse patterns of "the Other" and the need for teachers (especially white teachers) to vary their instructional strategies and styles so as to teach students the skills they need in order to enter the "culture of power" (Delpit 1988). I learned about Ogbu's (1989) notions of cultural discontinuities, and I became adept at understanding the different kinds of "Others" and the problems they might encounter in schools. At least once a year, I encountered McIntosh's (1989) "White Privilege: Unpacking the Invisible Knapsack," so that intellectually I knew I was "privileged," and I could tell you how that privilege was made manifest.

Now let me be clear: I do not completely discount the value of this kind of education. I am certainly not an anti-intellectual. I think this information is a necessary part of an educator's knowledge base. However, this knowledge alone is not sufficient for an antiracist, white educator.

White educators must also pay attention to how white students situate themselves in the study of race, culture, and education. At my school of education, as a general rule, the process within which material was presented did not provide a structured environment that encouraged us as white students to come to terms with ourselves, nor did it provide the opportunity to interact with white, antiracist role models who were doing or had done the same. It did not present the full truth. It was not focused enough. It did not go deep enough. It may have been politically correct, but it was not politically progressive. It did not get to the heart of the issues. It did not dare us to think critically about ourselves. As an institution and as a collective community of learners, we neglected our ethical responsibility to struggle to transform ourselves and to facilitate similar transformations in all white preservice teachers.

## The White Teacher as Ally

If we are to educate the white teacher as ally, we must "intervene in challenging students to critically engage with their world so they can act upon it" (Freire with Macedo 1995, 391). Like my personal environment, my graduate school of education never systematically provided me with the experiences or the role models to ensure the process of my own racial identity development and its critical connection to teaching. Nonetheless, I began to envision a new focus for myself as a teacher educator based on what I had needed myself: guiding white students in their understanding that multicultural education is not only learning about "them" but requires learning about "us" and the dynamic we create as we relate to one another. Moreover, the problem of racism is not outside of us but within us. One other significant idea white educators need to catch on to about "us" is that not only have our psyches suffered negative effects because of our own race-centered socialization but also that we can move beyond that. As allies, we can take positive action in support of our black colleagues, students, and friends. We can continue the history of white protest against racism and work for educational and societal change. We can join people of color in the work of replacing detrimental school practices such as the use of a Eurocentric curriculum, biased assessment practices, and tracking. We can untie our own tongues about the racist socialization we have undergone and explain our processes of redefinition. We can become positive, white, antiracist role models for our students and teach them to do the same for their students.

## LESSONS FROM MISSED OPPORTUNITIES

### Class Processes

To approach "multicultural work" from this angle is daunting because not only do we have scant material to draw from, but also because the process of resocialization is very complex and time consuming. It is extremely difficult to maintain a productive learning environment in which participants are experiencing considerable discomfort while grappling with the truth about themselves and white racism. Exactly what skills does a teacher need to frame the content and process in order to handle best the resistance that usually results from this approach?

The teacher's own self-actualization and skill at guiding the discussion process are critically important in this approach. The necessary understanding can come to students only when the teaching staff demonstrates deep self-knowledge and unwavering courage and patience. Unfortunately, missed opportunities are more common. For example, in a professional seminar for doctoral students at my graduate school of education, on the first evening of class after introductions, the professor asked us to take a few minutes and write about a time in our lives when we felt "different." After an hour or so, we presented our stories to each other. These stories were incredibly poignant, and in some cases they were passionately recounted. Considerable tension was generated as stories of racial and gender differences were relived, but their potential for instruction—for increased understanding—was enormous.

The esteemed and experienced professor was visibly shaken by some of the experiences and immediately called for a break in the class. She said that she was shocked with the intensity of our emotion and was completely unsure as to how to handle it. She was visibly paralyzed, and her paralysis eclipsed our dialogue. Her inability to handle our revelations actually suffocated the tension, and that fact silenced our learning. More important, because of the resulting silence, the misunderstandings among us were perpetuated and intensified. Obviously, this was not purposeful wrongdoing, but the professor's socialization, her inexperience in confronting her own whiteness and privilege, and her lack of self-understanding as a white woman assured her unwillingness to dialogue with us about it. It also prevented us from confronting those very issues for ourselves. Her opportunity to model for future educators how to deal with issues of race, class, and gender was irretrievably lost. Though she may have been well meaning, the professor herself was a victim and an example of the multicultural intellectualist. In subsequent class meetings, she diligently worked to keep the discussion and activities at an intellectual level—where participants were not personally and emotionally engaged, so no deep progress could be made. Because she protected her own comfort level, we did not learn to outsmart or outpace the ugliness of cultures in conflict. We learned to intellectualize and avoid the ugliness, and we walked straight into Nothingness.

## Research and Writing

Classroom settings are not the only milieu in which these important subjects can be broached and such critical opportunities seized. Research and writing processes provide obvious means to encourage students to delve into themselves and use their new discernment to improve their teaching. Early in my dissertation planning stage, I proposed a qualitative research study to be set in Louisiana to work with a sample of white teachers. The purpose of this study was to grasp the teachers' understandings of the significance that whiteness had in their professional identities and professional practices. I wondered: "How did these teachers see their race affecting their attitudes toward others and the classroom practices they developed?" A nationally respected faculty member in my department dismissed the proposed topic as "too difficult" and "not directly useful enough to schools and schooling." Another said it was "too politically charged" and "too negative," while a third called the topic "too close to my own experiences and passions" and therefore inappropriate as a research topic. In retrospect, I suspect that another explanation for these responses from white faculty members was, of course, their lack of interest or confidence in wrestling with this question.

Although confused and feeling stifled by the advice I was receiving, my own feelings of insecurity and intimidation caused me to accept their opinions as valid. Eventually I settled on a slightly less problematic and less threatening thesis topic: the metaphysical, epistemological, and pedagogical holdings of Catharine Macaulay, an eighteenth-century British, pioneering feminist. I say "slightly less problematic" because, even in this instance, some faculty members questioned my desire to study a woman in the field of philosophy—especially this "unknown woman whose work was probably not very strong."

## Informal Advising

Still eager to grow in my antiracist identity, I sought less systematized ways to take advantage of my surroundings such as classroom discussions and dissertation research, and in some instances even these were discouraged. At one point, when I was working on a short research paper for a history of education class, I inadvertently came into contact with the work of Lillian Smith, a committed southern journalist, essayist, and novelist. In her book *Killers of the Dream* (1949), Smith systematically confronted and examined her society's concepts of race, gender, and sexuality. I was inspired by Smith's honesty about racism in her southern community, her lyrical perception of her own experience and of the transcendent meaning it held. I pored over the details about how it affected her own thinking. I respected her efforts in *South Today*, a literary magazine she edited and in which she wrote articles between 1936 and 1945, and I wanted to study her life and her work. One professor strongly deterred me from doing so because "neither she nor her work was scholarly enough."

## Educating the White Teacher as Ally

From the preceding "missed opportunities" we can identify several teacher characteristics we would want to develop in the white, antiracist role model. At their best, these teachers would be: (1) cognizant of themselves in relation to history and place (Kincheloe and Pinar 1991), that is, in this case, able to define and acknowledge their own whiteness; (2) willing to initiate, and able to hold a group in, discussions of racial issues and education, even emotional and confrontational ones; (3) cognizant of the ways curriculum and projects can be used to address students' unarticulated beliefs about the connections between race and education; and, (4) aware of the opportunities for supporting students in their racial identity development even in situations of informal advising and contact.

To be an effective white teacher in a classroom committed to the personal and professional development of our white students, I must embark on my own process of healing racism and have some understanding of the complexities, the pain, the potential satisfaction, and the transformation that the process probably would entail. I must undertake a process of critical self-inquiry and begin to focus on myself as a racialized person living in a particular social context with a dark history. Step by step, and in some very real ways, we must all redefine our personal identities and enlarge our professional purposes as teachers.

In the context of teaching prospective and in-service teachers about culture and education, I have learned to expect that white people who first come face to face with the concepts of racism and their own complicity in maintaining a system from which they benefit, will feel not only very uncomfortable but also deeply wounded in the process of exploring it.[3] Most of us are not at all receptive to seeing ourselves—and, more important, who and what we represent—as the problem. We educators and our students actually may have been taught the very opposite.

In order to move beyond denial and feelings of guilt and helplessness, we must help ourselves to experience a form of healing. Some of it we can do alone, reading and thinking, but some of it requires honest dialogue with others we trust.[4] It is more than intellectual work; it is a work of the spirit. The need for this work cannot be denied as nonexistent or dismissed as irrelevant political correctness. Foremost in schools of education, it must be acknowledged as a substantial issue and faced seriously, as much with the heart as the mind. To intellectualize or to ignore this problem will not diminish its pernicious effects. On the contrary, it will entrench them.

As white educators, we need to understand ourselves critically in relation to "the Other." We need to challenge ourselves—to *change* ourselves—to understand ourselves differently from how we may have been taught. We need information, a safe holding environment for open, sometimes confrontational, dialogue, time for reflection and feedback, and strategies and action plans for immediate implementation. Moreover, we need to learn to practice new responses in real settings. This should be required work for prospective teachers, policy makers, administrators, academicians, researchers, and the like. It should be set into the conceptual frameworks that drive entire schools of education. It should be an obvious, and steady, thread through courses, field experiences, and advising. We cannot leave it to the initiative of individual students or serendipitous events.

## IN CONTEXT

I first began teaching classes called "Multicultural Education," "Antiracist Education," "Multiethnic Education," and "Cultural Foundations of Education" at the graduate-school level in the summer of 1992. I have taught these courses and correlated undergraduate courses to both preservice and in-service K - 12 teachers in the United States and in Bangkok, Mallorca, and Cyprus. The overwhelming majority of my students have consistently been White and female, and I have been eager to engage them in a focused study of the social construction of schooling within a particular society, the significance of whiteness/oppression, and the urgent professional implications of understanding these complex and challenging ideas.

I have entered into this work believing that many white people, or whichever people represent the dominant group in a particular culture (for example, Irish Protestants in Northern Ireland, northern Italians in Italy and Sicily; the Chinese in Taiwan; the Canadian English speaker in French-speaking Canada; the mainland U.S. citizen in Puerto Rico) have had a socialization similar to mine. However, often at the beginning of the course, students respond to the course content as just so much "political correctness." They sometimes elaborate by saying that this work, although required for state certification, is irrelevant to them for two reasons: (1) They do not perceive themselves personally as racists nor can they identify bias in their dealings with any students, and in these two regards this work is superfluous for them; and (2) they do not teach many students of color, and their white students, like them, have little need of "multicultural understanding."

Before I can engage in the necessary work with prospective white teacher allies and future role models, these learners and I must first come together in seeing the need for the work. We must come together because in each instance when a discussion of superior, racialized thinking occurs, we will be working together to break down those barriers that serve to block the psychological and intellectual receptivity of the learners' minds and hearts.

Obviously, one critical prerequisite for the white, antiracist professor is to hold a clearly defined antiracist, educational philosophy reflecting his or her political commitment. Emerging from such a philosophy, the professional role model works within a particular pedagogy to attend simultaneously to certain key dimensions of the teaching/learning realm in order to maximize the possibilities for students to see themselves in context and transform their teaching motives and methods. These dimensions are: (1) the creation of a particular kind of learning environment; (2) the creation of a particular kind of student-teacher relationship; and (3) the exploration and co-construction of a particular knowledge base that may demand concrete changes in practice.

## Learning Environment

The driving force for the development of my classroom environment is Parker Palmer's (1983, 69) assertion that "to teach is to create a space in which obedience to truth is practiced." In this space, I sit with my students in a circular pattern regardless of whether we number 10 or 35. In order to employ concepts of dialogue and problem-posing education (Freire with Macedo 1995), I have found that any other physical arrangement is distracting. Participants must be able to see each other, to hear each other, to understand each other, as we engage over a text. Moreover, we must have opportunities to practice responding to each other face to face and heart to heart about differences of experience, opinion, or interpretation, especially when these differences are culturally based.

In addition to the physical space, the psychological atmosphere in which we work is a critically important aspect of the learning environment. It is my responsibility, as the professor, to provide a holding environment for containing stresses and encouraging adaptive efforts, where learning is most apt to occur (Heifetz 1996, 103). Some unspoken questions that must be answered in practice are: Is it safe to be honest about race? Is it safe to disagree with my professor and with my colleagues? Who is talking? Who is not talking? How is this conversation related to education or educational practice? Must I talk? How welcome are personal feelings and experiences related to the "content" of the class? A learning space must include an air of hospitality, openness, and boundaries (Palmer 1983, 71). It must be a place where "strange" thoughts are welcome but the accepted boundaries of respectful discourse are clearly established.

The professor also must help the students pace their psychological and intellectual learning efforts. In the ideal situation, students in the class participate evenly and are most likely to learn multiple perspectives seeing themselves and each other as knowers. However, certain discourse patterns must be recognized and openly acknowledged as less than optimally effective. For example, it is not uncommon for a small number of students to dominate the class "air time" or for a small number of students to remain imperviously quiet. In both cases, the professor must make participants aware of the significance of this dynamic so that each can learn to balance speaking and listening. Moments of silence are not uncommon, as students haltingly learn to listen, discuss, disagree, question, confront, and change each other. The professor must have the patience and the restraint to allow for this creative silence.

The professor also must achieve his or her own balance of speaking and listening. Aside from the work associated with framing questions, redirecting the focus of discussions, and managing the tension that arises in confrontational moments, the professor must consciously monitor how much time he or she—as the "authority figure"—takes up in class discussions and how many students' questions he or she automatically offer answers to. At the same time, I think it is very important to try to remain present in the discussion as a person with personal experiences relevant to the topic and not purely as a professor. Our roles as teachers should not be a "mask that we put on to hide who we are, but part of a structured space that respects our freedom to be ourselves, explore ideas, generate knowledge, create beauty, and grow" (Noya 1995, 168).

When teaching educators, every one of these issues related to the classroom dynamic and the discourse patterns is relevant to discussions because these issues are all critically relevant to our understanding of difference, of the educational implications of difference, and of the teacher's role in accomplishing the adaptive work required in today's educational settings. At those times when we experience a clashing of interpretations over a text or concerning our own classroom processes because of racial, ethnic, cultural, or gender differences, the group must learn, assisted by the professor's modeling, how to take advantage of the learning opportunities and engage each other with respect and receptivity. We must always remember that we do this work to gain understanding and to construct valuable knowledge that we can use as teachers.

## Student/Teacher Relationship

The student/teacher relationship is founded, developed, and maintained on respect and love—for ourselves and for each other as human beings. As I create and attempt to sustain meaningful discourse on how race and identity affect teaching and learning in educational settings, I understand Paulo Freire's argument that dialogue "cannot exist in the absence of a profound love for the world and for people [or] without humility." Aside from love and respect, it requires more—"it requires an intense faith in humankind, faith in [students'] power to make and remake, to create and to re-create, faith in their vocation to be more fully human" (Freire with Macedo 1995, 70-71). This level of faith demands not only courage from the teacher but also an ability and willingness to model risk taking in the learning sphere.

The respect I have for students must go beyond a more or less abstract, positive feeling. It must be visible to students and completely tangible. The most obvious manifestations are very important— coming to class, preparing thoroughly for class, responding carefully and quickly to students' work, and guarding the tone of my voice in conversation with students. My attention to my own development also indicates the deepest respect for my students. I must strive to be consistently introspective and open in order to ensure my own development as a person and as a professional. I must feel connected to the heart of the curriculum and find avenues of enthusiastic expression of its content. I must abandon the authoritarian protection as "professor" and risk true relationships with the human beings who are students. The ultimate challenge is to understand that teaching is never a neutral act and that because of this, the student/teacher relationship is very sacred.

## Knowledge Base

The truth we pursue is to know ourselves, to be able to read our worlds, and to fashion our professional practice because of this knowing. Three types of knowledge comprise the fundamental basis of understanding for the antiracist, white teacher as ally. Although they are embedded in and discussed throughout this chapter, however, I would like to reiterate them here. They are:

1. Knowledge of self. The white teacher as ally must first understand his or her own culture and grasp "how our cultural perspectives shape our thinking and actions" (Hidalgo, 101). This self-knowledge also must include an understanding of oppression and the role the individual and the individual's representative group plays in the perpetuation of oppression.
2. Knowledge of the Other. The white teacher as ally must understand the present-day experiences of those people who are oppressed in his or her host society. He or she also must be able to perceive the educational implications (both positive and negative) for students due to such contextual and identity factors as race, class, ethnicity, or gender.
3. Knowledge of how to take action and to lead. The white teacher as ally must be an educator who understands the politics of education and can take action in a professional setting to establish, extend, and protect the institution of the school in its constructive role to aid in the intellectual and social development of young people.

## CONCLUSION

White educators, preservice as well as in-service, usually have good intentions for correcting the societal mistakes that exist in school settings. However, if their socialization mirrors mine, often they instinctively adopt, as one of their purposes for teaching, a messianic complex toward the children of oppressed groups. In doing so, they miss critical opportunities to work with white students. One of my aims in classes for preservice teachers is to disrupt this response. I focus on three objectives: (1) exposing preservice teachers to the obvious and more subtle workings of racism, sexism, and classism within their own attitudes and behaviors; (2) increasing their understanding of racist practices at work in systems of education and the accompanying effects on students; and (3) working with students to construct concrete strategies they can use to remedy the effects of racism and to contribute to dismantling systemic racist practices. This kind of knowledge provides preservice educators tremendous potential to influence their effectiveness as teachers, counselors, and administrators—and as people. Moreover, it gives them a sense of social agency and hope that opens their thoughts to playing the role of the professional, white, antiracist educator.

According to statistics regarding the racial composition of the teaching force, the vast majority of teachers are white (U.S. Department of Education 1995). Yet at most of the schools of education I have known, the institution, the administration, and faculty members did not consistently insist that a process of abandoning racism and defining a positive, white, professional identity occur for all of its preservice white educators. Classes in curriculum, in assessment, in statistics, in research, in psychology of the adolescent, in philosophy—none of these systematically addressed the issues of race or class in critical ways and from the perspective of whiteness.

In one very real sense, schools of education benefit from maintaining their exclusively intellectualist stance on issues of diversity and preserving the status quo. Training new generations of workers in this manner ensures the perpetuation of a racist system. I worry about this for other colleagues who will follow me through academic programs. I worry for all of the many, many students each of these teachers, administrators, policy makers, and teacher educators will encounter. I envision multiplied and amplified lost opportunities growing out exponentially—an infinite mass of educators and educated marching straight into Nothingness. As professional educators striving to be white allies in the struggle for social justice, we cannot allow that vision to stand undisturbed. We must change the direction of this sorrowful march.

## NOTES

1. The challenge to understand racial issues and to promote the racial awareness of white students has been more or less consistent in all of the predominantly white secondary and postsecondary institutions with which I have been associated. I have seen the difficulties I identify here in the majority of schools and academia.
2. The word "ally" has a specific meaning in this context. An ally is someone who takes on the struggle against discrimination and racist practices and systems because of skin color, language difference, gender, etc. even if it is not his or her own personal struggle. The basis of our allied relationships, I believe, rests in our understanding of how the person or group to which we are allied is affected by individual discriminatory actions and a discriminatory system.
3. See the work of Beverly Daniel Tatum. In one article she applies a theory of racial identity development in creating strategies for overcoming student resistance to talking about issues related to race in a class called the "Psychology of Racism." In a subsequent piece she focuses her research on white students.
4. See the work of bell hooks. In her book *Teaching to transgress* (1994), she speaks of the vicissitudes and success she has experienced as she creates a classroom climate and "transformative pedagogy" aimed at respecting multiculturalism.

## BIBLIOGRAPHY

de la luz Reyes, M. (1992). "Challenging Venerable Assumptions: Literacy Instruction for Linguistically Different Students. *Harvard Educational Review* 62, no. 4.

Delpit, L. (1988). "The Silenced Dialogue: Teaching Other People's Children." *Harvard Educational Review* 58, no.3, pp. 28-27.

Freire, P. with D. Macedo. (1995). "A Dialogue: Culture, Language, and Race." *Harvard Educational Review* 65, no. 3, p. 391.

Heifetz, R. (1996). *Leadership Without Easy Answers.* Cambridge, MA: Harvard University Press.

Hidalgo (1995). "Multicultural Teacher Introspection." In *Freedom's Plow.* Perry, Theresa and Fraser, James (eds.). New York: Routledge.

hooks, b. (1994). *Teaching to Transgress.* New York: Routledge.

Kincheloe, J. L., and Pinar, William F. (1991). *Curriculum as Social Analysis: The Significance of Place.* Albany: State University of New York.

Macedo, D. (1993). "Literacy for Stupidification: The Pedagogy of Big Lies." *Harvard Educational Review* 63, no. 2.

McIntosh, P. (1989, July/August). "White Privilege: Unpacking the Invisible Knapsack." *Peace and Freedom.*

Noya, G. R. C. (1995). "Young People's Perceptions of Teachers and Their School Experiences: Two Dialogues." Ph.D. dissertation, Harvard University.

Ogbu, J. U. (1989). "Cultural Discontinuities and Schooling." *Anthropology and Education Quarterly* 13, no. 4.

Palmer, Parker J. (1983). *To Know as We Are Known: A Spirituality of Education.* San Francisco: Harper Collins.

Perry, Theresa and Fraser, James. (eds.). (1995). *Freedom's Plow.* New York: Routledge.

Rodriguez, R. (1982). *Hunger of Memory: The Education of Richard Rodriguez.* New York: Bantam Books.

Smith, L. (1949). *Killers of the Dream.* New York: W. W. Norton.

Tatum, B. D. (1994). "Teaching White Students About Racism: The Search for White Allies and the Restoration of Hope." *Teacher's College Record* 95, no. 4.

———. (1992). "Talking About Race, Learning About Racism: The Application of Racial Identity Development Theory in the Classroom." *Harvard Educational Review,* 62, no. 1.

U. S. Department of Education, National Center for Educational Statistics. (1995). *Digest of Educational Statistics 1995.* (NCES Publication 95-029, Table 66). Lanham, MD: U. S. Dept. of Education.

X, Malcolm, with Alex Haley. (1964/1987). *The Autobiography of Malcolm X.* New York: Ballantine Books.

# NINE

# Perspectives of the Curriculum of Whiteness

**Ladislaus Semali**

Familiar notions are those least examined. For many people, "whiteness" surely fits that category. This fact is perhaps best illustrated by my own story about living in the United States. This brief account explains my lifelong relationship with whiteness and how it has positioned me in life today. I am a college professor who teaches at a white university. Both my undergraduate and graduate education were undertaken in North America. Since my arrival in the United States from Tanzania, I have steered my activities to reflect my African heritage whenever it was convenient for me and followed the rules and avoided making any waves that might point me out or indicate my uniqueness. Upon reflection, I now realize how I am able to go in and out of my African heritage to position myself within the African culture while at the same time claiming my place in a white institution. My upbringing as an African and schooling in pre-independence Tanzania predisposed me to take for granted what it means to be educated in a neocolonial setting and perhaps not to question "whiteness." My story takes place within spaces of identity formation where I encountered silencing, a place where accepting silence and not questioning were rewarded with platitudes. I continue to encounter silencing today, as part of the colonial legacy that haunts me and promotes years of paralysis.

It was not until I arrived in the United States that I was made aware of the "curriculum of whiteness." One day, while jogging with a colleague, I had a conversation about my experiences in attending school in the United States. I recounted in the story how upon arriving from Tanzania, I was classified as an "alien," a foreigner, and an international student. Such labels hurt my feelings but I preferred to suffer silently rather than vent my discomfort. I recalled how this new identity positioned me in a new light relative to my peers. My fellow "aliens" and I were placed in host families during the first two weeks after arrival. I suppose the intention of this practice at this all-white university was to introduce newcomers like myself to the American way. And therefore, what a better way to do it than to be totally immersed in a family setting? I must admit, this was a good arrangement, because without it I would not have known where to begin to look for housing, transport, or groceries, particularly the kinds of foods that were typical to the diet I am used to. By the same token, being placed in a host family was strategic in terms of socialization and a systematic introduction to hamburgers, apple pie, and milkshakes. Soon after these introductory experiences, I was given a book on how to survive at a university. This book, organized like a recipe manual, covered everything from emergency matters, to ombudsman, to "how-to" stuff, like "first date," etiquette at the movies, and other social functions. These experiences did not mean much at the time. As presented, the manual emphasized "survival." And since I wanted to survive at this institution, I embraced everything totally. Naturally, I needed help, help to understand and decode the cultural norms of the curriculum of whiteness. One of my professors remarked: "You must watch more television to make up for what you missed all these years of village life." According to my American host family: "You are no longer the village boy, you are now a gentleman."

In retrospect, the lessons I learned—for example, from cultural theorist Edward T. Hall's *The Hidden Dimension* (1966), a book assigned for my reading and study—were illuminating and reaffirming of the curriculum of whiteness. Hall's text focused on interpersonal communication practices and emphasized the differences that abound between the diverse racial groups but especially between Whites and non-Whites. It provided clues about use of language, body language, signs and symbols, and by implication insinuated that in order to succeed in the white culture, a newcomer like me must become familiar and learn all these idiosyncrasies. Because I was such an eager international student, I did not realize then how this curriculum was inscribed in everything I was going to do later in graduate school. As one of the international students on campus, I was often invited to participate in camping, beach parties, and weekend sorties. We were instructed very carefully in areas from table etiquette to dancing, to first-date procedures and movie-house etiquette. Now I understand that these experiences did not provide the knapsack tools needed for my survival and success at an all-white university but pushed me to assimilate by abandoning my language habits and African identity. I viewed Hall's hidden dimensions of a Western culture part of an important curriculum of graduate school. But after telling these stories to my jogging partner, I realized that there was another way to look at those events as they built up into my life, particularly my identity and how I position myself in life today. My partner was quick to point out that what I had experienced was an assimilationist approach to the "curriculum of whiteness." The ideology of whiteness permeated everything, from notions of discipline, to blind obedience, docility, and not questioning authority.

And even then, it was not until I read bell hook's *Outlaw Culture: Resisting Representations* (1994), Frances Rains's (1996, Spring) article, "Holding Up a Mirror to White Privilege (1996)," and Peggy McIntosh's piece, "White Privilege and Male Privilege (1992)," that I understood what my partner was talking about. Since then I have examined other works, for example: *Race Matters* by Cornel West (1993); *The Racial Crisis in American Higher Education* by Philip Altbach and Lomotey; "Struggling with Labels that Mark My Ethnic Identity" by D. M. Cruz (1995); and "Power and Knowledge" by Teresa Cordova. These works and others that I have read recently offer compelling insights and have provided the backdrop of the reflection in this chapter. In addition, these works help to articulate what I have failed to voice for many years. These years of suppressed voice could also serve as indicator of my naïveté. While I may be naive about the pervasiveness and oppressive nature of whiteness, I certainly am not unaware of oppression. How could I forget colonial domination, particularly the kind that was inscribed in the textbooks I read in elementary school, the pain of studying a colonial language at the expense of learning other African languages? But realizing that these activities were part of a coherent curriculum of whiteness is not so obvious. Colonialism continues to haunt us today, and its legacy of whiteness is imprinted in our identities. To this day, my African culture continues to be despised and continues to be perceived as exotic (read primitive), a subject vigorously studied by anthropologists in the academy where I teach. Through this colonial legacy I have been complacent to despise my African culture as inferior in order to fit in a "white" institutional landscape or to continue to have access to the privilege that might be accorded to me. At times my race was despised too, while I looked on.

What follows is an account of my realization of the "curriculum of whiteness." Taking time to hold up a mirror to white privilege provides a teachable moment for myself and to the many others like me, riding along the wave of "privilege." At this juncture, this realization is an important one. It is a reflection of how I became aware that I had been riding along without looking up to my rearview mirror. When I did check that mirror, what I saw was a systematic curriculum of whiteness. It might be characterized as (1) a culture of denial, (2) a sense of frustration, (3) a period of uncertainty, (4) a feeling of powerlessness, and (5) a moment of failure. But what most struck me at this time of realization is the extent to which I had been conditioned to "see" and the realization of how oblivious I was to the fact that systems of domination are interlocking and interdependent. Silence and compliance are critical to maintaining them. It is in the course of speaking about them that we learn about how and why they persist. Let me comment on parts of this awareness.

## A CULTURE OF DENIAL

The culture of the United States is fascinated with individualism and with the potential of technology to solve social problems. Individualism is highly valued; students are taught early on in school to aspire to be individuals in their thinking and acting. This "worldview" coincides with the culture of denial about the cultural implications of consumerism and commercialism. It helps to create a myth about the exploitative needs of colonialism, oppression, and domination as long as there is a critical gain to the individual. Domination or oppression is couched in terms of competition to secure appropriate resources, whether it is land, knowledge, or privilege. While force often is applied to impose these unequal relations, ideology attempts to convince people of these unequal relations and to legitimize the superiority of one race over another. And in doing so, ideology attempts to convince people of the validity of these unequal relations by showing the appropriateness of the roles individuals play in those relations. Therefore, people who identify with whiteness and participate in relations that reinforce it and the exploitation that goes with it are accomplices in forms of social injustice. A culture of denial arises among those who refuse to accept this role of accomplice. Equally, denying that exploitation exists in unequal competition is denying fairness and privilege.

This culture of denial is made manifest and expressed in many forms in our society. A few examples will illustrate. References to whiteness abound all around us, in contexts ranging from politics to media advertising. For some critics, the curriculum of whiteness is a piece of liberal mythology. For others, the profile of the curriculum of whiteness is approximately as follows: white, Western, "civilized," male, adult, urban, middle class, heterosexual, and so on. This profile has monopolized and dominated all other curriculums, including the definition of humanity in mainstream Western imagery. The constant denial of the existence of such a curriculum of whiteness relegates oppression or "white" supremacy to a triviality. For example, the question of school integration has been increasingly assaulted through hostile court decisions, the dismantling of affirmative action, continued white resistance, and growing black cultural nationalism. These events are not easily understood by those unfamiliar with the history and the persistent racial tensions in the United States. In other terms, what have these events to do with the curriculum of whiteness? Is a national dialogue on race possible, given the nature of this curriculum of whiteness?

According to Thomas H. Kean, president of Drew University in Madison, New Jersey, and member of the advisory board for President Clinton's Initiative Race and Reconciliation, a national dialogue on race is long overdue. "As we look around at the country we love, we see schools that are more segregated in my state than they were 30 years ago. We see neighborhoods that continue to be made up of simply one ethnic group or one race. We see clubs and we see even churches where we don't have a chance to commingle with people who are not like us" (quoted in *New York Times,* 1997, 28). President Clinton's initiative coincided with a major event in the history of America's racial struggles: the integration of Central High School in Little Rock, Arkansas, 40 years ago. To achieve that, President Dwight D. Eisenhower deployed troops to protect nine black students attending the school, which was all White. Today, the notion of "racist America" seems to be, for many college students, something of the deep past. For others, President Clinton's recent visit to Central High School and the repetition of television images of those dark days is like opening up old wounds and is deemed counterproductive. Neither does any good to build better race relations. However, for the many residents of Little Rock, this event was symbolic. By holding the doors of the school open forty years later for the nine African American students whose attendance at Central High triggered mob lynching, the President of the United States sent a strong message about national reconciliation.

With a new wave of African and African American superstars enthralling white America through its VCRs and movies, the debate continues as to what it means to race relations. There are those who think race is no longer fate but fashion. It's perhaps not difficult to convince a newcomer to America that racism is something out of the past, particularly after watching movies such as *The Color Purple* and *Forrest Gump*. Some news commentators cannot resist quipping after any one of such movies. Quietly they surmise, "God made Eddie Murphy to tackle the funny bone of mass white audiences who are tired of being made feel guilty about a 'racist America,' which 'has not existed for many years now, and is, indeed a piece of liberal mythology'" (Bayles 1989, 618). These remarks echo those of William F. Winter, former democratic governor of Mississippi and a prominent member of President Clinton's Advisory Council who fought for equal opportunity and better relations between the races. He said, "Most white people seem to think we've come further than most black people think we have. The twin goals of achieving racial equity and the elimination of racial prejudice continue to recede before all the advances that we have made. The fault line of race is the paramount factor in keeping us from realizing our full potential as a people" (quoted in *New York Times*, 1997, 28). Perhaps what is not readily examined in such commentary is how to locate the fault line of race and how "whiteness" is implicated. What is frustrating is that whiteness is not static or in any one place.

## A SENSE OF FRUSTRATION

Can we pin down "whiteness"? Why is it so difficult to arrest whiteness? Whiteness is a shifting, strategic category with a persistent if indefinite extreme, "blackness," a norm against which it resonates (Gresson, 1996). According to Aaron D. Gresson, whiteness is not limited to physical characteristics like hair texture, skin hues, nose shape, lip and hip size, and the like. Whiteness is about the position that the category of "White people" happens to occupy in people's minds and in individual psyches. It is a norm against which everything is compared or matched with rewards and privileges commensurate with it. Ultimately, it is about white privilege. And yet the place from which the power of whiteness is exercised is often elusive. When we try to pin it down, the center seems to be somewhere else. Yet we know that the center of power, elusive as it is, exerts real power over the whole social framework of our culture, our identity, and over the ways that we think about its rewards. Andre Lorde calls this center the mythical norm, defined as "white, thin, male, young, heterosexual, Christian and financially secure" (Lorde 1978). As Lorde implies, the combination of these characteristics describes a status with which we are all familiar. It defines the tacit standards from which specific "Others" can then be declared to deviate. While that myth is perpetuated by those whose interests it serves, it also can be internalized by those who are oppressed by it. Thus, whiteness mutates from overt constructions in which open and favorable coverage is given to arguments, positions, and spokespersons who are in the business of elaborating an openly racist argument or advancing a racist policy to those apparently naturalized representations of events and situations relating to race, whether factual or fictional, that have racist premises and propositions inscribed in them as a set of "unquestioned" assumptions.

Authors like Gloria Anzaldua, bell hooks, and Kobena Mercer have stressed in their writings the role of independent cultural traditions in creating a positive self-identity. Gilles Deleuze and Felix Guattari have argued that the invisibility of the dominant group in its own definitions means that the very concept of race has meaning only in terms of a system of oppression and, further that any concept of "pure" race ignores this reality: "there is no race but inferior, minoritarian, there is no dominant race, a race is not defined by its purity but rather by the impurity conferred upon it by a system of domination" (Deleuze and Guattari

1986, 12). Simply put, "whiteness" is a theory of racial superiority to rationalize the right to exploit the "non-White." Thus the curriculum of whiteness pursues the systematic exploitation and dehumanization of one race of people by another. Rhetoric apart, the "race question" is about *whiteness* and its pervasive curriculum of domination and subjugation of culture, knowledge, and power (Deleuze and Guattari 1986).

## A PERIOD OF UNCERTAINTY

Even though "racism" and "white" privilege have been around for a long time, different individuals manage to deal with such situations differently, oftentimes depending on their own positions of power, cultural context, and sense of "identity." For example, working in higher education and being an academician is a position of power and privilege. I work so hard to play by the rules that I also tend to overlook how I am equally implicated in certain ways, particularly in maintaining the systems of domination—for example, my tacit participation as an intellectual and academician in an educational system that tokenizes multiculturalism in classrooms; my enjoyment of ethnic jokes, especially when the ethnic group being taunted is not my own; my silence on those occasions when privilege was accorded to me as a male in the face of ignoring female counterparts; or my condoning the language of complicity in matters of racism, sexism, and classism in the media, textbooks, and in language arts. As explained by bell hooks, we cannot choose to oppose or change imperialism and become negligent regarding other -isms. More specifically, she lays out the dilemma by writing:

> It has always puzzled me that women and men who spend a lifetime working to resist and oppose one form of domination can be systematically supporting another. I have been puzzled by powerful visionary black male leaders who can speak and act passionately in resistance to racial domination and accept and embrace sexist domination of women, by feminist white women who work daily to eradicate sexism but who have major blind spots, when it comes to acknowledging and resisting racism and white supremacist domination of the planet. Critically examining these blind spots, I conclude that many of us are motivated to move against

domination solely when we feel our self-interest directly threatened. (1994, 243-244).

I suppose what I see in my rearview mirror as a metaphorical retrospection is the constant effort of positioning myself relative to "whiteness" rather than confronting it as a form of domination; and such positioning is comparable to what hooks calls the "blind spot" in my critical vision of social change. My return to the United States in the mid-1980s to undertake doctoral work made it possible for me to begin to unravel the many contradictions I had experienced in the 1970s while attending undergraduate studies here. It was an awakening of sorts. Attending undergraduate classes with my American counterparts was challenging, but because I was eager to learn and to excel, much of what I saw as racist or contradictory to what my beliefs did not seem to matter. At the time, I believed that confronting racism would conflict with "doing" school. In addition, higher educational institutions did nothing to increase my peers' limited understanding of racism as a political ideology. Instead, professors systematically denied us the space to question, teaching us to accept racial polarity in the form of white supremacy. The examples are just too numerous to recount here.

## A PERIOD OF POWERLESSNESS

Because of the difficulty of pinpointing "whiteness," a critique may not be as clear-cut as may seem necessary. For instance, what does it mean for educators to educate young, privileged, predominantly white students to divest themselves of white supremacy if such work is not coupled with work that seeks to intervene and change "internalized racism that assaults people of color"? (hooks 1994). What does "whiteness" mean when one group is willing to repudiate the domination in one form while supporting it in another? For example, white men who take sexism seriously but are not concerned with racism or vice-versa or black men who are concerned with ending racism but do not want to challenge sexism? What can school leaders do to arrive at a just, more humane world? These contradictions point to the complexity of the subject matter, and together they paint a bleak picture of the future of race relations. However, Hall (1991) challenges us to courageously surrender participation in whatever sphere of coercive hierarchical domination we enjoy through individual and group privilege.

In this chapter I have discussed the specific role of language as an instrument of power. For example, the ideologies of whiteness are best understood in the context of power relations. Power in contemporary society habitually passes itself off as embodied in the normal as opposed to the superior. This is common to all forms of power, but it works in a peculiarly seductive way with whiteness, because of the way it seems rooted, in commonsense thought, in things other than ethnic difference. Hall (1991) explained that we have to "speak through" the ideologies that are active in our society and that provide us with the means of "making sense" of social relations and our place in them. The transformation of ideologies is thus a collective process and practice, not an individual one. Largely, the processes work *unconsciously,* rather than by conscious intention. They work most effectively when we are not aware that how we formulate and construct a statement about the world is underpinned by ideological premises; when our formulations seem to be simply descriptive statements about how things are (that is, must be) or of what we can "take for granted." Hall seems to think that since race, like gender, appears to be "given" by nature, racism (and for that matter whiteness) is the most profoundly "naturalized" of existing ideologies. For instance, some people point to the Judeo-Christian use of the colors white and black to symbolize good and evil, as carried still in such expressions as "a black mark," "white magic," to "blacken the character" and so on. Curiously enough, as Hall indicates, all these uses of color, and the images, artifacts and use of language that emerge from their interaction, form a continuous, whole landscape in which these images coalesce to form unconscious formulations of simply descriptive statements about how things are. And, therefore, they essentially are taken for granted. It is this everyday portrayal of "how things are" that makes critique desirable.

## A MOMENT OF FAILURE

Besides denial, frustration, and uncertainty, there is a lot more in the blind spots of the rearview mirror. A sense of frustration is perhaps one blind spot that has blurred the vision of many educators like me. What can I do? How can I go about changing oppression and domination in my classrooms: oppressive curricula, ideas, ideologies, and ways of knowing? What framework might I use to examine the curriculum of whiteness in the American school context? The intolerable level of minority failure in school has to do with the fact that the curriculum suppresses minority, particularly African American, cultural heritage: those symbols, arts, music, images, folklore, history, and their contributions to the history of this nation. Black students fail because schools assault their identities and destabilize their sense of self and agency. For the proponents of Western civilization, the curriculum of whiteness and its Western cultural emphasis in schools is colorblind. They argue that black students fail because of the cultural deprivation that exists in their homes and in their communities. According to E. D. Hirsch, Jr. (1987), broad cultural literacy would help disadvantaged black youths enter the mainstream. Literacy in the canon of Western civilization would be the best antidote for failure among the black poor. Therefore, inducting them into the curriculum of whiteness would provide them with the cultural literacy that is missing in their homes and would enable them to excel. However, this assimilationist view excludes the recognition of the African American heritage, or all other nonwhite heritages, particularly when it comes to the role that language plays in the curriculum of whiteness.

In this chapter, I have examined the apparatuses that generate and circulate the ideologies of whiteness in the American classroom. I seek to expose the continued unconscious colonization of the mind that pervades textbooks and schooling. Examples drawn from my own education in the United States and the interplay between concrete examples and explanatory theories illuminate the definition of white privilege. The apparent invisibility of whiteness in the curriculum is yet another indication of the extent to which whiteness masks the definition of its norms—class, gender, heterosexuality, nationality, and so on— while it also masks the notion of whiteness itself as a category to be confronted. In short, whiteness is a pervasive and insidious privilege inscribed in the curriculum from textbooks to table manners, to dress code, decorum, and comportment. It is imperative, therefore, to take note of the parallels of the great struggle over whiteness that are taking place in the American education system instead of denying them. The challenges to the ethnocentric view of the world, marginalization of non-European people, the politics of "Other," and the debate over multiculturalism in the curriculum are only a part of the struggle.

## CONCLUSIONS

In this chapter, I have outlined my reflections of a curriculum of whiteness. As I thought through male privilege as a phenomenon with a life of its own, I realized that since hierarchies in our society are interlocking, most likely the phenomenon of white privilege was similarly denied and protected, but alive and real in its effects. A critique of whiteness brings omissions into the foreground. It exposes blind spots and bottlenecks in even the most radical and ameliorative of approaches to social themes of "exploitation," "domination," "resistance," and "human emancipation." In such critique, we must ask: Who produces educational theory? About whom? And for whom? What social and ideological functions does educational theory serve? And how is it socially deployed with respect to policies and programs that address and "target" nonwhite children or minority youths in classrooms? Feminist scholar Peggy McIntosh (1992, 71) relates white privilege to an invisible weightless knapsack of special provisions, assurances, tools, map guides, code books, passports, visas, clothes, compass, emergency gear, and blank checks. So who is to challenge white privilege systems? Who is to bring about change? How might one acquire this knapsack of tools?

The white students I have encountered in my classroom admit that they had been taught about racism, which puts others, particularly non-Whites, at a disadvantage. Few had ever been taught to see white privilege, which puts them at an advantage. It seems Whites are carefully taught not to recognize white privilege, as males are taught not to recognize male privilege. As echoed by Hall, one of the ways in which ideological struggle takes place and ideologies are transformed is by articulating the elements differently, thereby producing a different meaning: breaking the chain in which they are currently fixed. The problem of non-Whites' invisibility can be understood as a condition of their relative lack of power to represent themselves to themselves and to others as complex human beings, and thereby to contest the bombardment of negative, degrading stereotypes put forward by white supremacist ideologies and perpetuated through the media. Hall has talked about these responses as attempts to change "the relations of representation." Perhaps it is not too much to hope for a future in which we can recognize differences without seizing them as levers in a struggle for power. But all of us must be involved in making this future. Men cannot disassociate themselves from "women's issues," and white people cannot declare themselves indifferent to racial politics. It is too easy for a "sympathetic" self-effacement to become another trick of quiet dominance.

## BIBLIOGRAPHY

Altbach, P. G. and Lomotey, K., eds. (1991). *The Racial Crisis in American Higher Education.* Albany: State University of New York Press.

Andaldua, Gloria. (1987). *Borderlands—La Frontera: The New Mestiza.* San Francisco: Spinsters-Aunt Lute.

Bayles, M. (1989). "The Problem with Post-Racism." In G. Colombo, R. Cullen, and B. Lisle (eds.), *Rereading America. Critical Contexts for Critical Thinking and Writing.* New York: St. Martin's Press.

Caplan, P. J. (1994). *Lifting a Ton of Feathers: A Woman's Guide to Surviving in the Academic World.* Toronto: University of Toronto Press.

Chan, S., and Wang, L. C. (1991). "Racism and the Model Minority: Asian-Americans in Higher Education." In P. G. Altbach and K. Lomotey (eds.), *The Racial Crisis in American Higher Education.* Albany: State University of New York Press.

Córdova, Teresa. (1997, Fall). "Power and Knowledge: Colonialism in the Academy." In *Taboo: The Journal of Culture and Education.* vol. 2, pp. 209-234.

Cruz, D. M. (1995). "Struggling with the Labels That Mark My Ethnic Identity." In R. V. Padilla and R. Chavez (eds.) *The Leaning Ivory Tower: Latino Professors in American Universities.* Albany: State University of New York Press.

Deleuze, G., and Guattari, F. (1986). *Nomadology: The War Machine* (New York: Semiotext[e]; cited in R. Ferguson, Gever, M., Minh-Ha, T., and West, C., *Out There: Marginalization and Contemporary Cultures.* New York: New Museum of Contemporary Art, 1990.

Gresson A., III, (1996, Spring). "Postmodern America and the Multicultural Crisis: Reading Forrest Gump as the Call Back to Whiteness." *Taboo* 1, 11-33.

Hall, Edward T. (1966). *The Hidden Dimensions.* New York: Doubleday.

Hall, S. (1991). "The Whites in their Eyes: Racist Ideologies and the Media." In G. Bridges and R. Brunt (eds.), *Silver Linings: Some Strategies for the Eighties.* London: Lawrence and Wishart.

Hirsch, E. D. Jr. (1987). *Cultural Literacy.* Boston: Houghton.

hooks, b. (1994). *Outlaw Culture: Resisting Representations*. New York: Routledge.

Lorde, A. (1978). *Movement in Back*. Oakland, CA: Diana Press.

McIntosh, P. (1992). "White Privilege and Male Privilege: A Personal Account of Coming to See Correspondences Through the Work of Women's Studies." In M. Andersen and P. H. Collins (eds.), *Race, Class, and Gender: An Anthology*. Belmont, CA: Wadsworth Publishing.

Mercer, Kobena. (ed.). (1988). Black Film/British Cinema, ICA Document 7. London: Institute of Contemporary Arts.

Rains, Frances. (1996). "Holding Up a Mirror to White Privilege: Deconstructing the Maintenance of the Status Quo." In Taboo: The Journal of Cultural Education. vol. 1.

*New York Times,* (1997, Sept. 28 p. 28). From Steven Holmes, "Scholar Takes on His Toughest Study of Race."

West, C. (1993). *Race Matters*. Boston: Beacon Press.

———. (1982). *Prophesy Deliverance! An Afro-American Revolutionary Christianity*. Philadelphia: Westminster Press.

# Culture and Pedagogy

# TEN

# Developing a Media Literacy of Whiteness in Advertising

## Daniel R. Nicholson

## INTRODUCTION

The cultural curriculum of the United States is fraught with advertisements. From T-shirts and bumper stickers, to Internet web pages and corporate renamed stadiums, as well as within the various forms of media that surround us, advertising is an almost inescapable institution; and it is an institution projecting images of what it is to be White in America. The New York City Department of Consumer Affairs conducted a survey of over 11,000 ads in 27 magazines and of 22,000 pictures in 157 catalogs and found that:

> while African-Americans comprise 12% of America and 11% of the readers of magazines, only 3% of all models in magazine ads were black; the pattern is similar with Latinos and Asians. And the few minority figures to appear were overwhelmingly cast in stereotypical roles: athlete, musician, menial worker, object of charity, or child.... [I]f Americans don't see people of color as consumers in the periodicals that surround us, many

whites may continue their comfortable ignorance while minorities will be reminded of their status as second-class citizens. (Green 1991, 1)

Many facets of culture and society can be revealed by addressing an advertisement as a "cultural artifact" (Frith 1995). Information about marketers' intent and intended target market may be discerned; but often these sales messages are intertwined with social messages relating to power and oppression. With the aid of 20/20 hindsight, one can easily see the racism and sexism manifest in (especially) pre - civil rights advertisements. However, if one were to shift her view to more contemporary advertising, the inherent oppression may not be quite so obvious. As Henry Giroux (1994, 23) states, "Cultural workers need a new map for registering and understanding how power works to inscribe desires and identities and create multiple points of antagonism and struggle."

It is my intention to facilitate a "media literacy" (Kellner 1995) that will enable consumers to see their position and subjectivity with regard to whiteness within the greater framework of contemporary capitalism— utilizing advertisements as pedagogical tools toward that end. Aware of their positionality as expressed through advertisements, consumers will be better informed about the consequences and implications of the choices they make through their purchases or nonpurchases.

I endorse a counterhegemonic position that goes beyond John Fiske's (1989) acts of "resistance"—that is, using a product for something unintended by its producers in order to foster a sense of control within one's own life. "Counter-hegemonic movements . . . imply a 'clear theoretic consciousness' which enables people to comprehend fully and act on their discontent" (in Lather 1984, 55). Furthermore:

> Counter-hegemonic work is inherently educational work. The charge is to "work incessantly to raise the intellectual level of an ever growing strata of the populace" (Gramsci 1971, 340). The educational process is not one-dimensional, however. Its central component is its inclusive concern for intellectual, moral, cultural, political, and economic change. The task of counter-hegemonic groups is the development of counter-institutions, ideologies, and cultures that provide an ethical alternative to the dominant hegemony, a lived experience of how the world can be different. Counter-hegemonic forces work to stymie consensus, to present alternative conceptions of reality, to develop the ripeness of subjective conditions that is a

precondition for the struggle toward a more equitable social order. The entry point in terms of individual consciousness is the disjuncture between received versions of reality and lived contradictions (Lather 1984, 55-56).

Media literacy thus would enable a distinction between "resistance" sold in the marketplace and counterhegemonic "resistance" that works toward creating a radicalized democracy. This form of media literacy understands that creating a radicalized democracy requires much more than patronizing corporations that appear to critique the social formation of whiteness, as the Diesel Jeans and Workwear advertising campaign attempts to do.

## THE PHILOSOPHIES
## OF AN ADVERTISING CAMPAIGN

One of the goals of advertisements is to create a favorable image for the company doing the advertising. By expressing popular sentiment within the context of an ad, advertisers hope consumers will attribute that sentiment to an overall philosophy of the company paying for the ad. In the postmodern scheme of things, part of identity formation has come to rely on expression of self through purchases consumed and/or adorned. For instance, Ralph Lauren signifies a sort of casual elegance and Levi's a relaxed, "go-with-the-flow but remain your own person" mentality.

In his book *Disturbing Pleasures* (1994), Henry Giroux analyzes several Benetton ads that depict real-life images of such things as a dying AIDS patient, a terrorist car bombing, a soldier holding skeletal remains, as well as other staged photographs depicting racial integration (3-22). Giroux asserts that "[a]ll of Benetton's ads depend upon a double movement of decontextualization and recontextualization" (17). That is, the images are taken out of their original context, therefore losing a great deal of their original signifying properties, and then recontextualized as part of an advertising campaign. This recontextualization applies a whole new set of signifiers to the photographs, replacing history with whatever significance the now-present Benetton logo carries. Benetton asserts such an act is "raising awareness" of important issues (16), but by decontextualizing, dehistoricizing, and recontextualizing, "the ads sim-

ply register rather than challenge the dominant social relations reproduced in the photographs" (17).

The Diesel Jeans and Workwear campaign, on the other hand, seems
to take Benetton's "issue awareness" motif a step further by making an
effort to create ads that "challenge dominant social relations." Many of
Diesel's ads attempt to represent the positionality of its models, who are
oftentimes people of color, in relation to dominant white patriarchy—
that is, throughout this campaign, the social dominance of whiteness is
continually alluded to and parodied. At this level, the ads work as
pedagogical tools for exposing what may be very difficult for much of
white America to fathom: the privileged nature of their race.

Novelist and literary critic Toni Morrison writes in *Playing in the
Dark* (1992) of the literary canon and its presumed white readership.
She also calls attention to how issues of race are presented in terms of
effects on the recipients of racism and not how racist acts affect and
position the perpetuators. The race of whiteness and its acts are
assumed as a given progression in history, and Others are regarded in
terms of how they measure up to the white yardstick—while whiteness
remains unexamined. The result: "images of blackness can be evil *and*
protective, rebellious *and* forgiving, fearful *and* desirable—all of the
self-contradictory features of the self. Whiteness, alone, is mute,
meaningless, unfathomable, pointless, frozen, veiled, curtained,
dreaded, senseless, and implacable. Or so our writers [of American
literature] seem to say" (Morrison 1992, 59).

The Diesel Jeans and Workwear ads attempt a sort of iconographic
"strategic rhetoric," in the language of authors Nakyama and Krizek
(1995), that deterritorializes the terrain of whiteness and exposes relations of power that have remained invisible (perhaps only to other
Whites) for far too long. That is, the ads make visible the invisible nature
and privilege of whiteness and the power and ideology that accompanies
it. The ads play with the notion of "color evasiveness" (Frankenberg
1993, 14)—the notion that all Americans are given the same opportunities for success because we are all the same under the skin (a.k.a. color
blindness). Lack of success is attributed to personal shortcomings
unrelated to skin color and a society founded on slavery and colonization.
The advertisers at Diesel seem to be aware of the myopic stance behind
color evasiveness and work to expose relations of subjectivity and power
along the axes of race and age, effectively critiquing the *race* of whiteness.

If this is the philosophy Diesel wishes to express, to whom would it appeal? I believe the appeal is intended for those who are discontent with the social, political, economic, and cultural situation the overbearing tyranny of whiteness has caused, those who are interested in the formation of a radicalized democracy, and those who are subject to or are appalled by continuing race oppression. This is a wide market (one hopes) and not exclusive to people of color. It is very clever on the part of Diesel's advertisers; however, like Benetton's, Diesel's ads signify much more than their advertisers intended.

## DIESEL'S TARGET MARKET

One of the reasons I chose to work with the Diesel campaign is because I believe it is directed at a very specific target market—the ethnically diverse (Macalister 1994, Miller 1993, Ritchie 1995) market that has come to be known as Generation X. I will provide support for this argument further later, but first I would like to provide some background.

The term "Generation X" originated as the name of a 1980s glam-rock band founded by Billy Idol, but more recently it has come to signify a segment of the population characterized in Douglas Coupland's 1991 novel *Generation X: Tales for an Accelerated Culture*. The three main characters of this book are pushing 30 years old and are "underemployed, overeducated, intensely private, and unpredictable." This novel invoked an understanding that this so-called Generation X was indeed a nation-wide phenomenon. Coupland introduced terms such as "McJob"[1] and "Poverty Jet Set,"[2] which are quite accurate in describing congruencies among this generation. But for those who reside outside Coupland's frame of reference—those who didn't find some form of support or comfort in his insights and all-too-obvious revelations, or those who never bothered actually to *read* the book—"Generation X" has come to signify a group of young adults too lazy and/or apathetic to go out and get a "real job" and a "real life."

Richard Linklater's 1992 film *Slacker* was another precursor to the onslaught of attention this age group is receiving. In *Slacker* the camera seems to randomly follow recent college graduates, temporary drop-outs, and graduate students (all mostly white males) as they live their lives in Austin, Texas. The common theme running among the numerous and never-to-return-to-the-screen-again "stars" is the desire to espouse their personal conspiracy theories. Those who take the word "slacker" at face value (a person who shirks work or obligation) miss the point. In fact, a book by Sarah Dunn titled *The Official Slacker Handbook* (1995) likens the slackers of the 1990s to the youths of the 1960s in San Francisco, the 1920s youths in Paris, and the 1790s youths in Cambridge. Linklater's slackers are individuals questioning their forthcoming roles in a society they see as sick and in need of major reform. Does one disregard what she deems as important just for the sake of taking some fundamentally contradictory, albeit societally approved job in order to pay back student loans? Or does one continue to cohabit among like-minded cohorts, making ends meet and waiting for something to happen?

Advertisers have been interested in the social phenomenon "Generation X" since the 1992 American Magazine Conference in Bermuda, when advertising executive Karen Ritchie delivered her "Farewell Boomers! Hello Generation X!" speech (Huhn 1993). While delivering a media presentation on the future, Ritchie "realized there was a world beyond Baby Boomers she knew nothing about" (ibid., M14).[3] This realization and subsequent research earned Ritchie "expert" status with regard to marketing to Generation X, and she proceeded to inform her fellow ad executives of their neglect toward a major buying force. Of course ads always have been directed at this age group, but this time something was different—these twentysomethings weren't the standard Baby Boomer's advertisers and marketers had targeted. Perhaps this segment necessitated further research, further understanding.

*Newsweek* (Giles 1994) reports that Xers have a highly sensitive "bullshit alarm." Ritchie attributes this to the fact that during the 1970s, Saturday morning cartoons were so advertising intense they had to be addressed by federal legislation. "The first time you realize the super toy you wanted is really only four inches tall you learn a hard lesson. We created a whole generation that believes advertising is lies and hype" (70).

Generation X's awareness of being a target market is of major concern in the industry. An article in the December 6, 1993, *Marketing News* is titled " Xers know they're a target market, and they hate that." The article states, "marketers have been made to face up to the painful reality that this generation knows what marketers are up to *and* wants nothing to do with them" (Miller 1993, 2). In fact, one of the chapters in Coupland's book, *Generation X,* is titled "I Am Not a Target Market."

It becomes apparent that Generation X is typified by advertising/ marketing trade journals and popular fiction/nonfiction books as "jaded with traditional advertising, tired of the same old stale images, and bored with and cynical toward advertising manipulation" (Kellner 1995, 254). When Generation X became a bona fide target market (see Huhn 1993), discussion circled around how to reach this media-savvy, advertising-critical, anticonsumerist, and ethnically diverse market. Armed with demographic and psychographic information, very intelligent and talented advertisers and marketers attempt to penetrate the wall of resistance this target market is heralded to possess. I intend to expose advertising techniques that attempt to circumvent this resistance and, by so doing, add to the arsenal of opposition against the oppressive nature of consumption-based capitalism.

## SELLING IDENTITY TO GENERATION X

> Advertisements are selling us something else besides consumer goods: in providing us with a structure in which we, and those goods, are interchangeable, they are selling us ourselves.
>
> —J. Williamson (1978)

> Every American counterculture has had it out for advertising since advertising became a cultural power, but this generation of young malcontents is taking it personally
>
> —D. Goldman (1993)

The "ourselves" of the Generation X market is characterized as antiestablishment, antimaterialist, and antiadvertising (Coupland 1990; Rushkoff 1994). How does one go about projecting this identity? Some of the ways, which have become "trademark" Generation X, are traditional-format scoffing "grunge" and "alternative" music, retro (that is, old) clothing, "fashion-neutral" flannel shirts, and, of course, an ongoing aura of irony and an ever-present aura of apathy.[4]

The questions I am more concerned with are: How do advertisers go about selling this identity back to the "ourselves" of Generation X? And how are advertisers attempting to circumvent the animosity Generation X holds for them? One method is "the wink"[5]— or self-referentiality within an advertisement. The advertisers want the reader to recognize that "we know you know what we're trying to do, but because we're letting you know we know, it makes it okay—because we're so hip to your hipness. Get it?"

Douglas Kellner (1995, 254) has posited a second strategy: "forc[ing] the consumer to work at discerning the brand being sold and at deciphering the text to construct meaning." Doing this requires basic deconstruction/semiological skills on the part of the consumer in order to ascertain the intended product or message. These skills are reputed to be among the Generation X repertoire: "Exposed to consumerism and public relations strategies since we could open our eyes, we GenXers see through the clunky attempts to manipulate our opinions and assets, however shrinking. When we watch commercials, we ignore the products and instead deconstruct the marketing techniques. This is what we love about TV. We have learned that 'content' means lies, and that in context lies brilliance" (Rushkoff 1994, 5).

A third strategy is the commodification of "resistance" itself. These ads parody white patriarchy while positioning their products in terms of multicultural and/or antiestablishment scenarios, allowing the consumer to purchase a "resistant" identity along with the product—these ads, in effect, *provide* an "oppositional reading" (Hall 1980). The surface message of these ads may be oppositional and therefore possibly considered counterhegemonic, but the surface image is only a fraction of the story: "Certainly, visual images can be openly resistant to dominant discourses in a culture [such as white patriarchy], serving a counterhegemonic function, however these images are nonetheless produced within a dominant ideology and it is the relation of that dominant ideology to the form of resistance in a visual image that is of particular importance to the scholar of visual communication" (Shields 1990, 25).

It is of particular importance to the discerning consumer, I would argue. "Media culture [advertising] provides resources for identity and new modes of identity in which look, style, and image replaces such things as action and commitment as constitutives of identity of who one is" (Kellner 1995, 259). Moreover, purchasing a resistant identity merely contains activism within the confines of the marketplace. That is, buying into this form of "resistance" "translates the possibility of agency to the privatized act of buying goods rather than engaging in forms of self- and social determination" (Giroux 1994,18).

## A CLOSER LOOK AT SOME DIESEL ADS

The Diesel Jeans and Workwear ad campaign combines these three strategies at various levels in effort to create a positive association between their products and their intended target market, Generation X. I will proceed to analyze a sampling of these ads, individually at first and then as a whole. Through the course of analysis I will describe on an individual basis how and why these ads are intended for Generation X and then will discuss the use of the campaign as a pedagogical tool toward indicating the cultural messages pertaining to whiteness it presents and represents. In order to facilitate this process I will use Dyer's three levels of meaning (Dyer 1982 in Frith 1990) as a template:

> 1. Level 1 is comprised of the primary subject matter. In the case of an advertisement this might be the colors, shapes, people, product, typography, and other basic components of an ad. Generally speaking, this might be thought of as the "face value" of the ad.

> 2. Level 2 relates to the secondary or conventional subject matter, which reflects the wider culture. In relation to an advertisement, this might involve how the models in the ad are relating to each other or to the product.

> 3. Level 3 can be described as "those underlying principles which reveal the basic attitudes of a nation, a period, a class, a religious or philosophic persuasion—unconsciously qualified by one personality and condensed into one work" (G. Dyer 1982). This third level refers to the ideologies of the culture from which the advertisement has been generated (Frith 1990).

Level 1 is concerned with the ad's basic composition. Level 2 exemplifies the advertisers' relationship with Generation X, and Generation X's relationship with whiteness and other facets of society. And level 3 exposes broader cultural implications.

## Levels 1 and 2

A level 1 reading of the first ad reveals a surface textuality with a postmodern aesthetic; it depicts seemingly fragmented scenes melded together to create an eye-catching montage with no discernible significance; in fact, one may have trouble deciphering exactly what is for sale. The four people on the couch and the young boy sitting against the wall seem to be the only ones aware of the camera. This combined with the fact that the four on the couch are cast under an additional source of illumination would indicate they are the models for this product line. The Diesel insignia in the top left corner, the Diesel logo in the bottom left corner, and the little white box that looks something like a government warning on a pack of cigarettes but rather proclaiming a "Guide to Successful Living" are the only instances of printed text and are unable to generate even a fraction of the "meaning" the visual components offer.

The "allegory within the image" (level 2) positions the models in a room created to resonate with Generation X. Artifacts of mass-produced culture adorn the walls: a velvet painting depicting a matador going in for the kill, a landscape painting that looks as if it must have been stolen off the wall of a motor lodge, Elvis tapestries and painting combined with the plastic flowers of a Barbie Doll shrine; also a shag carpet remnant. These are emblematic of a recycling and reusing of culture in order to create a new one: a culture of kitsch. The big-screen TV supports the statement that technical equipment is the one consumer category Generation X is willing to spend their few dollars on (D. Goodman, 1994). It also indicates an immersion within media culture.

The floor mat in the bottom right corner "welcomes" the reader to a playground poised for deconstruction. One of the points of interest is the older white-haired man practicing his golf putting into the open legs of the young woman in her underwear while the older woman, easily perceived as the man's wife, tends to her knitting and pretends not to see. The location of the man's golf bag on the opposite side of his "wife" makes it clear that the knitting woman is indeed an integral part of the putting scene. This scenario alludes to the blatant patriarchy, the high divorce rate, and the take-what-you-can-get and suffer-the-consequences-later attitude Generation X experienced while growing up. Tattooed anarchists, a fascist dictator, children, guns, dogs, a woodchuck, a putting patriarch, and subjected women all comprise the periphery of the room—when one lives in the "Diesel world," *these* are the things that are marginalized. Of course there is a price of admission into the Diesel world; one doesn't just belong, one needs to *purchase* the identity of a Diesel Jeans and Workwear consumer.

What sets this ad, and perhaps the whole campaign, apart is the use of additional characters/stories that practically *beg* for further deconstruction and meaning-making. Diesel advertising director Marchiori Maurizio says their "Successful Living" series depicts two worlds: "One is the Diesel world, and one is the world around Diesel. We let people decide which one is better" (*Newsday* 1993). Throughout the course of the campaign one will notice that "Diesel world" inhabitants are primarily people of color. "[T]he oppressed can see with the greatest clarity not only their own position but also that of the oppressor/privileged, and indeed the shape of social systems as a whole" (Frankenberg 1993, 8). In this particular scenario, three of the five Diesel models are people of color and are defining themselves against the differing and "marginalized" white forms of fascism. Maurizio, or his research assistants, has gone to great lengths to identify forms of oppression experienced by Generation X and then to encode them within the context of the advertisements in a manner that would allow the target market to identify and decode the "two worlds" and their corresponding messages. Morrison (1992) made note about the ways that Whites define themselves against notions of blackness in much of the literary canon; however, in this advertisement we can find a sort of reversal of that situation. The would-be marginalized are now at the center, differentiating themselves from the white margins.

A level 1 reading of the second ad finds the same three instances of Diesel symbols and yet another montage of seeming meaninglessness. The Diesel models (a.k.a. Generation X) are the ones lying prone as result of a four-car pile-up; all but one of the victims are people of color—"the people born between 1965 and 1968 constitute the most ethnically diverse group of young folks in U.S. history" (Levine, 1994), and Diesel's advertisers, for better or worse, have capitalized on this.

A level 2 analysis tells a story familiar to Generation X: Hazards of a world they did not create strike them down as their obese predecessors (mostly White) kick back in lawn chairs, chomp on popcorn, and passively observe. The instruments of destruction, the automobiles, have left *white* skid marks en route to their destiny of creating a gigantic, automotive X.

The visual story is also replete with stereotypes I believe the advertisers included for the benefit of Generation X's renowned deconstruction abilities. The "Japanese tourists" on the left side of the ad take advantage of the "photo opportunity." (The two tourists lying down are merely posing as opposed to being victims.) The African American woman in the back of the blue car is expressing a ravenous sexuality despite her misfortune of being in an accident. And a white "ambulance-chasing lawyer" complete with a brief case that says "1-800-SUE THEM" fills out a form on behalf of one of the unconscious victims.

This ad hopes to win the hearts of Generation X with its use of "the wink." By employing the blatant use of stereotypes, the advertisers are admitting to having relied on these techniques in the past. However, with a new audience so sharp and wise to the ways of advertising, these techniques are reemployed "nostalgically" for the reader's amusement. The overt function of the stereotype may have changed, but it still serves the purpose of conveying a message.

The third ad features two African American models in Diesel garb. They are set within a very metallic environment also occupied by sunbathing senior citizens and tanning beds. The three Diesel icons are the only instances of printed text.

A level 2 story once again positions Generation X against its forebears. The African American Generation X representatives bite their lips and try not to laugh as the white (?) senior citizens worship the Sun God. The winter/summer relationship of the people in this ad is given an ironic twist as the winter folk don summer garb and the summer "kids" are dressed more for winter.

The yellow circle hanging on the wall signifies the ozone hole this older white generation has induced, through which they are able to more directly reap the offerings of the Sun God. The lackey in the soda-jerk outfit waits, with paintbrush and bucket of baby oil (also with the ozone hole emblem) in hand, to slather these fools as they attempt to make their skin look more like that of the people they've spent their whole lives oppressing.

The ridiculously reflective and artificial environment amplifies the unnaturalness of this entire scene. The silver "moon boots" worn by the female Diesel model serves to anchor her and her friend within this otherworldly environment. Whether they like it or not, the "Diesel world" and "the world around Diesel" are not as separate as one would hope. This ad plays on the fear of environmental degradation and the hopelessness of waiting for the winter generation to make amends. This older, and white, generation seems to openly welcome the infractions in the environment it has incurred, even as it ironically utilizes the technology-created "safer" artificial sun of the tanning beds.

The last two ads I have chosen for analysis are departures from the previous formats. Instead of portraying the Diesel and non-Diesel world, they depict clothing line in a context of hyperexaggerated whiteness.

The first of these two ads positions a stereotypical white sitcom nuclear family in a bright shiny modern kitchen, circa 1955. The wife and husband comprise almost the entire right half of the ad. They touch each other with loving affection as they share in the task of making green Jell-O. The grade-school-age girl and boy sit at a white plastic kitchen table while they observe their parents. "The family that prays together, stays together" is written underneath the Diesel insignia. There is also a paragraph at the bottom of the page that reads:

> Do you know that your children (and yourself) are being brainwashed every day? And that your tax dollars are spent on violent, pornographic, anti-Christian TV series, records, movies and advertising? Yes, it's true. And it's all over the place! Let's remove that shameful mask of moral blindness and put an end to all this—once and for all! It's time to start paying some RESPECT to decent old-fashioned family values like shyness, good vibrations and innocent dates. Why not do the right thing, and wait for the ring? The joy and inner feelings you experience in a hard working and morally correct family are unbeatable! Those are the feelings that made this world of ours so great. And those are the feelings that will guide mankind into its future—FIRST CLASS. Isn't that what we all want?

One could easily perceive this ad appearing in a mid-century issue of *Life* magazine.

A level 2 reading of this ad tells the reader this is a parody of traditional white values. Initially, this may not be apparent to all readers. A quick glance at this ad may lead one to think this is another manifestation of what Aaron Gresson (1995) has termed "recovery rhetorics." "Engagements with 'white ethnic' heritage that either romanticize the past or evade race privilege in the present continue to 'deculturalize' and therefore 'normalize' dominant cultural practice" (Frankenberg 1993, 234-235). In this instance, the visual depiction may be a remembrance of "the way things were" and an attempt at reclamation toward "the way things ought to be." Its effect, the recovery of the Great American Dream—or put more precisely, the White Man's Great American Dream, as "whiteness and Americanness seem comprehensible only by reference to the Others excluded" (17).

While this is one possible interpretation, I believe it is the advertiser's intent to utilize the concept of rhetorical reversal, or "persuasion through reversed meanings" (Gresson 1995, 24-25). The ad is *not* intended to valorize the Great American Dream; the allegory within the ad is rather a tongue-in-cheek critique of the unnamed norm of whiteness and alludes to the ridiculousness of holding such ideals as a paramount expression of success in the United States. The ad is engaged in a form of self-referencing by depicting an advertising style and technique of a bygone era and, by doing so, heightening the realization for an advertising-savvy reader that these ads are as ineffectual today as are the morals and traditional white values this ad pretends to purport.

The last ad features an extended black family enjoying a Christmas celebration in an upper-class and incredibly antiseptic living room where the walls, carpet, furniture, lampshades, Christmas tree, and wreath are white. Even the dog and the butler are white. The grandfather is holding up a Diesel T-shirt he apparently just unwrapped and the text, besides the usual three Diesel icons, reads in quotes, "A Diesel T-shirt? Just what I always wanted!" Beneath that, written in smaller text, as if in a whisper, is the statement: "The first signs of chronic depression are often extremely well disguised."

Once again the ad seems to be begging for deconstruction. What "wider culture" is reflected here? The story suggests that this black family has attained "the American Dream" by "assimilating . . . into the [mainstream] of U.S. society" (Frankenberg 1993, 13). But why the stark whiteness of the surroundings? The "black" people in the "white" world create a dissonance not unlike that created by the black actor portraying the working-class identical twin brother of an affluent white man in the film *Suture*. Such attempts call attention to the futility of what Frankenberg terms color evasiveness—the assertion that: "we are all the same under the skin; that, culturally, we are converging; that, materially, we have the same chances in U.S. society; and that—the sting of the tail—any failure to achieve is therefore the fault of people of color themselves" (14). The dissonance created by a black family in a high-income (albeit "white-ified") home illuminates an understanding for the reader that, for some reason or another, "it just doesn't seem natural." Of course the next step is to question *why* it doesn't seem natural, which will bring the potential Diesel consumer full circle to the re-realization that U.S. society is unjust and oppressive to much of its citizenry. This ad, in effect, conducts a parody of color evasiveness. If color evasion was actually possible, this ad would be depicting a perfectly normal-looking scene, which, I believe most would agree, it does not. (The ad would be rendered ineffectual if it did.) The ad appears to display a counterhegemonic element, critiquing a liberal notion of race equality (that is, color evasiveness); however, as the next section will show, there is more to be read into the intentions of Diesel and its advertisers.

The comment "The first signs of chronic depression are often extremely well disguised" suggests that despite the pleasant expressions on the people in the ad (except for the butler), something is amiss. Could it be that although this family has succeeded in assimilating to the unnamed white norm (Frankenberg 1993, 17), they find their lives are still lacking? Or perhaps it's *because* they have succeeded in assimilating that their lives are lacking. In writing "Blacks and the Identity Crisis," Gresson quotes author Orrin Klapp:

> The American Negro is in a parallel predicament as he struggles toward equality, though, in his case, the question is more pertinent because he is moving directly in the very situation where identity problems seem to thrive. No doubt his answer would be, "Give us the Thunderbirds and split-level homes, and we'll worry about the identity problems later." Moreover, it must be admitted that to trade a stigma on identity and menial status for a mere confusion about identity may be a bargain. (Klapp 1969, 5 in Gresson 1995, 31)

Gresson goes on to write, "We now know that these Black aspirations to the mainstream were more than a 'mere confusion about identity'" (31). Perhaps the "chronic depression" this family is inferred to be experiencing is a manifestation of assimilating to upper-class white culture. Perhaps the collective history of this "American Dream" contains too much oppression, thereby creating dissonance for peoples whose own collective histories have been subject to violently zealous white aspirations.

In the postmodern scheme of things, history may be disengaged but never lost. The civil rights movements of the 1960s gave way to "personal-choice rhetoric" (Gresson 1995, 13) of postmodern ideology and thereby curtailed further collective effort toward a "recovery of race." Gresson defines recovery of race as: "(1) recovery of a collectively shared set of ideals by which to conduct civil relations; and (2) recovery of a mutually binding interracial code of morality" (4). The self-interest that falls out of personal-choice rhetoric, as opposed to recovery of race, "encourages a neglect of a historically real collective oppression in the racial, economic, and political spheres" (6). Is the family in the ad able to enjoy the benefits of a white standard of success while others who share the same collective history continue to struggle in order to survive? Is this the cause of "chronic depression"? This ad is a fine pedagogical tool for addressing race issues; however, it is important to develop a media literacy that moves beyond decoding messages purposefully encoded by the advertisers, to one that questions *why* Diesel has chosen this approach and what its implications are.

When perceived as a cultural artifact, this campaign can be an effective pedagogical tool for exposing the invisibility of whiteness as well as other (albeit related) cultural, political, economic, and environmental criticisms concerned citizens hold for American culture and society—as this indeed appears to be the advertisers' intent. They combine the first two strategies, the wink and intended deconstruction, in order to speak to the target market. The wink says, "We know *most* people won't understand these ads, but because of your deconstruction abilities, we know *you* will." The advertisers then go on to encode criticisms that, once decoded, will resonate with socially cognizant members of Generation X.

## Level 3

It's the third level of analysis that reveals the real value of this campaign as a pedagogical tool for inciting counterhegemony. The advertisers have granted their audience an authority of "cultural critic," as they provide ready-made, deconstructable critiques of whiteness. But they only intend the reader to take this cultural analysis up to a certain point. The ideology from the advertisers' own agenda (level 3) is a profit-oriented one—this is a fact that should not escape media literacy.

The truly media literate will recognize that the advertisers of this campaign have appropriated the multicultural nature and resistant, antiestablishment attitudes of Generation X and commodified them for the purpose of selling multicultural and resistant, anti-establishment identities in order to make money for Diesel. They rely on the frustration—or *weltschmerz*—of their target market and offer an outlet through which they can express this discontentment; and by doing so, they attempt to capitalize on/profit from the critical sensibilities of Generation X. Social activism is replaced by fashion and resistance is contained within the marketplace.

This campaign, and others that employ similar tactics, can be further utilized as a pedagogical tool for exposing consumer capitalism's ability to accommodate resistant niche markets while simultaneously maintaining the status quo. These advertisements also can serve to distinguish between, in the language of John Fiske, "resistance" and counter-hegemony. If a person wishes to project an aura of resistance, she may buy into this campaign; however, if she wishes to engage in an action toward facilitating a radicalized, multicultural democracy, she must think and act in terms of counterhegemony. In a marketplace democracy, *money* can be thought of as *votes,* and counterhegemonic acts entail understanding what one is voting for. The media-literate person who understands the distinction between resistance and counterhegemony will realize that the revolution cannot be bought at the mall.

While the Diesel Jeans and Workwear campaign provides wonderful pedagogical tools for ferreting out "hidden" aspects of white privilege, and in that respect is an enjoyable element of our cultural curriculum, it is nevertheless an inextricable component of consumption-based capitalism. This campaign is hegemony in the guise of counterhegemony: It attempts to lure the socially discontent into their product line as a means of showing resistance to white patriarchy, and as any good capitalist— and media-literate individual—knows, "[r]ebelling, properly managed, is not only not a threat to the social order, but it also can be appropriated for the benefit of the status quo" (Kincheloe 1995, 95).

A critical pedagogy that works to expose manifestations of white privilege—particularly when those manifestations are in the guise of liberation or statements of discontent—is a step toward effecting social change. If one becomes media literate and learns to read the messages of oppression found in the advertising, which constitutes a huge portion of the environment of our reality, other forms of oppression, and their equally pervasive nature (in terms of advertising), will come to be recognized. The pervasive nature of advertising initially can symbolize the pervasive nature of oppression; however, as skills for reading the media are expanded into skills for reading culture, forms of oppression become more clearly visible and a symbolic association is no longer required.

When a political-economic critique is included in such an analysis, resources potentially available but currently under the control of corporate conglomerates are realized. A comprehensive and sustainable reallocation of these resources could foster the rich and diverse society that constitutes a true and real democracy. Teaching people to move forward with their daily cultural analysis by reading media texts extensively and critically—rather than by participating in existing forms of ineffectual would-be resistance (that is, buying Diesel jeans)—will open new awareness of undue subjectivity and will serve as a catalyst toward the demand for an egalitarian society.

Developing a media literacy of whiteness involves an understanding of the institutions that perpetuate and normalize the invisibility of whiteness. The critical sensibilities that are recognized as a component of the target market Generation X create a starting block for further development of such an understanding. The institution of advertising has begun to modify its appeals in an attempt to communicate to this "problematic" market more effectively, and by doing this, the advertisements present themselves as rich pedagogical tools. Encouraging students of our cultural curriculum to read beyond the criticisms "overtly" manifest in such advertisements, to develop a media literacy that extracts the *latent* messages found in these ads (level 3), will foster a deeper understanding of what it means to be White—or *not* to be White—in our culture and society as well as deeper understandings of our various positions within consumption-based capitalism.

## NOTES

1. "A low-pay, low-prestige, low-dignity, low-benefit, no-future job in the service sector. Frequently considered a satisfying career choice by people who have never held one" (Coupland 1991, 5).

2. "A group of people given to chronic traveling at the expense of long-term job stability or a permanent residence [or a savings account or a "0" balance credit card]. Tend to have doomed and extremely expensive phone-call relationships with people named Serge or Ilyana. Tend to discuss frequent-flyer programs at parties" (Coupland 1991, 6).

3. Founder of *Spin* magazine, Bob Guccione Jr. has been quoted, "Waking up to the discovery of 46 million people [Generation X] is like all of a sudden noticing France" (Wice 1994, 285).

4. The term "*weltschmerz*" is perhaps more descriptive in this instance: "mental depression or apathy caused by comparison of the actual state of the world with an ideal state."

5. I learned of "the wink" through interviews with some creative minds in advertising.

# BIBLIOGRAPHY

Coupland, D. (1991). *Generation X: Tales for an Accelerated Culture*. New York: St. Martin's Press.

Dunn, S. (1995). *The Official Slacker Handbook,* New York: Warner Books.

Dyer, G. (1990). "What Do Advertisements Mean?" In *Advertising as Communication*. London: Metheun.

Femia, J. (1975). "Hegemony and Consciousness in the Thought of Antonio Gramsci." *Political Studies* 23, no. 1, 29-48.

Fiske, J. (1989) *Reading the Popular*. Boston: Unwin Hyman.

Frankenberg, R. (1993). *The Social Construction of Whiteness*. Minneapolis: University of Minnesota Press.

Frith, K. (1995). "Advertising and Mother Nature." In Valdivia (ed.), *Feminism, Multiculturalism, and the Media: Global Diversities*. Thousand Oaks, CA: Sage.

———. (1990). "Undressing Advertisements." Paper presented at the Association for Education in Journalism and Mass Communication, Minneapolis, MN.

Giles, J. (1994, June 6). "Generalizations X." In *Newsweek*, 62-72.

Giroux, H. (1994). *Disturbing Pleasures: Learning Popular Culture*. New York: Routledge.

Goldman, D. (1993). "The X Factor." In Douglas Rushkoff (ed.), *The GenX Reader*. NewYork: Ballantine Books.

Goodman, P. (Dec. 6, 1993). "Marketing to Age Groups Is All in the Mindset" *Marketing News,* Vol. 27, No. 25, p. 4.

Gramsci, A. (1971). Selections from the Prison Notebooks of Antonio Gramsci. Trans. Q. and G. Smith.New York: International Publishers.

Green, M. (1991). *Invisible People: The Depiction of Minorities in Magazine Ads and Catalogs, A Study*. New York: New York City Department of Consumer Affairs.

Gresson, A. D. III (1995). *The Recovery of Race in America.* Minneapolis: University of Minnesota Press.

Hall, S. (1980). "Encoding/Decoding." In Hall, Hobson, Lowe, and Willis (eds.) *Culture, Media, Language: Working Papers in Cultural Studies, 1972-79.* London: Unwin Hyman.

Huhn, M. (Dec. 6, 1993) "Karen Ritchie." *Adweek,* M14-M16.

Kellner, D. (1995). *Media Studies: Cultural Studies, Identity and Politics between the Modern and the Postmodern.* New York: Routledge.

Kincheloe, J. (1995). *Toil and Trouble: Good Work, Smart Workers, and the Integration of Academic and Vocational Education.* New York: Lang.

Lather, P. (1984). "Critical Theory, Curricular Transformation and Feminist Mainstreaming." *Journal of Education,* 166, no. 49-62.

Levine, J. (July 18, 1994). "Generation X." *Forbes,* Vol. 154, No. 2, pp. 293-294.

Macalister, K. (May 1994). "The X Generation." *HR Magazine.*

Meehan, E. (1991). "'Holy Commodity Fetish, Batman!': The Political Economy of a Commercial Intertext" in R. Pearson and W. Uricchio (eds.) *The Many Lives of Batman: Critical Approaches to a Superhero and His Media.* Newbury Park, CA: Sage, pp. 47-65.

Miller, C. (1993, Dec. 6) "Xers Know They're a Target Market, and They Hate That." *Marketing News,* 2.

Morrison, T. (1992). *Playing in the Dark: Whiteness and the Literary Imagination.* New York: Vintage.

Nakayama, T., and Krizek, R. (1995). "Whiteness: A Strategic Rhetoric." *Quarterly Journal of Speech* 81, 291-309.

Ritchie, K. (1995). *Marketing to Generation X.* New York: Lexington Books.

Rushkoff, D. (1994). *The GenX Reader.* New York: Ballantine Books.

Shields, V. (1990). "Advertising Visual Images: Gendered Ways of Seeing and Looking." *Journal of Communication Inquiry,* 25-39.

Wice, Nathaniel. (1994). "Generalizations X" in Douglas Rushkoff (ed.), *The GenX Reader.* New York: Ballantine, pp. 279-286.

Williamson, J. (1978). "The Currency of Signs." *Decoding Advertisements: Ideology and Meaning in Advertisements.* New York: Marion Boyer Publishers.

# ELEVEN

# Whitewashing "The Strip"

## *The Construction of Whiteness in Las Vegas*

### Barbara G. Brents and Melissa J. Monson

In a racially imperialist nation such as ours, it is the dominant race that reserves for itself the luxury of dismissing racial identity while the oppressed race is made daily aware of their racial identity. It is the dominant race that can make it seem their experience is representative.

—bell hooks (1981)

**M**ost people don't believe it when we tell them we live in Las Vegas. The long-standing image of Las Vegas as "abnormal" has been so entrenched in the American consciousness that it is impossible for people to fathom that normal people live here. Those who style themselves as aficionados of high culture, especially (until very recently) academics, scoffed at the tacky, Sin City, overdone image of Las Vegas. Others have difficulty containing excitement at the chance to indulge in the kitschy, Sin City, extravagant image of Las Vegas. We who live here have a repertoire of responses to these outsiders, ranging from the equally scoffful "I can't go near the Strip, the sexual exploitation makes me sick," to the defensive "off the Strip are normal residential neighborhoods, we even have more churches per capita than anywhere in the world," to the gleeful "from my backyard I can see the New York City skyline, a pyramid, and a castle!"

Regardless of how one ends up analyzing Las Vegas, people seem to start with an analysis of what it is not, and it's not normal. What is most telling in these constructions of "the normal" is the invisibility of race. Listening to ourselves and others defend and define "normalcy" in and around Las Vegas makes it clear to us that there is a whitewashing of the Strip, a decoloring of Las Vegas, that is evidence of racial stratification qualitatively different from (but inseparable from) the surface visibility of gender stratification. In this chapter we will discuss three ways the Strip is whitewashed. The first is in how we, both residents and visitors, construct "normalcy" around and in opposition to the Strip. The second is in the iconography of the vacation resort and the ways that it constructs itself both around and against "normalcy" in order to make visitors feel comfortable. The third is how the iconography constructs woman and how the women of Las Vegas construct themselves in and against this image.

Behind the question of how analysts, visitors, and residents construct "normal life" in Las Vegas, a city fraught with contradiction and bedlam, lies deeper questions of how one constructs identity in a race-, class-, and gender-segregated society. In struggling to forge an identity against the image of Las Vegas, we found ourselves equating certain experiences to the boundaries of "normal." As our project progressed, it became increasingly apparent that the ways in which we initially conceptualized Las Vegas and how we defined "being normal" in this environment were largely contingent upon racial stratification, or more specifically upon our being White. The "normal" was constructed by "Othering" or distancing ourselves from the experiences of those not like us. These "Othering" dichotomies not only reflect material segregation; they also hide and ignore issues of race and ethnicity.

Likewise, as we began to look closely at the iconography of the Strip casinos and resorts, it became clear that while it defined "normalcy" in a different way, it too was predicated on "Othering" people of color. This is especially evident in exotic themes that surround most resort hotels.

Finally, when we began to reflect upon feminism, it became apparent that the construction of sexuality that either enraged or intrigued us was in fact a construction of a white sexuality, and that our response to it was one framed largely in ways that ignored race.

This chapter then is based on our experiences as residents here. Melissa has lived in the area since age 12, with a brief respite to get an undergraduate degree at Oregon State, and now is an employed academic. Barb has lived here nine years, time spent entirely from the perspective of an employed academic.

Our major points follow Ruth Frankenberg (1993) in that race privilege is lived but not seen by Whites. We live in a segregated material environment where the Strip is one of the largest employers of people of color. Discourse of and about Las Vegas mitigates against attention to this racial segregation. In other words, race is hidden in the structure of occupations, in the images of Las Vegas, and in our discourse about it. The iconography constructs normalcy, even as we construct normal identity against it. In so doing, as hooks says, we white people make our experiences representative.

## CONSTRUCTING THE STRIP AS OTHER

While most people link their identity at least in part with their place of residence, we who live in Las Vegas are faced with a unique dilemma. While tourists flock here to enjoy the spectacle and indulge in the oddity, they can go "home." For residents, to embrace as part of our identity the image of Las Vegas is to embrace its hedonistic desires of the flesh, wanton indulgences, moral bankruptcy, greed, corruption, and objectification of women. So an illusion of normalcy, in this context, is often established by defining oneself against these elements. Instead of critically unpacking the cultural iconography of the Las Vegas Strip, its image is flatly rejected.

In listening to Las Vegas residents talk about their connection with the culture of the Strip, we found many people, like ourselves, attempted to downplay its importance, by constructing the Strip as "Other" and defining identity against it. Many of the white academics we spoke with stressed how little they thought about the Strip and how easy it is to become oblivious to the images as one "drives through" the Strip zone. The attempt to distance oneself from the image of the Las Vegas Strip was not limited to white academics; those from the working class and/ or people of color also sought to define their own normalcy by juxtaposing their identity with that of the stereotypical Strip lifestyle. In the words of one African American woman, "I avoid it. Lights and gambling don't do anything for me . . . I don't like the party life." The creation of such dichotomies allows one to maintain a sense of "normalcy" by establishing in-group/out-group boundaries. It is as if to say "We are not like them, we may gaze at the oddity, even enjoy the occasional dip in, but we are not connected with the oddity. We are the good people." This need to dissociate from the Strip culture in order to be "normal" is no more apparent than when expressed by those who earn a living on the Strip. For example, a topless dancer, Barb, that I was talking to after her set, stressed "I am a normal mother and wife when my husband picks me up after work." (Again, "I am not like them.")

Women striving to be "normal women" are faced with an even more pressing need to dissociate their self-identity from the Strip. The sex industry is a major contributor to the culture of the Las Vegas Strip. Images of strippers and exotic dancers; scantily clad cocktail waitresses on giant billboards, and taxi cabs carrying pictured advertisements for the Topless Girls of Glitter Gulch cross our paths daily. The zone around the Strip is infused with images of women readily available for objectification. The saturation is so complete that many Las Vegans, both men and women, claim not to even notice the images any longer. However, the normalization or the everyday nature of sexualized, objectified, airbrushed images does not make us immune to them. Las Vegas iconography has constructed "woman" so completely that to be a woman in this town dictates that one either embraces or rejects these images in constructing one's own self as a woman.

But what is it specifically that we are rejecting or embracing about these images as we attempt to construct our identity as "normal" women? Often outright defensive rejection of the Las Vegas Strip entails ignoring critical issues of race and class inequality by rendering them invisible. The following illustrates one such instance in which the work of women on the Las Vegas Strip was trivialized and "Othered" by a group of women attempting to define their own sense of self. The warning of bell hooks against the normalization of the experiences of the dominant race seems particularly prophetic.

"I'll never forget a meeting I attended a few years ago," Barb recalled.

> Amie Williams, an award-winning documentary filmmaker was trying to raise money to shoot a documentary about women in Las Vegas. She had

called a meeting of about 15 "women" in Las Vegas, those with an interest in women's issues, those whom she thought might help financially with the project or help her get a handle on what being a woman was all about in this town. Many of the women were professional women. You know, the kind with clothes I could never figure out how to wear, lawyers, executives, and spouses of such types.

Amie started out explaining the film's concept. Las Vegas employs more women than any city in the country. Women's work contributes to the myth and spectacle that is Las Vegas, but she hoped to examine how women in Vegas find their voices against this domination of male aesthetic and imagery. She then showed a 15-minute set of clips to give people a sense of things. "Stripped and Teased: Voices of Vegas Women" showed strippers, it showed showgirls, it showed housekeepers marching downtown in a union rally. It interviewed a successful Realtor who originally came to Las Vegas to be a stripper. I was impressed with the attempt to frame the Strip in some more complex fashion than the center of debauchery, and especially its attempt to place the very women objectified by the Strip as subjects.

Well, not everyone agreed. "What about the women who don't work on the Strip?" "Good women have worked hard to do important things in this town in spite of the image of the Strip." Others jumped in: "You are contributing to the exploitation of these women and all of us when you start from these typical Las Vegas stereotypes." Some of us pointed out that the Strip provided important high-paying jobs for women that couldn't be ignored. But others began to cast these high-paying jobs as "easy money." Then some women began to discuss the Strip as a place where our youth could be led astray. Decent kids could make so much money parking cars that they might be deterred from going to college or even finishing high school.

Something bothered me about this turn in the conversation, but I couldn't quite figure it out. I felt the defensiveness that everyone who lives here faces. But this was different. My on-the-spot analysis was that this distancing was based on class bias and moral judgments against women working on the Strip as dancers and waitresses.

Then, an African American woman who I hadn't seen at these "women's events" before began to speak. She told of bringing her young children to town as a single mother and getting one of her first jobs as a maid at one of the casinos. Without this job she would have been unable to support her family. Then it became clear who she was: Hattie Canty, president of the Culinary Union, one of the largest and fastest-growing service workers' unions in the country. She said her constituency, dealers, housekeepers, cocktail waitresses, food service workers, included single mothers who had an opportunity they otherwise wouldn't have had. And to speak of the Strip's high-paying jobs as "easy money," as if only middle-class high school kids benefited, was a luxury only these white women could afford.

I hadn't thought of it that way before. Obviously, when I and the rest of the white women in the room thought of women working on the Strip, we thought of topless dancers and showgirls and cocktail waitresses in skimpy outfits. These sexualized females were the "women" of the Strip. And when we thought of jobs on the Strip, none of us thought of these jobs as the best possible jobs people of a certain class, other than our own, could hold.

Hattie Canty pointed out how race and class privileges invisibly frame much of the discourse "Othering" the Las Vegas Strip. We live in a segregated material environment where the majority of jobs for people of color are segregated from the majority of jobs for white people. But more than that, we live in a society where the life experiences of the dominant group are made to seem representative of all. This discursive environment in which white women construct "normalcy" mitigates against our conscious attention to racism, by hindering us from seeing beyond the monolithic characteristics ascribed to the Strip and questioning the very notion of "normal." Specifically we fail to recognize which jobs are available off the Strip and for whom, and which jobs are available on the Strip and for whom.

The gaming industry is among the largest employers in Las Vegas. Half of all workers work in the service sector. There are currently 90,000 hotel rooms in Las Vegas, and more than 29 million visitors come each year. It is not incidental that gaming is also the largest employer of ethnic and racial minorities. The Culinary Union, which organizes approximately 85 to 90 percent of nonmanagement jobs in casinos, reported that in July 1996 its membership consisted of 31.3 percent white, 29.7 percent Hispanic, 14.4 percent black, 11.1 percent Asian, and 16.6 percent unknown. Many working-class as well as middle-class women, women of color as well as white women, cited the growing number of available jobs as the major reason for moving to Las Vegas. Additionally they indicated low cost of living, cheap food, and affordable entertainment (in some of the low-end casinos) as a factor in moving here.

In not recognizing the ethnic makeup of those whose livelihood depends on the Strip, the issue becomes whitewashed. For professional middle-class educated white women, the Strip as "Other" is the Strip of easy money as opposed to "not the Strip," where hardworking white people who can get jobs using their intelligence should go. The Strip is exploitation of women as opposed to "not the Strip," where self-respecting white women who can get jobs using their minds and not their bodies should go. In this context, normalcy is framed as a white, middle-class concern much in the same manner as oppositions of body vs. mind through attention to the exploitation of women's bodies are framed, and as oppositions of "hard-earned" vs. "easy" money, greed, and excess are framed. While white women easily recognize the construction of women in these discursive regimes, we often remain blind to the construction of middle-class whiteness in these images.

That these constructions embody whiteness was made clear to us when almost all of the women of color whom we spoke to responded to the Strip, not in terms of its portrayal of women but in terms of its potential for jobs. White women academics framed responses to the Strip first in terms of its portrayal of women. So at the same time as residents and tourists alike construct an image of normalcy in opposition to Las Vegas's image, the city continues to survive and grow because of it. It is undeniable that the Strip provides tens of thousands of people with jobs, a large percentage of whom are ethnic minorities. Further, when we "Other" the Strip altogether, important questions of occupational segregation, wages, and work conditions, and underlying issues of race and class are hidden. In constructing this image of a "normal" person in opposition to the Strip, we are in effect denying the significance of working-class and ethnic minorities in developing the character of the city.

## THE LAS VEGAS VACATION EXPERIENCE—
## TAKING THE "POST" OUT OF COLONIALISM

The answer to this dilemma is not the uncritical acceptance of the Las Vegas Strip. The Strip's cultural icons have been whitewashed. As pointed out earlier, a large percentage of workers on the Strip are people of color, but if one were to judge the ethnic makeup by images alone, Las Vegas appears to be dominated by white faces. From billboards, to advertisements, to flyers, the image portrayed is one of white America enjoying the excitement of a Las Vegas vacation. The invisibility of people of color on the Strip is nowhere more conspicuous than it is within the context of the exotic thematic nature of most Las Vegas casinos. These resorts strive to re-create the atmosphere of faraway exotic paradises, while maintaining the illusion of whiteness by concealing reminders of race and class exploitation. This task is largely accomplished by making the service workers themselves so unobtrusive as to be invisible.

The Las Vegas vacation experience is an attempt by resort businesses to create an environment where the visitor feels comfortable gambling. The stage is set with lots of food, drinks, scantily clad women, dark windows, and no clocks, all of which encourage indulging in bodily and libidinal pleasures that "normal" civilization back home would deny. A lot of side businesses, including nude dancing clubs and the pornography industry, also thrive in this climate. To help encourage this libidinal subculture, most of the Las Vegas resorts are constructed around images of exotic storybook places where your senses can be tantalized, you can indulge, be waited on, and enjoy wild spending sprees guilt-free. The experience is predicated on a dichotomy between the familiar and the unfamiliar, on the civilized and the uncivilized, on Othering (us versus them). That "uncivilized," unfamiliar image is the nonwhite Third World. The Las Vegas Strip is lined with all the favorite Third World getaways of the rich and famous, where the spoils of colonialism go to the victor unrepentantly. It is a world where the tourist can enjoy all the exotica of traveling to a Third World tropical island paradise, or the exotic reaches of South America or Saharan Africa, and still be able to drink the water and be surrounded by familiar middle American people (read: white culture). In fact, one giant billboard beckons visitors to "Feast, Plunder, and Valet Park." Very few casinos and hotels don't draw on this Third World theme. From the Middle East, Asia, and Africa—the Aladdin, Algiers, the Luxor, Sahara, the Dunes, the Sands, the Desert Inn, the Mirage, El Morocco, Shalimar, Gold Coast, the Barbary Coast, the Tropicana, Imperial Palace. From Latin America—Fiesta, Hacienda, El Cid, El Cortez, Rio, El Rancho, St. Tropez, San Remo.

Beyond just being exotic, these resort themes allow us to enjoy the fruits of colonialism without the guilt of imperialism. The images beckon the tourist to revel in the "feast and plunder" side of the hedonistic desires of the flesh. It is the indulgence that is based on the exploitation of the nonwhite world. Relatively few of the hotel/casino/resorts embody Western European themes without the theme of colonizing the Third World; exceptions include the Riviera and Caesar's Palace (although Caesar did his share of conquering), and some newer resorts, such as the Monte Carlo, Riviera, Excalibur, and New York-New York.

The other predominant motif on the Las Vegas Strip is that of the Wild West—Arizona Charlie's, Apache Motel, Boomtown, Buffalo Bill's, Binion's Horseshoe, Chaparral, El Dorado, Eureka, Frontier, Gold Rush, Gold Strike, Gold River, Golden Nugget, Longhorn, Sassy Sally's, Santa Fe, Silver City, Silver Nugget, Westward Ho, Whiskey Pete's, Railroad Pass. Such a theme also evokes freewheeling, lawless days when the men gambled and the only women were prostitutes. Hedonistic desires again are indulged. However, unspoken in these images, and at their very root, is the United States' own internal colonialism, the taking of the "wild" West through a succession of manifest destiny, massacre, and "Othering" Native and Mexican Americans.

A quick walk through any of these casinos reveals that what remains familiar about this particular exotic is all the Middle American people you see working. The girl next door is your cocktail waitress. Your neighbor's mom will get your iced tea in the buffet. Your friendly neighborhood mailman or grocer is your valet. This image of Middle America is promoted to the extent that many of the tip workers wear name tags with their hometown listed, to help identify with the tourists. The vast majority of these folks are White. The point here is that the hook that makes Las Vegas both exotic and palatable, the elements that are comfortable, familiar, and civilized, are images of white middle-class culture.

Melissa recalls: "Two years ago, when I was in Chicago, I was struck by the ethnic split in the service industry. While Las Vegas is inflicted with this same racial segregation, somehow it seemed more evident in Chicago." According to the Las Vegas Convention and Visitor's Bureau, in 1995, 79 percent of visitors to Las Vegas were White, 7 percent were Black, 7 percent were Asian/Asian American, and 6 percent were Hispanic/Latino. The images of colonization become all the more stark in contrast to figures that show only 31.3 percent of people serving these tourists are White. Perhaps capitalism is the answer—in Las Vegas everybody's money is the same color, green. However, based on conversations with people of color and upon my own observations, this also does not appear to be the case. While money is certainly important, the color of money does not erase the color of one's skin . . . treatment is qualitatively different.

What strikes me most about service workers in Las Vegas casinos is their virtual invisibility. In an attempt to create fantasy worlds, worlds where there is no dirt (in the casinos at least), no unfulfilled need, no human misery, the casino industry must conceal it. Litter is unobtrusively removed, drinks magically appear, change is only as far away as the nearest cashier, or it will come to you if you prefer. Service workers move through the casino undetected. Someone, a man or more likely a woman of color, stealthily sweeps up discarded nickel wrappers, makes sure your room is clean by the time you return, fills your water glass or quickly removes your plate. The vast majority of people of color work in the invisible occupations, the non-tip work, maids, kitchen workers, table bussers, gardeners, and so on, while white employees tend to be the most visible, waitresses, dealers, pit bosses, and the like. The structure of casino work promotes the image of a white Middle America. The maintenance of this image hides the guilt-inducing trappings of the Third World, poverty and exploitation, making the Vegas service worker the quintessential invisible minority.

The invisibility of ethnic minorities on the Strip contributes to the whitewashing of Las Vegas iconography and subsequently to the dismissal of significant issues surrounding racial and class inequality. Even organizations attuned to exploring and eradicating segregation have played to the tendency of normalizing the white experience while ignoring the experiences of others.

## WHITEWASHING SEXISM

And I'll thank you Mrs. White Man for worrying about
Barbie's breast and waist measurements without ever letting
your pretty little white head consider the fact that if feminism
is about Barbie-looking you, it still doesn't get around to me.
—Four Women with a Mac (1994)

As we discussed earlier, Las Vegas is almost synonymous with a particular construction of "woman." From the low-cut tops and high-cut bottoms on the cocktail waitresses' uniforms, to the sometimes-topless showgirls, to the strip clubs, to the prostitution, and to the billboards advertising all this, the dominant image is that of woman as object for the male gaze. The billboard fantasy image of the "perfect" body is enforced upon women working in various sexualized jobs. The average age of dancers on the Las Vegas Strip has been estimated at less than 25. Many casinos do not provide cocktail waitresses with uniforms larger than size 14. And some of the more upscale topless dancing clubs even furnish their dancers with low-interest loans for breast reconstruction or augmentation.

When white feminists interpret the Strip, we often center on what stands out most to us: woman as sexual object. Almost all of the white academic women we spoke to responded to the Strip in terms of the sexual portrayal of women. One student characterized Las Vegas as "the city of sin, where women are more oppressed and exploited than perhaps anywhere else in the world." Another student said, "The women represented in this town by the casino industry are ones without any known important qualities besides a good body and a pretty face." Another said, we are "inundated with examples of the inequalities in gender identity, female objectification, and distortions of female representation." Only one of these white women noted the exploitation of nonsexualized women—those in the invisible service sector; none recognized that the images of which they spoke were largely of white women.

On the Las Vegas Strip, as elsewhere in the country, the "ideal" woman is, among other things, fair skinned with blond hair and blue eyes. In the Las Vegas Yellow Pages, there are 81 pages of "Entertainers"; 397 photos of the entertainers one can purchase while spending time in Las Vegas are depicted. Of these photos, 3 percent (13) are men, 93 percent (over 300) are women, 2 percent (8) are Black, 7 percent (27) are Asian, roughly 1.5 percent (6) are Hispanic, and 90 percent are White. Two-thirds are blonde. And lest there be any doubt that the characteristics of the ideal sexy Las Vegas glamour girl include skin color, of the 41 nonwhite images of women, one-third are clearly marked as not white. Half of the Asian women are clearly labeled "China Dolls," "Lovely Orientals," "Oriental Girls Know Secret Ways of Pure Pleasure." And one of the black women is marked in an ad called "Salt and Pepper."

Women of color are clearly being objectified in different ways than white women are. Racial stereotypes are added to sexual stereotypes to produce a qualitatively distinct form of sexual objectification. In both the absence of women of color and in the differential labeling of them, they are presented as less than "normal." When this disparity is not recognized by white feminist theorists and activists, it hinders the building of alliances. The goal here, of course, is not to equalize exploitation by balancing sexist images along race lines. It does, however, beg some important issues to be addressed. Why is it that the images of the Las Vegas Strip are primarily White? How does this affect the development self-concept for women of color as well as for white women? What does the whitewashing of sexist images mean in terms of feminism? More specifically, what does it mean when white feminists concern themselves with these images without recognizing the racial stratification inherent within them?

Barb says:

I remember when I first moved to Las Vegas, I became involved with a campaign to pass a statewide law protecting women's right to an abortion. The initiative passed. I remember I was impressed with the main organization, at how savvy these women were, how proper, how politically astute, how politically connected, they were organized, they had money, they had packets of talking points, they had lots of volunteers. But once again I felt inferior because I didn't know how to dress like they did.

Up until very recently, I thought the movement was so successful because people really cared about the abortion issue. Gender can be an organizing factor, I thought happily to myself. But the fact that I felt in a different league than most of the women I was meeting has since made me realize how upper middle class and White the organization was. Even though the abortion issue is a race and class issue, I am afraid that the success of this organization was because race and class were invisible. In a Western state priding itself on Western individualism and an antigovernment sentiment, the issue of keeping government off our bodies was the issue that mobilized most of the women I was meeting. I'm not saying that all successful movements in Las Vegas are or must be White. I am just utterly amazed at how blind to the raced and classed nature of the organization I was.

In the pieces of the Las Vegas feminist community that we are familiar with, there are woefully few women of color involved as activists.

Slowly, white feminists are recognizing that hierarchies of race and class as well as gender define the diverse conditions of women and that continuing to construct "woman" as a universal is to construct a white image. But until we recognize fully that the ways in which we, as white women, construct the category "woman" are part of our construction of whiteness, it will be very hard to make race visible.

## CONCLUSIONS

Whitewashing the Strip has serious material consequences. The racial character of the town is ignored. The contributions of people of color are ignored, as are the problems associated with racial segregation.

In many ways, Las Vegas is a relative success story for a service sector economy. Those lucky enough to hold unionized jobs have some of the highest-paying service sector jobs in the country. They have contributed to one of the strongest and fastest-growing local unions in the country during a time when unions are losing ground. Thanks to Culinary Union contracts, the average pay for a union maid is $10 an hour, in addition to medical benefits and pensions. This is enough to allow more service workers than average across the country to own homes in certain areas of the city. Currently, there are nearly 90,000 hotel rooms in Las Vegas, and the influx of Hispanic and Latino/Latina workers is making it economically possible to build the four megaresorts currently under construction for more than $1 billion each.

However, people of color are still confined to the lowest-paid, least-secure jobs in Las Vegas. Four to six thousand people have moved to town each month for the past ten years with the promise of jobs in all these new casino projects. Yet new casinos routinely overhire, and after three months they typically lay off hundreds of workers. About one-third of Nevada workers earn wages below the poverty line, and disproportionately these are people of color.

Likewise, blanket understandings of racial "minorities" often minimize differences and dynamics between them. African Americans are a shrinking percentage of culinary members, getting fewer and fewer of the well-paid union jobs. Up until 1992, shortly after the Las Vegas riots in the aftermath of the Rodney King decision, there were no banks and no large grocery stores in West Las Vegas, where the highest concentration of low-income African Americans is. Language issues are increasingly at the forefront of politics, and a large percentage of housekeeping staffs speak only Spanish. A recent immigration sweep of a Hispanic Las Vegas neighborhood took many legal immigrants to the police department, mainly because they did not speak English.

Las Vegas, like most service economy cities, is facing serious problems in affordable housing and homelessness, with minorities again being disproportionately represented. In 1990, 22,600 people were homeless in Clark County, not including hotels and motels filled with families recently evicted or unable to afford deposits. Sixty-eight percent of workers in Las Vegas do not make enough to qualify for the median-priced home. Growing ranks of working poor, particularly minority female-headed households, have trouble finding affordable rental housing. And all this is coupled with Nevada paying among the lowest welfare payments in the country.

Constructions of normalcy and the "Othering" that comes with it portray white middle-class images as representative of everyone and hides these sorts of issues from the view of white culture.

Increasingly, the gaze of cultural analysts is turning to Las Vegas as the old line between high culture and pop culture melts into analyses of postmodern culture. Las Vegas is the postmodern, thank you very much, finally something we can be proud of. The ignoring and disdain of pop culture is what lies behind the academic Othering of Las Vegas, and this new gaze is sorely needed to understand that which capitalism-run-amok has wrought. As a flyer for an upcoming College of Architecture Symposium on Las Vegas advertises, "Las Vegas is, and has been, in the forefront of the evolution of new urban environments and perhaps best personifies the material construct of a postmodern city." But as the Othering of Las Vegas gives way to an embrace, we must take care that we don't just embrace the whiteness and render racial stratification invisible once again.

## BIBLIOGRAPHY

Four Women with a Mac. (1994). "Bitter with a Touch of Kahlua." In Elena Featherstone (ed.), *Skin Deep: Women Writing on Color, Culture and Identity*. Freedom, CA: Crossing Press.

Frankenberg, Ruth. (1993). *White Women, Race Matters: The Social Construction of Whiteness*. Minneapolis: University of Minnesota Press.

hooks, bell. (1981). *Ain't I a Woman?: Black Women and Feminism*. Boston: South End Press.

# TWELVE

# Okie Narratives

## *Agency and Whiteness*

**Clinton B. Allison**

## INTRODUCTION

This chapter is about Okies, a much-maligned group of rural white people from the upper South and the Southwest who, suffering from drought and depression, fled to California on Route 66, the road of flight, in the 1930s. Perhaps no white group has been so despised and marginalized in America, certainly none with roots so deep in American soil. Their ancestors were mainly Border Scots and Scotch Irish, and they had been in this country since before the American Revolution; yet, in the 1930s and 1940s, for privileged white Americans they were an Other.

It was not simply a matter of social class; they were not just the "poor white trash" scorned historically by African Americans and white southerners alike. Ruth Frankenberg (1993, 198) tells us that there are two kinds of Whites: "those who are truly or only white, and those who are white but also something more—or is it something less?" Mexican Americans, as an example, are something more, or less. And Okies (who like most disparaged people were named by the dominant cultural group) represented something more than class and something less than ethnicity.

What follows are narratives of white experiences. The story of three Okie families who traveled Highway 66, "the mother road," to California:

Steinbeck's fictional Joads; the Tathams, subjects of a recent major book on Okies; and my own family, the Allisons. I conclude by analyzing the Okies' rise in status and their political and ideological migration from New Deal Democrats to New Right Republicans.

## THE JOADS

Americans' images of the Great Depression come largely from three sources: Dorothea Lange's widely reprinted documentary photographs of gaunt women and their barefoot children, John Steinbeck's novel *The Grapes of Wrath,* and the Henry Fonda movie based on it, a black-and-white film that seems more and more like a documentary as the decades pass. Steinbeck gives us a morality play. Desperately poor Okies are victimized by distant, faceless monsters created by corporate America. The Okies (ignorant, incredibly naive, and perhaps even a tad stupid) are devoured by bankers and factory farmers. These monsters "don't breathe air, don't eat side-meat. They breathe profits; they eat the interest on money. If they don't get it, they die the way you die without air, without side-meat. It is a sad thing, but it is so. It is just so" (Steinbeck 1939/1976, 41).

Already living in poverty, the Joad family is "tractored out" of eastern Oklahoma when corporate banks seize small subsistence farms and turn them over to farming conglomerates that bulldoze houses and barns to destroy any resistance by demoralized farmers. The diesel tractors were "snub-nosed monsters, raising the dust and sticking their snouts into it. . . . The man sitting in the iron seat did not look like a man; gloved, goggled, rubber dust mask over nose and mouth, he was part of the monster, a robot in the seat" (45).

Seduced by widely distributed circulars promising work at good wages, the Joads, like tens of thousands of actual families, headed for California in a worn-out vehicle along Highway 66. Grampa and Gramma die along the way. The Joads were lied to about the promised land. In a despicable but successful strategy to keep wages low, the labor contractors' circulars had brought to the fields many times the number of workers that were needed. Despite crop-picking by the whole family including the kids and the oh-so-pregnant Rose of Sharon, not enough work could be found to keep the Joad family's bellies full. They faced starvation in California.

They also suffered the humiliation of being set aside as an inferior species of humans, Okies. Ma first heard the word in a conflict with a deputy sheriff, a goon on the payroll of the growers: "[W]e don't want you goddamn Okies settlin' down.' . . . She looked puzzled. 'Okies?' she said softly. 'Okies'" (275). In Steinbeck's account, the privileged were afraid of the Okies whom they had enticed to California. They needed to dehumanize the migrants in order to protect themselves. For the Chamber of Commerce types, Okies became "white niggers." "These goddamned Okies are dirty and ignorant. They're degenerate, sexual maniacs. These goddamned Okies are thieves. They'll steal anything. They've got no sense of property rights. . . . We can't have them in the schools. They're strangers. How'd you like to have your sister go out with one of 'em?" (363). Sometimes Steinbeck makes the nigger metaphor explicit: "Why, Jesus, they're as dangerous as niggers in the South! If they ever get together there ain't nothin' that'll stop them" (304). And it wasn't just the owning class and their hired goons that used the epitaph. "Them goddamn Okies got no sense and no feeling," a filling station worker tells his helper: "They ain't human. A human being wouldn't live like they do. A human being couldn't stand it to be so dirty and miserable. They ain't a hell of a lot better than gorillas'" (284). Children didn't go to school, not only because their labor was needed in the fields, but because of their treatment by other children with shoes and socks "an' nice pants, an' them a-yellin' 'Okie'" (435). (The debased place of African Americans is not questioned in *The Grapes of Wrath*.)

The Okies were also victims of the Holiness churches they brought with them, according to Steinbeck. A particularly mean-spirited, gossiping Pentecostal troublemaker spoke in tongues: "Her eyes rolled up, her shoulders and arms flopped loosely at her side, and a string of thick ropy saliva ran from the corner of her mouth. She howled again and again, long deep animal howls. Men and women ran up from the other tents, and they stood near—frightened and quiet" (412). The "holy roller" preachers, watching for sin in innocent fun and condemning the Okies' acceptance of modern ways, were major villains. In one sensible camp, the inhabitants refused to let preachers take up a collection, and none were heard from again. The most decent and enlightened character in *Grapes* was Casy, a holiness preacher who had "lost" his religion, found revolutionary politics, and, as a result, could be a helpful minister to his fellow Okies.

Besides Casy, Steinbeck's strong characters were women. Okies came from a largely patriarchal southern society; but in the dislocations of the new world, women found it easier than men to change and adjust. Ma took control on the way to California because she was the strongest one: "The eyes of the whole family shifted back to Ma. She was the power. She had taken control" (218). Later the family viewed Ma with "a little terror" because of her strength (294). Pa, surprising even himself, was too dispirited or too overwhelmed by changes to effectively resist: "Funny! Woman takin' over the fambly. Woman sayin' we'll do this here, an' we'll go there. An' I don' even care" (541).

*The Grapes of Wrath* is a powerful anticapitalist sermon. "When I was a kid my ol' man give me a haltered heifer an' says take her down an' get her serviced," a character says. "I done it, an' ever time since then when I hear a business man talkin' about service, I wonder who's getting screwed" (155). Instead of growers spending money on workers' wages, it went for goons and guns to keep the workers in bondage. And the Okies' anger grew as they became hungrier. A young Okie is talking to Mr. Hines, a large landowner: "'Mr. Hines, I ain't been here long. What is these goddamn reds?' 'Well, sir,' Hines says, 'A red is any son-of-a-bitch that wants thirty cents an hour when we're payin' twenty-five!' Well, this young fella he thinks about her, an' he scratches his head, an' he says, 'Well, Jesus, Mr. Hines. I ain't a son-of-a-bitch, but if that's what a red is—why . . . we're all reds'" (383). Steinbeck looked to revolution as a result of anger generated by social and economic injustice. Marx, Lenin, and other revolutionaries "were results, not causes," Steinbeck warns (194). "In the souls of the people the grapes of wrath are filling and growing heavy, growing heavy in the vintage" (448).

## THE TATHAMS

My Okie experience was, for the most part, forgotten, or sublimated, until I read Dan Morgan's *Rising in the West: The True Story of an "Okie" Family from the Great Depression Through the Reagan Years* (1992). When I read a review of Morgan's book in *The New York Times Book Review*, I thought it looked interesting but forgot about it until I found it, deeply discounted, at Books-A-Million. It is a first-rate study and deserved more readers than its fate on the sale table suggests. Morgan, a reporter for the

*Washington Post,* based the study largely on extensive interviews with members of the extended Tatham family. Part of my interest in the book resulted from similarities between the Tathams and my family. Oca, the central character, is the same age as my father, and they resemble each other in many ways. Bill, a multimillionaire entrepreneur and the most prominent of Oca's sons in the book, is a year older than I. We resemble each other hardly at all. They left for California on Route 66 in 1934; we made the trek two years later.

Like the fictional Joads, the Tathams began their odyssey from Sallisaw in eastern Oklahoma. Although they were poor and the dust storms of the "dirty thirties" were devastating, they were not dusted out or tractored out; but, according to Morgan (xv), they "simply drifted out." Morgan pictures them more as pioneers than as victims of corporate greed. In a somewhat Frederick Jackson Turnerian interpretation, he describes them as pioneers, descendants of the Scotch Irish who settled the backwoods and mountain South, and who had been moving every generation or two since. When times become hard, a previous generation of poor southerners had GTT—gone to Texas—as my Tennessee and Mississippi great-grandparents did. They were marginalized generation after generation as hillbillies, rednecks, or Okies. The Tatham family (and mine) were always moving, and, like mine, some members of the Tatham family returned home to Oklahoma during postwar prosperity.

The Tatham's trip resembled the Joads; Oca's brother, Vernon, said it was worse. Sixteen people with $50 among them traveled in a small truck with homemade seats and sides. And, like the Joads, they had a wreck going up a mountain, breaking Oca's arm and sending Cora, his mother, to the hospital with cuts; but the "old Chevy was Okie-tough. The engine ran and there were no leaks and not even a flat" (55).

The Tathams were often desperately poor during their first years in California, but they did not face Steinbeck's specter of starvation. And if growers were far from generous, they were not monsters either. The Tathams quickly found work, and a grower provided them with a dry block house with indoor plumbing and a gas stove. And when work ran out and they were forced onto relief, a California social agency treated them respectfully. "They treat you almost like a *customer* down there," Oca told his wife, Ruby, after he had been given "a new mattress, some blankets, and a 'family box' of canned milk, ham, and flour" (76). And unlike the Joads, the Tatham children went to school. The family didn't want school officials to think that they could not afford to feed their children, and Ruby sent them with lunches even when the kids said that lunches were provided by the school. Finally, one of the children convinced her mother that she did not have to be ashamed to let them eat at school: "Mama, this is California. They get a free hot lunch every day" (73). Times got harder in the late 1930s with a right-wing reaction against welfare, making relief harder to get.

In the Tatham family, the women more often than the men worked in the fields, picking cotton or fruit. The large ranches had their own labor camps, "segregated by race and nationality." There were two "Jap" camps, a "Filipino" camp, a "Mexican" camp, and an "American" [Okie] camp. Each group had its own mess hall with food prepared by a cook of their heritage (104). Most Okies were too individualistic and too opposed to their "red" taint to join farm-labor unions; besides, they saw fruit picking as a temporary expedient. Okies were used as strikebreakers and "field-labor militancy subsided" with their arrival (111). Many years after their fruit-picking days were over, the Tathams reserved special hatred for César Chavez and the United Farm Workers.

Regardless of their own circumstances, native Californians could look down on Okies. Job discrimination was widespread: "We don't hire no *Okies*. Them people'll rob you blind" (77). Wise migrants learned to ditch their Oklahoma license plates as soon as possible and try to keep their Oklahoma brogue under control. "The successful Okie had to have some of the qualities of the guerrilla fighter," Morgan writes, "blending into his surroundings and calling as little attention to himself as possible" (77). Oca quickly mastered the art. He taught his children to avoid Okie slang, and he rejected much of Okie culture, including country music with its twangy guitars. Years later, visiting cousins from Oklahoma were advised by Oca's children, "Say you're from Dallas" (198). On the other hand, transplanted Okie culture, particularly Oklahoma humor, helped make life bearable in California.

A strong sense of family was a part of Oklahoma culture that was preserved for succeeding generations. The extended family stayed close and other members migrating from Oklahoma received help. Within a few years of Oca's and Ruby's arrival, most of their relatives and friends from Oklahoma were living within a few miles of each other in California. One point of agreement between Steinbeck's novel and Morgan's study is that strong women held the families together; although like Ma in *Grapes,* they often were circumspect in doing it. "The women, in particular, liked California," Morgan writes, "and their views counted. Oklahoma women often gave the orders and took the men in tow when their confidence faltered" (161).

A part of Okie culture that Oca and the other Tathams of their generation did not reject was their holiness, Pentecostal religion. Steinbeck and most New Deal liberals (as well as progressives before them and leftists after them) saw fundamentalist or evangelical religions as detrimental to the social and economic progress of the underclass. Steinbeck must have been disappointed when the first social activism of some migrants was against storeowners who opened on Sunday, not against factory farmers. For the Tathams and many other Okies, Pentecostal religion gave meaning to their lives, as sharecroppers in Oklahoma, as migrant workers in California, and, later, as businessmen, although speaking in tongues (a sign of baptism by the Holy Ghost) was silenced as status and wealth increased. Oca, who had been more than a tad of a hellion in his youth, selling moonshine and womanizing, responded to a Morgan question: "Did we need the church in the Depression? You bet we did. What else did we have? We had no one else to turn to. We couldn't turn to our landlords. And you know something? We were full of joy—more joyful than people whose faces were hanging down to their stomach, who hated Pentecost" (133).

By the 1960s, members of the Pentecostal churches were growing in status and changing the names of their congregations to "Christian Center" and others that concealed their roots in the holiness tradition. These institutions were often the nucleus of the evangelical megachurches that increasingly became homes for the new religious right. Pentecostals were especially effective with television ministries, including Pat Robertson, Jimmy Swaggart, Oral Roberts, and Jim Bakker, all of whom received financial support from the Tathams. Swaggart was Oca's favorite preacher until his sexual escapades became public, and he regularly gave to Oral Roberts until Roberts claimed to have had a vision of a 900-foot-tall Jesus telling him to build a medical center in Tulsa. Photographs in Morgan's book show Bill shaking hands with Pat Robertson and Jerry Falwell with his arms around Oca. One of Oca's sons, Dick, became a prominent new-right, evangelical pastor and television evangelist, and, in his retirement years, Oca was a missionary to and a financial supporter of Pentecostal churches in Mexico.

Steinbeck left the Joad family in an abandoned barn facing starvation—hopeless. In contrast, the Tathams experienced growing afflu-
ence—a "rising in the West." Part of their success was Oca's natural talent
as a trader; as a child in Oklahoma, he traded his younger brother's suit
for a dog. Shortly after arriving in California, he noticed a disparity in
the price of potatoes between where they were grown and nearby
localities. He started selling potatoes to other migrants in the fields;
within six weeks he had made enough to order a new Ford pickup. He
began dealing in used tires, wheels, and junk; and within a couple of
years he had several trucks and was hiring drivers. He soon developed
subdivisions of inexpensive houses, created a water company, and later
owned nursing homes. In the early years, despite growing wealth, the
family still lived very simply; money went into further investments.

Son Bill did even better as an entrepreneur. By the 1970s he was worth
many millions. His Consolidated Industries operated the Belcor chain of
nursing homes, eventually owning 45 homes. He had interests in banking,
commercial real estate, health clubs, pharmaceuticals, and other enterprises. Eventually he became rich enough to lose a sizable fortune with a
franchise in the United States Football League, much to Oca's chagrin.

Rather than the left-wing revolutionaries Steinbeck hoped for, the
Tathams became right-wing reactionaries. In 1932, Oca cast his first
presidential vote for Franklin D. Roosevelt. The other members of the
family also voted New Deal Democratic, but they slowly drifted to active
participation in New Right politics. Morgan argues, rightly I think, that
the Okies' move to the right was motivated more by social issues than
by their pocketbooks; even poorer Tathams became reactionaries. Oca
saw culture and family life degenerate decade by decade. Rock and roll
in the 1950s was "demon possessed" (224). He was highly offended by
the prayer decision of the early 1960s. "We'll finally be like the
Communist nations where no one will be allowed to pray," he complained (223). He agreed with other social conservatives that a woman
working outside the home was the beginning of the destruction of the
American family, despite the fact that his wife, mother, and sister had
worked in the fields during the depression. "They really had to work,"
he said. "But, boy, they was going to have their kids right by their side"
(223). Despite the relief that he had received during the depression, he
became increasing critical of welfare. His relief was "a temporary helping
hand," not a way of life.

Pentecostals traditionally had been wary of politics. But Oca was part of the generation that made them a political force in America. Fervently anti-Communist, in part because it was anti-Christian, he found his first political hero in Barry Goldwater. He gave money and campaigned for him, buying and giving away copies of Goldwater's *The Conscience of a Conservative*. He found his fellow Okies more receptive with Reagan but was particularly excited by Pat Robertson's run for the presidency in 1988.

Culture changes, even though whiteness and blackness remain. Many of the grandchildren and great-grandchildren of Oca and Ruby are in the upper-middle class. Most who are old enough are college graduates; granddaughters work full time in professional jobs; they married outside their Okie culture and Pentecostal faith, and six of their 11 married grandchildren have been divorced. They are no longer Okies.

## THE ALLISONS

I am/was an Okie. I was less than a year old in 1936 when my family moved from western Oklahoma to California. I have only repressed memories of the trip. With the coming of war prosperity and to avoid the draft of my father, we returned to Oklahoma in 1941. Like many other Okies, we moved back and forth, returning to California after the end of World War II in 1946 and going "home" to Oklahoma again in 1949.

My story is based on my memories, family folklore, and a rambling several-day interview with my mother in April 1996 that broke all known rules of ethnographic interviewing. Part of their culture, as Morgan points out, is that Okies are storytellers and truth tellers; but they tell about events, about what happened, not about feelings.

Depression and drought forced us off the land that my young parents were farming. The dust bowl was dreadful west of the 100th meridian. Mother's most vivid memory of their condition was being paid $25 by the federal government to shoot each of their starving cows. There were too many to butcher; there was no way to refrigerate the meat; and besides, the cattle were lean and tough. Steinbeck's Joads were faced with human villains—factory farmers who tractored the Joads out and monster bankers who secured the land for the large owners. My parents' remembered experience is much different. They blame nature and remain grateful to the local bankers whom they believe stood by them. A leftist defending bankers is as incongruous as a feminist defending rapists, but I remember how proud my father was of a letter of recommendation written by the local banker, "Pete" Thurman. He carried it with him for years and loved to show it; it began: "Clinton Allison is a responsible and hard working young man who has been doing business with me since he was old enough to do business."

My 22-year-old father hitched to Colorado then caught a freight train to California. Unexpectedly, the train went on into Mexico; he jumped off when he decided that the landscape was too peculiar to be California. An old woman fed him beans and tortillas and helped him catch a freight back to California. After a month as a Los Angeles movie theater janitor, he made enough money to send a bus ticket for my mother and me. At first we lived with Uncle Fritz, Aunt Flossie, and Grandfather Pitts Bills, who had moved to California in 1929. Grandpa Pitts seems never to have worked. Aunt Flossie dipped chocolates in a Hollywood shop and worked behind the counter at lunch. A regular customer tipped her a dime every day. The streetcar fare to her work was seven cents; the tip paid her way. Mother, then 20 years old, worked as a baker and a waitress, walking a mile or so to work. As with the Joads and Tathams, the women held the family together.

Like the Tathams, family and friends from Oklahoma re-created a supportive community in California. Many high school friends of my parents migrated at the same time they did. They furnished each other a place to stay, helped others find jobs, and partied together on Saturday night. Highway 66 was a two-way street, and family and friends were continuously moving and visiting. One of mother's cousins drove the 1,500 miles to California to sell a car; the price was better there. Mother remembers the period as a time of youthful fun with warm friends and close-knit family relationships. (Historians are cautious about such memories; they understand that humans need to remember a pleasant past. And it was a better time for Mother because she was young.)

Like the Tathams, the Allisons' church moved with them. Rather than the exuberant, faith-healing, talking-in-tongues Pentecostals of the Joads and Tathams, my family, like many other western Oklahomans, were members of the rule-following, legalistic, fundamentalist Church of Christ. They insisted on the strictest interpretation of the gospels: one cup at communion, no instrumental music, and lay preachers; one misinterpretation of the scriptures could mean eternal damnation. They were contemptuous of the "holy rollers" of Pentecostal faiths. But, meeting in storefronts and other temporary facilities, the Church of Christ, like the Pentecostals, gave Okies a community while at the same time setting them apart from the broader culture.

Unlike the Tathams, my family did not work in the fields. Mother claimed that it was those who picked crops who were called Okies. (Because my sister was born in California, Mother called her a prune picker.) Despite vocal skepticism from me, Mother, in a pronounced Oklahoma accent, denied being treated badly or characterized as an Okie in California. I asked her if she knew an Okie joke. She responded: "How can you tell if it's a rich Okie? They have two mattresses tied to the top of their car." Perhaps children remember emotional hurts better than do adults. I remember, from our second time in California, my eyes stinging after having been called an Okie, a classmate telling me that his mother told him he couldn't play with Okie kids, and practicing my "California" pronunciation on a walk home from school.

In 1941, Grandfather Allison bought us a farm and sent us $100 to return to Oklahoma. As Morgan points out, Okies and others of the upper South tend to be isolationists and rarely very gung ho about foreign wars. Several young men in my family became enthusiastic farmers when farming became the source of a draft deferment. (My father moved to the right over the years and I to the left, and we often raised our voices in opposition to each other's fool ideas, but we quarreled less about my opposition to the Vietnam War than most other things.) Our old car broke down in Arizona on the way east, and Dad sold it for another $100. Mother has fond memories of the Greyhound Bus Line; we rode to Oklahoma with trunk, pillows, and six suitcases, at no extra charge for my sister and me.

We returned to California after World War II in 1946. I asked Mother why. She said that Aunt Flossie and Uncle Fritz came for a visit and wanted us to go. Times were still hard on the farm. Mother said, "Why not?" and she and my sister returned with them. Dad and I went later in our 1937 Chevy, taking the southern route rather than Highway 66 for a change in scenery. We again moved in with Aunt Flossie, Uncle Fritz, Grandpa Pitts, and Aunt Flossie's teenage daughter from a previous marriage. The daughter attended a Catholic school and had converted to Catholicism. In the hallway outside her room she hung a large picture of the crucified Christ, complete with a vivid bleeding heart. It was the most bizarre and fascinating thing that my young fundamentalist eyes had ever seen. We were to share expenses, but we often didn't have enough money to pay our share. The household money was kept in a vase in the kitchen cabinet. Aunt Flossie called it the kitty; I thought it a funny name even though discussions about the kitty were usually very serious.

Even when times were hard, and they often were, we did not experience the hopelessness, victimization, and lack of agency of Steinbeck's Joads. Part of the answer was in the strength and determination of my mother and part was in the gifts of my father. Like Oca, my dad was short, handsome, and smart. He had more schooling than most Okies. Expelled from Southwestern State Teachers College for "helping" some high school classmates with their freshman biology course, he attended Chillicothe Business College in Missouri for a year, and he took night classes at Long Beach State College during our the first sojourn in California. He was chronically gregarious, a storyteller much like a Garrison Keillor character. People would gather around for his stories: "What did he say? What did he say?" He first found a job working with Uncle Fritz on a construction project but was fired for making fun of the foreman. Hired as a janitor for the Security National Bank in Los Angles, he soon worked his way up to manager of the eight-floor building. Most of the janitors and maintenance workers were Italians and African Americans. Dad, young and tough, loved to tell how he had the workers empty their pockets when they came to work: "You get your razors back when your shift is over." After the second return to Oklahoma and another unsuccessful try at farming, he became a successful traveling salesman of building materials and eventually a building contractor in Oklahoma City. He divorced my mother just before their fiftieth wedding anniversary.

My parents' generation has kept close contact with those who stayed in California. Highway 66 has been replaced by I-40, and 60 years after the Okie migration, 80-year-olds travel annually or semiannually back and forth from California to Oklahoma by car, RV, or, increasingly as they age, air. They know the names of each other's great-grandchildren. Never have immigrants kept a closer tie with the old country.

My family was Democratic by conviction and birthright—after all, it was Hoover's depression and Democrats were for "the little guy." The first time I saw my father cry was when I brought in the newspaper announcing FDR's death. Like Oca, Dad moved from being a New Deal Democrat to a Reagan Republican, and like Oca, it was not primarily because he became affluent. Okies were populists, individualists, hard workers, and, as Morgan (1992, 219) writes, "suspicious of 'upper crusts.'" For reasons I found hard to understand then, Kennedy infuriated my father, and he viewed "The Great Society" not as a continuation of the New Deal but as a devil's compact between socialists and the chronically lazy. Oca and my father are examples of a generation of white males lost to progressive politics and found by the New Right.

## CONCLUSION: WHITENESS COUNTS

Mother hated *The Grapes of Wrath*. Several times as a child, I heard her complaining about the novel and the Henry Fonda movie based on it. From her description, I supposed it was a mean-spirited, anti-Oklahoman book. I read it the summer after high school graduation; it was far too controversial and much too racy to be assigned to high school students, particularly in 1950s Oklahoma. I thought it wonderful. Steinbeck's language and descriptions were magic for me, such power in words. (But I am not to be trusted as a literary critic; after all, I delight in Carl Hiaasen novels.) And Steinbeck was sympathetic to Okies; they were both the oppressed and the heroes of the story. Mother was simply wrong, I decided; she, lacking sophistication, had misread the story. Eighteen-year-olds' mothers are notoriously unsophisticated.

In my interview, I asked Mother again about *The Grapes of Wrath*, and she confirmed her displeasure. Had she really read the book? She said she had read the book and seen the movie, and she reiterated that it put Oklahomans down. In preparation for this chapter, I reread *The Grapes of Wrath* after 40 years. I now realized the source of my mother's hostility. Yes, the language is powerful, and the Okies are oppressed. But they are also treated as simple, ignorant, and superstitious. Steinbeck's Okies are sometimes persons of courage and strength, but they are also an innocent, native species. Steinbeck patronized them. The Joads were not people mother knew; her reality and that of the Tathams was much more complicated.

The larger context in which the story was told was also more complicated. *The Grapes of Wrath* is magnificent, enduring literature, and "literary license" was necessary to tell a story with profound truths. But it is not a documentary on the Great Depression, nor did Steinbeck intend it to be. Depression and the subsequent suffering of Okies and others were a result of the failure of unbridled capitalism, but not in the direct, simple way that Steinbeck presents. Economic and social depression cannot be reduced to monsters and victims. (And the story of corporate bankers and factory farmers tractoring out sharecropping farmers owes much more to conditions in Steinbeck's native California valleys than to the hills of eastern Oklahoma.)

The Okies had much more agency than Steinbeck suggests. The frontier myth has some explanatory power here. The Okies were independent as hell, and they may have been the last of the traditional American pioneers: poor westward-moving rural folk who were often anti-intellectual and anti-aesthetic but who often were also innovative and entrepreneurial. Not all Okies had the strength or luck to exchange their oppressed position to one of privilege, but many did; and many others moved into or were pushed by people of darker color into the middle class; they were beneficiaries of racism. They succeeded not only because of their agency but because they were White. Their identity as Okies was temporary. They were oppressed and humiliated, but they were not permanently unwhitened. "Notwithstanding a complicated history," Frankenberg (1993, 203) writes, "the boundaries of Americanness and whiteness have been much more fluid for 'white ethnic' groups than for people of color."

The experiences of Okies verifies again that culture is dynamic and that whiteness counts; it still confers privilege. Not only have the grandchildren and great-grandchildren of Okies disappeared into the white middle class, but also in many ways Middle America has become "Okie." White conservative, middle America's favorite music is country. (The favorite country singer of former Okies is Merle "I'm an Okie from Muskogee" Haggard. Born in California of Okie parents who were from around Muskogee, his songs are vaguely reactionary and antiestablishment.) The former Okie-type fundamentalism and Pentecostal churches have metamorphosed into the fast-growing evangelical megachurches that are changing the face of American Protestantism. And few among my leftist colleagues do not fear the political power of the religious right as exemplified by the Christian Coalition that is well on its way to capturing control of one of America's two major political parties.

# BIBLIOGRAPHY

Frankenberg, R. (1993). *White Women, Race Matters: The Social Construction of Whiteness*. Minneapolis: University of Minnesota Press.

Morgan, D. (1992). *Rising in the West: The True Story of an "Okie" Family from the Great Depression through the Reagan Years*. New York: Alfred A. Knopf.

Steinbeck, J. (1939/1976). *The Grapes of Wrath*. New York: Penguin Books.

# THIRTEEN

# Once Upon a Time When We Were White—A Rather *Grimm* Fairy Tale

**Karen Anijar**

Once upon a time, in a world far, far away, we had our eyes fixed toward a future. A future brimming with possibility (our porcelain cup had runneth over). Ph.D. in hand, job on the coast, I was returning to my mother's homeland—a place I knew only through a too-often-told story of a candle on Olivera Street. No wonder she was so often silent. She never told us exactly *what we were.*

We left our home in Greensboro, North Carolina, good-byes all said. We packed up the Budget-Rent-A-Car, sang one last chorus of "Dixieland" (with our eyes firmly fixed on Disneyland), and we headed west. We were, indeed, a pale imitation of *The Grapes of Wrath,* almost everything we owned was loaded on the truck, my red Mazda hitched to the back. We headed toward the "Golden State." As I look back upon the cross-country trip, upon the past two years of my life, at the shattered puzzle pieces of my once-slippery identity—I remind myself: "All that glitters is not gold."

The desert creates mirages, and illusions. The sands shift and swirl creating new configurations, new alliances. One day I was sitting in North Carolina, a week later I am Los(t) in Angeles. I had no idea that when I entered the credit card class in suburban California, the politics of race would become so peculiarly overdetermined.

We drove through Tennessee: alas, no time to stop for my Velvet Elvis and make my pilgrimage to Graceland. Through Arkansas: "Gee, if Clinton is President, don't you think he could fix the roads?" We not so merrily bumped along. Our bottoms became sore. The throbbing pain kept us awake through the never-ending boredom of Oklahoma. We drove rapidly through a tiny part of Texas, to my family in New Mexico. I barely remember Arizona.

Finally, seven days later, we screamed in delight, "Eureka, we've found it!" Oh, how I desperately desired to get rid of it! On the Mojave Desert we realized that the phone connection had been severed. We were riding on a moonscape of apprehension. High above the world, we wanted to turn around and run home. All was not as it seemed. It was all downhill from there. We lost our brakes on the Cajon Pass (and for those of you who do speak Spanish, clearly, you could understand my child's confusion between Cajon and another word . . . which anticipated just what was needed to live here in the land of the ubiquitous sun-dried tomato). I do not know how *not* to be white.

A month ago I sat with a friend from Miami who is currently living in Beverly Hills. He has become a famous L.A. (as in Latin American) television personality. We sat at the Ritz-Carlton "doing lunch." The place reminded me of the gilded ghettos of country club life I recall from that part of my youth spent in Barranquilla. At the time we were both afraid of the rise of Pat Buchanan while nostalgically recalling our youth in our tropical paradise (lost). "Americans." We both shook our heads with contempt, snickering sarcastically. Americans are just so individualistic, so psychological, so ahistorical. All of a sudden I started to laugh. My friend understood. We sat under an umbrella of privilege complaining about Anglos, while being served by a very indigent-looking man. We are white! We are American. Such is the story from the border. It is real, as real as the San Andreas Fault on which I live. I can see it, and it grows. When we fall into the Earth who will remember that we were here?

If I can eat jalapeno bagels with cilantro pesto hummus cream cheese, why must I Spic' N' Spanish only? (See Perez-Firmat 1994). This is what I have learned through hands-on pedagogy, living on the rugged terrain of the San Gabriel Mountains (forged out of granola): cry and/ or get angry. I cry when I go to Pomona and realize the California curriculum that mandates bilingualism cannot be translated into English. Bilingualism is nilingualism.

> Just as bilingue is someone who speaks two languages . . . nilingue is someone who doesn't speak either: "Ni espanol, ni ingles." Such a person is a no-lingual, a nulli-glot . . . occasional Spanish utterances are shot through with anglicisms: falta for culpa, introducir for presentar, parientes for padres, . . .
> . . . In Spanish to know a language well is to dominate it. But my mother tongue has it backwards. People don't dominate languages, languages dominate people . . . English and Spanish battle[d] each other to a tie (a tongue tie). (Perez-Firmat 1994, 46-47)

My tongue tied, I trip and I fall, and I cannot get up.

Children cannot compete, because they cannot speak, they cannot negotiate the terrain on equal footing. The language does indeed dominate people. In Los Angeles the nilingual education programs produce another generation destined for the sweatshops, another generation of low paying jobs, another generation of gardeners for the lawns of Beverly Hills. Frankfurt school philosopher T. W. Adorno once said: "Only he who is truly at home inside a language can use it as an instrument" (Perez-Firmat 1994, 47).

Alas, *aqui* the only instrument we can play are primitive ones, very valuable handmade objects, demonstrating a Peace Corps of neobenevolence. We are "folk," which means less than civilized. The farther we move from the epicenter of the Anglo vortex, the more savage we become, the quainter we become. I feel a mariachi band blossoming from my being; it is an alien feeling. For it is not in people's definitions of themselves but *who* has the author-ity to define who and what *they* are.

This is truly problematic. We are working within an essentialist framework that, much like a natural disaster, huffs and puffs and blows the house apart. Leaving those without the *common* sense to be able to construct their own categories and define their own conditions (which does require a certain amount of privilege), left in the shambles of a condemned building. The building sold out from under them, they are homeless. Homelessness within two languages (see Perez-Firmat 1994) is instrumental to the economy of Los Angeles. If one has an "accent in two languages" (46) unable to speak either, the silence becomes immobilizing, precluding changes in political practices. It is the politics of whiteness that has raped (oops, robbed) U.S. (us) of selfhood (even though the concept of a radically individual selfhood is a Western European concept). Selfishly, I want my privilege back.

I was invited to a Cinco de Mayo festival, where the students performed a cumbia to the sounds of that great Mexican songbird Gloria Estefan. To paraphrase Shakespeare: Something isn't kosher in Denmark. At one school I learned about Swedish Christmas customs. (We ate Swedish meatballs.) The teacher had a flag of Israel up because during the next week the children were going to be exposed to the "Israeli Christmas: Hanukkah" (Hanukkah?) I tried to explain politely that Hanukkah had nothing to do with Christmas, and the holiday did not emerge in Israel. But she told me I was wrong, she showed me her multicultural workbook. (I guess I was just suffering from false consciousness.) What could I possibly know about the holiday? I didn't write the workbook.

The celebration of the multicultural and calls for diversity merely create a "Museum of Natural History" tour, for the emphasis of Otherness comes under the benevolent plantation embrace of the satin sheets of the Hollywood movie set. It isn't a melting pot; it is a melted pot. It is a Velveeta cheese curriculum. A professor I know told me that acknowledging the categories is better than ignoring them, a little bit is better than nothing. I resist; I know that I cannot be a little bit pregnant.

"Multiculturalism has produced if anything an even greater rush towards utopian thinking" (Chicago Cultural Studies Group 1994, 114). Utopianizing is a conservative impulse understood as "reactionary on the grounds that it sought to impose an ideal plan upon reality rather than seeking in that reality the means of social change" (Levitas 1990, 59). An impulse that *vive la différence* and diversity arguments tend to inculcate particularly when instrumented in schools.

Within these colonized terms (for example), bilingualism and biculturalism make those of us who fall in between the hyphens' bisected entities. Bi-lingual, bifurcate, bi-sect, dis-sect, and we are dying. You are embracing us to death. Ni-culturalized in a balkanized metaphor. (See Perez-Firmat1994 and Regalado 1995.) People are not collocations of objective characteristics. Nothing is fixed. We are all in the process of changes and exchanges.

Benetton's ads combined with the racial structure of antebellum Louisiana in California. One drop of blood, yes, indeed one drop of blood *y no puedo hablar en ingles.* (Problem is, I can't speak Spanish either!) My son, an alumnus of the Randolph County North Carolina Happy Heifer 4-H Club, sits in a school in Rancho Cucaracha (a revolutionary song, whose power was lost under the sign of the dancing cockroach), perplexed. It is an unanticipated world. How could I have prepared him to survive? I know what to do in hurricanes; I have no idea what to do in an earthquake. I know how to surf my hyphens, not be swallowed by the spaces. There remains a blurry netherworld between "description and prescription . . . reality does not match the theory" (Gillborn 1995, 10). I could also label this habitat, this suburban sprawl, "Rancho Cookie Monster," where Disney is ubiquitous and the Avon lady roams the Amazon. It's a small world after all.

All the narratives in this chapter are a mixture (a melange, a mongrelized multicultural stew) of teacher education candidates and white supremacist web sites.*

> Although some blacks and liberal whites concede that non-Whites can, perhaps, be racist, they invariably add that non-Whites have been forced into it as self-defense because of centuries of white oppression. What appears to be non-white racism is so understandable and forgivable that it hardly deserves the name. Thus, whether or not an act is called racism depends on the race of the racist. What would surely be called racism when done by Whites is thought to be normal when done by anyone else. The reverse is also true.

> I made good grades, good test scores and did not get into the college of my choice. I know it is racism. Affirmative action has made it impossible for white men to get ahead in this world.

> Here, then, is the final, baffling inconsistency about American race relations. All non-Whites are allowed to prefer the company of their own kind, to think of themselves as groups with interests distinct from those of the whole, and to work openly for group advantage. None of this is thought to be racist. At the same time, Whites must also champion the racial interests of non-Whites. They must sacrifice their own future on the

---

* I am purposely not citing who said what; in the few cases in which names are included, pseudonyms are used

altar of "diversity" and cooperate in their own dispossession. They are to encourage, even to subsidize, the displacement of a European people and culture by alien peoples and cultures. To put it in the simplest possible terms, white people are cheerfully to slaughter their own society, to commit racial and cultural suicide. To refuse to do so would be racism.

My first quarter in California, a not-so-young man who lost his job in Silicon Valley decided to become a teacher. He too is an immigrant, from a more Aryan sort of nation. He had a solution to the immigrant problem: Zyclon-B gas. You can't flunk someone for ideology. "But who will teach the children?"

On the seventh day, educational technicist Madeline Hunter proclaimed: "White is all there is!" Everything must fit into a category. If it doesn't, it cannot exist in the schools. Let us now focus on and review "whiteness," let us guide its practice. What are the outcomes? What are the conclusions?

The metropolitan mosaic of Los(t) Angeles is a static metaphor. I have always thought when something does not change, when it remains static, it is dead. Discourse can never be a hypostatized "thing" that in its stasis produces the "dead thing like shell," "the naked corpse." (See Clark and Holquist 1984; Morson and Emerson, 1990.) Meaning is unstable; it is polysemous. Life is unstable; it, too, is polysemous. What Bakhtin terms centrifugal forces "compel movement, becoming and history; they long for change and new life," as opposed to centripetal forces, which "urge stasis, resist becoming, abhor history, and desire the seamless quiet of death" (Clark and Holquist 1984, 7-8), ought to be considered. Centripetal forces reduce "cultural life to a static system of categorical relationships which leave untouched many critical factors involved in the construction of cultural exchanges" (Quantz and O'Conner 1988, 95). Recognizing that nothing can ever be reduced to the categorical may "provide the only meaningful escape from an endless oscillation between dead abstractions" (Morson and Emerson, 1990).

You must grout mosaics, even metropolitan ones; they are stuck in the cement. They must be firmly braced just in case the earth moves. The only way to change a mosaic is to break the tile. "Don't cry for me, Argentina." Evita, even if Madonna does play you in the movie, you too are not white. Ricky Ricardo had no name; he was a double diminutive.

(See Perez-Firmat 1994.) But, of course, anything that is foreign is made diminutive. If I cannot be grateful, I cannot be. If I am part of more than one mosaic, I must be broken apart. Identity cannot be slippery in Los(t) Angeles, you must choose sides. Either way, *mi hija,* you lose. Welcome to the world of the walking dead.

Undoubtedly California is the boldest leap of all into the ontological void. "Nothing Theory"—a post-Newtonian idea—"the universe is one of those things that happen from time to time," please pass the sun-dried radicchio, do you want a latte or a double espresso? It is all image (and I do despise that word). La-de-da. Perhaps it is as Tennessee Williams said (I admit paraphrasing), "a vacuum is a hell of a lot better than some of the stuff nature replaces it with." So, if the world exists merely because it is superior to nullity, then California really is the dream. It surrounds us, it is in us, it is Hegel's pure being. Having no qualities it remains a vacant void (again I am paraphrasing an article from Harpers' magazine).

Staring into the void of history, filled with mirages, I have stepped behind the Orange Curtain. If I close my eyes and click my heels three times, can I ever go home again? I may be an insect, but I am not a *gusayno.* Somewhere over the rainbow coalition, high above the heights of Hollywood, the screams of the children still cannot be heard. Whiteness is a color, an opaque color.

## PART TWO:
## NOW THAT THE PRIVILEGE HAS PASSED ME BY . . .

I'll define "whiteness" as a state of mind caught between preparedness and being a total idiot about the world. It is an instance of knowing exactly what alpha and beta is without knowing exactly what it is. It is a separation of oneness with nature and total absurdness. It is a disconnection with life while we wait for Tara to return. It is walking through the wilderness with miles to go before your feet. It's never really knowing you were a child all along when you thought you were an adult. It's not knowing that the baggage we come clothed in (that is, our skin) is not our bag at all. It's John Travolta dancing all night on Saturdays never really knowing the true meaning of dance. It's never hearing the trees breathe and seeing the rivers as crystal lakes. It's never quite getting the get-with-it-ness that we're supposed to all get. It's definitely not me or you but the "them" that's been terrorizing the U.S. It's the down-home grind of pigs' feet and caviar mixed up as Sunday fare. It's oblivion and darkness. A black cube without the white. It's like seeing white without the color. You're blind and you know it. Hope that's enough. If not I could add others.

—Arts Educator

The Heart of Whiteness (forgive my Joseph Conrad pun) is not easy to find. It is not a "thing" to latch on to. It is not like an artichoke heart, it is more like an onion.

Ron Gonzales and I carpool together. On the drive from the university to our respective homes, I told Ron what I had written in the first part of this chapter. I also said that I was beginning to feel a tad bit skin-o-frenic about the whole project. Ron looked at me and responded: "No, no . . . you have got it all wrong! You are looking at this from the wrong perspective!" "This is academic," I reply. "No, whiteness is more metaphysical! You need to ask yourself: Do white people have souls?" "What? I am not thinking in terms of theology," I answered. Ron responded: "Do white people have souls, or maybe soles? Can you see the soles of a white person's feet? Maybe it is sol's. Do white people radiate presence of being from the sol? Or do they just wear Italian leather on their soles?" We descended into limericks. Whiteness must be more than two very tired teachers, making up bad poetry, while trying to discuss a white metaphysic as opposed to a white politic.

Something was bothering me. It was a visceral reaction. I reacted when I wrote the first part of this. I was asked to write a chapter on whiteness. I am reacting to whiteness. But I cannot define whiteness. Who or what is "white"? [W]hite culture is the hidden norm against which all racially subordinate groups differences are measured . . . at the same time it can be used to imply that whites are *colorless,* and hence without racial subjectivities, interests, and privileges . . ." (Roman 1993, 71).

My parents once bought my little sister a Simon and Garfunkel record: "Mrs. Robinson." I told them I distinctly heard in the chorus: "Go cook a Jew, Mrs. Robinson." Horrified, they threw out the record. Who knew that Simon and Garfunkel were Jewish? Do we sometimes hear what is not there? Concurrently, we refuse to listen to what is there.

of territory. Viewed in biological terms, ethnic diversity is prelude to destruction.

We as white Americans have gone soft; we've lost our values, lost our direction. Our society is going the way of ancient Rome, permeated with laziness, greed, lust, gluttony, etc. We must come together before it is too late, because very soon the time to defend ourselves from this black onslaught will arrive. We will have to stand and fight for our families and our way of life; we must begin preparation now. If we fail, we have no one to blame but ourselves.

The Protestant Ethic and the spirit of capitalism, with its undergirding sense of I-ness, is *fundamental* to this. Alas, I wish that you wouldn't blame yourselves. Victim blaming has never accomplished much. I will be generous; it isn't your own fault that you failed. I won't tell you that you need to stop being lazy and get jobs! You need to stop lusting after our exotic women! You need to stop looking at the material; after all, "If you work hard, the world can be yours! Do you white people want a handout?" I'll be liberal and express an ethos of care and altruism: It is your static version of family values, it is your emphasis on anti-intellectualism, it is after all a policy failure, it is a Reagan legacy, a Newt-onian inheritance. It smells like Limbaugh-ger cheese (which is why you are soft—too many fatty foods). I am offended by the smell, but I won't blame you, if you would have only asked for some help! I would have given you advice. I mean, I worked hard to get where I am today. You can do the same.

Europeans are underbreeding themselves into extinction. Like other animals, humans are driven by the urge to reproduce their kind. . . . In California, "Anglos" will soon be one among many minority groups; in the 21st Century the same may be true of the whole United States. This is not due to any quirk of national character. Human reproduction appears to be determined more by economics than nationality.

Gaia, the Earth-mother, moves in mysterious ways. The penalty for becoming an overdeveloped mega-industrialized state may be national extinction. I have, until now, believed that this would be the consequence of emission of noxious fumes and the killing effect of urban stress. If a species becomes dominant, Nature destroys it.

I do understand that, honestly. I am, I am beginning to see "the light." At Duke University I had the good fortune of going to the lemur center. I saw an aye-aye there. It is hard to picture an aye-aye because they are almost extinct. We cannot language what we cannot see. Is it that we cannot articulate whiteness because whiteness is disappearing? It is all in the linguistic theory, not in the anthropological construction. Because whiteness is extinct or almost extinct or erased by ethnicity, we use other words to talk around whiteness.

There has been much talk of America disappearing. Disappearing, that is, as a world power, as a military leader, even as a dominant economic force. But there hasn't been so much talk about an even more serious vanishing act—that of the American people themselves. Recently, in a crowded Miami Airport, I watched a bewildered young GI listening to the machine-gun bursts of Spanish announcements. "I would like to get back to America," he wailed. It was hard to accept he was in it.

Whites have let themselves be convinced that it is racist merely to object to dispossession, much less to work for their own interests. Never in the history of the world has a dominant people thrown open the gates to strangers and poured out its wealth to aliens. Never before has a people been fooled into thinking that there was virtue or nobility in surrendering its heritage, and giving away to others its place in history.

There is a war against white people.

As a supporter of the white race, as an ex-government employee with one of the nations' "elite" organizations . . . The simple fact is that there are two "foes" targeted, and that is the White race and the Christian religion.

Whiteness is becoming extinct because there is an all-out war against whiteness. Sometimes I miss things. I forget to put stamps on the mail, I forget which day the garbage pick up comes. But a war? I don't know when the declaration of war was sounded, but it would have been nice if someone would have let me know this. Am I trying to define the dodo bird? Or has millennialism combined with ecology in a clean-cut and clear-cut white fantasy?

According to U.S. Census projections, by the year 2050 one third of the U.S. population of 400 million will be due to post 1965 immigration. At this point American Whites will be on the verge of becoming a minority, and will already be a minority among the young. And of course, in another 50 years or so Whites may well be a small minority, merely a beleaguered elite struggling to maintain their position in what is essentially just another crowded, miserable Third World country. (Note that 400 million is only a "most likely" projection; the worst case for 2050 is 500 million.)

Am I trying to locate El Dorado? Pat Linn (a friend, colleague, and mentor) sees whiteness under a paleontological rubric. I was a card-carrying member of the North Carolina Fossil Club. I loved waking up early in the morning to go to phosphate mines and sift through the sands to find my treasures. I collect sharks' teeth and vertebras. Fossils are safe, they don't bite. Believe me, the sharks have big teeth, with serrated edges that even after millions of years can give a Ginsu knife a run for its money.

But I still cannot find the heart of whiteness. I ask myself why I should bother if it will no longer exist in a few years. It seems as silly as trying to find the cure for smallpox! Yet I did promise myself and the editors of this book: I will write on whiteness!

Some of you may already be aware that an all-out war exists on our People, our culture, our heritage, and our very existence. We are living in the era of State-sanctioned hypocrisy and double standards. America must have separation of church and State, and integration, yet our largest beneficiary of foreign aid (Israel) remains a racial/religious State. It is wrong and racist for White people to have any White organizations, yet all non-Whites are encouraged to have them. The most important thing that you can do to ensure our survival is to educate yourself! . . . There is not a Straight White male on Clinton's cabinet! And it goes on and on. . . .

I go on too, to seek my destiny with the Wizard of Whiteness (or the grand wizard of the Klan). I make sure to use my second husband's name (Bradford) . . . I make sure to keep the e-mail short and to the point: "I am writing a chapter on a book about whiteness. Can you please give me a definition of who is White and who is not?" Follow the white brick road . . . (you wouldn't want to follow the Yellow Brick Road, now would you?). It is really a *straight* path. On my way to seek the wizard, it seems that I am not alone in my conundrum.

I have been put in doubt about my own racial identity: I am a white German citizen, living in the French-talking part of Switzerland. My father has been a officer in the German army, however, I heard that he could have had some Jewish forefathers. His superiors in the army didn't know that, of course. My mother had a Jewish father. I think I must be half Jewish, more or less. However, I speak perfectly well the German language, I have a German passport, etc. . . . However, I would like to have your opinion: am I an Aryan, or no?

—Leopold Farmer

The clarion call for the rise of an Aryan homeland beckons and the issues, as in one drop of blood, are exceedingly complex. Namely, who will be allowed access once the evil darkening of this great nation, indeed the world, is stymied.

My grandmother was one fourth Cherokee. Does this prevent me from being part of the great movement that will sweep across this nation? Am I welcomed here?

—Carl Ruby

Where do I fit in? I am a blond-haired, blue-eyed white male. I am exceptionally right-wing. I believe in the following:

1. Mixing of the races will eventually lead to the extinction of the Caucasian race.
2. Blacks are the primary cause of all crimes.
3. Immigration is undermining America's foundation.
4. An armed society is an honest society.

I maintain a cache of weapons, ammunition, and I firmly believe that one day I will need to use these in order to defend my family, property, and self.

My family's lineage includes Confederate soldiers, Klan members, slave masters, etc. I am also a proud member of Sons of the Confederacy and Florida Pioneers. The other half of my family (my mother's side) are Jewish immigrants from Russia. I am Jewish. I was Bar Mitzvah'd. I am marrying a Jewish girl in less than three weeks. She feels the same way I do about most issues.

My questions are as follows:

1. There are a lot of white people in my position, ones who are "disqualified" from the white nationalist movement by a RELIGION, not a race.

2. Am I precluded from all "activities" because I am Jewish, as I will proudly admit, even though I would make most Stormfront readers look like tree-hugging homos?

I want straight answers, no BS. Where does everyone stand on this issue? Unfortunately, I don't have time to write a well-thought out letter and I have a couple of coworkers with wandering eyes. Please respond.

—Blaise

Although I really did want to answer Leopold, Carl, and Blaise, I decided it would distract me from my mission. Finally, after three months of searching, I found the definitions I was seeking:

All Whites are descended from European immigrants, and we are not actually "White." The term European-American has political significance for two reasons. First, it recognizes that most people in the U.S. of European extraction have intermarried to such an extent that it is no longer possible to identify American Whites as "Irish" or "German" or "Italian." But more important, use of the term "European-American" is intended to recognize that White elites in the United States have exploited differences based on religion and European national origin to divide European-Americans, with the intention of rendering us unable to defend ourselves against non-White demands.

Another site provided me with an even more in-depth explanation. It provided more than scientific (a.k.a. eugenist) descriptions but biblical definitions as well:

An Aryan is a person of Indo-Hittite (Indo-European) ancestry. Germans, Kelts, Slavs (Russians), Kurds, Persians (Iran = Aryan), India Aryans, etc. are more or less pure Aryans. Not all "Whites" are Aryans. Semites (Jews and Arabs), Basques, Caucasians, and southern Europeans, etc. are part of a race which about 35,000 years ago emigrated from Africa to Eurasia, where they miscegenated with or exterminated the Neanderthals, before the Ice Ages. Glaciers cleansed northern Europe by pushing people south, which is why the pre-Aryans of Europe are referred to as the Mediterranean race, and why the Aryan race of Northern Europe (the origin of most "white" Americans) has remained pure enough to maintain the most powerful Aryan civilization. The ancient Aryan civilizations in the Middle East and southern Europe, once the most powerful in the world, have declined due to miscegenation with Mediterranean's.

I now understand why I have to tweeze my eyebrows so often. I am not quite human; I am related to Neanderthals. I go to the mirror to check my frontal lobes.

I can't clean. I burn myself when I iron. And whenever I make the beds, well, the sheets sort of fall off (which would be a problem for me at Klan meetings). But now I understand it isn't my fault that I can't be like Donna Reed, it is my lack of domestication: my Neanderthal ancestors. I have been merely passing as human.

White = American = Straight = Christian (Protestant only) = Human. There must be an equal sign and not a hyphen.

My name is Jorge Peterman Veras of Spanish and German ancestry. I am a white Puerto Rican. The reason I am writing to you is the following, I would like to know why we Puerto Ricans being of mostly European heritage are always been discriminated by the KKK and other white groups, these groups label us as Non-Whites, and this is very much annoying for most of us. We are also White and nobody can take that away from us, no matter what language we speak. We don't have to prove our color to anybody. But for all of those ignorants out there who cannot differentiate what is or who is a White person; do me a favor pick up an anthropology book or dictionary and look under different race and maybe you could see where the Spanish people belong. Please stop this nonsense. Just because we have a different culture from White Americans doesn't make us less White.

One very important contribution that us Spanish people made in World War II was that we were Germany's ally, and we were and are more extremist than you concerning race related subjects. Read our history and you'll find out thank you; PS. Most of us Hispanics believe in White nationalism.

Well, Jorge, you are incorrect. Some very enlightened groups do recognize that Hispanics may well be White. After all, "Hispanic" is a construction created by the census bureau. It frightens me that the Nazi Party has a much more sophisticated analysis of the ambiguity of the definition than most multicultural books I have read, than the liberal discourse I have heard, or than what I have observed in schools. A young man explained: "When the drugs come from Columbia, blame the Latino and Mexican race, not Whites." There are differing Hispanic races? (It would have been nice for the author-narrator to be able to spell Colombia correctly.) So now there is not just one, but two? This is a new metaphor—Race as Juicy Fruit Gum (you got two—two races in one!). Gloria Estefan really got it wrong; we are *not* brothers held together by a common language.

*Stormfront,* the Nazi web site, recognizing the need for multicultural understanding among white brothers, maintains English, Spanish, and German versions. Let us not forget that the president (for eternity?) of Paraguay was named Strossner, the liberator of the southern part of South America was named O'Higgins, one of my favorite journalists is named Jacobo Timmermin (Oops, he was Jewish—Sorry. Does this mean he can't be White or can't be Hispanic? Or both? Or one? Or none?). If I think back to friends from Colombia and other countries from "Latin" America, their last names were: Warner, Froheberg, Shmucklevinsky, Holtz, Marconi, Italiano, and Sigendorf. Perhaps white people are alive and well and living in Latin America. However, if I stop in Puerto Rico to find the enigmatic white person, please realize I will not be Jorge's brother or sister, and I will never use the soap in Jorge's house, and I have no intention of buying a used lampshade from him.

> The census bureau classifies half of all Hispanics as White. White Nationalists generally feel the same way. That portion of the Hispanic population that blends in and displays no hostility of a personal or political kind may remain. That group of Hispanics who want to see the Southwestern U.S. annexed to Mexico would not be welcome.

Once again White becomes political. Only the Hispanics who *do not* recognize that the Southwest cannot be extricated from Mexico and who, like tumbleweed, can blend into the landscape can claim whiteness. This is clearly a very interesting geographic tradition. Must be a white thing. Must be a natural sort of geographic feature. There are mountains, mesas, and *tapados*. On one side we have the good Latinos who are White.

So many of the Nazi, Skinhead, and Aryan Nation pages reach out for their Spanish-speaking brethren. In some ways it is heartrending and gratifying. If you let your Spanish-speaking brothers stay, do they have to do windows or just the lawn?

Concurrently, white people, who have been abused, berated, had their country stolen from them and are at risk of extinction, now have to contend not only with Montezuma's revenge but also with Hitler's revenge. I guess it could really be described as a white man's version of Jewish guilt in the I-told-you-so vein:

> There is a sense in which current immigration policy is Adolph Hitler's posthumous revenge on America. The U.S. political elite emerged from the war passionately concerned to cleanse itself from all taints of racism or xenophobia. Eventually, it enacted the epochal Immigration Act (technically, the Immigration and Nationality Act Amendments) of 1965. And this, quite accidentally, triggered a renewed mass immigration, so huge and so systematically different from anything that had gone before as to transform—and ultimately, perhaps, even to destroy—the one unquestioned victor of World War II: the American nation, as it had evolved by the middle of the twentieth century.

Accidental immigration? The United States destroyed? The white man does believe in evolution, the statement said: "the American nation evolved." That should put the creationist argument to bed for a while.

> Consider crime. Right now 25 percent of the prisoners in our federal penitentiaries are immigrants. Thirty-five to forty percent of the heroin that comes into this country is smuggled in by Nigerians, and U.S. law enforcement officials estimate that an incredible 75 percent of all Nigerians in this country are engaged in some sort of systematic fraud. . . . The list goes on and on, with different ethnic groups tending to specialize in different crimes.

I would like to know what type of crime the white person engages in, what is the white person's specialized crime? Is it polyester? Or could it be transgressing the boundaries of good taste and wearing shorts in the summer?

Tuberculosis is on the rise again, mostly due to immigration. Exotic tropical diseases are starting to be reported in the U.S., again due to immigration. Public health officials estimate that 10,000 people would probably die within months if yellow fever, endemic in Africa and South America, were to reestablish itself in New Orleans.

No wonder the poor white person is hiding out.

KEEP FIGHTING FELLOW WHITES, OR WE WILL FACE EXTINCTION!!!!!!!!!

Has anyone else out there noticed the dramatic increase in interracial dating over the past couple of years? It seems to me that many white women are no longer interested in dating white men. A day doesn't go by when I don't see one or two mixed couples. . . . on weekends I often see over a dozen. What is going on here? Is it just a "fad"? Is it happening all over the country or is it just here in the shadow of Wash DC?

I'm a single white male—I'm told I'm attractive, that I have a good sense of humor. . . I'm reasonably athletic, gainfully employed and what I want more than anything else on earth is to be a husband. But, I seem to be lacking a quality a lot of white women are looking for: black skin.

Could it be that the white man, apparently the most elusive of all creatures, has been hiding from white woman?

Minorities have a better chance for education and jobs through anti-White "Affirmative Action" legislation enacted by a traitorous government out to appease minorities. Minorities turn the streets of our cities into urban jungles, unsafe for you or your children to walk in. Our people exist in fear behind locked doors.

White children are so estranged from their proud Aryan heritage that many take up acting Black and become social degenerates. Children believe that "White and Proud" is an alien concept. White American youth take Blacks and other non-Whites as their heroes and role models. White Aryan Americans are victimized in the land of their forefathers because of the color of their skin. White men and women are so guilt-ridden that they allow minorities to have power over them.

Burdensome racial preference schemes in hiring, racial preference schemes in university admissions, racial preference schemes in government contracting and small business loans. Beyond quotas there is the denial of rights of free speech and of due process to Whites who are critical of these governmental policies. We have special punishments for assaults committed by Whites if the motives might be racial. In addition, Whites pay a proportion of the costs of the welfare state that is disproportionate to what they receive in benefits. But the most exploitative aspect of the situation is that neither the racial quotas, the business preferences, the loss of freedom of speech, nor the disproportionate contributions to the welfare state have managed to sate the appetites of non-Whites living in the United States. The more Whites sacrifice, the more non-Whites demand. Many Whites are beginning to believe that no amount of tribute, other than mass suicide, would satisfy the non-White demands.

When Blacks do not perceive me as a racist because I love my heritage, my anger will stop. I do not hate on the basis of skin color. There are far better reasons to hate someone than the color of their skin. Not allowing me to be proud of my European heritage is at the top of the list.

I write this on the morning of the so-called "Million Man March" on Washington, and would like to make a few points by relating some experiences on the way to work this morning. First off, let me preface this by saying that I do not "hate" other races, but I am proud to be Aryan. I took public transportation to work this morning, a relatively short subway ride. As the journey progressed, I noticed more and more Blacks boarding the train bound for the "Million Man March" site. I felt a mob mentality take over, as is common where Blacks congregate. The black mob begin to shout, verbally abuse, and generally harass the white commuters. I heard such things as "It's time to take over" and "You can't hide from this."

As I took note of all this, I wondered if the white people were hiding under the luggage racks. Next time I am in D.C., I will play Glenda the Good Witch and tell them to come out from their hiding spaces (or closets), the tornado is over.

These people hate us, and they want blood. My point is this: These people were clearly together and spoke with one voice. I have yet to witness white-collar average Joe American exhibit this sort of cohesiveness; we're all too busy taking care of our own asses. White America, it's time to wake up and smell the slime. We've given blacks every opportunity in the form of affirmative action, quotas, welfare, public dole; you name it. It's not opportunity they want, they want control of the country. They want to see all whites enslaved or hanging from trees.

You want to push us out of our own country!

I am not a racist, but I hate this whole idea of being squashed into one super-culture with everyone else. I am not african-american or latin-american. I am white, if anything I am a European-American . . . The more Whites sacrifice, the more non-Whites demand. We are being exterminated, and squeezed out of our country.

I want to ask white people how these conclusions were made. Much like the movie *On the Beach,* there is no response, the connection once again is severed, high on a moonscape of apprehension, and ultimately there is only silence. My next-door neighbor is on vacation. He forgot to take his flag down. It is blowing in the slight morning breeze. There was a bumper sticker circulating in Miami several years ago that said: "Will the last American to leave Miami please take the flag?" Guess he forgot.

> [The West] has not yet understood that whites, in a world become too small for its inhabitants, are now a minority and that the proliferation of other races dooms our race, my race, irretrievably to extinction in the century to come, if we hold fast to our present moral principles.
> —Francois LeBeau

The great American melting pot is already changing hue, and Whites in cities as diverse as Detroit and Miami are experiencing the oddity and strangeness of being outnumbered in their own communities. In California, a state with a population of 26 million, White pupils are a minority in the public schools, accounting for a mere 31.4 percent. Whites only account for 58 percent of California's population. In New York State, 40 percent of the children in elementary and secondary schools are non-White and the figures may exceed 50 percent in a decade. A recent investigation by Time Magazine points out that in San Jose, bearers of the Vietnam surname Nguyen outnumber the Joneses in the telephone book by fourteen columns to eight. The West has, in fact, been re-won by another race, and the same thing is happening in the East, South and North. . . .

> Any attempt to preserve the integrity of the White race, in their view, constitutes the most vile form of racism and bigotry, and anyone advocating such a plan must be pilloried as a dangerous criminal.

What does it say for us as educators, as teachers, as parents, as people when I cannot distinguish between Nazi web sites and those of teachers, future teachers, parents, and professors?

> What makes me so sick about this whole teacher education program is that I am supposed to learn all about the Hispanics, the Blacks, and the Asians, when do you think that it will stop and they will learn to be Americans like the rest of us? Do you know sometimes when I go downtown nobody speaks English!

> It's almost a crime to be White and proud. Government works for big business and the minority, forgetting the White majority. Politicians and government leaders fail to emphasize the importance of quality education, squandering millions of tax dollars, with the only results being illiteracy and an alarmingly high drop-out rate. Interracial dating is being promoted by Hollywood and television. White Aryan girls lower themselves, feeling pressured into race-mixing with non-Whites to be "politically correct" and accepted by friends.

Having journeyed into the heart of whiteness, I am petrified by it and of it. My child used to have a pet dinosaur named "Him." "Him" was used to "break nightmares" and chase the monsters from underneath his bed. I wonder if that is where the white people are hiding. I look under the bed. There are no white people hiding. No-one is there. (I also check the closet, given the many homophobic comments I heard—thou dost protest too much.) I cannot see the whites of their eyes, so I cannot shoot. The invisibility of whiteness may make it linguistic, or may make it paleontological, or may make it a phantom. I still cannot write about whiteness, or on whiteness, or define whiteness, I can't find him anywhere (whiteness must be a he), I think he is a poltergeist—an authentic poltergeist.

Feeling thwarted in my mission, I decide to go out and listen to some music. Ron is playing with his band at a nearby saloon. I am sipping my coffee, my eyes gazing down, reflecting. . . . Suddenly I focus in on the music and hear: "Play that funky music, white boy." I look up, thinking perhaps there is still some hope. But all I see is Ron singing the song. I walk outside and hum to myself "Where have all the white boys gone?"

## BIBLIOGRAPHY

Bakhtin, M. (1984). *Problems of Dostoevsky's Poetics.* Ed. and trans. C. Emerson. Minneapolis: University of Minnesota Press.

Chicago Cultural Studies Group. (1994). "Critical Multiculturalism." In *Multiculturalism: A Critical Reader.* London: Blackwell.

Clark, K., and Holquist M. (1984). *Mikhail Bakhtin.* Cambridge, MA: Harvard University Press.

Gillborn, D. (1995). "Racism, Identity and Modernity: Pluralism, Moral Anti-Racism, and Plastic Ethnicity." *International Studies in Sociology of Education,* 5, no. 1.

Levitas, R. (1990). *The Concept of Utopia.* New York: Syracuse University Press.

Morson, G., and Emerson, C. (1990). *Mikhail Bakhtin: Creation of a Prosaic.* Stanford, CA: Stanford University Press.

Perez-Firmat, G. (1994). *Life on the Hyphen: The Cuban-American Way.* Austin: University of Texas Press.

Quantz, R. and O'Conner, T. (1988) "Writing Critical Ethnography: Dialogue, Multivoicedness, and Carnival in Cultural Texts." *Educational Theory* 38 (Winter), 1: 95-109.

Regaldo, J. (1995). "Community Coalition Building." In M. Baldassare, (ed.), *The Los Angeles Riots.* Boulder, CO: Westview.

Roman, L. (1993). "White Is a Color! White Defensiveness, Postmodernism, and Anti-Racist Pedagogy." In C. McCarthy, and W. Crichlow, (eds.), *Race Identity and Representation.* New York: Routledge.

# FOURTEEN

# Computer-Assisted Racism

*Toward an Understanding
of "Cyberwhiteness"*

**Vicki K. Carter**

Do not enter, snowy heron, in the valley where the crows are
    quarreling.
Such angry crows are envious of your whiteness,
And I fear that they will soil the body you have washed in
    the pure stream.

                       —Korean poem

Although the sijo (a traditional Korean poetic form) prefacing this
chapter may have been written as early as the twelfth century, its imagery
and the purity symbolized by the concept of whiteness are quite
contemporary. For decades, white America has sought to preserve its
"pure stream" by ignoring, withdrawing from, or constructing spaces
inaccessible or hostile to the quarreling residents of the valley; white
flight from city to suburb serves as one familiar scenario. This ongoing
separateness has been accomplished, in part, by physical, social, and
today virtual constructions of reality.

In metaphoric terms the poem could be interpreted in a variety of ways, but in a multicultural context it has much affinity to concepts of whiteness as they are currently being examined and refined. Consider the historically cyclical meanings and locations of the valley, the pure stream, the quarreling angry crows, and the snowy herons as they relate to a society at this moment in the process of being redefined by hyperreal educational methods, virtual classrooms, educational software, and distance education—a society that still manages to avoid and refrain from acknowledging the valley or the crows. The unexamined pristine whiteness existing within Western society is reproduced by and within its technologies, its citizens and students washed anew in a pure stream situated in the realm of cyberspace, a stream representing the newest form of white America's flight to suburbia.

In 1984 William Gibson's novel *Neuromancer* introduced the idea of "cyberspace," a referent to a constructed, infinite world of navigable information. This chapter will argue that currently the pedagogical overlap between a critical multiculturalism beginning to be practiced and technologically mediated education operating within the terrain of cyberspace is infinitesimal and yet must be seen as a crucial dimension of a conceptual exploration of whiteness. While cultural workers acting in solidarity with marginalized groups that seek justice, fairness, and equality struggle inside the confines and trappings of conventional school structures, education mediated through Internet technologies is being promoted and funded by educational administrators, political power structures, and commercial ventures in accord with the United States government's agenda to network the country. If the whiteness existing in cyberspace is to be identified and confronted along with other locales of whiteness, traditional disciplinary fringe areas surrounding these new cultural and educational "neighborhoods" must be recognized, negotiated, and crossed.

This chapter links contemporary technological infrastructures with whiteness as framed by Toni Morrison (1993) and Ruth Frankenberg (1993). It also investigates ecological and social aspects of education mediated by technologies and provides examples of cyberspace whiteness. Finally, commentary on mainstream views toward the technological infrastructure vis-à-vis "cyberwhiteness" is presented as an agenda for moving beyond the status quo.

## FRANKENBERG AND
## MORRISON—WHITENESS AND CYBERSPACE

Frankenberg's book *White Women, Race Matters* (1993) and Toni Morrison's *Playing in the Dark* (1993) are among several contemporary works examining multiculturalism and introducing the concept of whiteness. The perspectives of these two authors, while not directed toward technology as a topic, assist in exploring connections between whiteness and today's multidimensional technologies. For example, in the second of Frankenberg's two-part analysis of the life-shaping influence of race, cultural environments interpreted via historical, social, and political discourse are considered. This analysis applied to computers and networks is exceptionally appropriate with respect to forms of neoexpansionism and neocolonialism facilitated by technologies. Eurocentrism and contemporary configurations of cultural imperialism are sweeping into new cyberterritories and terrains just as they swept into America when it was a new nation. Cyberspace, viewed as ownerless but ideologically Western and White, is ripe for shaping and sustaining the same underlying oppression as that which constituted America's pioneer days.

Frankenberg's contemplation of whiteness as delimited by a locale of structural advantage, a standpoint, and a set of assumed normative unbounded cultural practices is appropriate and eminently applicable to an analysis of technological discourses. Her observations about the relationship of people of color to systems of domination fit technological systems generally and educational technologies in particular. Systems of domination and unmarked white cultural practice are the means by which non-Whites are expected to engage the institutions of a society "structured in racial dominance" (1993, 234). In corporate and academic America, classed, raced, and gendered systems interact negatively, sometimes violently, with people who do not or cannot automatically participate in them. Instructional systems and new social media such as the Internet are also systems of domination and cultural normativity as yet unmapped onto the current critique of racial and multicultural theory and pedagogical practice. In contrast to the commonly accepted idea of technology as inherently neutral and the Internet as a site of democracy and revolutionary social perspectives, technologically facilitated spaces may well be the newest forms of white havens where turmoil can be left behind and, concurrently, where a dramatic effort to protect and project whiteness as a normative pervasive cultural practice can be enacted and recovered. In a similar vein, scholar Joe Lockard (1996, 6) writes: "Cyberspace is unmistakably signed with Euro-American whiteness. Online monoculturalism reiterates the external racism prevalent in American social structures. Middle-class America, confronted with diversity, has retreated to cyberspace."

Author Toni Morrison offered insights into literary devices, rhetorical tactics, and topics for critical investigation embedded within her examination of the Africanist presence in American fiction. Morrison's perspective on the soil of America as a new world, a pristine land proclaiming the ideals of freedom while erasing from consideration its unfree slave population, was both poignant and eerily transportable to the new spaces being created by means of technological constructions such as the National Information Infrastructure. Given that networking, computer software, and instructional systems are full-blown forms of text and discourse, Morrison's methods of examining literary devices and tactics and her linguistic taxonomies are especially useful for a thematically similar critique of cyberspace.

Morrison (1993) theorized that until recently, the overarching assumption of writers of American fiction, regardless of their own ethnicity, has been that the reader is White. Research into educational software has corroborated this assumption, finding that the "reader" is assumed to be male as well (Huff and Cooper 1987). In other words, like American literature, American software often may be complicit in acts of racism, classism, and gender bias. Morrison outlined several linguistic strategies employed as recipes to portray and reference Blacks in books for and about white people. Technologically mediated education, now in a formative period comparable to the nascent years of American literature, bears many similarities to these strategies. Stereotypes abound in educational software and web-based instruction; the flat, weak, one-dimensional images and representations magnify stereotypical characterizations. Nonwhite characters are often erased and displaced and the technique of "collapsing persons into animals" (68) is an almost-mature art form. By turning people into cartoon-like characters and animals, issues of inclusion and diversity can be avoided. Morrison also believes difference is deliberately magnified in texts, foreclosing the civilizing process and, in effect, excluding history "as a process of becoming" (68). From Morrison's perspective, then, technological educational worlds as forms of text and literature will also extend history forward into what has come to be termed virtual reality and, as she points out, truly extend civilizing processes infinitely. As technology and cyberwhiteness are analyzed further, Morrison's efforts to focus on and notice the creator or author must be applied to hyperreal contexts as well, so that on the World Wide Web it also becomes possible "to avert the critical gaze from the racial object to the racial subject; from the described and imagined to the describers and imaginers; from the serving to the served" (90).

## SOCIAL AND ECOLOGICAL ASPECTS OF EDUCATION MEDIATED BY TECHNOLOGY

In order to make them meaningful in an educational context, technology and whiteness must be examined, albeit with extreme brevity, from a broader social and ecological perspective using techniques and structures akin to those introduced by Frankenberg (1993) and Morrison (1993). As previously noted, the Internet or cyberspace is analogous in many ways to the establishment of an independent America over 200 years ago. Morrison's description of American literature in its formative years is comparable to the "text" and discourse created by the Internet and educational technologies. Morrison describes a young America as "pressing toward a future of freedom" (33), a "flight from oppression and limitation to freedom and possibility," a "vision of a limitless future, made more gleaming by the constraint, dissatisfaction, and turmoil left behind" (34). So often technology and educational technologies in particular are praised as inherently democratic and pluralistic, creating equal opportunities for learning and promoting social reform. Yet how very strongly these two descriptions of the creation of new places and spaces evoke thoughts of the herons and the crows. In fact, many veteran users of the Internet and technology are already bemoaning the fact that great masses of the networking "unwashed"—both White and non-White—are invading their pure stream. As theorist D. Goodman (1995) states, the Internet elite are now having "to contend with the flood of newbies onto their previously comfy Internet" (10), resulting in "an exodus of the more knowledgeable folks to other areas" (11), different, quieter, undefiled, and more pristine spaces to build anew. These sorts of withdrawals may be viewed as simply a recovery of "white nerd" space, but the reality may be more like the concept of Aaron Gresson's (1995) recovery of race, a maneuver to get back a threatened positionality and reinforcing an assumed area of entitlement where whiteness is central and where its images are powerful.

Winner's (1986) description of Long Island bridges constructed with clearances so low that inner-city buses cannot be accommodated is a clear and (pun intended) concrete example of a technology supporting politics and power—a very recent example of fundamental American whiteness caught in the act of protecting its purity and isolation. Even laundry products are marketed with the attitude that whiteness is so highly desirable that more and more whiteness has to be the laundry-doers' ultimate goal. In today's capitalist society, it is not surprising that technologies and techniques of all types are imbued with politics and power, for they not only change the social, but they also reflect and contain the social. After all, technological products built, distributed, sold, and employed are those deemed valuable and acceptable, thereby configuring power and politics squarely within economic architectures. And so it is easy enough to see and understand the purpose and ramifications behind the Long Island bridges and the subtler message conveyed by the quest to achieve the whitest wash possible. On the other hand, the complexities and even the size of information and educational technologies such as networks and computers constructed with microchips so small they cannot be seen by the naked eye are much less tangible than bridges and clothing, more difficult to grasp, identify, and interrogate. Scientist D. Gelernter (1989, 66) provides a transitional analogy from bridges to microchips when he writes: "What iron, steel and reinforced concrete were in the late 19th and early 20th centuries, software is now: the preeminent medium for building new and visionary structures." And as scientist D. Hess (1995, viii) says, "the complexities of how national cultures continue to reproduce themselves in new settings" are misunderstood, ignored, or remain unobserved. Such is the case today with cyberspace and the whiteness located within its networks, computers, and information systems.

An ecological understanding and approach to technology further magnifies its effects. Technologist A. Feenberg (1991, 7) suggests technologies are a cultural form, a system "that restructures the entire social world as an object of control," in essence making subject into object. Postman (1992) employs an ecological metaphor in describing technology not as something that is added or subtracted but instead a factor causing the world to be different and permanently changed. In other words, as computers and networks become a part of what constitutes an ordinary day, new environments with different paradigms and changed conditions for survival are created, a change equivalent to introducing movable type and overlaying air traffic and its support systems upon most of the world's continents. Following these kinds of ecological shifts, existing institutions begin to struggle with the power of, resistance to, and proselytizing elements of newly introduced technology. Often metaphors surface, employed to describe the new technologies. For instance, computers often are portrayed as automated filing cabinets. Icons associated with electronic mail systems resemble old-fashioned mailboxes. Messages are graphically represented as stamped envelopes. The National Information Infrastructure is known as the "Information Superhighway." These metaphors are intentionally backward facing and familiar so that people feel safer and less threatened by change.

Computers and networks in a postmodern world cross borders that traditional technologies, disciplines, and practices do not. They function not just as tools and devices for blue-collar assembly lines and pink-collar clerical work but also as sites and locations, as border-usurping virtual communities. Computers become doorways to cyberspace and to cyberwhiteness as well. They are the metaphorical thresholds to cyberspace's elite white territories, places of privilege, and "New Age weekend getaways for higher consciousness" (Hess 1995, 116). Cyberspace is a comfortable place to be White because of its normative cultural practices. Authors J. Brook and I. Boal (1995) believe the white flight into cyberspace was motivated by some of the same desires and anxieties as the white migration to the suburbs. And so far the Internet does remain a relatively inaccessible economic and cultural locale; it is another border to cross in an allegedly borderless environment for non-Whites. Comfortably white cyberspace is a significant part of today's technoculture that demands a thoughtful ecological analysis of how cultural hegemony is being reproduced and a traditionally conservative whiteness is being retrenched, retained, and maintained within a space typically marketed as a locale for free speech and open access.

## EDUCATIONAL CYBERWHITENESS

Examples of whiteness and erasure of nonwhite minority populations abound in software available at every level of instruction, in public, private, and higher education, in instruction delivered at a distance, part of institutionally and commercially developed software, and in resources on the Internet. For example, there are several sites on the World Wide Web (WWW) providing children's stories and songs; all the characters are white. Advertised on the WWW are pamphlets or manuals providing instruction on myriad topics such as child care, planning for water systems, and shop safety; all the cover photography depicts white men, women, and children engaged in these activities. A children's step-by-step video guide to their first garden is packaged portraying an idyllic scene with two white children surrounded by flowers, green plants, pumpkins, turtles, and a little bunny rabbit. The subjects of the artwork for an on-line children's poetry presentation are not only all white, but all blond and mostly male. In a children's "paint" module, the kids holding the paintbrush are White. In tutorials for learning the alphabet and mathematics, letters become animated and turn into blond little girls or dolls, X rays (for the letter X) are of a white male, and an ear of corn, the letter "E," transforms into a human ear—a white ear, of course. The images packaged with mathematics and memory-enhancing software modules are white professors and blond men. The popular (and award-winning) software *Where in the World is Carmen Sandiego?* is replete with stereotypical images of marginalized groups.

The instances just described are only a few examples of much of the "learning" software offered to young students and are manifestations of Frankenberg's and Morrison's theoretical positions. Unfortunately, these examples would not raise many eyebrows; most educators create and design their products according to a white, male, Western European model. In fact, even many females adopt male stereotypes. Research on sex bias in educational software found that male *and* female teachers envision and describe their students as male. Furthermore, because "the world of computers and computing technology is mostly inhabited by men, and social-psychological research indicates that the expectations an individual has about another person can shape his or her interaction with that person" (Huff and Cooper 1987, 519), it is not surprising that software is developed and presented in male-oriented formats. These formats—game-oriented software, for example—can discourage women and minorities who consequently have less chance to become skilled with it. Software design, moreover, can affect in-school or on-the-job performance outcomes for non-Whites and non-males in addition to the difficulty using and understanding instructional products built within this genre (Fiske and Taylor 1984).

Imagine for a moment three instances in which the economics of opportunity costs are being discussed. In a traditional classroom the teacher might describe a scenario in which a young man was trying to decide whether to leave home and rent his own apartment. This scenario is already easily construed as a white dilemma; however, given a classroom setting, it is possible students could imagine an African American, Asian, or Native American young man. If these circumstances were presented in a critically multicultural classroom environment, the scenario would be discussed in terms of race and gender cognizance, power, and privilege. Now, consider a second instance in which an instructor has added a multimedia component to the classroom. The situation is the same, except audio-visual representations show two young white men standing outside a large suburban single-family home discussing the opportunity costs of renting an apartment. Without a doubt, race and cultural assumptions are now visibly present but can still be recognized and explored. In a third scenario a student is at home, connected to the Internet, working through a tutorial on opportunity costs. Once more, video and audio components contain affluent, white, suburban young men conferring about renting an apartment, but in this case the opportunity for dialogue and confrontation is completely missing. In this third example the venue is elitist, racist, and basically precludes opportunity for dialogue. Has this technologically mediated educational format made learning better, more democratic, active, or meaningful?

In the world of business and industry, training and technology-based job aids have become commonplace. In a series of training modules on wastewater treatment developed for a diverse group of blue-collar plant personnel, a white "guide" leads students through the program even though most of the workers who avail themselves of the training materials are non-White. In a presentation on "doing good instructional design," the presenter describes cultural sensitivity as a design requirement while at the same time displaying slides containing clip art full of white people, except for one slide. In this one instance, a black woman is present in the group, but the background on the slide is also black, effectively erasing the woman from the visual composition.

Evidence to the contrary notwithstanding, mediated educational modules are not all racist and unconsidered. For example, an excellent case study learning module addressing integration in post-Apartheid South Africa is available on the Internet. Just like textbooks, some software products can be more inclusive and supportive of racial identities and diversity issues than others. However, it is not just images that are at issue but also more subtle hidden agendas, codes, and curricula comprising instructional designs created by practitioners in these fields, practitioners who are mostly white men and white women. The subtler messages encoded within the designs are unwittingly aided by the complicity of educators who may not be practitioners of a critical multiculturalism, who are comfortable with (or oblivious to) the status quo, and who often are highly technophobic.

Typically, issues of access are paramount—if not singular—when the web, educational technologies, and supporting hardware and software are examined. Availability, cost, and accessibility of technology for marginalized groups are obvious obstacles for uniformly providing these types of resources to schools and educational institutions. Distribution of technology in minority communities and acquisition of specialized forms of "literacy" required to make use of technology vary significantly between black and white households. In one statistical "for instance," home computer use differed from Whites to Blacks by a ratio of 26.9 million to 1.5 million ("High-Tech Redlining" 1995). Communications networks deployed into black and minority communities may well be a theme-and-variation on the interstate highway system begun decades ago; they represent the potential for continuing the destruction of black and minority culture and community.

## EXPANDING THE VIEW OF THE STATUS QUO

In spite of the perception that the Internet is universalistic and democratic, in practice the web is a hegemonic locale where considerations of who is represented and who is not remain unacknowledged. Moreover, the limitations and structures of technology in many ways narrow the idea of presence and voice. Although there are sites created by underrepresented and marginalized groups and other sites (such as Computerusers Against Racist Expressions and the Center for the Study of White American Culture, Inc.) that understand that white culture is not necessarily *American* culture, these are far outnumbered by other pages full of unexamined whiteness and white privilege. Many ultra-conservative organizations have constructed elaborate sites promoting white nationalism, white power, and an Aryan society. Even educational efforts such as Internet art museums, the Online Book Initiative, the ALEX catalog of electronic texts, and Project Gutenberg contain very few works by African Americans. These few examples help to expose the Internet as another technique to omit or "write out" roles associated with the marginalized and the narratives of alterity, essentially to erase the problems associated with race, class, and gender.

Mediated education and cyberworlds are too often sites of coloni-zation, recolonization, and racial recovery for a white culture rather than venues for implementing traditional educational objectives of empowerment, democracy, and liberation. Drawing on a critical philosophy of education, educational technologies as text and discourse must be examined alternatively via critical questions, such as post-structuralist Cherryholmes' (1988) admonition to ask whose authority is represented in discourse and who is listening. Whose speech is permitted and authorized and who does not speak? Educator Patti Lather (1991) believes a reader also speaks via a text; if so, how do students react when their very presence and their voices do not even exist in the text? Where are their possibilities and what violence and harm occurs as a result of the absence of possibility? As previously described, Morrison (1993, xii) feels the presence and intentions of the author—his or her "blindness and sight"—are elements of the activity and image-producing process involved in the struggle to interpret text and discourse. Educational practitioners and cultural workers must always be suspicious, looking closely and asking themselves whether all parties are present in mediated forms of learning and whether full opportunity for dialogue exists as part of their "products," that is, the texts being created. Educators and cultural workers cannot assume universality or presume community within any text, for to do so is to ignore multiple forms of power and privilege.

Even critical educators often are not fully cognizant of the impact of the World Wide Web upon education and teaching and learning practices. Although Simon (1992) questions technology as a practice of semiotic production, he fails to critique technology itself as a location of text outside of the classroom. Similarly, Cherryholmes (1988) examines the asymmetrical connections between reader and text but also adheres to traditional classroom interactions as sites of textual production and power. Joe Kincheloe (1993, 86) critiques the tidal wave of electronic information and hyperreality, stating "class and racial inequalities are perpetrated by new technologies and at the same time rendered more impervious to exposure by the removal of those with limited access to information from those who produce it." Kincheloe's analysis of the effect of image and the nature of today's information formats goes further than that of Simon and Cherryholmes, but it stops short of engaging the contribution of educational technologies to class and racial inequalities outside the confines of the traditional classroom.

Describing the modern discourse of prediction, systems, and control, Borgmann (1992), perhaps inadvertently, illuminates an ironic relationship among critical pedagogy, critical multiculturalism, and technological systems. Borgmann feels nonsubstantive shell-like "objectified and disavowed versions of ourselves" have been left "in the universe we are trying to understand and shape. We vacate our first-person place and presence in the world just when we mean to take responsibility for its destiny" (2-3). Borgmann's description is an apt one, as whiteness is examined because it seems as if at the very historical moment when a critical multiculturalism is beginning to be introduced as practice into traditional classroom environments, whiteness has begun to move on to alternate and less easily critiqued time and space. There is little recognition that computer networks and instructional materials delivered on computers and at a distance are sites of cultural imperialism, recolonization, racism, patriarchy, or whiteness. In many cases these circumstances are unconsidered and unintentional results of course material design and development, but, nevertheless, they have the effect of exacerbating what is already a world of comfortably ensconced white folks satisfied with, if not actively sustaining, a hegemonic positionality. If a vision of a different future is attainable, the social and physical realities of mediated education must be recognized as significant factors that represent and order educational processes.

## CONCLUSION

Where are critically oriented multiculturalists vis-à-vis the Internet and educational technologies? Is there a Cornell West, bell hooks, Aaron Gresson, or Toni Morrison writing about or problematizing techno-logically mediated education? Are there feminist, Hispanic, gay/lesbian, or physically challenged presences involved in critiquing these cultural terrains? Are there spaces for dialogue and ways to respond to messages promulgated through technologically mediated environ-ments that raise possibilities for human interaction, intervention, and choice? Mostly not. Educators who practice a critical pedagogy focus almost entirely on the traditional classroom and a face-to-face educa-tional environment as their paradigm. Cultural studies as an arena for social and educational commentary concentrate on the effect and affect of "popular" media such as television, film, and music accessed via traditional means. Meanwhile, as critical pedagogy and critical multi-culturalism explore the accouterments of whiteness, a "virtual" white-ness is being perpetuated at an astonishing rate in the instructional systems, educational technologies, and instruction delivered through "our" National Information Infrastructure.

As a relatively small group of educators think through the pedagog-ical issues of multiculturalism, and an even smaller group of educational technology professionals consider the ethics and morals of their praxis, a formidable cadre of instructional designers, instructional programmers, distance educators, and commercial providers, most of whom are white men and white women, are developing technologically mediated instruc-tion. These practitioners are reproducing images in cyberspace framed by their own unexamined whiteness and reproducing a social construc-tion of reality cloaked by its own invisibility. Except for issues of access to technology and infrastructure, the various realms of educational technology research and practice seldom engage in paradigm-changing dialogue or interrogate issues of diversity and multiculturalism. At most, within these disciplines difference is "appreciated" and marginalizing systems are accepted as normative instead of their centrality being questioned. Consequently, as the seeds of critical multiculturalism and pedagogy start to become rooted in traditional classrooms, a form of uncontested, unproblematized cultural imperialism grows unchecked in the less familiar terrain of cyberspace—part of "that cultural space with the most political significance of all, the dominant space called whiteness" (Frankenberg 1993, 231).

As agendas for critical multiculturalism are developed and implemented, workers in consonance with these agendas must keep in mind the quarreling crows and the snowy herons described in the poem at the beginning of this chapter. Educators and cultural workers must become "critical friends" willing to contest and erase the boundaries imposed by disciplines and special interests so that the valleys, landscapes, and pure streams in the terrain of cyberspace do not remain unexamined domains, reproducing injustices of race, class, and gender inscribed by the purity of whiteness.

## BIBLIOGRAPHY

Borgmann, A. (1992). *Crossing the Postmodern Divide.* Chicago: University of Chicago Press.

Brook, J., and Boal, I. (1995). Preface. In J. Brook and I. Boal (eds.), *Resisting the Virtual Life: The Culture and Politics of Information.* San Francisco: City Lights.

Cherryholmes, C. (1988). *Power and Criticism: Poststructural Investigations in Education.* New York: Teachers College Press.

Feenberg, A. (1991). *Critical Theory of Technology.* New York: Oxford University Press.

Fiske, S., and Taylor, S. (1984). *Social Cognition.* Reading, MA: Addison-Wesley.

Frankenberg, R. (1993). *White Women, Race Matters: The Social Construction of Whiteness.* Minneapolis: University of Minnesota Press.

Gelernter, D. (1989, August). "The Metamorphosis of Information Management." *Scientific American,* 66.

Goodman, D. (1995). "Education and the Internet: The Coming Challenge to Internet Culture." *Syllabus* 9 no. 3, 10-12.

Gresson, A. D., III. (1995). *The Recovery of Race in America.* Minneapolis: University of Minnesota Press.

Hess, D. J. (1995). *Science and Technology in a Multicultural World: The Cultural Politics of Facts and Artifacts.* New York: Columbia University Press.

"High-Tech Redlining." (1995, March-April). *Utne Reader,* 73.

Huff, C., and Cooper, J. (1987). "Sex Bias in Educational Software: The Effect of Designers' Stereotypes on the Software They Design." *Journal of Applied Social Psychology* 17, no. 6, 519-532.

Kincheloe, J. (1993). *Toward a Critical Politics of Teacher Thinking.* Westport, CT: Bergin & Garvey.

Lather, P. (1991). *Getting Smart: Feminist Research and Pedagogy With/in the Postmodern.* New York: Routledge.

Lockard, J. (1996). Virtual Whiteness and narrative diversity. *Undercurrent.* Available World Wide Web URL: http://darkwing.uoregon.edu/~heroux/uc4/4-lockard.html.

Morrison, T. (1993). *Playing in the Dark: Whiteness and the Literary Imagination.* New York: Vintage Books.

Postman, N. (1992). *Technopoly.* New York: Vintage Books.

Simon, R. (1992). *Teaching Against the Grain.* New York: Bergin and Garvey.

Winner, L. (1986). *The Whale and the Reactor.* Chicago: University of Chicago Press.

# FIFTEEN

# The Learning Organization

*Reproduction of Whiteness*

**Sharon L. Howell**

The learning organization is a Eurocentric construct that naturalizes whiteness as the unspoken cultural norm against which success is measured. Socioeconomic exploitation and hardship are ignored within this monocultural perspective. While holding out the promise of participation, empowerment, and collaboration within a culture of trust and equity, issues of power and control are ignored. Here I use Whirlpool Corporation as an example of a learning organization in the process of development to illustrate the unnamed structural and cultural norms of whiteness.

## A LEARNING ORGANIZATION IN THE MAKING?

Growing up in St. Joseph, Michigan, across the river from Benton Harbor and world headquarters of Whirlpool Corporation, I was aware of the gradual change in the racial makeup of the community. During the 1950s, the small African American community was located mostly in Benton Harbor with the poorest living in the "flats," a slum area on the edge of the large open-air fruit and vegetable market near the downtown area. Throughout the 1950s and 1960s, the African American community increased in size as more and more of the migrant labor that followed the fruit and vegetable crops from Florida north into Michigan each year remained in Michigan. In 1968, the City of Benton Harbor, as a part of a federally funded municipal betterment program, condemned the "flats" and the market. This enabled the city to get rid of the unsightly slums on the edge of the downtown area and to move the market to the edge of town and closer to the newly constructed I-94 interstate highway, which replaced rail transportation for the shipment of fruit and vegetables. Cottages and rooms once rented by tourists visiting the House of David, a religious community on the edge of town, became a source of inexpensive housing rented by the week and month by the displaced African Americans (Adkin 1990). Gradually, the African American community increased in size, moving into the older sections of Benton Harbor as white families moved across the river to St. Joseph and into the neighboring townships along Lake Michigan. By 1990 African Americans represented 92.9 percent of Benton Harbor's population with 83 percent residing in single-parent households, the highest percentage of single-parent households in the United States (Horowitz 1995). This pattern of population movement paralleled Detroit, Chicago, and numerous other large urban areas; the number of African Americans in the city and older suburbs increased, as did the number of Whites located in the newer suburban areas. The much-criticized legally enforced segregation of the South became the de facto pattern in the North, an economic and social form of segregation rather than legally enforced segregation.

Also like Detroit and other Midwestern urban areas, the area experienced a decline in the number of manufacturing jobs. Whirlpool Corporation, founded in 1911, is the leading manufacturer of home appliances in the world. As the corporation expanded, it turned to the South in search of locations where labor was cheaper and the unions were not as strong and adversarial. Employing 40,000 people worldwide, Whirlpool now has manufacturing facilities in 11 countries and markets its products in 140 countries (Marquardt 1996). While Whirlpool still has its world headquarters in Benton Harbor, it is important to note that no manufacturing takes place there anymore. All manufacturing occurs in areas where labor is cheaper.

Interestingly, Whirlpool Corporation is identified as a leader in employee empowerment and globalization through organizational learning, an example of a corporation in the process of becoming a learning organization. In 1989 Whirlpool first expanded outside the United States and Canada when it purchased N.V. Philips in the Netherlands. Until this time, the management of Whirlpool was homogeneous, comprised of white middle-class males from the Midwest (Marquardt 1996). Then, almost overnight, this expanded staff was defined as having diverse cultural backgrounds. To mold this newly diversified management group into a team, an annual Worldwide Leadership Conference was started in 1990. The first conference was held in Montreaux, Switzerland, with 150 top managers from 16 countries. The goal of this leadership conference was to develop a unifying corporate vision and to enable this diverse group to learn together to produce and market home appliances in the most efficient way possible (Marquardt 1996; Watkins and Marsick 1993). According to chief executive officer David Whitwam, "We made those 150 people accountable for educating all 38,000 people around the world. When going global, you have to communicate to everyone what the company vision is and what the long-term goals are. And then you have to follow through and design processes that force the interaction to continue" (Marquardt 1996, 115). This conference established the vision of global learning and a values statement that reads in part:

> We, the people of Whirlpool, aren't "in" the company; we "are" the company. As such, we recognize our individual responsibility to assure our collective success by practicing and promoting the following values. . . .
>
> Business with Integrity
>
> We will pursue our business with honor, fairness and respect for both the individual and the public at large . . . ever mindful that there is no right way to do a wrong thing. . . .
>
> Commitment to the Common Good
>
> We will serve responsibly as members of all communities in which we live and work, respecting cultural distinctions throughout the world. We will preserve the environment, prudently utilize natural resources and maintain all property we are privileged to use. (Marquardt 1996, 116)

## THE CORPORATE DISCOURSE ON ORGANIZATION AND ECONOMIC RESTRUCTURING

The organizational development plans implemented by Whirlpool Corporation followed the path taken by many corporations trying to increase market share and thus shareholder value. Organizational structures of the industrial age and the workplace training that supports these structures are based on the concepts of modernist science in that they follow the Cartesian theory of separation of mind and body: managers think and workers act without questioning. Characteristics of this paradigm include performance outcomes that are observable and quantifiable with learning based on deficits detected in the learner. This is a model of a smooth-functioning machine with clear lines of authority, nonoverlapping jobs, and rational systems of delegation and control. The training component, whether provided by traditional schooling or in the workplace, emphasizes individual skill development with a clear distinction drawn between personal and work-related development.

In contrast, the postindustrial age creates changes that range from simplicity to complexity, from a mechanical to a holographic model, from predictability to unpredictability, and from objectivity to multiple perspectives. The external environment now represents fast-changing technology and a more diverse workforce. The emerging paradigm recommended to replace the Cartesian dualism of the industrial age represents the integration of personal and work-related development: an organizational model based on lifelong learning, with a focus on collaboration and teamwork.

In the search for competitive advantage in an increasingly global marketplace, organizations have embraced an evolving set of management strategies to ensure quality. Quality involves measurement and conformance of both the product and the worker to a set of standards as defined by the customer. Organizations demand new education and training initiatives that develop responsible, adaptable workers with appropriate communication, thinking, and problem-solving skills. Focusing on quality, team approaches to work organization depend on enterprising workers capable of lifelong learning. Most recently these management strategies have fallen under the umbrella of organizational learning. Learning is the construction and reconstruction of meaning for the continuous transformation of the organization. A learning organization, according to its advocates, is the ideal organizational model to meet the fast pace of change necessitated by the movement from the industrial age to the postindustrial age and the requirements of global realignment (Handy 1990; Redding and Catalanello 1994; Senge 1990; Watkins and Marsick 1993).

The learning organization, a concept popularized by Peter Senge (1990) in his book *The Fifth Discipline: The Art and Practice of The Learning Organization,* can be defined as "organizations in which people continually expand their capacity to create the results they truly desire, where new and expansive patterns of thinking are nurtured, where collective aspiration is set free, and where people are continually learning how to learn together" (3). Rather than following one fixed path, the learning organization is focused on the ability of its workers and thus the organization to learn and change faster than its competitors. The discourse of the learning organization, with a focus on customer satisfaction, is presented as a neutral management philosophy, purporting to tap the job knowledge of those closest to the actual processes. Workers involved in the decision-making process feel empowered, viewing themselves as valued contributors to the organization, who continually strive to improve their productivity. There is no longer a need for an adversarial relationship between labor and management (Katzenbach and Smith 1993; Scholtes 1988; Senge, Kleiner, Roberts, Ross, and Smith 1994; Walton 1986; Watkins and Marsick 1993).

## RACE AND THE LEARNING ORGANIZATION

Whirlpool Corporation, within the learning organization discourse, illustrates issues related to unequal power differentials as viewed through the lens of unnamed structural and cultural norms of whiteness. The learning organization literature presents a value-neutral organizational construct focused on market issues of competition and increasing shareholder value while ignoring issues of power and inequality. Until the middle of the twentieth century, social and economic inequality with the resulting differential in power and privilege was supported by law. The civil rights movement of the 1960s changed the legal status of minorities, thus masking the continued social and economic inequalities in work and community (Ferguson 1984). "While it is true that the nature of racist oppression and exploitation has changed as slavery has ended and the apartheid structure of Jim Crow has legally changed, white supremacy continues to shape perspectives on reality and to inform the social status of black people and all people of color" (hooks 1989, 114). According to Ruth Frankenberg (1993), racism as viewed from a position of race privilege focuses on the Other as a construct external to the dominant white culture. The discourses of essentialism and color/power evasiveness are identifiable across the learning organization literature and within the concepts of empowerment, teamwork, and quality. "Whiteness, as a set of normative cultural practices, is visible most clearly to those it definitively excludes and those to whom it does violence. Those who are securely housed within its borders usually do not examine it" (228-229). The color/power evasiveness of the leadership within the organizational culture in the United States represses racial awareness and the identification of White as a distinct race that is dominant in relationship to other races. In actuality, whiteness is a place of privilege and dominance. A white European male culture controls the structure and discourse within the organization while those without power, for example, minorities, are stripped of their subjectivity. The literature on learning organizations fails to recognize issues related to race within the context of the unidentified cultural norm of whiteness. The leadership's single-minded focus is on the organization's ability to survive and profit within the global market; ignored are the increasing levels of poverty and suffering at the one extreme and the massive accumulation of wealth by the few at the other extreme. In addition, it is never questioned whether the end result is desirable. People become "human resources," just another economic commodity, to be combined with capital and other forms of material resources to produce increased wealth for the providers of the capital.

The civil rights movement of the 1960s was accompanied by increased demand for equal rights from other minorities as well as high levels of immigration from non-European countries (Rubin 1994). Also, the collapse of Fordism created a threat to the structural norm of the white patriarchal organizational culture. Teamwork, empowerment, customer service, and quality—tools of the learning organization—while ostensibly diminishing the androcentric hierarchical organizational structure by giving more control to those close to the work, tacitly serve to recover the pre-1960s hegemony of white patriarchy. The rhetoric of recovery focuses on individual opportunity and commitment within the myth of manifest destiny and the superiority of the white European population of the United States (Gresson 1995).

The initial upheavals and restructuring of the post-Fordist marketplace were experienced first by African Americans who migrated to the cities of the North in ever-increasing numbers during the 1940s and 1950s as the invention of the mechanical cotton picker and the South's full economic recovery from the Civil War eliminated the need for widespread use of sharecropping. African Americans found employment in urban areas as unskilled factory workers with hopes of moving into higher-paying skilled jobs. However, technological advances beginning as early as the 1950s decreased the number of unskilled jobs available in manufacturing, creating high unemployment rates among African Americans and cutting off millions from entry into the largely white middle-class mainstream of life in the United States. The impact of automation resulted in the loss of more than 1,500,000 blue-collar jobs between 1956 and 1962, mainly in the unskilled entry-level jobs that African Americans hoped to fill. Beginning in the mid-1950s, new automated manufacturing plants were located in suburban industrial parks away from strong union plants in the urban areas. This was the beginning of the trend that first moved manufacturing from north to south and then overseas. African Americans who made up about 25 percent of the workforce in the urban areas were hit by both the relocation of the factories to the suburbs and automation, which reduced the need for unskilled labor (Rifkin 1995). Increased unemployment can be the result of restructuring within the capitalist marketplace as workers move from one industry to another. The recession of 1979 to 1982 hit African Americans before they had recovered from the recession of 1973 to 1975. There was also a structural crisis of declining productivity during this period, with the United States unable to compete with industries in West Germany and Japan. The government implemented its usual programs to sustain employment, but this time the multinational corporations closed factories permanently and began to move production to cheaper labor markets in the Sunbelt and to Third World countries (Jennings 1992, 152-153). The government actually has encouraged the movement of manufacturing overseas with programs sponsored by the U.S. Agency for International Development that encourage capitalist forms of economic development. The number of workers employed in manufacturing dropped from 26 percent in 1970 to 18 percent in 1991 with a predicted drop to 12.5 percent by the turn of the century (Rubin 1994, 223-224). The transformation of the economy has some individuals predicting a future of increasing joblessness for increasing numbers of people (Rifkin 1995; Steinberg 1996).

This phenomenon of increased automation and of the movement of the factories to areas of lower labor costs was generally ignored until it began to affect white workers. The underclass, portrayed as Black, urban, and largely irresponsible and lazy, threatens to become increasingly White and suburban. Unemployed white blue- and white-collar workers do not recognize how much they have in common with unemployed African Americans. An atmosphere of fear now prevails as the dominant white culture seeks to place blame for their declining standard of living on the Other, primarily racial minorities within the United States and underpaid workers in other countries (Rifkin 1995; Rubin 1994).

## GLOBALIZATION AND COMMITMENT TO COMMUNITY

Within the learning organization literature, "globalization" refers to the restructuring of organizations that results from the turmoil and increased competition caused by dynamic global markets. "Globalization represents the converging of economic and social forces, values, and opportunities. Pundits have called globalization the root cause for change in the 1990s and beyond" (Marquardt 1996, 3). Cultural diversity is discussed only in relationship to the differences in values and customs between countries. Also, the learning organization literature identifies commitment to community as integral to creating a learning organization and as key to survival. "Learning organizations recognize that many benefits accrue by involving the community as a part of the learning process, such as (1) the enhancement of the company's image in the community, (2) the generation of greater community interest in working for or buying from the company, (3) strengthening of the quality of life in the community, (4) the preparation of a future workforce, and (5) the opportunity to exchange and share community resources" (112). In the new worldview, ". . . the commitment required to build learning organizations goes beyond people's typical 'commitment to their organizations.' It encompasses commitment to changes needed in the larger world and to seeing our organizations as vehicles for bringing about such changes" (Kofman and Senge 1993, 6-7).

In the case of Whirlpool Corporation, the white male leadership became interested in their ability to work with a multicultural workforce after expanding into international markets. Before the Dutch company was purchased, most of the senior management had never left the United States. The design of the first global leadership conference forced managers to mix with their counterparts from other countries, to push them out of their ". . . 'cultural cocoons' . . . It was at this conference that the vision of a global learning company and the values of 'commitment to people,' all people, began to emerge" (Marquardt 1996, 114-115). This commitment included not only Whirlpool's 40,000 employees, customers, and partners, but also the global community at large. Yet, while the corporation talks about a commitment to all people, Benton Harbor, the community of its origin, suffers increasing levels of poverty and the crime and discontent associated with poverty.

Frankenberg (1993, 44) defines racial social geography as "the racial and ethnic mapping of environments in physical and social terms and enables also the beginning of an understanding of the conceptual mappings of self and other. . . . " Outside of corporate philanthropy, the predominantly white leadership does not see the need for cultural learning within its organization before expanding outside the United States. From a position of dominance and power, the values and customs in the United States, in Benton Harbor, and within the corporation represent the unspoken norm of white Eurocentrism. Race and cultural differences are seen only in relation to the leaders' contact with employees and customers in other countries. These cultural differences are at a distance, not in the corporation's own backyard within the local community.

As noted, the leaders of Whirlpool have developed a corporate values statement that includes a commitment to community. Their commitment to the common good pledges to "pursue our business with honor, fairness and respect for the individual and the public at large . . . [to] serve responsibly as members of all communities in which we live and work, respecting cultural distinctions throughout the world . . ." (Marquardt 1996, 112). The corporate leadership apparently sees no contradiction between the values statement and the conditions it has helped to create in the community where their corporate headquarters is located. Like other manufacturing corporations, Whirlpool has moved its production and assembly plants to areas where cheaper, more compliant labor is available. Ironically, with the drive to increase profits, apparently no thought has been given to moving management functions and positions to locations in the Third World where cheaper labor is also available. As with commitment to cultural diversity, community is seen through the lens that makes invisible the Other. The commitment is to the white middle and upper-middle class, not to the underclass made up primarily of African Americans in Benton Harbor.

## CONFLICTING AGENDAS

The concepts that underlie the learning organization, including the various iterations of Total Quality Management (TQM), collaboration, teamwork, and empowerment, often come into direct conflict with the strategic initiatives of most organizations. Not only do these programs conflict with the traditional hierarchical, patriarchal Eurocentric model of management, but they also are in direct conflict with the economic model of the firm that seeks to maximize shareholder wealth, emphasizes individual self-interest, places a high priority on individualism and accountability, and keeps power in the hands of the few at the top (Grant, Shani, and Krishnan 1994).

Bensimon (1995), however, places TQM within modernist discourse, a systemic modernism that requires emphasis on customer satisfaction, reduction in variation, and the ability to measure satisfaction. The concepts of customer, variation, and measure are shaped by those who control and therefore shape the discourse—those in positions of power. While writing from within the framework of higher education, Bensimon's analysis is equally applicable to the corporate world. Within the literature of the learning organization, the focus is on the leaders and managers of the organization, despite inclusive talk of empowerment and participation from all levels. The learning organization focuses on change at the top, still placing emphasis on a hierarchical structure controlled by the few. Recognition of a multicultural workforce and society is generally limited to brief comments related to the need to understand other cultures in order to be competitive within the global marketplace (Kofman and Senge 1993; Marquardt 1996; Senge 1990; Watkins and Marsick 1993). Whirlpool's leadership conference included only the select few from top management who, in the words of CEO Whitwam, "We made accountable for educating all 38,000 people around the world" (Marquardt 1996, 115).

While remaining unnamed, the leaders and managers are predominately white males coming from the upper levels of the socioeconomic scale who are charged with making sure the rest of the organization complies with the dictates of management: Their mission is to "follow through and force the interaction to continue" (115).

Quality as defined by customer satisfaction is a reflection of the interests, values, and beliefs of those with power, the stockholders and leaders of the organization. Minorities are not identified as customers.

> Historically, subjectivity has been the privilege of those with the power to control institutionalized discourses, which for the most part have been white males. Thus, the subjectivity of women, as well as that of racial, ethnic, and sexual minorities, is recognized as long as it reflects the norm. The subordinate position of women and minority groups . . . deprives them of subject status in the discourses that structure the practices and processes to which they must conform in order to succeed (Bensimon 1995, 599).

Groups excluded by the organization at large also are excluded from teams. The failure of teams within organizations is blamed on the skill deficits of individual team members. Problematizing individual team members assumes a fixed definition of success based on set standards. This deficit model places blame on the individual and fails to take into account alternative forms of knowledge. There are conflicting messages within organizations: regarding, say, ". . . competitive individualism versus cooperation, short-term financial returns versus quality improvement, and control and accountability versus participation and risk taking" (Brooks 1995, 43-44).

## CONCLUSION

There is a danger of the concept of a learning organization becoming another master narrative, another attempt to create a totalizing system based on instrumental rationality and the cult of efficiency. Many organizations have undergone extensive restructuring in an attempt to remain competitive in the fast-changing global market. These organizations utilize cheap labor provided by ethnic minorities and women, a segment of society long silenced by a dominant white patriarchal culture. Efficiency still means "the maximum yield that could be produced in the shortest time, expending the least amount of energy, labor and capital . . ." (Rifkin 1995, 49). Multinational corporations, such as Whirlpool Corporation, are still reducing the number of full-time workers employed in the United States. Increasingly they are relying on cheaper "leased or temporary—even 'use and throwaway'—workers" (Rothwell and Kazanas 1994, 28). At the same time, workers are expected to take more responsibility for their own lives, careers, and job changes. Two recent articles in *Newsweek* speak to the growing fear and insecurity created by the large number of layoffs that are affecting not only the African American community but also white blue- and white-collar workers (Samuelson 1996; Sloan 1996).

> There's something different in the air these days when it comes to people's jobs. Yes, we've had corporate layoffs ever since business was invented. We've had greedy and isolated and insensitive chief executives. . . . Not to mention hungry shareholders and anxious workers. But lately, all these usual suspects have combined in a way that forms something new and nasty. Call it "in-your face capitalism." You lose your job, your ex-employer's stock price rises, the CEO gets a fat raise. Something is just plain wrong when stock prices keep rising on Wall Street while Main Street is littered with the bodies of workers discarded by big companies. . . . (Sloan 1996, 44).

Large segments of the white community are now experiencing what it might be like to be the Other—African American or some other minority. High unemployment among African Americans in Benton Harbor has been blamed on the individual, not on lack of opportunity or access, things that the white population take for granted. Now the white population is feeling the same pinch.

Organizational learning uses a model of continuous self-directed learning at the individual, group, and organizational level, a Eurocentric ideal based on individualism. Learning based on interdependence found outside the dominant white cultural perspective is not readily incorporated into organizational culture. Within a learning organization the lip service given to collaboration and teamwork not only contradicts this norm of individualism, but it fails to recognize the power differentials within self-directed work groups. Dialogue required for a collaborative model is not possible within a socioeconomic framework of inequality where those at the margins are silenced. Negotiated team consensus based on the core values of the dominant white culture rationalizes work behaviors that become acceptable because they are created in the name of the team. The concept of a learning organization, based on the unspoken and unwritten norm of a dominant white culture, does not adequately address the reality of a workforce that is increasingly multicultural.

## BIBLIOGRAPHY

Adkin, C. E. (1990). *Brother Benjamin: A History of the Israelite House of David.* Berrien Springs, MI: Andrews University Press.

Bensimon, E. M. (1995). "Total Quality Management in the Academy: A Rebellious Reading." *Harvard Educational Review* 65, no. 4, 593-611.

Brooks, A. K. (1995). "The Myth of Self-Directed Work Teams and the Ineffectiveness of Team Effectiveness Training: An Argument with Special Reference to Teams that Produce Knowledge." *36th Annual Adult Education Research Conference: Conference Proceedings.* Edmonton: University of Alberta.

Ferguson, K. E. (1984). *The Feminist Case Against Bureaucracy.* Philadelphia: Temple University Press.

Frankenberg, R. (1993). *White Women, Race Matters: The Social Construction of Whiteness.* Minneapolis: University of Minnesota Press.

Grant, R. M., Shani, R.; and Krishnan, R. (1994). "TQM's Challenge to Management Theory and Practice." *Sloan Management Review* 35, no. 2, 25-35.

Gresson, A. D., III. (1995). *The Recovery of Race in America.* Minneapolis: University of Minnesota Press.

Handy, C. (1990). *The Age of Unreason.* Boston: Harvard Business School Press.

hooks, b. (1989). *Talking Back: Thinking Feminist, Thinking Black.* Boston: South End Press.

Horowitz, C. F. (1995). "Searching for the White Underclass." *National Review* 47, no. 17, 52-56.

Jennings, K. (1992). "Understanding the Persisting Crisis of Black Youth Unemployment." In J. Jennings (ed.), *Race, Politics, and Economic Development: Community Perspectives.* London: Verso.

Katzenbach, J. R., and Smith, D. K. (1993). *The Wisdom of Teams: Creating the High-Performance Organization.* New York: Harper Business.

Kofman, F. and Senge, P. M. (1993). "Communities of Commitment: The Heart of Learning Organizations." *Organizational Dynamics* 22, no. 2, 5-23.

Marquardt, M. J. (1996). *Building the Learning Organization: A Systems Approach to Quantum Improvement and Global Success.* New York: McGraw Hill.

Redding, J. C. and Catalanello, R. F. (1994). *Strategic Readiness: The Making of the Learning Organization.* San Francisco: Jossey-Bass.

Rifkin, J. (1995). *The End of Work: The Decline of the Global Labor Force and the Dawn of the Post-Market Era.* New York: G. P. Putnam's Sons.

Rothwell, W. J. and Kazanas, H. C. (1994). *Improving on-the-Job Training: How to Establish and Operate a Comprehensive OJT Program.* San Francisco: Jossey-Bass.

Rubin, L. B. (1994). *Families on the Fault Line: America's Working Class Speaks About the Family, the Economy, Race, and Ethnicity.* New York: HarperPerennial.

Samuelson, R. J. (1996). "Are Workers Disposable?" *Newsweek* 127, no. 7, 47.

Scholtes, P. R. (1988). *The Team Handbook: How to Use Teams to Improve Quality.* Madison, WI: Joiner.

Senge, P. M. (1990). *The Fifth Discipline: The Art and Practice of the Learning Organization.* New York: Doubleday Currency.

Senge, P. M., Kleiner, A., Roberts, C., Ross, R. B., and Smith, B. J. (1994). *The Fifth Discipline Fieldbook: Strategies and Tools for Building a Learning Organization.* New York: Doubleday Currency.

Sloan, A. (1996). "The Hit Men." *Newsweek* 127, no. 9, 44-48.

Steinberg, S. R. (1996). "Interview with Stanley Aronowitz." In J. L. Kincheloe, S. R. Steinberg, and A. D. Gresson III (eds.), *Measured Lies: The Bell Curve Examined.* New York: St. Martin's Press.

Walton, M. (1986). *The Deming Management Method.* New York: Perigree Books.

Watkins, K. E., and Marsick, V. J. (1993). *Sculpting the Learning Organization: Lessons in the Art and Science of Systemic Change.* San Francisco: Jossey-Bass.

# SIXTEEN

# Giving Whiteness a Black Eye

*An Interview
with Michael Eric Dyson*

**Ronald E. Chennault**

Michael Eric Dyson is one of the foremost intellectuals living in the United States today. His brilliance as a cultural critic is matched by his ability to communicate with audiences of all stripes. No wonder: His responsibilities as a scholar, father, educator, clergyman, activist, and husband (among other roles) require him to interact with different groups of human beings in a variety of settings. Dyson is the author of numerous publications, including the recent *Race Rules: Navigating the Color Line* (1996). In what follows, Dyson shares his views on whiteness with Ronald Chennault, one of the editors.

CHENNAULT: Let me start by just talking a little bit about what the other authors in *White Reign* have done. Generally, they have done three things: tried to describe what they understand whiteness to be or what the content of whiteness is; identified some of the forms that whiteness takes in the multiple locations in which it manifests itself; and attempted either to redefine what whiteness should be or to spell out ways to combat the oppressiveness that is a part of whiteness, thus trying to rescue its productive content. Based on that synopsis of the work of the others, why don't we start, if it's okay with you, with what you perceive whiteness to be or what you understand whiteness to mean.

DYSON: Well, I think when we talk about whiteness in the context of race in America, we have to talk about whiteness as *identity*, whiteness as *ideology*, and whiteness as *institution*. These three elements are complex and impure; they bleed into one another. Still, as categories of analysis they can help us get a handle on the intensely variegated manifestations of whiteness.

In speaking of whiteness as identity, I am referring to the self-understanding, social practices, and group beliefs that articulate whiteness in relationship to American race, especially, in this case, to blackness. I think whiteness bears a particularly symbiotic relationship to blackness; in one sense, whiteness is called into existence as a response to the presence of blackness. Only when black bodies—through slavery on to the present—have existed on American terrain has whiteness been constituted as an idea and, indeed, an identity-based reality. White people's sense of themselves as being White is contingent upon a negation of a corollary blackness and on the assertion of that blackness as the basis of a competing racial identity.

White people who understand themselves through narratives of race do so in response to the presence of African "Others" on American terrain. As a result, I think that white identities have been developed unconsciously and, hence, for the most part, invisibly within the structures of domination in American society. That is to say, for the most part, whiteness has been an invisible identity within American society, and only recently—with the deconstruction and demythologization of race in attacks on biologistic conceptions of racial identity—has whiteness been constituted as a trisected terrain of contestation: over ethnicity, over ethnocentrism, and over the way groups manufacture and reproduce racial identity through individual self-understanding. I think whiteness in that sense has only recently been called into existence as a result of questions about the social construction of race, the social reconstruction of biology, and, in general, how we have come to talk about race in more complex terms.

When I talk about whiteness as ideology, I'm referring to the systematic reproduction of conceptions of whiteness as domination.

Whiteness as domination has been the most powerful, sustaining myth of American culture since its inception. In other words, the ideological contamination of American democracy by structures of white domination is indivisible from the invention of America. Another way of saying this is that the invention of America and the invention of whiteness are ideologically intertwined because the construction of narratives of domination are indissolubly linked to the expansion of the colonial empire: America as the new colony. America found its roots in response to an *intraracial* struggle with Europe over the power of representation (that is, how citizens should be granted official voice and vote in the polis) and the representation of power (how cultural institutions like churches and schools should no longer be exclusively regulated by the state). The United States was brought into existence as a result of an intraethnic war between white, Anglo-Saxon Protestants and American colonists who rejected their political deference to Europe and defended their burgeoning sense of nationhood and personal identity.

In that sense, there is a fissure in whiteness that is not articulated as such because it happens within the borders of ethnic similarity. This civil war of white ethnicity generated the fissuring of the state at the behest of procreative energies of emancipation. But that emancipation, at least in terms of its leaders' self-understanding, was not ethnically or racially constituted; it was viewed as the ineluctable conclusion to a fatal disagreement over issues of primary political importance, like freedom, justice and equality.

At the same time, ironically enough, the expansion of American culture, especially the American State, was fostered primarily through the labor of black slaves and, to a lesser degree, the exploitation of white indentured servants and the oppression of white females. From the very beginning of our nation's existence, the discursive defense and political logic of American democracy has spawned white dominance as the foundational myth of American society—a myth whose ideological strength was made all the more powerful because it was rendered invisible. After all, its defenders didn't have to be conscious of how white dominance and, later, white supremacy shaped their worldviews since there was little to challenge their beliefs. Their ideas defined the intellectual and cultural status quo. In that sense, the white race—its cultural habits, political practices, religious beliefs, and intellectual affinities—was socially constructed as the foundation of American democracy.

In terms of the genealogy of American nationality, whiteness and democracy were coextensive because they were mutually reinforcing ideologies that undergirded the state. When we look at the Constitution and the Declaration of Independence, the implicit meanings of white domination were encoded in state discourse. State discourse was not only articulated in the intellectual architecture of the Constitution and the Declaration of Independence; it was also written into the laws of the land that eroded the social stability of African American people, first as slaves, then as subjugated victims of the state through debt peonage, sharecropping, Jim Crow law, the retraction of the welfare state, and so on.

Also written into the laws of the land were the explicit articulation of black racial inferiority and the implicit assumption of white racial superiority. These two poles were reproduced ideologically to justify white supremacy; the mutually reinforcing structures of state-sponsored racial domination and the ideological expression of white racial superiority solidified the power of white people, white perspectives, and white practices. As a result, whiteness in its various expressions was made to appear normative and natural, while other racial identities and ideologies were viewed as deviant and unnatural.

The final component of my triad is the institutional expression of whiteness. The institutions I have in mind—from the home to the school, from the government to the church—compose the intellectual and ideological tablet upon which have been inscribed the meanings of American destiny. Let's focus on one example of how whiteness has been institutionally expressed: the church. First, "manifest destiny" found an institutional articulation in the church, even though our country's founders ingeniously disestablished state-sponsored religion and thereby encouraged radical heterogeneity within American religion. While ostensibly free from state rule, religious communities were not impervious to secular beliefs; the theological discourse of many faiths actively enunciated the ideology of white domination.

Not only did manifest destiny bleed through the theological articulations of the churches, but the belief in blackness as an innately inferior identity galvanized the missionary activities of most religious communities as they sought to contain and redeem the black slave's transgressive body, since many believed blacks didn't have a soul. With the overlay of theological verity added to embellish the ideology of white supremacy, black identity became the ontological template for the reproduction of discourses of racial primitivism and savagery. The black body became a contested landscape on which the torturous intersections of theology and ideology were traced; it was at once the salvific focus of the white missionizing project and the foremost example of what unchecked transgression could lead to.

These elements of whiteness—identity, ideology, and institution—are articulated and reinforced over space and time. They substantiate the argument that Whites don't understand themselves in abstraction from the cultural institutions and the critical mythologies that accrete around whiteness. What we've witnessed over the last decade is a crisis in the myth of whiteness; that is, it has been exposed as a visible and specific identity, not something that is invisible and universal. Whiteness has been "outed," and as a consequence of its outing, it has to contend with its own genealogy as one ethnicity among other ethnicities, as one race among other races. We are now seeing a proliferation of ideas, articles, books, plays, and conferences that question the meanings and significations of whiteness. As part of that process, we've got to understand what whiteness has meant and to specify what it can or should mean in the coming century.

CHENNAULT: Now, given this "outing" of whiteness, would it be your opinion that the concept of whiteness will continue to be studied, that it won't be just a fleeting academic interest?

DYSON: That's right. I think we can rest assured that the extraordinary interest in whiteness won't taper off too much. First, there are masses of Whites who are absorbed by the subject, a sure index of its staying power. There are also a great deal of African Americans, Native Americans, Latinos, and Asians—and other subaltern, aboriginal, and colonized peoples—who are deeply invested in reversing the terror of ethnography: of being the disciplined subject of an often intellectually poisonous white anthropological scrutiny. Many minorities yearn to return the favor of interrogation, if you will, though not in nearly as punishing a manner as they've received. Many members of these groups simply seek to unveil the myths of universality and invisibility that have formed the ideological strata of white supremacy.

They also seek to reveal a fundamental strategy of white supremacy: forging belief in the omnipotence of whiteness. This belief maintains that whiteness secretes a racial epistemology whose function is akin to omnipotent narration in fiction: It unifies the sprawling plot of white civilization; it articulates the hidden logic of mysterious white behavior; it codifies the linguistic currency through which the dramatis personae of white cultures detail their intellectual idiosyncrasies and emotional yearnings; and it projects an edifying white racial denouement to the apocalyptic conflict between whiteness and nonwhiteness. One consequence of an investment in the omnipotence of whiteness, and in the unitary racial sentiment that it enforces, is that many minorities have been ontologically estranged from what might be termed the *Dasein* of American race—the racial order of being that defines national and, more fundamentally, human identity.

The great irony of American race—that is, within the discursive frame of whiteness as an invisible entity—is that the condition for racial survival is racial concealment, a state of affairs that produces a surreal racelessness that stigmatizes all nonwhite identities. Thus racial and ethnic minorities face a triple challenge: They must overcome the history and ongoing forces of oppression; they must eradicate the demonization of racial identity-qua-identity that whiteness generates; and they must help excavate the historical and ideological character of whiteness in the sedimenting fields of cultural and social practice.

Another reason I think that the examination of whiteness will not diminish quickly is the sheer variety of white identities, behaviors, texts, and practices that the current phase of whiteness studies has uncovered. Such variety gives the lie to whiteness as a singular and fixed phenomenon. Whiteness must be viewed as destabilized loci of contested meanings that depend on different articulatory possibilities to establish their identities and functions. Whiteness is now up for grabs; it is being deeply retheorized and profoundly rearticulated. Whiteness is no longer simply good or bad. In any case, either formulation is a *reductio ad absurdum* that underwrites a rigid, essentialist view of race.

Contemporary studies of whiteness explore the complex character of white racial identity and practice. Such studies examine whiteness in multifarious modes: as domination *and* cooperation, as stability *and* instability, as hegemony *and* subordination, and as appropriation *and* co-optation. By no means am I suggesting that a narrow ideological binarism lies at the heart of whiteness; I simply mean to accent the interactive, intersectional, and *multi*lectical features of whiteness with other racial and ethnic identities as they are elaborated in intellectual inquiry. Even if such studies are viewed as faddish, we must remember that many substantive intellectual engagements began as trends.

Then too, one of the advantages of the *subject(ed)s* of whiteness now *objecting* it—that is, constituting it as a legitimate object of discursive interrogation and thereby objecting to the power of whiteness to iterate domination by remaining amorphous and invisible—is that we demystify the mechanisms by which whiteness has reproduced its foundational myths. We also get a better sense of how whiteness has helped construct blackness and how whiteness has helped to construct Latino/a, Native American and Asian identities as well.

We must recognize that current studies of whiteness—especially the groundbreaking writings of white scholars such as David Roediger, Theodore Allen, Noel Ignatiev, and others—are building on the often unacknowledged tradition of black critical reflection on the ways and means of whiteness. To be sure, whiteness studies in its present modes— in terms of the scopes of interrogation, disciplinary methodologies, paradigms of knowledge, theoretical tools of analysis, historical conjunctions, and material supports that make this an ideal intellectual climate for scrutinizing white identities—unquestionably mark a significant scholarly, perhaps even disciplinary, departure in cultural studies of race and ethnicity. But such studies would be impossible, or at least highly unlikely, without the pioneering work of figures like W. E. B. Du Bois, Langston Hughes, Zora Neale Hurston, Fannie Lou Hamer, and on and on.

To be fair, a number of the "new abolitionist" writers have scrupulously acknowledged their debt to this hidden black intellectual tradition. For instance, David Roediger acknowledges that Du Bois was the first to write, in his magisterial tome *Black Reconstruction,* about the "psychic wages of whiteness," arguing that even poor workers derived a psychological benefit from their whiteness. Current whiteness studies will only be strengthened as they refer to those texts and figures in black life, and in other minority communities, who have aided in the demythologization of a homogeneous, uniform whiteness.

I think that the study of whiteness will be around for some time because it can give us crucial historical insight into current cultural debates. For example, contentious discussions about the labor movement and its relationship to identity politics would be greatly benefited from a vigorous examination of the role white racial identity played in the formation of the American working class. Despite their economic disadvantage, poor white workers appealed to the surplus value that their whiteness allowed them to accumulate in the political economy of race. Many poor workers invested their surplus valued whiteness into a fund of psychic protection against the perverse, impure meanings of blackness. They drew from their value-added whiteness to not only boost their self-esteem but to assert their relative racial superiority by means of what may be termed a *negative inculpability:* Poor Whites derived pleasure and some cultural benefit by *not being the nigger.*

Their negative inculpability prevented poor Whites from being viewed as the ultimate cause of harm to white civilization—despite the social problems to which their poverty and class oppression gave rise. Their negative inculpability redeemed poor Whites, at least partially, by granting them powers to deflect their degraded status through a *comparative racial taxonomy:* Poor Whites could articulate the reasons for their superiority by naming all the ways they remained white despite their economic hardship. Negative inculpability and comparative racial taxonomy were racial strategies by which poor Whites appropriated the dominant meanings of Whiteness, and the ideology of white domination while obscuring the intellectual and material roots of their own suffering. Of course, in objective, empirically verifiable ways, poor Whites had much more in common with poor Blacks: degraded social status, depressed wages, and stigmatization through social narratives of "the deserving poor" that blamed the poor for their plight. Such studies are of utmost importance in explicating the complex intersections of race, gender, and class in the labor movement and in contemporary cultural politics.

In order to solidify the intellectual foundation of whiteness studies, we should distinguish among at least three economies within whiteness: an *economy of invention,* an *economy of representation,* and an *economy of articulation.* Economies of invention explore how and when the multiple meanings of whiteness are fashioned. Economies of invention permit us to excavate, for instance, the construction of Irish as a white ethnicity, as Noel Ignatiev has done; the making of the white working class, as David Roediger has done; and the invention of the white race, about which Ted Allen has written. Economies of invention address the foundational myths of white ethnicity as they are articulated through metaphysical claims of white superiority. Economies of invention help us narrate the means by which culture has colluded with ideology to reproduce whiteness. They help us understand how cultural privilege is assigned to an accidental racial feature like whiteness and how such privilege gives credence to philosophical arguments about the inherent goodness and supremacy of white identity.

Economies of invention encourage critics to stress how the project of whiteness was constructed on a labor base of exploited indigenous Americans and enslaved Blacks. The irony is that enslaved Blacks supplied material support and social leisure to white elites as they constructed mythologies of black racial inferiority. Economies of invention also accent a factor I discussed earlier: the symbiotic relationship between white and black identities, practices, and cultures in the construction of the material and cultural means to express whiteness.

In this matter, Orlando Patterson's important book, *Freedom,* is crucial in pinpointing the intellectual function of an economy of invention in interrogating the historically and socially constituted meanings of whiteness. Patterson argues that Western conceptions of freedom—and, one might add, the epistemic crucible of Western culture and identity—are contingent upon, indeed, articulated against, the backdrop of slavery. In other words, there's no such thing as Western freedom without a corresponding articulation of slave identities; there's no ideal of freedom within American culture in particular, and Western cultures in general, without the presence of the corollary slave subject that was being constructed and contained within the narrative of freedom to begin with. Economies of invention help us to comprehend the extraordinarily intricate construction of white identities in the interstices of hybrid cultural contacts.

Economies of representation examine how whiteness has been manifest, how it has been symbolized, how it has been made visible. Economies of representation highlight how whiteness has been embodied in films, in visual art, and in branches of culture where public myths of white beauty and intelligence have gained representative authority to rearticulate the superiority and, especially, the desirability of whiteness. Economies of representation pay attention to the erotic visibility of white identities and images—that is, how whiteness has been fetishized as the ideal expression of human identity.

Economies of representation also underscore the cultural deference paid to white identities, images, styles, and behaviors even as they cast light on the scorn heaped on nonwhite identities in a key strategy of defensive whiteness: demonizing the racialized other as a means of sanctifying the white self; devaluing nonwhite racial identities through stereotypical representations as a means of idealizing white identities; and bestializing the expression of eroticism in nonwhite cultures while eroticizing racial others for white pleasure and consumption.

Finally, economies of articulation name the specific sites of intellectual justification for white superiority and supremacy. From selected writings of Thomas Jefferson, David Hume, Immanuel Kant, Abraham Lincoln, and Woodrow Wilson to the writings of Dinesh D'Souza (a white superiorist in brown skin), Charles Murray, Arthur Jensen, William Shockley, and Richard Herrnstein, beliefs in the pathologies and corruptions of black culture and, by extension, in the inherent rightness of whiteness have deluged our intellectual landscape.

Economies of articulation specify how, from the Enlightenment to *The Bell Curve,* ideas of black inferiority have been expressed with vicious consistency. Indeed, *The Bell Curve* argues black intellectual inferiority through a tangle of pseudoscientifically manipulated data, leading to what cultural theorist Raymond Franklin has termed "statistical myopia." Economies of articulation isolate the philosophical architecture and rhetorical scaffolding that joins white superiorist and supremacist thinking to social and cultural practices. Economies of articulation show how myths of value neutrality, ideals of Archimedean-like objectivity, conceptions of theory-free social science, notions of bias-free scholarship, and beliefs in heroically blind moral explanations are deployed to defend—and to coerce others outside of its ideological trajectory to defer to—white civilization. These three economies help us to determine, define, and demystify the meanings of whiteness and to make sure that the study of white identities, images, and ideologies rests upon a critical intellectual foundation.

CHENNAULT: So, then, what about whiteness being discussed outside the confines of academia, or what about the influence of these scholarly discussions on others not in the academy? How can that happen or how is that happening?

DYSON: I think it certainly is happening. One flagrant example is in the cultural discourse about "white male anger," which, according to its apologists, is the legitimate bitterness of white men who have been unfairly denied employment because of affirmative action. Debates about white male anger take place in employment arenas, especially fire and police stations, where white men, we are told, have had enough. White male anger has focused on black bodies as its *objet de terreur,* its target of rage. In the minds of such men (and their wives and daughters), Blacks occupy wrongful places of privilege in the job sector because of their color. Black progress symbolized in affirmative action policies constitutes reverse racism for many Whites. This is an extremely volatile occasion outside of the academy, where the meanings of whiteness are being fiercely debated.

There were also discussions—sometimes explicit, more often veiled and coded—about whiteness in the recent ordeal of the bombing of the Murrah Federal Building in Oklahoma City and in its aftermath, the trial of Timothy McVeigh. McVeigh became a flashpoint in the resurfacing of a virulent, violent whiteness that had to be contained for at least three reasons. First, the racial violence that McVeigh symbolized transgressed its historic ethnic limits by, in significant measure, being directed toward other Whites. Second, by intentionally targeting the American government, McVeigh's white racial violence shattered an implicit social contract where the nation absorbed (that is, excused, overlooked, downplayed, underestimated, and so on) extralegal racial violence more readily if it was aimed at black or other minority bodies. This was an ideological relic from earlier generations when extralegal white racial violence actually served the interests of the state, or at least multitudes of its officials, by discouraging black insurrection, protest, or rebellion against the legal strictures of white supremacy. Finally, McVeigh's violence had to be contained, even eradicated, because his poor white rebellion against state authority threatened to symbolically contaminate "purer," more elite expressions of white ethnicity.

One really gets a sense, from many of the white cultural discussions of McVeigh, of the ethnic betrayal many Whites feel in the Oklahoma City bombing. Judging by what I've read, McVeigh viewed himself as part of a tiny outpost of pure patriotic rebels whose patriotism was expressed in the logic of radical *antipatriotism:* One must blow up the state as it is to get to the state as it should be. I think that McVeigh believed he was reviving a heroic vision of whiteness that he thought was being suppressed within the institutional matrices of American democracy and "legitimate" government. Apparently in McVeigh's thinking, the only legitimate government was to be found in the guerrilla gangsterism of his supremacist, antistatist comrades. They are the real

Americans, not the namby-pamby politicians and state officials who cater to racial minorities and who endanger the freedom of religious minorities like the followers of the late cult leader David Koresh.

What's fascinating about McVeigh is that his actions articulate in the extreme the logic of repressive, hegemonic whiteness that hibernates within the structures of legitimate government: vicious attacks on welfare and its recipients; brutal attacks on black progress and its advocates; heartless attacks on the crime-ridden black ghetto; and exploitative attacks on the alleged pathologies of black culture. All of these claims and more have been launched by governmental officials. The cumulative effect of such attacks is the implementation of policies that punish the black poor and stigmatize the black middle class, and the legitimization of crude cultural biases toward black citizens.

Figures like Timothy McVeigh become hugely discomfiting manifestations of the hidden animus toward blackness and civility that such discourses of attack encourage. McVeigh is the rabid reification of the not-too-abstract narratives of hatred that flood segments of white talk radio. Bob Grant, Rush Limbaugh, and many other lesser lights discover a living embodiment of their vitriolic, vituperative verbiage in McVeigh. McVeigh is the monster created by the Frankensteins of white hatred. And there's a great deal of shame in him because he's out of control and destroying his creators. In this regard, it's crucial to remember a salient fact: Frankenstein is not the name of the monster but the name of the monster's *creator*. The real terror, then, are the mechanisms of reproduction that sustain and rearticulate ideologies of white supremacy and that sanction the violent attack on black and other minority identities.

Finally, debates on whiteness beyond the academy occur in the construction of cultural conversations about "poor white trash." Interestingly enough, Bill Clinton figures as a key subject and subtext of such conversations. For many, Clinton is our nation's *First Bubba,* our country's *Trailer Trash Executive,* our nation's *Poor White President.* It tells on our bigoted cultural beliefs and social prejudices that Clinton—who is a Georgetown University alumnus, a Rhodes Scholar, an Oxford University and Yale University Law School graduate, and now President of the United States—could be construed in many quarters as a poor white trash, cracker citizen. The study of whiteness prods us to examine the means by which a highly intelligent man and gifted politician is transmuted into "Bubba" for the purposes of intraethnic demonization.

Then too, Clinton, or at least his legal representatives, relied on the same prejudice that befell the president in their legal battles over sexual harassment with a very different victim in the poor white trash wars: Paula Jones. The intriguing subtext in Clinton's fight against Jones's suit was not about the hierarchy of gender, where a male's prerogative in defining a sexual relationship is under attack through the discourse of sexual harassment. An even more powerful subtext was that Jones was a "po' white trash 'ho." By being so designated, Jones's sexual ownership of her body was much less prized in the popular mind-set than Clinton's ownership of his sexual self. As a result, Jones's believability was unfairly compromised by her degraded social and gender status. Beyond considerations of her relationship to political forces that oppose Clinton, Jones's status reinforced the perception that gender and class cause one to be assigned a lower niche on the totem pole of poor, white identity. And there are many, many more places where whiteness is being discussed far beyond the boundaries of the academy in ways that scholarly studies of whiteness are barely beginning to catch up to.

CHENNAULT: Speaking of President Clinton, what about his recent addresses on this issue of race? Do those serve in your mind as useful or productive means of expanding the public discourse on whiteness and race?

DYSON: Well, I think it's important that the President of the United States help set the tone for how discourse about race will proceed. If we have any chance of rescuing the productive means by which race is articulated, we certainly have to have the "First Pedagogue" in place. And Clinton in that sense becomes a figure of estimable symbolic and even moral worth in setting a healthy tone for the debate about race. And the means that he has ingeniously seized upon—which has been discussed in not altogether dissimilar ways in philosophical circles by Michael Oakeshott, Richard Rorty, and others—is that of conversation. The will to converse about race is motivated by an overriding concern: How can we adjudicate competing claims about race without tearing the essential fabric of American democracy that is embodied in the slogan *E pluribus Unum,* "Out of many, one"? If we're already fractured at the level of identity, and this fractured identity is reproduced through mythologies of racial superiority and inferiority—or through narratives of Whites being victimized by Blacks in identity politics, affirmative action, multiculturalism, or political correctness—how can we justly resolve disputes about relative victimization within the larger framework of American democracy? It's a very messy business, and one that certainly calls for the president to become a leader in these matters. But his shouldn't be the only or even the dominant voice. Still, Clinton has created space for the conversation to take place.

It's important that Clinton open up the space of conversation about race; it's infinitely better than shooting or stabbing or killing one another. It's better than black men killing each other in the streets of Detroit or Chicago. It's better than black people being beaten and killed by white policemen in New York or Los Angeles. It's better than Latinas being victimized by the ideology and institutional expressions of anti-immigrant sentiment. Conversation certainly is superior to destroying one another and our nation.

Still, we mustn't be naive. One of the supreme difficulties of discussing race in America is our belief in the possibility of morally equivalent views being reasonably articulated and justly examined. The implicit assumption of Clinton's ideology of race conversation is that we are having debates among equals, or at least among people who have been equally victimized in American culture. But this is a torturous belief that obscures history and memory. We've got to unclog the arteries of collective American political memory.

In regard to race, we are living in the United States of Amnesia. We've got to revoke our citizenship in the State of Denial. That's an extraordinarily disconcerting process, partly because what is demanded is the rejection of a key premise of liberal racial discourse: Whites, Blacks, and others share a common moral conception of racial justice, an ideal that regulates social practice and promotes the resolution of racial disputes. The politics and history of race have not supported this belief. To shift metaphors, what we've got to do is graft the skin of racial memory to the body of American democracy. That demands skillful rhetorical surgery and the operation of an intellectual commitment to truth over habit. In the conversation of race, we really must be willing to discover new ideas and explore ancient emotions. We can't simply shout our prejudices louder than someone else's defense of their bigotry.

If we're going to have real progress in thinking and talking about race, we must not reduce racial issues to black and white. Race in

American culture is so much more profound and complex than black and white, even though we know that conflict has been a major artery through which has flowed the poisonous blood of white supremacy and black subordination. There are other arteries of race and ethnicity that trace through the body politic. The tricky part is acknowledging the significant Latino, Asian, and Native American battles with whiteness that have taken place in our nation while admitting that the major race war has involved Blacks and Whites.

The political centrality and historical legitimacy of dealing with the mutual and dominant relations of whiteness to blackness in the development of what Michael Omi and Howard Winant (1994) call "racial formation" is simply undeniable. But such a view must be balanced by paying attention not only to other racial and ethnic conflicts but also to the intraracial, interethnic differences that reconstitute racial and ethnic identity and practice. It's extremely important to get such a complex, heated, and potentially useful dialogue started.

A nagging question, however, remains: Who gets a chance to come to the race table to converse? Will poor people's voices be heard? What about young people's voices? In the conversation on race, there is the danger that we merely reproduce a liberal ideology of racial containment—that is, mute the radical elements of race that might really transform our conversation and practice. Such a prospect appears inevitable if we refuse to shatter our ideological and intellectual grids in order to hear the Other. What we don't need is the crass and deceitful politics of toleration that masks the sources of real power, that conceals the roots of real inequality, that ignores the voices of the most hurt, and that is indifferent to the faces of the most fractured. What we need is *real* conversation, the sort where hidden ambitions are brought to light, where masked motives are clarified to the point of social discomfort.

Such an aim of honest, hard conversation is what the so-called opponents of political correctness should have in mind when they launch their sometimes pedantic, always pejorative broadsides against the assertion of racial, ethnic, gender, class, and sexual difference. Instead, their ostensible desire to push beyond received racial truths ends up being an operation of rhetorical sleight-of-hand: They end up reasserting in new terms much older biased beliefs. That's why I'm so skeptical about many of the critics of so-called political correctness—they simply dress up bigotry in socially acceptable form by calling it "anti-P.C.," when indeed it's the same old P.C.: the PoppyCock of socially sanctioned racial disgust.

What we have to do, then, is to aim at a raucous debate where the impoliteness of certain people must be permitted because their pain is deep and unheeded. We must surely shatter the rituals of correctness and civility in order to hear from those whose voices have been shut out, where the ability even to articulate pain and rage has been delegitimized through social stigma. That's the only way we have a chance of striking a just racial contract with our citizens. Taking all of what I've discussed into consideration, I think the conversation on race is a step in the right direction.

CHENNAULT: That gets us away from what Toni Morrison refers to as the "graceful" liberal practice—in the past, at least—of talking about people as if they were raceless, which we at one time thought was the best way. But what you're suggesting is that that doesn't work.

DYSON: That's right, such a move simply doesn't work. As Du Bois said, there's no way to deal with race without going through race; there's no way of overcoming race without taking race into account. What we've had in our nation for too long is a willed ignorance about race; on one reading, it's a perverse application of philosopher John Rawls's notion of the "original position" in the social contract where we are placed behind a veil of ignorance in order to execute justice in the social realm. Well, when we've misapplied this model to race, it has been quite disastrous. It's failed primarily because we can't justly assume a statutory ignorance about race and because the means to apply racial justice fall disproportionately into the hands of those against whom claims of injustice have been convincingly levied.

Further, the assumption of racelessness fails to account for the contents and identities of race that have always played a role in fashioning American views of justice. This is why I think identity politics must be given a historicist, materialist, and genealogical reading. Identity politics has been going on from the get-go in American culture, indeed, in cultures the world over. Aristotle and Plato, and their followers, were ensconced in identity politics; Descartes and Kant, and their followers, were negotiating identity politics; Foucault and Derrida, and their followers, are embroiled in identity politics; and Julia Kristeva and Luce Irigiray, and their followers, are unquestionably involved in identity politics, though they, as I suspect the others I've named, would vehemently deny it.

That's because many of them are or were transfixed by the dream of transcendental truth, Enlightenment rationality, deconstructive practice, or semiotic analysis that, for the most part, severs questions of identity from questions of racial politics. What we must come to see is that even when we deal with intellectual or theoretical issues, they refer to—although by no means are they reduced to or equated with—considerations of identity, even if such considerations are not explicitly articulated. The disingenuous character of too many debates about identity in America is that they deny this process.

After generating a genealogy of identity—that places our own accounts of universalism versus difference into historical context, and that acknowledges that identity politics occur in a variety of intellectual and social settings —we can press forward to an adequate and fair criticism of identity politics. As things stand, too many critics wrongly argue that we must move beyond narrow frameworks of identity to get to this universal identity. I have in mind the most recent writings of Todd Gitlin (1995) and Michael Tomasky (1996). I share some of Gitlin's and Tomasky's concerns about the cultural dead ends of vicious identity politics that enshrine tribal preferences over the common good. But right away I disagree with them about what constitutes tribal preferences, how they can be justly eradicated, and what constitutes successful expressions of universal identities in the social and cultural realm.

In regard to whiteness, Gitlin and Tomasky fail to acknowledge that the particular identities of white people were rendered universal by a cultural and political process that punished Blacks and other minorities for seeking to come into their own: their own identities, their own cultural repertoires, their own linguistic and rhetorical facilities, their own styles of survival, and so on. Until we are able to concede this point, we won't get far in this debate about identity, about racelessness, and about the proper role that race should play, both in the American public sphere and in private institutions.

CHENNAULT: Do you see any contradiction between Clinton's inviting everyone to the table to talk about race and yet not listening to all those voices in making policy—welfare reform, for instance—and excluding the very voices that we need to be hearing from?

DYSON: There's no question that there's a deep contradiction in Clinton's methodology. Further, there's no question that in the past Clinton has not been above race baiting through very subtle semantic distortions and ideological gyrations. This surfaced in Clinton's first run for the presidency, when his crass opportunism got the best of him as he attacked rap artist Sister Souljah for her violent racism without providing a thicker account of the conditions that shaped her comments, something Clinton was clearly capable of effectively pulling off. It surfaced when Clinton, during his first campaign, sent coded signals to alleviate white fears by suggesting that he and Gore would focus their policies on rescuing suburbia and Middle America. It surfaced as well when Clinton failed to justly read the complex writings of his close friend, Lani Guinier, thereby encouraging her unjust demonization as a "quota queen." It surfaced with Clinton's support for a vicious crime bill that, like the welfare reform he supported, targeted black men and women with vicious specificity. And on and on.

More important, Clinton has failed to understand that if we as a nation are to have a successful conversation about race, it must be seconded at the level of public policy and political implementation. The conversation about race must perform a crucial educational function as well. Unfortunately, I think that too often Clinton has caved in to the American tendency to demonize what Malcolm X termed the "victims of democracy." Clinton has heartily advocated a neoliberal rearticulation of the ideology of racial tolerance that has largely served to hurt the black and Latino poor. One of the great problems with neoliberal race theory is that it writes the check of its loyalty to the black and Latino poor against the funds of conservative rhetoric and social policy. Bill Clinton certainly has a troubled history when it comes to race, a matter about which we must be forthright.

Clinton symbolizes, ironically enough, many white Americans who are well intentioned about race but who constantly make faux pas in their quest to do the right thing. Of course, in Clinton's case, his mistakes have cost millions of Blacks, Latinas, Native Americans, and other minorities dearly. Clinton's political position, his peripatetic bully pulpit, has given him the authority to amplify his intentions as well as the contradictions of his racial beliefs. But he is as representative of the misguided rhetoric of neoliberal race thinking as we're likely to get. The mixed blessing of such representation is that we get a clear glimpse of just how difficult it will be for the average white American to adequately confront the history and continued function of white supremacy, especially as it is manifested in neoliberal intolerance of radical black insurgence against racism. The bitter irony is that in Clinton black folk are being hurt by friendly fire. The bitter reality is that we have no choice but to find ways to work with him, as limiting as that may be, in the hope of reconstructing racial destiny in American culture.

CHENNAULT: In addition to what you've already mentioned, how do you in specific ways talk about whiteness, such as in your writing, your public lectures, your classroom?

DYSON: As I've lectured across the country, I've witnessed the resistance by many Whites to identify and name whiteness in its supremacist ideological mode. Many Whites believe that white supremacy is old news—which, of course, it is, but they fail to see how it's also today's news—and many believe that pointing to it is divisive and adds to the racial and cultural Balkanization that we're told we're living through. It's extremely difficult to break the hold such a perception has on many Whites. So, one of the strategies I try to adopt—in lectures, sermons, speeches, op-eds, articles, book reviews, and books—is the imaginative redescription of white supremacy in its cultural and ideological manifestations.

I also think it's important to emphasize the heterogeneity of whiteness, to stress how the meanings of whiteness are not exhausted by discussions of domination or supremacy. One of the good results of constructivist views of race—and in American culture, "race" has usually signified "black"—is that whiteness is increasingly viewed as a source and site of racial identities and practices. As much as I admire and appreciate the important work of David Roediger, Noel Ignatiev, Mab Segrest, and other new abolitionist thinkers, I think we have to proceed cautiously with the project of reconstituting white identities through their abolition. We have to pose a multipronged question: Do we want to abolish whiteness, or do we want to destroy the negative meanings associated with white identities? I think the latter is what we should aim for.

Of course, Roediger, Ignatiev, Segrest, Allen, and other new abolitionist writers would concede that the whiteness they have in mind to abolish is precisely the socially constructed, culturally sanctioned, ideologically legitimated value of white supremacy that has been a scourge to our nation. In that sense, perhaps they'd agree that we don't want to destroy white identity—because then we'd have to destroy those meanings of whiteness that have been mobilized to resist supremacist thought or, for that matter, to abolish whiteness. Rather, we want to abolish the lethal manifestations of white identity. The salient issue is whether we can completely and exclusively identify whiteness with destruction, negativity, and corruption. In any case, I applaud their desire to reject white skin privilege and to historicize social and racial identities.

Moreover, Roediger, Allen, Ignatiev, and the new abolitionists have got an extremely useful point; whiteness has been manifest in our nation in hegemonic, destructive, and, at times, evil ways. Although many Whites are loath to admit it, whiteness in its supremacist mode, which has been its dominant mode, has polluted our moral ecology through slavery, colonialism, imperialism, and genocide. Still, I'm uncomfortable with the notion of destroying white folks and cultures, which, by the way, isn't what Ignatiev and the folks around the journal *Race Traitor* have argued. I do think we have a moral obligation to destroy white supremacy. We must speak and think about the rearticulation, reconstitution, and recasting of whiteness to expand, enhance, and embrace its more redemptive, productive features.

This is why cultural studies and theoretical interrogations of whiteness are crucial. Besides the work of the new abolitionists—including Roediger, Allen, Ignatiev, Segrest, John Garvey, Alexander Saxton, and many others—we should remember the important work of W. E. B. Du Bois, C. L. R. James, Thomas Kochman, Eric Foner, Lerone Bennett, Jr., bell hooks, Toni Morrison, George Lipsitz, Marilyn Frye, Vron Ware, Ruth Frankenberg, Adrienne Rich, and Peggy McIntosh. And much of the recent work on whiteness is indispensable in coming to terms with its complex cultural manifestations: the brilliant books of Henry Giroux and the important work of Fred Pfeil, Linda Powell, Becky Thompson, Michelle Fine, John Dovidio, Lois Weis, Robin D. G. Kelley, Annalee Newitz, Ron Sakolsky, Jesse Daniels, Melvin L. Oliver, Thomas M. Shapiro, Eric Lott, Michael Rogin, Barbara Ching, Mike Hill, Paul Kivel, Patricia Hill Collins, Sean Wilentz, Jennifer Hochschild, Michele Wallace, José Saldivar, Matt Wray, Laura Kipnis, and on and on.

We should also scrutinize, for instance, white studies of the underclass, which address, reflect, or extend the pathologization of the black poor; many also reveal how white critics make use of blackness—which is an intellectual strategy worthy of examination—and how they construct the ghetto and articulate black identity and moral norms against a rhetorical backdrop of implicit whiteness.

Or think of a brilliant text like Ann Douglas's (1995) *Terrible Honesty: Mongrel Manhattan in the 1920's*. Douglas shows in her book how black and white figures were working, playing, loving, and thinking together, how they were engaging across the white-black divide in ways that have been relatively hidden. Douglas's book is crucial to excavating a cultural tradition of interaction, exchange, appropriation, and influence between various forms of whiteness and blackness. Such works help us accent the stratified and complex character of whiteness while paying attention to the history of how whiteness became a socially useful, racially valued, and culturally hybrid identity.

CHENNAULT: I'm glad you brought that up because I did want to talk about rescuing the productive content [of whiteness]. That's an important dimension, so that we get away from some of the accusations of talking about whiteness in terms of it being an essentialized notion, or of oversimplifying what whiteness is, or of only allying it with domination.

DYSON: That's right. The importance of the studies of whiteness I've discussed above is that they uncover, indeed, re-cover, the contradictory, contested meanings of whiteness from hidden histories of racial practice. If we don't speak about the productive, transgressive, subversive, edifying meanings of whiteness, we're being intellectually dishonest. If we don't narrate those stories, we're doing a great disservice to the moral trajectory that our work of historical reclamation often follows. One of the most powerful ways of challenging and ultimately destroying the ideology of white supremacy, the myth of white superiority, and the narrative of white domination is to unearth sites of resistive memory, history, and practice. Then too, one way to rescue the productive meanings of whiteness is to accent transgressive whiteness: how Whites cooperated with racial "others" in the unmasking of white skin privilege, the subversion of forms of white power, and the destabilization of forces of white oppression.

I think that people tend to essentialize white identities because whiteness has been a consistently malevolent force in a great number of cultures over a long period of time. It is also true that white allies to racial emancipation have often sacrificed blood and body in expressing a redemptive disloyalty to oppressive meanings of whiteness. Hopefully, in a future that still appears too far away, white disloyalty to unjust privilege and power will fuse with the liberation struggles of oppressed people around the globe as we create a world where we can lay down the burden of race.

CHENNAULT: I want to return to something you mentioned earlier: that is, some other ways of discussing intragroup differences within whiteness, other than focusing on ethnic variation, like "I'm Irish and you're Italian," but focusing on gender difference and class difference.

DYSON: One of the benefits of, for instance, ethnographies of white cultures, practices, and identities is that we begin to get a fuller picture of differentiated whiteness. The fissuring and fracturing of whiteness, especially along axes of class and gender, gives us greater insight into how white cultures have adapted, survived, and struggled in conditions where their dominance was modified or muted.

It's also important to explore histories of white difference to highlight how whiteness has not been made by Whites alone. Part of what it means to be White in America is to be Black. As Ralph Ellison said: "I don't want to know how 'white' black folk are, I want to know how 'black' white folk are." If we completely, indiscriminately destroy whiteness, we're also destroying what Blacks and other racial minorities contributed—sometimes covertly, sometimes symbiotically, often in hybrid interactions, and occasionally in extravagant fashion—to white behaviors, identities, styles, and intellectual traditions. One of the great paradoxes of race is that whiteness is not exclusively owned or produced by Whites. White is also black. As we discover how black whiteness is, we discover how interesting and intricate whiteness is. We discover how Whites and Blacks have cooperated in very shrewd ways to produce alternative structures, rituals, and cultures to dominant whiteness.

Interrogating whiteness in the manner I've just outlined opens discursive space for a post-appropriationist paradigm of cultural and racial exchange. Such a paradigm accents the unbalanced power relations, racial inequality, and economic injustice that often mediate, say, black/white artistic exchanges, where black ideas, products, styles, and practices are stolen, borrowed, or appropriated without attribution or reward. But it also accents the revisioning of whiteness through the prism of black cultural practices, especially as white subjectivities are reconceived and recast in the hues of transgressive blackness.

That's why it's important to explore racialized *communitas* and *habitas*—where Whites live and commune—to understand the productive meanings of whiteness through the reproduction and rearticulation of the productive meanings of blackness. In this connection, it makes sense to examine the phenomenon of the substitute nigger or the "wigger"—the white nigger—Whites who have been viewed, or view themselves, as Black. What uses have they made of blackness? How has blackness allowed them to alter dominant modes of whiteness? How have their knowledge and cultural practices pitted ontological contents of racial identity against strictly biological or phenotypical ones? All of these lines of inquiry are opened up by fracturing and fissuring, by differentiating, whiteness.

CHENNAULT: In what ways has whiteness in the American context spread its tentacles globally or had some effect at the international level, in productive or in oppressive ways?

DYSON: Let me answer your question in two ways. First, I'll briefly address how the oppressive meanings of whiteness in the American context have global implications. Then I will address black skepticism about the uses of even productive whiteness to unmask and unmake itself.

There's no question that one of the most powerful claims—though it is often dressed in racially essentialist terms—that certain postcolonialist, black separatists make is that whiteness has screwed things up the world over. It's relatively easy to supply historical verification for such a claim; after all, the oppressive meanings of whiteness have destroyed minority hearth and home, and kith and kin, around the globe. Wherever it has taken root, oppressive, colonizing, imperialistic whiteness has subjugated or tyrannized native peoples, indigenous populations, and aboriginal tribes. Along these lines, American visions of white supremacy have exported well, inspiring, for instance, South African apartheid and modern varieties of European neocolonialism.

The problem with certain criticisms of oppressive whiteness is that they are grounded in discourses of biological determinism and genetic inheritance, turning out to be *The Bell Curve* in reverse: Whites are genetically incapable of humane behavior and sane social interaction. Other varieties of racial geneticism and biological determinism—such as that found in Frances Cress Welsing's (1991) *The Isis Papers,* a perennial best-seller in black communities—maintain that white supremacy grows from Whites' fear of genetic annihilation because they lack melanin, while Blacks, who possess it in abundance, are guaranteed survival. In such versions of reductive pseudoscience, white supremacy is genetically encoded and biologically reproduced. In light of such theories, it's understandable that antiracist critics of new abolitionism shudder when they hear of the need to abolish the white race, even if it's conceded that it's a social construction the abolitionists aim to destroy.

Still, we've got to admit that one of the most ingenious, and deceitful, strategies deployed by white supremacists is to insulate themselves from knowledge of white supremacy's evil, of its thoroughgoing funkiness. In this mode, a crucial function of whiteness is to blind itself to its worst tendencies, its most lethal consequences. And one of the ways that dominant whiteness does this is by adopting a facade of ignorance, innocence, or naïveté in the face of claims of its destructiveness. Whether such a facade covers the deep knowledge its advocates possess of white supremacy's ill effects is, and is not, relevant to how racial or ethnic minorities interact with Whites in general. On one reading, such knowledge is irrelevant, because even if the intent to harm does not exist, the malevolent consequences of white supremacy are just as real.

On the other hand, such knowledge is relevant when racial or ethnic minorities seek to forge coalitions with Whites who reject the perspectives, practices, and privileges of white supremacy. How can Blacks, or Latinas, be sure that such a rejection is abiding? The immediate response, of course, is that one must judge white allies, as one judges all people, by their actions. But this is precisely where matters get tricky: It is sometimes the actions of even the most devoted white allies that surprise, stun, shock, hurt, and disappoint Blacks, Latinos, or Asians. The claim to ignorance, innocence, or naïveté by white allies in the face of offensive action is the cause of no small degree of discomfort in the relations between Whites and racial minorities.

What is even more uncomfortable is when white allies make a merit badge of their resistance to what is increasingly thought of as the hypersensitivity of racial minorities. As a result, alleged white allies of

Blacks—for instance, Bill Clinton—parade their racial accomplishments as a gateway to legitimacy in black communities and as a passport to do harm. The new white abolitionists and other progressive white allies are the first to decry this variety of neoliberal racial manipulation. But a more difficult suspicion to overcome in many black communities is the historic pressure of whiteness to make virtues of its vices—and vice versa—even as it creates discursive space to deconstruct and demythologize its own socially constructed meanings.

That may explain why some Blacks are skeptical of even progressive versions of white studies: It may be a sophisticated narcissism at work, another white hoax to displace studies of, but especially by, the Others at the height of their popularity and power with an encroaching obsession with the meanings, identities, practices, anxieties, and subjectivities—and hence the agendas, priorities and preferences—of the Whites. On such a view, whiteness once again becomes supreme by trumpeting its need for demystification, dismantling, or abolition. Thus the cultural capital of otherness is bleached, and to thoroughly mix metaphors, the gaze of race is returned to sender.

We've got to keep such skepticism in mind as we attempt to unmake and remake whiteness. As we scan the globe where whiteness has left its mark, the most remarkable fact is not the willingness of Whites to become disloyal to their whiteness but the courageous rebellion of native, colonized, or enslaved folk who fought and, as best they could, remade the meanings of the whiteness they inherited or confronted. Their stories are worthy of serious study.

CHENNAULT: Related to that, let's talk about in particular a place you just came from—Cuba—and how you see that disguising of the "funkiness" of whiteness functioning in the United States' relations with Cuba and the role that whiteness might play in our relationship with that country.

DYSON: I'll answer that in a couple of ways. First of all, the political measures that America has employed against Cuba are simply obscene. It is indefensible for America to treat a neighboring nation of beautiful people 90 miles away with such contempt while it grants China most favored nation status. Our relations with Cuba are hostile for one overriding reason: To put it crudely, America has been unable to kill Castro. He's like that little Energizer bunny: He just keeps on going.

Our foreign policy with the Soviet Union is far better, a fact that is more than a little ironic. We have thawed the thick ice that once froze Soviet-U.S. relations, and now, in our post–Cold War generosity, we've embraced the big bear we used to fear and hate, but we still can't embrace her cubs in Cuba.

The Helms-Burton act extends unjust American policies to their logical, imperialist conclusion. The embargo we have against Cuba not only punishes that nation, but it punishes other nations that might cooperate with Cuba. Our bullying has cost the people of Cuba dearly: extreme poverty, severely curtailed luxuries, evaporation of resources, shrinking of capital, and the deprivation of essential goods and services. In the guise of ostensibly just foreign policy, our relation with Cuba, especially as driven by Helms, is white supremacy in its reckless, destructive mode. America is not killing Castro; he's living well. We're hurting decent, beautiful everyday folk who love their country and who are proudly trying to extend the most democratic features of the Revolution: universal literacy, political representation of the poor, and government rooted in historical memory and national pride.

Finally, I think what's interesting is that most Cubans have a very different understanding of race than we have in the United States. Many white Cubans, and black ones as well, denied that they had a race problem. To our American eyes and ears, that was a hard claim to swallow. The Cubans *had* undeniably worked to remove vestiges of discrimination from its official quarters; still, many of the members of our delegation of black Americans understood that the rhetorical and representational battles that bewitch racial equity were still being fought. It is equally undeniable that white and black Cubans have been able to forge a Cuban national identity that overcomes, in important ways, the schisms of ethnic tribalism.

Even if it is not what we black Americans, imbued with the rhetoric of our own racial difficulties, think is altogether just, black and white Cubans at least have the real possibility of negotiating a livable racial situation. It may be what Ernest Becker (1967) termed a "vital lie:" a necessary deception that preserves the social fabric and keeps at bay the forces that destroy identity and community. The embargo has led to what the Cubans term a "special period," the time of austerity that has thrown their culture into sustained crisis. In such a period, it is perfectly reasonable that the Cubans understand race in the fashion they do to preserve the very survival of their nation. In many ways, they've done a much better job with race than we have under conditions of relative material prosperity.

CHENNAULT: Any closing comments on the past, present, or future of the study of whiteness?

DYSON: I have just one observation. As we look to the next century of whiteness studies, the field will mature and reconstruct its genealogy by pointing b(l)ack—to those great figures from W. E. B. Du Bois to Zora Neale Hurston, from Langston Hughes to Ralph Ellison, and from Nella Larsen to James Baldwin. Such a genealogy for white studies brings to mind something Fannie Lou Hamer said. Paraphrasing her, Hamer argued that the mistake white folk made with black folk is that they put us not in front of them but behind them. Had they placed us in front of them, they could have observed and contained us.

Instead, white folk placed us behind them, in what they deemed an inferior position. As a result, we were able to learn white folk—their beliefs, sentiments, contradictions, cultures, styles, behaviors, virtues, and vices. Black survival depended on black folk knowing the ways and souls of white folk. It's only fitting now that we turn to African American and Latino, Asian, and Native American scholars, workers, intellectuals, artists, and everyday folk to understand whiteness.

## BIBLIOGRAPHY

Allen, Theodore. (1994). *The Invention of the White Race, Volume One: Racial Oppression and Social Control*. London and New York: Verso.

Becker, Ernest. (1967). *Beyond Alienation: A Philosophy of Education for the Crisis of Democracy*. New York: George Braziller Incorporated.

Bennett, Lerone, Jr. (1984). *Before the Mayflower: A History of Black America*. Revised. New York: Viking Penguin.

Ching, Barbara. (1997). *Knowing Your Place: Rural Identity and Cultural Hierarchy*. New York: Routledge.

Collins, Patricia Hill. (1990). *Black Feminist Thought: Knowledge, Consciousness, and the Politics of Empowerment*. Boston: Unwin Hyman.

D'Souza, Dinesh. (1995). *The End of Racism: Principles for a Multicultural Society*. New York: Free Press.

Daniels, Jessie. (1997). *White Lies: Race, Class, Gender, and Sexuality in White Supremacist Discourse.* New York: Routledge.

Douglas, Ann. (1995). *Terrible Honesty: Mongrel Manhattan in the 1920s.* New York: Farrar, Straus, and Giroux.

Dovidio, John. (1986). *Prejudice, Discrimination, and Racism.* Academic Press, Incorporated.

Du Bois, W. E. B. (1935). *Black Reconstruction.* New York: Harcourt, Brace, and Company.

Dyson, Michael Eric. (1996). *Race Rules: Navigating the Color Line.* Reading, MA: Addison-Wesley Pub. Co.

Fine, Michelle; Weis, Lois; Powell, Linda C., and Wong, L. Mun (eds). (1996). *Off White: Readings on Race, Power, and Society.* New York and London: Routledge.

Foner, Eric. (1997). *African-American History.* 2nd Edition, Expanded, Reprint, Revised. Washington: American Historical Association.

Frankenberg, Ruth. (1993). *White Women, Race Matters: The Social Construction of Whiteness.* Minneapolis: University of Minnesota Press.

Frye, Marilyn. (1992). *Willful Virgin: Essays in Feminism, 1976-1992.* The Freedom, Crossing Press.

Garvey, John. (1996). *Race Traitor.* Noel Ignatiev and John Garvey (eds.). New York: Routledge.

Giroux, Henry. (1997). *Channel Surfing.* New York: St. Martin's Press.

Gitlin, Todd. (1995). *The Twilight of Common Dreams: Why America is Wracked by Culture Wars.* 1st edition. New York: Metropolitan Books.

Hill, Mike. (1997). *Whiteness: A Critical Reader.* Edited by Mike Hill. New York: New York University Press.

Hochschild, Jennifer. (1995). *Facing Up to the American Dream: Race, Class, and the Soul of the Nation.* Princeton, N.J., Princeton University Press.

hooks, bell. (1992). *Black Looks: Race and Representation.* Boston: South End Press.

Hume, David. (1826). *The Philosophical Works of David Hume,* Including All the Essays, and Exhibiting the More Important Alterations and Corrections in the Successive Editions Published by the Author. In Four Volumes. Edinburgh: Printed for A. Black and W. Tait.

Ignatiev, Noel. (1995). *How the Irish Became White.* New York: Routledge.

Jensen, Arthur Robert. (1973). *Educability and Group Differences.* New York: Harper and Row.

James, C. L. R. (1993). *American Civilization.* Malden: Blackwell Publishers.

Jefferson, Thomas. (1975). *The Portable Thomas Jefferson.* Edited and with an Introduction by Merrill D. Peterson. New York: Viking Press.

Kant, Immanuel. (1949). *The Philosophy of Kant: Immanuel Kant's Moral and Political Writings.* Edited and with an Introduction by Carl J. Friedrich. New York: Modern Library.

Kelley, Robin D. G. (1994). *Race Rebels: Culture, Politics, and the Black Working Class.* New York: Free Press.

Kipnis, Laura. (1996). *Bound and Gagged: Pornography and the Politics of Fantasy in America.* New York: Grove Press.

Kivel, Paul. (1995). *Uprooting Racism: How White People Can Work for Racial Justice.* Branford: New Society Publishers, Limited.

Kochman, Thomas. (1981). *Black and White Styles in Conflict.* Chicago: University of Chicago Press.

Lincoln, Abraham. (1905). *Complete Works of Abraham Lincoln.* Edited by John G. Nicolay and John Hay; with a general introduction by Richard Watson Gilder, and special articles by other eminent persons. New York: Francis D. Tandy Company.

Lipsitz, George. (1990). *Time Passages: Collective Memory and American Popular Culture.* Minneapolis: University of Minnesota Press.

Lott, Eric. (1993). *Love and Theft: Blackface Minstrelsy and the American Working Class.* New York: Oxford University Press.

McIntosh, Peggy. (1988). *White Privilege, Male Privilege: A Personal Account of Coming to See Correspondences through Work in Women's Studies.* Wellesley, MA: Wellesley College, Center for Research on Women.

Morrison, Toni. (1992). *Playing in the Dark: Whiteness and the Literary Imagination.* Cambridge, MA: Harvard University Press.

Murray, Charles, and Herrnstein, Richard. (1994). *The Bell Curve: Intelligence and Class Structure in American Life.* New York: Free Press.

Newitz, Annalee and Wray, Matt, eds. (1997). *White Trash: Race and Class in America.* New York: Routledge.

Oakeshott, Michael. (1989). *The Voice of Liberal Learning: Michael Oakeshott on Education.* Timothy Fuller (ed.). New Haven, CT: Yale University Press.

Oliver, Melvin L. (1995). *Black Wealth/White Wealth: A New Perspective on Racial Inequality.* New York: Routledge.

Omi. Michael, and Winant, Howard. (1994). *Racial Formation in the United States From the 1960s to the 1990s.* New York: Routledge.

Patterson, Orlando. (1991). *Freedom.* New York: Basic Books.

Pfeil, Fred. (1995). *White Guys: Studies in Postmodern Domination and Difference.* London and New York: Verso.

Powell, Linda C. (1996). *Off White: Readings on Race, Power, and Society.* (eds) Michelle Fine, Lois Weis, Linda C. Powell, L. Mun Wong. New York and London: Routledge.

Rich, Adrienne. (1995). *Dark Fields of the Republic, Poems, 1991-1995.* New York: W. W. Norton.

Roediger, David. (1994). *Towards the Abolition of Whiteness.* New York: Verso.

Rogin, Michael. (1996). *Blackface, White Noise: Jewish Immigrants in the Hollywood Melting Pot.* Berkeley: University of California Press.

Rorty, Richard. (1989). *Contingency, Irony, and Solidarity.* New York: Cambridge University Press.

Sakolsky, Ron (ed.). (1995). *Sounding Off: Music as Subversion/Resistance/Revolution.* Brooklyn, NY: Autonomedia.

Saldivar, Jose. (1997). *Border Matters: Remapping American Cultural Studies.* Berkeley: University of California Press.

Saxton, Alexander. (1990). *The Rise and Fall of the White Republic: Class Politics and Mass Culture in Nineteenth Century America.* London and New York: Verso.

Segrest, Mab. (1993). *Memoir of a Race Traitor.* Boston: South End Press.

Shockley, William. (1992). *Shockley on Eugenics and Race: The Application of Science to the Solution of Human Problems.* Washington: Scott-Townsend Publishers.

Thompson, Becky. (1996). *Names We Call Home: Autobiography on Racial Identity.* Edited by Becky Thompson and Sangeeta Tyagi. New York: Routledge.

Tomasky, Michael. (1996). *Left for Dead: The Life, Death, and Possible Resurrection of Progressive Politics in America.* New York: Free Press.

Wallace, Michele. (1992). *Black Popular Culture/A Project By Michele Wallace.* Edited by Gina Dent. Seattle: Bay Press.

Ware, Vron. (1997). *Beyond the Pale: White Women, Racism, and History.* New York: Verso.

Welsing, Frances Cress. (1991). *The Isis Papers.* Chicago: Third World Press.

Wilentz, Sean, ed. (1992). *Major Problems in the Early Republic, 1787-1848, Documents and Essays.* Boston: Houghton Mifflin Company.

Wilson, Woodrow. (1956). *The Politics of Woodrow Wilson, Selections from His Speeches and Writings.* Edited, with an introd., by August Heckscher. New York: Harper.

# Living with Anxiety: Race and the Renarration of Public Life

**Cameron McCarthy**

## INTRODUCTION

**Q**uestioning the positionality of "whiteness" and its devious articulations in contemporary life takes us to the threshold of the new dynamics taking place in the U.S. racial order at the end of the twentieth century. The contributors to *White Reign* alert us to new ideological configurations in our popular culture and civil life. They also foreground the dangerous rise of identity politics in the white suburbs and of middle-class narrowminded morality in the discourses of popular culture and public policy. In this afterword I want to expand on this topic and call attention to a broad pattern of racial instability, racial recoding, and racial incorporation taking place in American society as we enter the twenty-first century.

## LIVING WITH ANXIETY, LIVING IN NEW TIMES

We are living in new racial times, new racial circumstances. In these new times racial dangers have multiplied, but so have the possibilities for renewal and change. That is to say, we are living at a time when the racial order is being reconfigured in the tiniest crevices of everyday life. As the contributors have stressed throughout this book, we need new ways to talk about race and identity that will help us to better understand the powerful rearticulations that are taking place in popular culture and in the common sense of the whole body politic. As has been already emphasized, a significant new development is the growing anxiety and restlessness that characterize the white middle class. This tumult and restlessness are most strongly foregrounded at the level of the production of identities and representations. We are living in a time of the production of crass identity politics. By identity politics I mean the strategic deployment of the discourse of group distinctiveness in everyday struggles over political representation and scarce resources (the distribution of goods and services) in education and society. Far too often, identity politics are discussed in ways that suggest that only minority groups—particularly African Americans and Latinos—practice, promote, and benefit from the strategic deployment of identity. And the case is made further that minorities are the only ones who experience the effects of group politics in terms of the fragmentation of identity and symbolic and social disorientation and dislocation. This is manifestly false; white people also practice and benefit from identity politics. Nowhere is this more powerfully registered than in the popular culture. One only has to look at the respective coverage of Whites and minorities in television evening news to see the coordinating role the media play in the elaboration of white identity and the corresponding disorganization and subversion of minority identity formation.

In what follows, I try to understand these developments in racial identity formation and popular culture. I direct attention in this area to the twin processes of racial simulation (or the constant fabrication of racial identity through the production of the pure space of racial origins) and resentment (the process of defining one's identity through the negation of the other [Nietzsche 1967]) in popular culture and in education. I argue that these two processes operate in tandem in the prosecution of the politics of racial affiliation and racial exclusion in our times.

## RECODING RACIAL IDENTITY

In his book *Simulations,* postmodern theorist Jean Baudrillard (1983, 1) recounts a story told by the Latin American writer Jorge Luis Borges. It is the story of some special mapmakers, the Cartographers of the Empire, who draw up a map so detailed that it ends up covering the entire territory that was the object of the cartographers' mapmaking. Baudrillard uses the fable to announce the ushering in of the epoch of simulation—our age—the age in which the real is replaced by the hyperreal and the line between reality and fiction is forever deferred. The photo opportunity is our only contact with the president. The patriarch only blooms in autumn. The copy has in this case completely usurped the original. There is no place like home anymore in this new world order of boundary transgression and constantly collapsing global space.

I would like to take up the Borges story as a point of departure in my exploration of the articulation of race relations and racial identities in popular culture and in education at the end of the century. In doing so, I draw directly on Baudrillard's ostensible theme in the preceding passage that recounts the trials and tribulations of the emperor's cartographers—the theme of the centrality of simulation in our contemporary age. The idea of the copy that constantly recodes, usurps, and appropriates the original is a very precise insight on the way in which racial difference operates in popular culture and intellectual life. And it is this theme of simulation that I will want to return to in a moment. But let me say that I believe that the Borges's allegory is a fable about identity that I understand to be a drama of social crisis and recuperation, of exclusion and affiliation, of exile and return. Racially dominant identities do depend on the constant ideological appropriation of the Other. Racial identity, racial affiliation, and racial exclusion are the products of human work, human effort (Said 1993). The field of race relations in popular culture, but also in education, is one of simulation. The story of mapmaking is also a story, ultimately, of the excess of language that is involved in racial discourse. There is always something left over in language that never allows us to gather up our racial identities in one place and to fix them in invariant racial slots. The emperor needs the empire. The emperor exists for the fact of empire. Without it, he does not exist. Worst yet, as Baudrillard might suggest, without the empire, he does not know himself to exist. He is like the Devil-Landlord in writer Derek Walcott's "Ti Jean and His Brothers" (1970) who wants to drink at the pool of mortality. He wants to be human. But the peasants will burn down his Great House. The Landlord is a homeless Devil.

Understanding the operation of racial logics in education, paradoxically, requires an understanding of their constant simulation outside the laboratory of the educational field itself—in literature and popular culture, in the imaginary. It is this blend of the educational and the popular that I want to explore briefly here. One of the current difficulties in the educational literature on race relations is its refusal of the popular. American middle-class white youths and adults know more about inner-city Blacks through the media, particularly television and film, than through personal or classroom interaction or even in textbooks. And nowadays textbooks are looking intertextually more and more like television with their HD graphics and illustrations and their glossy, polysemic treatment of subject matter. In addition, anti-institutional educational projects, such as Teach for America[1]—with its mission to save the urban poor for God, for capitalism, and for country—are deeply inscribed in a language of the racial Other pulled off the television set, as we will see in a moment. We live in a time when "pseudoevents"—as historian Daniel Boorstin (1975) called media-driven representations in the 1970s—have usurped any relic of reality beyond that which is staged. Media simulations have driven incredibly deep and perhaps permanent wedges of difference between the world of the suburban dweller and his inner-city counterpart. Argues Boorstin (3) "we have used our wealth, our literacy, our technology, and our progress, to create a thicket of unreality which stands between us and the facts of life." It is these "facts of life"—notions of what, for example, black people are like or what Latinos are like—that are invented and reinvented in the media, in popular magazines, in newspapers, and on television and in popular films. In this sense, popular culture is always a step ahead of educational institutions in terms of strategies of incorporation and mobilization of racial identities. As authors such as Katherine Frith (1997) point out, by the end of the teenage years, the average student will have spent more time watching television than he or she has spent in school. It is increasingly television and film, more so than the school curriculum, that educates American youth about race.

## THE WAR OVER SIGNS

Even more crucially, to take up further the implications of Baudrillard's *Simulations*, contemporary conflicts in education and in popular culture are fundamentally battles over signs and the occupation and territorialization of symbolic as well as material resources and urban and suburban space. Central to these developments is the rise of resentment politics. In his *Genealogy of Morals,* Friedrich Nietzsche (1899) conceptualized resentment as the specific practice of identity displacement in which the social actor consolidates his own identity by complete disavowal of the merits and existence of his social other. This practice of ethnocentric consolidation and cultural exceptionalism now characterizes much of the tug-of-war over educational reform and multiculturalism. This battle over culture, self, and group has spread throughout society as a whole. Resentment and racial reaction therefore define school life; this can be seen in the extent to which a culture war over signs and identity has infiltrated the arena of everyday practices. Education is indeed a critical site in which struggles over the organization and concentration of emotional and political investment and moral affiliation are taking place. These battles over identity involve the powerful manipulation of group symbols and strategies of articulation and rearticulation of public slogans and popular discourses. These signs and symbols are used to make identity and define social and political projects.

An important feature of these developments is the radical recoding and renarration of public life now taking place. As I noted in "Reading the American Popular" (see McCarthy, 1997), traditional distinctions between conservatives and liberals, Democrats and Republicans, the Left versus the Right have collapsed. Radically distorting and conservative energies and drives have taken over the body politic, displacing concerns about inequality and poverty. Opportunistic discourses activated within the suburban middle class itself have mushroomed. These discourses center on the protection of the home and the defense of the neighborhood from inner-city predators. They narrate the preservation of the nostalgic ancestral record of the group and its insulation from the contaminating racial Other. These opportunistic discourses spawned within the last decade and half or so emphasize new priorities in the public arena: concerns with identity, history, popular memory, nation, family, crime, and so forth now drive the engines of popular will and the public imagination. This shift away from the issue of social inequality of the 1960s and 1970s has meant that America is now willing to spend more on law enforcement and prisons than it is on educating inner-city youth. On the other hand, some minority advocates seem more preoccupied with cultural assertion and cultural distinctiveness than with the bruising socioeconomic isolation of minority youths.

Let us turn briefly to the mise-en-scène of these cultural discourses associated with the tug-of-war of racial strife in the educational and social life of a divided society—the United States. In particular, we will examine four discourses of racial difference now in use inside and outside of education in which metaphors and symbols of identity and representation are the "issues at stake."

First, there is the *discourse of racial origins* (as revealed, for example, in the Eurocentric/Afrocentric debate over curriculum reform). Discourses of racial origins rely on the simulation of a pastoral sense of the past in which Europe and Africa are available to American racial combatants without their modern tensions, contradictions, and conflicts. For Eurocentric combatants such as William Bennett (1994) and George Will (1989), Europe and America are a self-evident and transcendent cultural unity. For the Afrocentric combatants, Africa and the diaspora are one "solid identity," to use the language of cultural theorist Molefi Asante (1993). Proponents of Eurocentrism and Afrocentrism are themselves proxies for larger impulses and desires for stability among the middle classes in American society in a time of constantly changing demographic and economic realities. The immigrants are coming. Jobs are slipping overseas into the Third World. Discourses of Eurocentrism and Afrocentrism travel in a time warp to an age when gods stalked the earth. These discourses of racial origins provide imaginary solutions to groups and individuals who refuse the radical hybridization that is the historically evolved reality of the United States and other major Western metropolitan societies.

The second example of the discourses of resentment is the *discourse of nation*. This discourse is foregrounded in a spate of recent advertisements by multinational corporate concerns such IBM, United, American Airlines, MCI and General Electric (GE). These ads both feed on and provide fictive solutions to the racial anxieties of the age. They effectively appropriate multicultural symbols and redeploy them in a broad project of coordination and consolidation of corporate citizenship and consumer affiliation. The marriage of art and economy, as cultural critic Stuart Ewen (1988) defines advertising in his *All Consuming Images,* is now commingled with the exigencies of ethnic identity and nation. These multicultural ads directly exploit difference—different races, different landscapes, different traditions and symbols. One moment the semiotic subject of advertising is a free American citizen abroad in the open seas sailing up and down the Atlantic or the translucent aquamarine waters of the Caribbean sea or lounging on the pearly white sands of Bermuda or Barbados. In another moment the free American citizen is transported to the pastoral life of the unspoiled, undulating landscape of medieval Europe. Yet another vista reveals our American Nostromo at one with the beautiful wild life of the forests of Africa—African forests that are just part of the scenery of one of our prominent entertainment parks.

GE's "We Bring Good Things to Life" ad is a very good example of this kind of racial recoding. In this ad, which is shown quite regularly on CNN and ABC, GE is represented as the benevolent corporate citizen extending American technology to Japan; it is shown bringing electricity to one Japanese town. Echoes of America's domination and vanquishing of Japan during World War II fill the atmosphere of this ad, thereby glibly eliding contemporary American anxieties about Japan's technological capabilities and possible economic superiority. Corporate advertising conducts its pedagogy via television, providing the balm for a troubled people in pursuit of origins. Ethnicity and race constitute some of the new productive locations for marketing—the new home ports for multinational corporations in search of harbor in the rough seas of international commerce.

Third, there is the *discourse of popular memory and popular history.* This discourse suffuses the nostalgia films of the last half decade or so. Films such as *Dances with Wolves* (1990), *Bonfire of the Vanities* (1990), *Grand Canyon* (1993), *Falling Down* (1993), *Disclosure* (1995), *A Time to Kill* (1996), and *Forrest Gump* (1994) foreground a white, middle-class protagonist who appropriates the subject position of racial "victim." For example, Joel Schumaker's *A Time to Kill* offers pedagogical insight about social problems concerning difference from the perspective of the embattled white suburban dweller. The problem with difference is, in Schumaker's world, symptomatic of a crisis of feeling for white suburban middle classes—a crisis of feeling represented in blocked opportunity and wish fulfillment, overcrowding, loss of jobs, general insecurity, crime, and so forth. The contemporary world has spun out of order, and violence and resentment are the coping strategies of white middle-class actors.

In *A Time to Kill,* Schumaker presents us with the world of the "New South," Canton, Mississippi, in which social divides are extreme and

Blacks and Whites live such different lives they might as well be on separate planets. But this backwater of the South serves as a social laboratory to explore a burning concern of suburban America: retributive justice. When individuals break the law and commit acts of violent antisocial behavior, then the upstanding folks in civil society are justified in seeking their expulsion or elimination. The film poses the rather provocative question: When is it respectable society's "time to kill"? Are there circumstances in which retribution and revenge and resentment are warranted? The makers of *A Time to Kill* say resoundingly "yes." This answer is impervious to class or race or gender.

In order to make the case for retributive justice, Schumaker puts a black man at the epicenter of this white normative discourse—what Charles Murray (1984) calls "white popular wisdom." What would you do if your ten-year-old daughter is brutally raped and battered, pissed on, and left for dead? You would want revenge? This is a role play that has been naturalized in society to mean white victim, black assailant— the Willy Horton shuffle. In *A Time to Kill,* the discourse is inverted: The righteously angry are a black worker and his family. Two redneck assailants raped his daughter. Carl Lee, the black lumberyard worker, gets back at the two callous criminals by shooting them down on the day of their arraignment. One brutal act is answered by another. One is a crime, the other is righteous justice. Crime will not pay. In this revenge drama the message of retributive justice is intended to override race and class lines. We are living in the time of an eye for an eye. The racial enemy is in our private garden. In the face of bureaucratic incompetence, we have to take the law into our own hands.

These films also retell national history from the perspective of bourgeois anxieties. Hence in *Forrest Gump,* the peripatetic Gump interposes himself into the raging decade of the 1960s, stealing the spotlight from the civil rights movement, Vietnam War protestors, the feminist movement, and so forth. Public history is overwhelmed by personal consumerism and wish fulfillment. "Life is," after all, "like a box of chocolates. You never know what you're gonna get." You might get Newt Gingrich. But who cares? History will absolve the American consumer.

The fourth example of resentment is the discourse of bourgeois *social voluntarism.* This is an example of what I wish to call positive resentment—a resentment based on what can best be described as a post-

Reaganite selfish idealism. One of the most powerful examples of this discourse is provided in Teach for America's (TFA) highly ideologically motivated intervention in the education of the inner-city child. This is a voluntarism that is backed by the leading corporations in the country, such as Xerox, IBM, Ross Perot, and Union Carbide. TFA's scarcely veiled agenda is to undermine and discredit teacher education preparation in the university and the teacher certification process as it presently exists. For TFA, the inner-city child is the tragic ballast weighing down the ship of state. In helping the inner-city child, the good TFA recruit can be projected as a timely hero rescuing society from inner-city degeneracy: crack, crime, and procreation. This is all powerfully represented in TFA's recruitment brochures and promotional literature. Of course, crime prevention tops the list of these Green Beret recruits. And crime and violence are presented in one recruitment manual as naturally residing in the heart of the inner-city child. Hence the TFA recruit must prepare himself for the pseudonormative task of crime prevention: "Let's . . . pretend that I'm one of your students, named [use your name] and we're going to act out a scene. So, don't tell me what you would do, just do it. Don't tell me what you would say, just say it. I'm going to take out a knife [your pen] in a non-threatening manner. School rules prohibit knives in the building, but some teachers look the other way. Begin" (Teach for America, 1990, 22). It is striking how TFA's representation of the inner-city child seems to be skimmed directly from the surface of the television set. The world of the inner city is available to the middle-class actor through simulation.

## CONCLUSION

Against the grain of historical variability, an irony now exists with respect to racial identity formation. That is, whereas educators insist on the master narratives of homogeneity and Western culture in their headlong retreat from diversity and hybridity, the captains and producers of the culture industry readily exploit the ambiguities of racial identity formation. Even cultural nationalism and Afrocentrism can sell goods and services well. A good example is the hot trading and hawking of the image of Malcolm X that took place in the early 1990s—the assortment of items, from the X cap to the glossy cover designs of magazines such as *Newsweek*, the *New*

*Yorker,* and the *New York Times Sunday Magazine* that have placed a bill of sale on the great icon. Needless to say, Eurocentrism also has been incorporated in advertising, as in the United Airlines ad that pitches a trip to a homogeneous imperial England free of the presence of the immigrant populations that have entered the Mother Country from every corner of England's once-vast commonwealth.

It is precisely this rearticulation and recoding that I call *nonsynchrony.* Racial difference and identities, as Edward Said (1993) points out, are produced. Therefore, I want to call attention to the organization and arrangement of racial relations of domination and subordination in cultural forms and ideological practices in the mass media and in education—what French intellectual Louis Althusser calls the "the mise en scène of interpellation." I am interested in the way in which moral leadership and social power are exercised in the "concrete" in this society and globally. In the past I have pointed to the impact of these discontinuities among differently situated groups of minorities. Here I have tried to draw attention to these dynamics as they operate in debates over identity and curriculum reform, hegemonic cultural assertions in advertising, popular film, and in the educational voluntarism of the much-publicized project called Teach for America, "our Peace Corps at home."

What do these examples of racial simulation and resentment tell us about the contemporary state of race relations in education and society? Collectively, they point to a generalized pattern of revision and recoding of our racial landscape. They also point to the instability in the elaboration of national racial categories and identities in late-century society. They, in part, invoke the new depthlessness, radical eclecticism, and rampant nostalgia of the age. In the shadow between truth and fiction lies the new reality of racial formation in our contemporary era. On the one hand, this is an age in which the emergence of subaltern racial minorities, their demands for democratic participation, and their assertion of their heritages and identities have precipitated a sense of moral panic and a series of quixotic and contradictory responses within the educational establishment that link conservative intellectuals and born-over-again liberals in the academy to some of the more vulgar anti-intellectual and fundamentalist political groups and traditions in this country. This is all summarized in what cultural theorists Stanley Aronowitz and Henry Giroux (1991) call "the politics of clarity" and the chants of political correctness and reverse discrimination that now provide the ideological cover for that special species of low-flying behaviorism that has been unloaded by the Right in all spheres of American cultural life. On the other hand, these new ethnicities are being rapidly colonized, incorporated, and reworked by a culture industry that radically appropriates the new to consolidate the past. Diversity can sell visits to theme parks as well as it can sell textbooks. Diversity can sell AT&T long-distance calling cards as well as the new ethnic stalls in the ethereal hearths of the shopping mall. And sometimes, in the most earnest of ways, diversity lights up the whole world and makes it available to capitalism.

But unlike Borges's map, the capitalization of diversity does not exhaust the subaltern imagination and the transformative character of new epiphanies. For this period of multinational capital is witness to the ushering in of the multicultural age—an age in which the empire has struck back and First World exploitation of the Third World has so depressed these areas of the world that there has been a steady stream of immigrants from the periphery seeking better futures in the metropolitan centers. With the rapid growth of the indigenous minority population in the United States, a formidable cultural presence of diversity exists in every sphere of cultural life. If this is an era of the "post-," it is also an era of the multicultural. And the challenge of this multicultural era is the challenge of living in a world of difference. It requires generating a mythology of social interaction that goes beyond the model of resentment that seems so securely in place in these times. It means that we must take seriously the implications of the best intuition in the Nietzschean critique of resentment as the process of identity formation that thrives on the negation of the Other. The challenge is to embrace the Other— to think of a politics that calls on the moral resources of all who are opposed to the power block. Indeed, as the purveyors of the identity politics of "white reign" assert themselves, they simply underscore their own vulnerabilities and fragilities. The floodgates have been opened and the swirling waters of difference now saturate the social field. This is the Age of Difference, the Multicultural Era. The Multicultural Era therefore poses new, although "difficult," tactical and strategic challenges to subaltern intellectuals and activists. A strategy that seeks to address these new challenges and openings must involve as a first condition a recognition that our differences of race, gender, and nation are merely the starting points for new solidarities and new alliances, not the terminal stations for depositing our agency and identities or the extinguishing of hope and possibility.

The white reign of terror is, ultimately, a new fascism spawned from the social and economic insecurities afflicting the working and professional classes of developed countries in the West. The task of subaltern progressives is always to read narrowminded identity politics back into the emerging socioeconomic and cultural conjuncture of late-century society. The new fascism is symptomatic of disorganized capitalism, and we must mount a new politics of persuasion and affect to confront it.

## NOTES

1. Teach for America is the much-talked-about voluntaristic youth organization that has sought to make a "difference" in the educational experiences of disadvantaged inner-city children. The organization, patterned on the can-do humanism of the Peace Corps, recruits graduates from elite universities and colleges around the country to serve two-year stints in inner-city public school districts desperate for teachers.

## BIBLIOGRAPHY

Althusser, Louis. (1971). "On Ideology and Ideological State Apparatuses." *In Lenin and Philosophy and Other Essays.* New York: Monthly Review Press.

Aronowitz, S. and Giroux, H. (1991). "The Politics of Clarity." *After Image* 19, no. 3, 5, 17.

Asante, M. (1993). *Malcolm X as Cultural Hero and Other Afrocentric Essays.* Trenton, NJ: Africa World Press.

Baudrillard, J. (1983). *Simulations.* New York: Semiotext(e).

Bennett, W. (1994). *The Book of Virtues.* New York: Simon and Schuster.

Berk, R. (1997). "Sight Seeing and Virtual Sightseeing: Tourism, Schooling, and Connectivity." Manuscript, Department of Educational Policy Studies, University of Illinois.

Boorstin, D. (1975). *The Image: A Guide to Pseudo-Events in America.* New York: Antheneum.

Ewen, S. (1988). *All Consuming Images.* New York: Basic Books.

Frith, K. (1997) (ed.) *Undressing the Ad: Reading Culture in Advertising.* New York: Peter Lang.

James, C. L. R. (1993). *American Civilization.* Oxford: Blackwell.

McCarthy, C. (1997). "Reading the American Popular: Suburban Resentment and the Representation of the Inner City in Contemporary Film." In C.

McCarthy, *The Uses of Culture: Education and the Limits of Ethnic Affiliation.* New York: Routledge.

Murray, C. (1984). *Losing Ground: American Social Policy, 1950-1980.* New York: Basic Books.

Nietzsche, F. (1967). *On the Genealogy of Morals.* Trans. W. Kaufman. New York: Vintage.

Said, E. (1993). "The Politics of Knowledge." In C. McCarthy and W. Crichlow (eds.), *Race, Identity and Representation in Education.* New York: Routledge.

Teach for America. (1990). *Teach for America Recruitment Manual.* New York: Teach for America.

Walcott, D. (1970). "Ti Jean and His Brothers." In D. Walcott, *Dream on Monkey Mountain and Other Plays.* New York: Farrar, Strauss and Giroux.

Will, G. (1989, Dec. 18). "Eurocentricity and the School Curriculum." *Baton Rouge Morning Advocate,* 3.

# CONTRIBUTORS

CLINTON B. ALLISON is Professor of Cultural Studies in Education at the University of Tennessee, Knoxville. He received his Ph.D. in History and Philosophy of Education from the University of Oklahoma. His research specialty is the history of southern education. His most recent books are *Present and Past: Essays for Teachers in the History of Education* and *Teachers for the South: Pedagogy and Educationists in the University of Tennessee.*

KAREN ANIJAR is Assistant Professor of Curriculum and Instruction at Arizona State University. She is the author of many journal articles and two forthcoming books: *Teaching Towards the 24th Century: The Social Curriculum of Star Trek* and *Paying Attention: The Political Economy of Nurture.* She is also the co-editor of *Taboo: The Journal of Culture and Education.* Her areas of research include consumerism, commodification, science fiction, and youth and popular cultural studies.

MICHAEL W. APPLE is John Bascom Professor of Curriculum and Instruction and Educational Policy Studies at the University of Wisconsin, Madison. He has worked with dissident groups, unions, activists, and educators throughout the world on democratic educational and cultural policies and practices. Among his recent books are *Official Knowledge* and *Cultural Politics and Education.*

BARBARA G. BRENTS is Professor of Sociology at the University of Nevada, Las Vegas. Her research interests include feminism, women, and work in Las Vegas.

VICKI K. CARTER is an instructional designer and a doctoral candidate in the Adult Education Program at Pennsylvania State University. Her research interests include socio-cultural practices surrounding work, particularly how core values of organizations and interests of employees are conceived and negotiated in workplace learning settings. Additional academic interests include interrogating the powerful political nature of technological systems, particularly in relation to critical educational practice.

RONALD E. CHENNAULT is Assistant Professor of Education at Alabama State University in Montgomery. He is the author of several articles and book chapters on cultural studies and pedagogy. His research interests surround issues of critical cultural studies, race, class and gender, and film studies.

MICHAEL ERIC DYSON is Professor at the Institute for Research in African American Studies, Columbia University and the author of *Between God and Gangsta Rap: Bearing Witness to Black Culture* (1997), *Boys to Men* (1997), and *Race Rules* (1997). He is an internationally known speaker, addressing areas involving cultural studies, Black studies, and race theory.

HENRY A. GIROUX is Professor of Education and Waterbury Secondary Chair at Pennsylvania State University. The author of numerous books and journal articles, his most recent books include *Disturbing Pleasures, Fugitive Cultures, Channel Surfing, Education and Cultural Studies,* and the forthcoming *Learning with Disney.*

SHARON L. HOWELL is a doctoral candidate in the Adult Education Program at Pennsylvania State University. Her research interests focus on critical perspectives on workplace learning related to quality management, organizational learning, and knowledge workers. She has been involved with a team of researchers over the past four years exploring the impact of the new work order on frontline workers. Recent articles and chapters include: "Creating contingency workers: A critical study of the learning organization" and "Complicity and control in the workplace: A critical case study of TQM, learning, and the management of knowledge."

JOE L. KINCHELOE is the Belle Zeller Chair of Public Policy and Administration at CUNY Brooklyn College and a Professor of Cultural Studies and Education at Pennsylvania State University. He is the author of numerous books and articles, including *Teachers as Researchers: Qualitative Paths to Empowerment; Toil and Trouble: Good Work, Smart Workers and the Integration of Academic and Vocational Education;* and *Changing Multiculturalism: New Times, New Curriculum* with Shirley Steinberg. His latest books include *How Do We Tell the Workers?* and *Fallen Arches: McDonald's Deconstructed,* with Allen Shelton. A well-known lecturer and international speaker, he travels frequently with Shirley Steinberg to present workshops and keynote addresses on popular culture, pedagogy, and issues of race, class, gender, and sexual preference.

FRANCES A. MAHER is Professor of Education at Wheaton College, where she coordinated the college's Balanced Curriculum Project, which integrated the study of women into introductory courses. She has written articles exploring the principles and practices of feminist pedagogy and co-edited a special issue of *Women's Studies Quarterly* on feminist pedagogy. She is the co-author, with Mary Kay Thompson Tetreault, of *The Feminist Classroom: An Inside Look at How Professors and Students are Transforming Higher Education for a Diverse Society.*

CAMERON McCARTHY is Research Associate Professor and University Scholar in the Institute of Communications Research, University of Illinois at Urbana-Champaign. He teaches courses in Media Theory and Cultural Studies. McCarthy is the author of *The Uses of Culture: Education and the Limits of Ethnic Affiliation.* He is also a coeditor of *Sound Identities: Youth Music and the Cultural Politics of Education* forthcoming this fall.

PETER McLAREN is an educational activist and Professor of Urban Schooling, Graduate School of Education and Information Studies, University of California, Los Angeles. He is the author of numerous books on the politics of education, critical pedagogy, and the sociology of education. An internationally recognized Marxist scholar, his work has been translated into Spanish, Portuguese, French, Catalan, Japanese, Hebrew, Polish, and German. Among his recent books are *Critical Pedagogy and Predatory Culture* and *Revolutionary Multiculturalism.*

MELISSA J. MONSON is a graduate student Instructor in Sociology at the University of Nevada, Las Vegas. Her research interests include feminism, women, and work in Las Vegas.

DANIEL R. NICHOLSON is a Ph.D. student in the School of Journalism and Communication at the University of Oregon. He has written journal articles and book chapters in the area of media studies. His interests within communication studies revolve around issues of political economy, critical cultural studies, and their intersections—particularly as they are manifest in consumer cultures.

MONICA BEATRIZ DEMELLO PATTERSON completed her Master's Degree in Educational Theory and Policy from Pennsylvania State University in 1995. Prior to her return to academic life, she worked professionally as an administrator and teacher in public funded daycare and Head Start programs, as well as a caseworker in child welfare. Today she finds herself both bodily and spiritually attached to her computer and infant son, while working at home to research affirmative action and race issues particularly as they pertain to higher education administrative practice. She continues to work toward the completion of her terminal degree in a long distance relationship enabled by technology and support for nontraditional kinds of workplace practice. She is interested in how modern aspects of life have become insidiously and subtlety informative in everyday action and thought to erase and replace what was once indigenous, vital, cyclic, and regenerative.

FRANCES V. RAINS (Choctaw/Cherokee & Japanese) is an Assistant Professor at Pennsylvania State University, with a joint appointment in Curriculum & Instruction and Educational Policy Studies/American Indian Leadership Program. Her research emphasis is in social justice and equity issues linked to race, class, and gender in American education, with special interests related to women of color and American Indian issues. She published an article, "Holding Up a Mirror to White Privilege: Deconstructing the Maintenance of the Status Quo," in *Taboo: The Journal of Culture & Education* and has a chapter, "Dancing on the Sharp Edge of the Sword: Women Faculty of Color in White Academe," in the forthcoming book *Everyday Knowledge & Uncommon Truths: Life Writings & Women's Experiences In & Outside the Academy.*

NELSON M. RODRIGUEZ is Assistant Professor of Cultural Studies in Education at Ohio University. He is the editor, with Leila Villaverde, of the forthcoming *Dismantling White Privilege: Pedagogy, Politics, and Whiteness.* He has also published on queer theory and education.

LADISLAUS SEMALI is Assistant Professor of Education at the Pennsylvania State University where he teaches Media Literacy to pre-service teachers. His work has been published in the *International Review of Education, Comparative Education Review,* and *Pennsylvania Educational Leadership.* He is coeditor of *Intermediality: Handbook of Teaching Critical Media Literacy.*

SHIRLEY R. STEINBERG teaches at Adelphi University in New York. She is an educational consultant and a drama director. Among the numerous books she has written and edited with Joe L. Kincheloe are *Measured Lies: The Bell Curve Examined; Thirteen Questions: Reframing Education's Conversation; Kinderculture: The Corporate Constructions of Childhood; Unauthorized Methods: Critical Strategies for Teaching;* and *Students as Researchers.* She is also the co-author, with Joe Kincheloe and Deborah Tippins, of *The Stigma of Genius: Einstein and Beyond Modern Education.* She is the Senior Editor of the electronic journal *Taboo: The Journal of Culture and Education* and co-edits four book series dealing with issues of critical pedagogy, popular culture, and children.

MARY KAY THOMPSON TETREAULT is acting Vice President for Academic Affairs at California State University, Fullerton. She is the author of *Women in America: Half of History,* a collection of primary source materials. In 1984 she received the Women Educators' Research Award of the American Educational Research Association for her study of the treatment of women in high school textbooks on U.S. history. She is the co-author, with Frances A. Maher, of *The Feminist Classroom: An Inside Look at How Professors and Students are Transforming Higher Education for a Diverse Society.*

CONNIE TITONE is Assistant Professor of educational foundations at the College of New Jersey. She is co-author, with K. Maloney, of the forthcoming *Thinking through Our Mothers: Women's Philosophies of Education.*